University of Michigan Publications

HISTORY AND POLITICAL SCIENCE

VOLUME X

THE YOUTH OF ERASMUS

PLATE I

Portrait of Erasmus by Holbein. The original is in the Louvre

THE
YOUTH OF ERASMUS

BY

ALBERT HYMA

UNIVERSITY OF MICHIGAN

ANN ARBOR
UNIVERSITY OF MICHIGAN PRESS
1930

PRINTED IN THE UNITED STATES OF AMERICA
BY THE PLIMPTON PRESS · NORWOOD · MASS.

PREFACE

"THE name of Erasmus shall never perish," said John Colet, dean of St. Paul's Cathedral in London, more than four hundred years ago. Colet was himself a great scholar and a man of sterling qualities, who, for years after his first meeting with Erasmus in 1499, could teach his friend many things, as the latter did not fail to acknowledge. But if the English dean had been told that in the course of four centuries his own name would pale beside that of the poor monk from the Low Countries, he would not have shown great surprise, nor would he have made any complaint. There was something about the Dutch scholar which made one feel intuitively that one stood in the presence of a mental giant, who was certain to leave a lasting impression on the minds of coming generations.

Much has been written about Erasmus and as yet not a single biographer has said the last word on many phases of his mind and character. Perhaps the time will never come when this great genius will be properly understood. Surely, among all the successful writers which Europe has ever produced, only a very few if any have been the object of so much unjustified abuse on the one hand and of so much unmerited praise on the other as was the case with that strange character whose uncanny power over words dazzled his admirers and confounded his enemies. And even now, when the clouds of religious fanaticism, of bigotry and superstition, seem to have been lifted from the scene of bloodshed and persecution which dimmed the star of Erasmus' genius, opinions about him still vary almost as much as in the sixteenth century.

It has seemed to the present writer that one problem still requires serious study. The youth of Erasmus, if scientifically illuminated and rightly interpreted, may explain much in his later life which thus far appears to have defied analysis. To Erasmus himself the first twenty years of his life were a bitter memory. His illegitimate birth, his unhappy childhood, his companionship

v

with "sordid minds," his disappointment with monasticism, his repeated illnesses — all these made him feel later that his youth had been wasted in a country and a climate not suited to his physical and mental needs. He wanted to forget his parents and his teachers, and he constantly aimed to cast a veil over his experiences in his former home, in school, and in the monastery. So he deliberately misrepresented some facts connected with this early period, with the result that his contemporaries and many of his biographers regarded the men who taught Erasmus and who were associated with him in the monastery as "barbarous."

About forty years ago a reaction set in, for it was becoming perfectly clear that Erasmus had not scrupled at telling several plain lies. In recent years much interest has been displayed in the labors of the Brethren of the Common Life, to whom Erasmus owed a goodly part of his elementary and secondary education. We now know that the brethren were not nearly so sordid and ignorant as they were depicted by their learned pupil. On the other hand, one should not yield to the impulse of condemning Erasmus before one has sufficient evidence against him. It will be the purpose of the following sketch to portray conditions in Erasmus' environment as plainly as the available sources reveal, and the remarks of Erasmus will be declared erroneous or misleading only when clearly established facts warrant such a procedure.

My task has been greatly lightened by the financial assistance rendered by the John Simon Guggenheim Memorial Foundation and by the University of Michigan. Equally valuable was the help received from generous scholars in Europe, among whom the following require special mention: P. C. Molhuysen, librarian of the Royal Library at The Hague; G. J. J. Pott, secretary of Gouda; H. A. Mulder, librarian, and S. H. van der Kraats, assistant librarian, Gouda; M. Schoengen, archivist, Zwolle; J. C. van Slee, librarian, Deventer; P. J. van Rosmalen, archivist, The Hague; L. Kruijf, archivist, 's-Hertogenbosch; W. de Vreese, librarian, Rotterdam; P. T. A. Swillens, archivist, Utrecht; and R. Flatscher, University Library, Innsbruck.

To no one, however, do I owe so much in preparing the present volume as to Dr. Eugene S. McCartney, editor of scholarly publications, University of Michigan. Not only was he instrumental in materially improving the text, but he enabled me to correct a considerable number of passages in my transcription of the manuscript version of the *Antibarbarorum Liber*, as it appears in the city library at Gouda. Furthermore, he detected errors in the copy I had made from the manuscript. But it need hardly be said that he is in no way responsible for the mistakes which may still remain in the printed copy.

To the Executive Board of the Graduate School of the University I also wish to express my thanks, for this body generously undertook to authorize the publication of my book for the University.

Finally, I am under obligation to Martinus Nijhoff, publishers, The Hague, who permitted me to reproduce a map of medieval Deventer.

A. H.

CONTENTS

Contents

ILLUSTRATIONS

PLATES

MAPS

PART I
THE BACKGROUND

CHAPTER I

THE AGE OF ERASMUS

ERASMUS was born between the years 1465 and 1470, approximately fifteen years after the fall of Constantinople and twenty-five years before the first voyage by Columbus to America. He died in 1536, or nineteen years after Martin Luther posted the celebrated Ninety-five Theses on the door of the Castle Church at Wittenberg, which act is said to have been the beginning of the Reformation. Erasmus witnessed the zenith of the Italian Renaissance; he beheld with raptured gaze the glory of exalted humanism, as prelates vied with princes in showering favors upon the men who helped restore the knowledge of the classics. But he also lived to see the rise of the German Reformation, and he observed with dismay the spread of intolerance and the decline of humanism. He lived in a time of storm and stress. His first years were spent in a country torn by civil strife and his last years saw such great nations as the Holy Roman Empire, France, and England engulfed by a wave of religious dissension and persecution, so that he felt constrained to seek rest in Switzerland. He first saw the light of day in the "Lowlands by the Sea," near the mouth of the river Rhine; and he closed his eyes for the last time in the "Oberland," where the same river Rhine takes its source.

The period between 1465 and 1535 — a most eventful period of "three score and ten years" — was above all a time of flux and change. It was in this period that the Middle Ages gave way to modern civilization, that human society in Europe underwent a combination of remarkable changes. Feudalism and serfdom now received a death-blow in several countries of western Europe; humanism spread beyond the Alps, and Italy ceased to be the one superior focus of higher civilization in Europe; scholastic philosophy was finally vanquished by humanists, mystics, and religious

3

reformers; and the invention of printing made possible a vastly increased circulation of books. In this period great "national states" were reaching maturity, such as Spain, Portugal, France, and England; the Turks occupied practically the whole of the Balkan Peninsula and Hungary, but were halted before the gates of Vienna; they also failed to extend their power into the East Indian Archipelago, thus enabling the Portuguese to build a colonial empire east of Africa; America was discovered and the principal routes of sea-borne commerce shifted from the Mediterranean to the Atlantic, thus hastening the decline of Venice and Genoa and the rise of Antwerp, Amsterdam, and London.

This period also marked the end of the political weakness and the beginning of the expansion of Europe, now on a much grander scale than in the days of Alexander the Great and of Emperor Augustus. Europe was at last to reap the fruits of the advantages which its physical geography had kept in reserve for the age of Columbus, Da Gama, Drake, Cartier, Gutenberg, Erasmus, Copernicus, Bruno, Da Vinci, Luther, Calvin, and Loyola. When Erasmus passed away in 1536, the master minds of Europe had definitely embarked upon the policy of conquest in the realms of politics, economics, learning, art, and religion. Asia and Africa had lost the contest with Europe, while America merely formed a field for exploitation and colonization. The day seemed indeed very far distant when the latter continent would compete successfully with Europe in any phase of human enterprise.

It must not be imagined that Erasmus was aware of all the great transformations which occurred in Europe during his lifetime; if his interests had been less narrow than they were he would probably have scattered his physical and mental energies and consequently his place in the history of civilization would have been very mediocre. Nevertheless his contempt of the common people and his indifference to economic and social developments could not prevent him from being affected by the latter. One cannot, therefore, fully understand the mind of Erasmus until one familiarizes oneself with the whole background of that mind. But it should also be remembered that a man who deliberately or involuntarily shuts his mind to a certain subject will absorb much less from it than his neighbor who displays an active interest in the same subject.

There is a tendency today in many places to underestimate the importance of the Christian Church and of religion at the end of the Middle Ages, because in our age men's minds appear to be drifting away from religious observances. One frequently hears the assertion that, although the great writers of the fifteenth century generally paid very little attention to political, social, and economic developments, the people as a whole were nearly as strongly subjected to the influence of these developments as they are today. Chroniclers in the fifteenth century recorded only those things in which they were interested, and therefore they presented a very one-sided picture of medieval civilization. Sound though this argument appears, the fact remains that the Christian Church was by far the mightiest institution of the Middle Ages and that the simple reason why Erasmus and Luther were the most celebrated figures during the first four decades of the sixteenth century is because they happened to discuss matters which aroused the greatest interest in the minds of thinking people.

Wherever Erasmus turned before he was forty he knew that everybody was born into the Church, just as today everybody is born a member of the State. There was in fact a great difference between the churches of his time and those of the present era. Shortly after the fall of the Roman Empire, when most European countries were being ravaged by hordes of barbarians, the Church had held out its hand of peace and order to millions of distracted Christians. It was the Church which restored order in Italy. It had assisted Charlemagne in building up his great empire. Its monasteries had preserved precious books, among others the Bible, the works of Aristotle, and of the Church Fathers. Its schools in almost all localities had been the only centers of learning. Thus it had richly deserved the privileges it enjoyed during the first five centuries of the Middle Ages.

Gradually the Church had grown exceedingly wealthy. Many a nobleman upon his death-bed had bequeathed part or all of his possessions to the Church. Not a few princes and rich nobles had deemed it expedient for the welfare of their souls to enter the ranks of the monastic orders. The monks had also found other ways of enriching the Church. They had secured immense tracts of land which had appeared of little value to the ignorant laymen, but which yielded bountiful crops, when once the swamps had been drained and the forests cleared. Around Rome the Papal States had grown up, controlled directly by the pope. In the twelfth and thirteenth centuries, the papacy had carried on a terrific contest for temporal supremacy with no lesser men than the emperors of the Holy Roman Empire, who in theory held all the countries of western and central Europe as their fiefs.

At the close of the thirteenth century, however, the power of the papacy began to wane. Most humiliating for the popes was the so-called Babylonian Captivity (1309–77) at Avignon, in France, where they were dominated by the French king. Equally distressing was the great schism (1378–1418), when there were two popes, one in Rome and one in Avignon. Then followed a period of twenty years in which the power of the papacy within the Church was contested by church councils, notably the Council of Basel (1431–33); but at the Council of Ferrara-Florence (1438–42), the pope was able to reassert successfully the claims of his greatest predecessors. His temporal power, however, continued to decline, particularly in France and England. Even in the Holy Roman Empire, where no great monarch stood ready to defend the national interests of the people, there was much discontent, and signs were not lacking that here too the pope could no longer strike terror into the hearts of princes, as had been the case in former days. In Russia and the Balkan Peninsula his authority had entirely disappeared since the middle of the eleventh century, because of differences in doctrine and church rites between the leaders in Rome and Constantinople. Europe possessed no longer one great Catholic Church, but two distinct branches, one called the Roman Catholic, the other the Greek, or Orthodox Catholic Church.

Nevertheless the Roman Catholic Church was exceedingly powerful, as almost every person believed that outside the Church nobody could be saved. For every individual in the Middle Ages the burning issue of his whole life was understood to be the possi-

ble salvation of his soul from eternal damnation. The only media-
tion between man and God was the Church. Such was the belief
of the vast majority of people. Life on earth was comparatively
short, and eternity had no end. Terrible was the prospect of the
trembling sinner, if the Church should fail to save him. Hence the
influence of the clergy and the importance of the seven sacraments.

There was much divergence of opinion concerning the efficacy
of these sacraments. The Church as an institution had undergone
many changes. Its creeds and its sacraments naturally had been
subject to a great deal of criticism. Within the ranks of the hier-
archy there had been intense rivalry. Church councils had sought
to limit the power of the pope, and even some of the greatest
cardinals had openly questioned several doctrines taught by the
popes and their followers. Heretics had risen in various countries,
some of whom had been put to death, while others had merely been
silenced or persuaded to modify their criticism. Abuses had crept
into the institution as a whole. National governments had begun
to restrict the power of the papacy. Finally, a number of mystics
had sought to secure salvation without the aid of the clergy. The
whole structure of the Church seemed to totter as the fifteenth
century drew to a close. Fifty years later it was felt by thousands
of observers that it would actually crumble to pieces.

The attacks on the papal power by humanists had been far-
reaching. The Emperor Constantine, who lived in the fourth
century, and who had moved his capital from Italy to Constantinople, was supposed to have presented the bishop of Rome with
the western half of his empire, in return for the assistance rendered
by the bishop in saving his life. Lorenzo Valla had proved that
this "Donation of Constantine" was simply a forged document.
Valla and many other Italian scholars further hurt the papal cause
by instilling into the minds of their numerous followers an attitude
of skepticism and disrespect for authority. A great number of
humanists made light of monastic discipline and the efficacy of the
sacraments. They belittled the value of the soul and the importance of life after physical death, and consequently taught that
people were foolish to be so intent on the salvation of the soul.
They were opposed to asceticism, and some of them were even in-

clined favorably toward paganism. Not all of their views and deeds led up to the Reformation, but they certainly helped to prepare the way for several phases of this movement.

The humanists were supported in their attacks on the power of the Church as an institution by many theologians and mystics who believed that the Church had become too materialistic, and that there was in the Church too much empty formalism, with too little emphasis laid on personal piety. The mystics, in particular, strove to warn their pupils against the reliance on what they called "outward deeds," as contrasted with inner faith, feelings, and emotions. Books like the *Imitation of Christ* emphasized the need of love and faith rather than "works." The mystics tended to weaken the power of the clergy by laying stress on the relation between the individual soul and God, in which relation the sacraments play a comparatively insignificant part. The influence exerted by the mystics is very difficult to measure, but it was great.

Almost all classes of people agreed that the Church needed a reformation. Conservative minds would be content with a small number of changes; radical thinkers naturally wanted more. Some were interested chiefly in political and financial issues, while others were almost solely concerned with spiritual problems. There was scarcely a thinking person to be found anywhere in Europe at the end of the Middle Ages who felt that the Church was a perfect institution.

Some of the abuses which in the opinion of every honest reformer needed correction were simony and nepotism. Both were widespread at the time, and they were openly practiced by the higher clergy in Rome and elsewhere. The papacy itself was in need of reform. For at least a century the popes had not been the type of men who could be considered proper representatives of Christ on earth. They were all subject to criticism, for they did not try to be spiritual guides for the people. One pope would lead an army to battle, another would spend most of his time in studying art and literature, while still another would do little more than indulge in selfish pleasures. To many people it seemed that Rome was about the last place where one should look for the center of Christianity.

Then there were a number of practices and doctrines which were considered faulty by certain reformers. As early as the thirteenth and fourteenth centuries the question had often been raised whether it was right to have so many feast days, whether pilgrimages, relics, "good works" in general, were as efficacious as some claimed. The sale of indulgences was prohibited in Spain by Cardinal Ximenez. Cusa, the German cardinal, had taught the Augustinian doctrine of justification by faith and the depravity of human nature. Some of the Brethren of the Common Life in the Netherlands had preached the doctrine of the priesthood of all believers, which was taught later by the early Protestants. They, in common with other loyal church members, had bewailed the indolence, ignorance, and immorality of certain classes of monks, priests, and bishops.

Far more radical were those reformers, or so-called reformers, who were condemned as heretics by the Church. Notable among these were the Waldenses, the followers of Peter Waldo of Lyons, who lived in southern France at the close of the twelfth century. They not only attacked existing abuses, but rejected several of the doctrines regarding the sacraments, and insisted on the reading of the New Testament in the vernacular. They resembled the Puritans of a later age in that they wished to simplify rites in the Church and to elevate morals generally.

Perhaps the most notable of all the radical reformers was John Wyclif, who taught for many years at Oxford, but who was silenced in 1378 because of his attacks on the power of the clergy, his repudiation of the doctrine of transubstantiation, and his relentless criticism of the abuses in the Church. He had a large following in England, and it is possible that he prepared the way for the spread of Luther's teaching early in the sixteenth century.

Bohemian students carried the doctrines of Wyclif from Oxford to Prague, where Hus taught them openly, and with such effect that the German professors and students finally left Prague for Leipzig (1409). Although Hus was condemned to die at the stake by the Council of Constance (1415), a large number of Hussites continued to teach his doctrines in Bohemia. Some of them rejected transubstantiation, indulgences, the confessional, and the worship of saints. They perpetuated the views of Hus long after he had been burned alive as a heretic. One day Luther himself was to exclaim: "We have all been Hussites without know- ing it!"

When Luther made this startling remark, he undoubtedly in- dulged in exaggeration, but it should be observed that at the close of the fifteenth century there was much confusion among clerics and laymen respecting the essential doctrines and rites of the Roman Catholic Church. The relation between Luther and Eras- mus was in a certain sense an illustration of this confusion. Eras- mus himself was deemed a heretic by many prominent churchmen. In common with Wyclif, Hus, Luther, and many of the humanists and mystics, he felt alarmed about conditions in the Church. After 1475 there was never a year in his life when ecclesiastical and religious problems did not arouse his lively interest. However, there were also times when they occupied only a secondary place in his mind. Even before he had attained the age of twenty he seemed to be consumed by a burning desire to devote himself to the revival of classical scholarship. It soon became his darling ambition to imitate the great Italian humanists, such as Petrarch, Valla, and Ficino. Well did he know that thousands of German scholars had crossed the Alps to sit at the feet of the celebrated teachers of Greek philosophy at Florence, and for years it was his favorite wish to go himself. Compared with the northern Nether- lands and with even the most prosperous districts in Germany, the city-states of Venice, Florence, Milan, and Rome certainly offered much to evoke admiration and envy in the hearts of trans- alpine "barbarians."

What did the northern countries possess with which to emulate the Vatican and the basilicas at Rome, and the palaces and cathedrals at Florence, Pisa, Bologna, Milan, and Venice? In all the Low Countries there was only one university, namely at Louvain, and even that institution had not yet attained much eminence. Whereas in Italy the Greek and Roman writers were worshiped almost as saints, in countries north of the Alps but little progress had been made in reviving classical learning. Throughout the fifteenth century, nearly all scholars in transalpine countries frankly admitted the superiority of Italian schools and of Italian art.

It is of course well known that the word Renaissance is French, and that it literally means re-birth. When the term Renaissance is taken in its widest connotation, it implies the revival of all forms of learning and comprises an intellectual movement which resulted in the discovery of America and India, in the exploration of vast continents and of the starry firmament, in the rise of modern science, the downfall of scholastic philosophy, the spread of classical Latin, the renewed study of Greek and of Plato, the invention of printing — in short, the conquest of humanism, or the revival of interest in human and physical and material things, as contrasted with the realm of the soul or spirit.

The humanists stressed what contemporaries called *humanitas*, or humanity — something neglected and even despised by the medieval scribes. The humanists taught that man has a perfect right to enjoy himself in this world, that human nature is not fundamentally bad and that human beings have great innate power, for which reason they need not be so self-depreciating. They exalted human nature, but were less interested in pure theology. They were opposed to asceticism, which is a system of thought directed toward the suppression of physical enjoyment. The ascetic loathes human nature and believes that the flesh is the ally of the devil. The humanist entertains a very different opinion concerning human nature. It should be observed, however, that the word humanist may be defined in different ways, just as is the case with the terms Renaissance and Christianity. Some men were named humanists simply because they devoted themselves to the study of classical literature, while others received the appellation because they broke with scholastic philosophy or with the old grammars.

Erasmus in his youth was strongly influenced by both humanism and asceticism, but as he grew older he became a typical humanist, though he always represented a type widely different from an Italian humanist like Valla. After he had passed the age of thirty he experienced a slight reversion to the principles of his teachers in the Netherlands. But he was never an ascetic, although he always sympathized with those humanists who chose to remain Christians. It seemed indeed quite possible for a scholar to combine the teachings of Christianity with the ideals of humanism. How this might be accomplished was a problem to which Erasmus devoted the best years of his life.

Those who have read all the printed works of Erasmus say that there is scarcely a place in all of his writings where he evinces an appreciation of the beauties of nature, or displays more than a fleeting interest in science, mathematics, geography, politics, economics, or sociology. He never knew what patriotism was and he despised the lower classes, although he himself was often poor. Hence he was able to concentrate all his energies on the study of Latin and Greek, with the result that he surpassed all his contemporaries as a writer of polished Latin, while his wit and his knowledge of human nature made him the dictator of intellectual Europe. To him it seemed folly to practice such virtues as self-sacrifice, humility, fidelity, and obedience. He had no desire to become either a martyr or a hero. It was his aim to live apart from the crowd, to avoid the scene of strife, and to ignore everything that hindered the progress of classical scholarship and religious reform. Just why he chose to adopt this course and how far he succeeded in achieving his aim may be gathered, in part at least, from the study of his youth.

CHAPTER II

THE BURGUNDIAN NETHERLANDS

ERASMUS was brought up in the Netherlands, or Low Countries, a district including not only the territory which now
forms the Kingdom of the Netherlands but also Belgium, Luxemburg, and a part of northern France. Strictly speaking, this district belonged partly to the Holy Roman Empire and partly to
France, but during the course of the fifteenth century the seventeen tiny states which were collectively styled Netherlands became nearly independent of both the emperor and the French
king.

At the opening of the fifteenth century most of the states, or
provinces, had become subject to three foreign dynasties, namely,
the houses of Wittelsbach (Bavarian), Luxemburg (Bohemian),
and Burgundy. The Bavarian house ruled in Holland, Zeeland,
and Hainault; the Bohemian house in Brabant, Limburg, and
Luxemburg; while the duke of Burgundy had held Flanders since
1384 and was gradually extending his influence, to the detriment
of the two rivals, who before long were to lose all their possessions
in the Netherlands.

Greatest of all the dukes of Burgundy was Philip the Good
(1419–67), who not only possessed the duchy of Burgundy and
Franche-Comté, or the County of Burgundy, but inherited
Flanders, Mechlin, and Artois from his grandmother Margaret;
and Brabant, Limburg, and Antwerp from his cousin Philip.
Through cunning, diplomacy, and force of arms he took possession
of Limburg and Antwerp (1430), which were to a certain extent
dependencies of Brabant; in the same manner he secured Holland, Zeeland, and Hainault (1433), and Luxemburg was added in
1451; Namur was bought from its count (1421) and the bishopric
of Utrecht was given to David, his natural son (1456). Of the

seventeen principalities which constituted the Netherlands, Philip actually possessed eleven, and he laid claim to Friesland, because the counts of Holland had for centuries regarded this district as a dependency of their county.

The reign of Philip the Good was of great importance in the history of the Netherlands. Gradually he increased his influence in the six districts which he himself could not occupy, so that by the end of his reign not only Utrecht, but also Gelderland and Liège formed little more than protectorates of the wily duke. His reign marked the end of feudalism in the Low Countries, for eleven separate principalities had been joined to form another "national state," controlled by one central government. Furthermore, Philip had withdrawn his possessions from the suzerainty of both the king of France and the emperor of the Holy Roman Empire. And what is still more significant, he had terminated the long series of social and political wars which had seriously hampered the expansion of trade and industry. There was only one task left for the duke of Burgundy, namely, the conquest of the territory between the Netherlands and the ancient duchy to the south.

Philip was not able to join the two great units, but when he passed away in 1467, his son, Charles the Bold (1467–77), firmly resolved to execute the plan and have himself crowned king besides. At first it seemed as if he would be successful, for the death of the Duke of Gelderland in 1473 enabled Charles to occupy this important duchy, and now he believed the time ripe for the creation of the kingdom of Burgundy. Had he not inherited the fairest provinces of the ancient kingdom of Lorraine, which once stretched all the way from the North Sea to the Mediterranean? In order to gain the good will of Emperor Frederick III he promised the hand of his only daughter, Mary, to the Emperor's son, Maximilian. In November, 1473, therefore, Charles was to be crowned king at Trier, but the day before the coronation the Emperor changed his mind and fled from the scene. King Louis XI of France, often named the "spider king," had informed the Emperor that Charles, his enemy, had no intention of keeping his promise. Against this cunning monarch the audacious but not highly intelligent duke was no match. He vainly attempted to increase his territories east of Burgundy, and in 1477 he was killed on the battle-field when fighting a Swiss army. At his death the French king pulled the whole duchy of Burgundy into his web, since Mary, Charles' heir, possessed neither soldiers nor finances with which to defend herself.

Shortly after the death of Charles the Bold his daughter married Maximilian, in accordance with the agreement between Charles and Frederick III. As archduke of Austria and prospective heir to all the Habsburg dominions, the bridegroom was expected to protect the Netherlands against the scheming "spider king." For the inhabitants of the Netherlands, however, the marriage was by no means an advantage. Maximilian and his successors remained true members of the illustrious house of Habsburg. The state so carefully constructed in the Low Countries by Philip the Good, even though it was enlarged later to include all the seventeen provinces, became and long remained a mere dependency of a great monarchy with its capital not in Brussels but in Vienna, and later in Madrid. The premature death of Charles the Bold and his lack of a capable successor were partly responsible for the subjection of the Netherlands to a number of monarchs who refused to identify their interests with those of the people in the Low Countries, and so it happened that the latter never formed a homogeneous state, not even in the reign of King William I (1815–30); and therefore a national consciousness did not develop in the country which gave birth to Erasmus until it had separated from the southern provinces and rose against the king of Spain (1568–1648). Had Erasmus been born two hundred years later he would have felt quite differently about his native country.

The death of Charles the Bold ushered in a period of civil war in the Netherlands. Suddenly the hand of a powerful ruler had been withdrawn and now there was no longer a standing army to quell insurrection and party strife. The bishopric of Liège was the first to rise successfully against the rule of Mary. She granted to Louis of Bourbon, the bishop, complete independence, which the bishopric maintained until the close of the eighteenth century. Gelderland, however, was less fortunate, while the other provinces inherited by Mary agreed to accept her rule on condition that she sign a document named the "Great Privilege," which wrung many concessions from her, but did not revive the old feudal governments. The dukes and counts were gone, never to return.

In 1478 Mary bore a son, Philip the Fair, who afterward married Joanna of Spain, and who became the father of the powerful Charles V, the modern Charlemagne. The birth of Philip created great happiness in the Low Countries, for it was hoped that he would some day restore order in the distracted provinces. Maximilian successfully continued the war with France, and when, in 1481, he made an alliance with King Edward IV of England the French king was compelled to resort to defensive warfare. But in 1482 Mary died and once more the country faced a grave political crisis. Everywhere attempts were made to deprive Maximilian of power. Particularly in Flanders he was strongly resisted. The city of Ghent compelled him to surrender the reins of government to a council of regents, and six years later (1488) Ghent started a new revolution. Maximilian tried to call a meeting of the States-General in Bruges, but this city also was hostile to him. The guilds of Bruges closed their gates to the German army which Maximilian had ordered to suppress the insurgents. They occupied the market square, and the illustrious archduke, who since 1486 had also been King of the Romans, was imprisoned in a grocery store! He now lost even the title of Regent of Flanders, but, once set free, he hastened to mete out revenge to the burghers of Bruges and Ghent, who after stubborn resistance had to surrender to his rule. In 1492 Maximilian was master of Flanders, and Ghent had lost its independence.

In the northern provinces also much fighting occurred. Civil war, held in check by Philip the Good and Charles the Bold (1428–77), broke out anew as soon as Charles fell on the battle-field. The two factions which before 1428 had arrayed themselves against each other, namely, the *Hoekschen* and the *Kabeljauw-schen*, now commenced another terrible war, causing widespread distress. The first-named party was opposed to the Burgundian house, while the other faction supported it. In Utrecht the bishop was defeated and it was not until 1483 that Bishop David, the son of Philip of Burgundy, was restored to power by Maximilian. In the former county of Holland a veritable guerilla war was waged. Two powerful noblemen fitted out an impregnable castle which formed a base of operations for plundering expeditions. Their fleet took Rotterdam in 1488 and their soldiers did untold damage in surrounding territory. Few countrysides suffered so much as the territory near Gouda where Erasmus at that very time was living in a monastery. One of his intimate friends, William Herman of Gouda, described the terrible conditions he had himself witnessed in a poem, which throws much light on this subject, as will appear. North of Gouda, particularly near the Zuider Zee, similar conditions prevailed. Pirates infested the latter sea, seriously interfering with traffic. Then followed a very bad harvest in 1490, which aroused thousands of farmers to frenzy, for it was not so much the weather as the fighting which had brought the country near to famine. In 1491 and 1492 the roving peasants entered various cities, where they destroyed much valuable property. Near Leiden they were finally defeated by troops which had been sent from Germany.

For fifteen years (1477–92) the archduke of Austria had failed to restore order. It was indeed a pity for Holland that Charles the Bold had so recklessly thrown away his life. Whereas before the year 1477 the cities of Amsterdam, Leiden, Dordrecht, Haarlem, Rotterdam, and Gouda had just begun to rival the Hansa towns of northern Germany, the period of anarchy which followed the death of Charles witnessed the devastation of miles of fertile fields and the destruction of thousands of homes, paralyzing trade and undermining the foundations of prosperity. In Holland the worst evils occurred between 1487 and 1492. It was in this very period that Erasmus resided in the monastery of Steyn, near Gouda, and it was at this time that he wrote his *De Contemptu Mundi*, or *On the Contempt of the World*, in imitation of Thomas à Kempis, praising monasticism, saying that in the quiet gardens of his house he found rest, and urging a friend of his to join him, inasmuch as in the world there was turmoil and misery, while the peace of the monastic grounds remained undisturbed! He afterward felt ashamed of this treatise, but those who have read about

the *Hoekschen* in Holland can understand perfectly the background of this composition. When civil war was ended, Erasmus
ventured forth from the quiet grounds of Steyn, for now he needed
the monastery no longer!

In 1492 the political crisis in the Low Countries had passed.
Maximilian had finally achieved his purpose. The central
government had been restored and the next year he could safely
intrust the reins of political power to his son Philip the Fair, and
direct his attention to affairs in the Holy Roman Empire, where
he was soon to become Emperor himself. In 1493 he made peace
with Charles VIII of France, who returned Franche-Comté and
Artois to him, and in 1494 he embarked upon the conquest of Italy.
In the Low Countries Philip the Fair was gladly hailed as Prince,
and during the twelve years of his reign (1494–1506) the burghers
of Flanders and Holland were content with their loss of political
autonomy, for they had learned to appreciate order and prosperity more than self-government. They could now apply themselves to the task of making the Netherlands the emporium of the
western world, the leader in scientific agriculture and the successful rival of Italy in the fields of commerce, industry, learning, and
art.

Professor Henri Pirenne has shown that during the late medieval
period (1000–1500 A.D.) the Low Countries were exceptionally
prosperous. Throughout this middle region French monastic
reforms, epics, and chivalry passed into Germany; and whatever
ideas came from Germany to France traveled mostly by way of
the Netherlands.[1] It was here that intellectual as well as religious
and commercial currents met and mingled; and from here they
issued forth. The Flemish towns were the first in transalpine
Europe to supplant the monasteries as chief seats of learning and
art.[2] Under the rule of the dukes of Burgundy, Bruges and Ghent
became the wealthiest cities north of the Alps, not excepting Paris
and London. In the middle of the fifteenth century the court at
Bruges outshone even the court at Paris.

---

[1] H. Pirenne, *Histoire de Belgique*, I (Brussels, 1902), viii-ix, 27, 30, 32, 156–158,
161–169, 244–245, 326–327, 336; II (Brussels, 1903), 178–180, 380–383, 394–395.
[2] H. Pirenne, *op. cit.*, I, 156–161.

"The most brillant court of Europe in the middle of the fifteenth century," says a noted French historian, "was that of Philip the Good, duke of Burgundy. No region was in fact so rich as the Netherlands, which belonged to him, and Philip was the most extravagant of all men. His reign was one long festival. His court, like that of the French kings after him, was a meeting-place of the noblemen of his immense domains; they imitated his vices and dissipated their possessions through extravagant expenditures. . . . His court was a prefiguration of the court at Versailles. Everything was so arranged as to enhance the majesty of the prince. It was here that the etiquette of the Christian monarchies was invented or at least developed." [3]

Like the despots of Florence, Milan, Verona, and Ferrara, the wealthy duke of Burgundy became a patron of learning and art. His famous library formed the nucleus of the Royal Library at Brussels. Dutch and Flemish musicians were the most renowned in all Europe, while in the field of printing the Netherlands achieved much. Some scholars still maintain that movable type was invented not by Gutenberg at Mainz, but by Dutch printers.[4] At any rate, during the second half of the fifteenth century the number of printing-presses increased rapidly throughout the Netherlands.

The vernacular literatures, however, seemed to be subject to a process of stagnation; neither Flemish nor French productions rose above the level of the mediocre and banale.[5] One can scarcely find a trace of patriotism in these writings, even though in France and Germany thousands of educated people displayed patriotic pride in cultivating their respective vernaculars. A national literature apparently could not thrive in the Netherlands. Only Latin, the universal language, was deemed worthy of those who knew how to write. This favor shown to Latin was a trait characteristic of the Burgundian Renaissance. "Like the language it employs," says Pirenne, "it is universal, and it responds to the

---

[3] Ch. Petit-Dutaillis, *Charles VII, Louis XI et les premières années de Charles VIII (1422–1492)*, in E. Lavisse, *Histoire de France*, IV, Part 2 (Paris, 1902), 170.
[4] P. J. Blok, *Geschiedenis van het Nederlandsche Volk*, I (Leiden, 1923), 636.
[5] *Ibid.*, p. 635.

essence of Belgian civilization. This level country, this territory open to all nations, this Burgundian state, could not live in isolation. In this region, toward which all European activity converged, the movement of ideas corresponded to the movement of merchandise and of capital. Just as Antwerp was the most cosmopolitan city of the sixteenth century, and Erasmus the most universal writer of his time, so the national character of the Low Countries, whenever they enjoyed a superior form of civilization, was original in that it was universal."[6]

[6] H. Pirenne, *op. cit.*, III (Brussels, 1912), 296.

CHAPTER III

THE "DEVOTIO MODERNA"

WHEN Erasmus was still a little boy he was sent to school in the city of Deventer, where he first became acquainted with the movement named Devotio Moderna. The term, which means "present-day devotion," originated in the fifteenth century, and was applied to the thoughts and labors of a large group of mystics and educators, mostly belonging to the Brethren of the Common Life and the Augustinian Canons Regular of the Congregation of Windesheim. The movement may be said to have originated with the life-work of Gerard Groote of Deventer (1340–84), and it was extinguished early in the sixteenth century when the storm of the Reformation submerged the spirit of Groote's teachings.

During the whole history of the Devotio Moderna the valley of the river Yssel, where Deventer was situated, remained the geographical center of the movement. It was here that Groote had founded the first house of the Sisters of the Common Life, and here he had collected a band of twelve disciples, who, with the exception of one backslider, solemnly vowed to continue the work of the beloved master. A plague had carried Groote away in the summer of 1384, but his influence remained a living force long after his death.[1]

How Groote was revered by his followers may be gathered from their eulogies, some of which are worth quoting. Thomas à Kempis, the author of the *Imitation of Christ*, claimed that Groote "illuminated the whole country with his life, words, ways and doctrine." John Vos of Heusden, a leader of the Devotio Moderna, remarked in 1424, when lying on his death-bed: "Groote was the first father of this our reformation, the source and origin of the

---

[1] On Groote, see A. Hyma, *The Christian Renaissance, A History of the "Devotio Moderna"* (New York, 1925), Chap. I.

21

Devotio Moderna; he was an apostle in his country who kindled the fires of religious fervor in the cold hearts of men, and drew them to God." And another leader, named William Vornken, called Groote the "Fountain of the Devotio Moderna," adding: "The fathers of the former congregation say, through what act of grace or miracle came it to pass that as master Gerard Groote was preaching and sowing the seed everywhere, there were added to him so suddenly and unexpectedly men of such kind and so great, for these were of one mind with him, and everyone of them in each city and place burned with the zeal with which he also burned to exhort and convert a people that was stiff-necked. O happy day on which that great Gerard was born among us, for he was the fount and source whence flowed the waters of salvation to our land, so that what before his time had been parched became a pool, and the thirsty land, springs of water."

A summary of Groote's activities as a religious reformer is found in a letter written to Pope Urban VI by William de Sarvar-villa, cantor of the University of Paris, shortly before Groote passed away. The word Groote means "great," wherefore the letter begins as follows: "Truly he was 'The Great,' for in his knowledge of all the liberal sciences, both natural and moral, of civil law, canon law, and of theology, he was second to no one in the world, and all these branches of learning were united in him. He was a man of such saintliness and gave so good an example of mortification of the flesh, his contempt for the world, his brotherly love for all, his zeal for the salvation of souls, his effectual preaching, his reprobation and hatred of wickedness, his withstanding of heretics, his enforcement of the canon law against those that broke the vow of chastity, his conversion to the spiritual life of divers men and women who had formerly lived according to the world, and his loyalty to our Lord Urban VI, — in all those things I say he gave so good an example, that many thousands of men testify to the belief that is in them that he was not less great in these virtues than he was in the aforesaid sciences."

Groote had reasoned that not only should the clergy be reformed, but laymen needed more religious fervor. His influence spread far and wide throughout the northern Netherlands, but it was most strongly felt and lasted longest in the institutions of the Brethren and Sisters of the Common Life and of the Congregation of Windesheim. The oldest institution was the first house of the Sisters of the Common Life at Deventer, to whom Groote donated the use of his ancestral home (1374). In 1379 he formulated for the sisters a simple constitution, written in the vernacular. Five years later the first house of the Brethren of the Common Life was founded near the city of Zwolle, which was located about ten miles north of Deventer. This institution, however, failed to develop for nine years, and therefore it may be said that the first real house of the Brethren of the Common Life was founded at Deventer shortly after the death of Groote. Most of Groote's intimate followers at Deventer made their living by copying books. During his lifetime their leader did not allow them to unite their funds, fearing that the mendicant monks would attack them for trying to found a monastic order.

Had Groote lived but one year longer, however, he would probably have witnessed the formation of the semi-monastic brotherhood of which he was actually the founder. On his death-bed he appointed as leader of the distracted disciples a man who for saintliness and integrity has seldom been surpassed in the Netherlands. This man was Florentius Radewyns, vicar in the ancient church of St. Lebwin's at Deventer, and for a period of seven years the teacher of Thomas à Kempis. Whereas Groote had considered himself too great a sinner to enter the ranks of the priesthood, he did not hesitate to urge Radewyns to become a priest. The latter was endowed with special gifts of devotion. No one was kinder than he to the poor, the sick, and the afflicted. He often went to visit the suffering. Many a meal he was wont to send to certain famishing families in the slums of Deventer. A list was kept by him of all the sick people in the city. The feeble-bodied and all others who through no fault of their own were in need of material assistance, he supplied with food and clothing, and the poorer class of schoolboys with pens, ink, and paper. One lenten season there was great scarcity of food and of work, so that an unusually large number of poor people came to Radewyns for help; whereupon he, finding himself unable to give assistance to so many at once, persuaded his friends and followers to add one hour a day to their work for the period of one week. The extra money thus saved he presented to the "Overseer of the Poor" at Deventer. During the month of May he was accustomed to gather herbs for the sick. He would invite all those people to his house who were afflicted with ulcers, sores, and other skin diseases. They were then given a bath in warm water, perfumed with aromatic herbs. A clean bed was also prepared for each patient, where they were told to rest themselves, after first having received a cup of wine.

Radewyns did not even shrink from lepers, and to the maimed and deformed he was particularly kind. "I once knew a leper," says Thomas à Kempis, "who used to abide outside the walls of the city. Florentius would often sit beside him and talk to him. I have seen," he continues, "one blind of an eye, and one lame of one foot, who were both converted by him." At times he was consulted by so many people that he had no time even to go to church. And who was there who could comfort the people as did Radewyns? Involuntarily their hearts were filled with new hope and happiness at one touch of his hand, or a single glance from those starry eyes which bespoke tender sympathy. The moment one approached him, one's troubles and anxieties would suddenly subside. What was there in this singularly attractive person to shed about him as it were a halo of almost celestial felicity? Was he so great an orator? Did he perhaps cast the hypnotic spell of fiery eloquence upon the fascinated crowds?

Among all the men Thomas à Kempis had met before he wrote the *Imitation*, Radewyns, he thought, was the one who had taught him most about the Cross of Christ. We should learn of him, Christ had said, by imitating him. And how could we imitate him best? By taking his yoke upon us, the yoke of humility and charity. One should try to sympathize with the poor and afflicted, visit the sick, comfort orphans and widows, and be ready to perform the most humble tasks at home. We should never seek our own good, Radewyns used to say, but rather consider only our neighbor's welfare. Thus one might become a Christian, in his opinion. And Radewyns was wont to practice what he preached.

He was always ready to take an active share in his neighbor's sorrows. Naturally, his feeling of pity was instinctively felt by all who came near him. Thomas à Kempis himself had often experienced a thrill of rapture simply in being near his teacher and master. A few words from Radewyns' lips would comfort all. "This," says Thomas à Kempis, "I have often tried and experienced myself." Is it any wonder that Thomas à Kempis, who had spent several years in Radewyns' presence, often used to look upon his stay at Deventer with a feeling of reverence and intense gratitude? Florentius Radewyns was a man who lived the ideals of the *Imitation of Christ*.

For fifteen years Radewyns was rector of the brethren at Deventer (1385–1400). It was a time of steady growth and fruitful labor, although at the end of the rectorate the men had to meet a twofold crisis, namely, a terrible pestilence which compelled most of them to leave Deventer for a while, and attacks by mendicant monks, who asserted that it was wrong to lead the common life without taking monastic vows. But the storm soon passed; the exiled brethren returned and the criticism of the hostile monks was rendered innocuous by a treatise composed in the brethren-house, entitled *On the Common Life*, setting forth the reasons why the brethren chose to live together, why they surrendered private property, and why they still declined to join the monastic orders.

The author of this learned treatise was Gerard Zerbolt of Zutphen, a quiet sort of scholar, who preferred to sit in his cell and write rather than do much preaching. Although he was but thirty-one when he died in 1398, he had nevertheless accomplished a great task, for two of his compositions were later to attract much attention in foreign countries. He wrote the *Spiritual Ascensions* and *The Reformation of the Faculties of the Soul*, which exerted considerable influence in France and Spain. Ignatius Loyola was one of many mystics who derived spiritual sustenance from these remarkable productions of Gerard Zerbolt.[2]

---

[2] To P. H. Watrigant belongs the credit of having called attention to the striking similarity between the *Spiritual Ascensions* of Zerbolt and the *Rosary of Spiritual Exercises* of John Mombaer on the one hand and the *Spiritual Exercises* of Garcia of Cisneros and of Loyola on the other. See especially the following

The brethren-houses of Deventer and Zwolle until the year 1520 were the two chief centers of the Devotio Moderna outside the monasteries. All the other houses of ,the new brotherhood were founded, either directly or indirectly by these two. As early as the year 1395 Radewyns was asked to found a congregation at Amersfoort, while in 1403 a house was established at Delft. The institution at Zwolle was instrumental in the founding of houses in such cities as 's-Hertogenbosch, Doesburg, and Groningen. In Germany there were also a considerable number of brethren-houses, while in the southern Netherlands there were at least nine. In France, however, no houses appear to have been established.

The Sisters of the Common Life also succeeded in founding a large number of houses, particularly in the Yssel valley. At Deventer they had five houses; at Zwolle there were six, and in many other places there were daughter institutions. Altogether the sisters counted approximately ninety houses, or twice as many as the brethren possessed.

The preface to the constitution of the brethren-houses at Deventer [3] and Zwolle [4] reveal the purpose of their founders.

---

compositions of his: *La Genèse des Exercitia Spiritualia* (Amiens, 1897); "La Méditation méthodique et l'école des frères de la vie commune," *Revue d'ascétique et de mystique*, 1922, pp. 134–155. Another Jesuit scholar named Codina has tried to prove that Loyola was independent of the Devotio Moderna. See his *Los origenes de los ejercicios espirituales de S. Ignacio de Loyola* (Barcelona, 1926). But his arguments have failed to convince other Jesuits. Cf. the reviews in the *Rev. d'asc. et de myst.*, 1927, p. 82, and in the *Nouvelle Revue théol.*, 1927, p. 634. An interesting study on this subject is also the book by P. Groult, entitled *Les Mystiques des Pays-Bas et la littérature espagnole* (Louvain, 1927); see pp. 53–54 and 130–145. Groult expounds the theory that John Ruysbroeck is the real father of the Devotio Moderna rather than Groote, but he does not appear to have acquainted himself fully with the labors of Groote and his followers.

[3] The Deventer constitution was printed for the first time in A. Hyma, *The Christian Renaissance*, pp. 441–474. It was not known until recently that this constitution had been used in the brethren-house at Deventer, and a few scholars in the Netherlands still believe that it is not the original version. However, the preface of the document shows that it was composed after 1413, the first chapter proves that it was not preceded by another written constitution, and therefore it is unquestionably the original written constitution. Although in this document a few phrases seem to reveal dependence on rules used at Zwolle, one does not exaggerate in saying that the Deventer constitution was the model after which the rules in all other brethren-houses were patterned.

[4] This constitution has been reprinted in M. Schoengen, *Jacobus Voecht Narratio*, pp. 239–273.

"Our house was founded," each document reads, "with the intention that, in imitation of the Primitive Christian Church, priests and clerics might live there, supported by their own labor, namely, the copying of books, and by the returns from certain estates." The constitutions state further that the brethren were to rise between three and four o'clock in the morning (later shortly before five), preparing themselves at once for prayer and reading. During meals they were expected to maintain silence, in order that they might pay proper attention to the reading of the Bible. After supper they could do as they pleased in their rooms till eight o'clock, but at eight all guests had to leave the house, the doors were shut fast and after half an hour of silence the brethren went to bed.

On Sundays and holidays certain passages in the Scriptures were read and explained and in this connection there was opportunity for general discussion, when each member of the house could freely express his opinions. Schoolboys as well as adults from all walks of life had free access to these numerous meetings (for holidays were plentiful), where discussions were held in the vernacular. Because of the short speeches or sermons provided by the brethren, they were often called *Fratres Collationarii*. Another popular name was that of *Hieronymiani*, "Jeromites," because of their liking for St. Jerome, while in Germany the name *Nullbrüder* or *Kugelherren* was frequently applied to them.

Unlike many of the monks, the Brethren of the Common Life, with rare exception, preferred a busy life of "good works" in the cities to peaceful meditation in the country. "We have decided," wrote the brethren at Zwolle in 1415, "to live in cities, in order that we may be able to give advice and instruction to clerics and other persons who wish to serve the Lord." Each house should if possible have four priests and some other members of the clergy, while the number of laymen was not specified. If somebody applied for admission, the brethren were required to examine his physical condition and his mental equipment. He would be asked whether he could write, and whether he loved to read books. In case he seemed a promising candidate he would be permitted to remain in the house on trial for one year, and after this period he might become a real member on condition that in the presence of a notary-public and some witnesses he swore to relinquish all claims to private property. No one, however, was expected to remain against his wishes, although property once surrendered was not restored to the original owner.

The Brethren of the Common Life counted many enemies in the ranks of the friars, and one learned monk in particular, named Grabow, caused them considerable worry. At the Council of Constance, however, they were warmly defended by no less a prelate than Gerson, chancellor of the University of Paris.[5] In 1431 their mode of living was officially approved by Pope Eugene IV, who instructed the archbishop of Cologne and the bishops of Münster and Utrecht to protect the brethren in their respective bishoprics.[6] And well he might, for the brotherhood was exceptionally loyal to all men placed in authority, while its members conscientiously strove to adhere to the accepted teachings of the Roman Catholic Church.

The Brethren and Sisters of the Common Life as a group may be called practical mystics, in distinction from such mystics as Ruysbroeck, Tauler, Suso, and Eckhart. Whereas the latter approached the pantheists, the former were unwilling or unable to seek union with the divine spirit through passive quiescence. Love for their neighbor impelled Groote and Radewyns and their followers to labor among laymen in busy thoroughfares. Their highest aim, however, was the reformation of the Church, which could most effectively be accomplished, they reasoned, by educating the young. Theodore Herxen, the successful rector at Zwolle (1410–57), wrote several treatises on the subject of "drawing boys to God." [7]

Groote had already taken steps to encourage learning in schoolboys, often inviting them to his house, where he had them copy books for him and talked with them about their work at school and about their plans for the future. At Deventer and Zwolle he cultivated the friendship of both teachers and employers. He was

---

[5] J. L. Connolly, *John Gerson* (Louvain, 1927), pp. 187–188.
[6] M. Schoengen, *Jacobus Traiecti . . . Narratio*, pp. 515–518.
[7] P. H. J. Knierim, *Dirc van Herxen* (Amsterdam, 1926), pp. 105–119.

particularly interested in an educator named John Cele, who for a period of about forty years was in charge of the public school at Zwolle, where he was intimately related to the Brethren of the Common Life. So successful was Cele that about eight hundred boys flocked to his school from many scattered localities, among them Cologne, Trier, Louvain, Saxony, Flanders, and Frisia. He did pioneer work in dividing the school into eight grades and intrusting the work in the seventh and eighth grades to specialists. Again, he led in the field of religious instruction. "The kingdom of heaven," said Cele, "consists not in knowledge and speech, but in work and virtue." He taught his pupils to pray both in the vernacular and in Latin. From the Gospels and other books of the New Testament he selected the plainest and most helpful sayings, and dictated these in a loud voice to the whole school, whereupon the pupils were instructed to memorize the texts and to apply the contents to their own lives.

Encouraged by the example of Groote and Cele, the Brethren of the Common Life turned their attention more and more to the field of education. It seemed so difficult to make much impression on adults, particularly those members of the clergy who deliberately neglected their flocks or led lives of vice. If the Church was to be reformed effectively, the ranks of the clergy would simply have to be filled from year to year with young men who not only had been properly educated, but were trained to imitate Christ.

Before the year 1450 the number of brethren who actually taught school was very limited. The majority of the members in each house made their living by copying books, but shortly after the invention of printing, manuscripts became less expensive. After 1475 it was found necessary to seek other sources of income, and now many Brethren of the Common Life became teachers. It may not seem surprising, therefore, that until recently many historians in Europe gave misleading descriptions of the interests displayed by the brotherhood in education. Some maintained that the brethren paid practically no attention to pedagogy, while others asserted that in most cases each house conducted a school of its own.

The brothers at Deventer never possessed a school, nor did

those at Zwolle and Münster, although in these three places were found the best and largest schools in the Netherlands and western Germany, as well as the most important brethren-houses. Without the presence of the Brethren of the Common Life in these cities the schools located there would certainly not have surpassed those in such places as Cologne, Trier, Strassburg, and Mainz. It must not be imagined, however, that a school flourished less because it was not owned by the brotherhood. The latter possessed schools at Doesburg, Ghent, Gouda, Grammont, Groningen, 's-Hertogenbosch, Liège, Magdeburg, Marburg, Nijmegen, Rostock, and Utrecht, but none of these equalled Deventer, Zwolle, and Münster. The chief factor on which the success of these schools depended was the presence of dormitories of the brotherhood which housed the pupils. The celebrated school at Deventer was that of St. Lebwin's, or the cathedral school, while at Zwolle Cele taught in the public school. So it did not matter whether a school was either privately owned or public.

Until the middle of the fifteenth century the Brethren of the Common Life were not affected by the educational theories of the humanists. Their methods remained thoroughly medieval and their textbooks differed not at all from those used in smaller centers of learning. But after 1455 a few of the most progressive brethren came in touch with humanistic principles, while near the close of the century the educators in their midst evinced a rather surprising liking for the teachings of such bold writers as Valla and Ficino. Though it may not be proper to say that the Devotio Moderna absorbed the teachings of the leading humanists, it certainly is true that many brothers openly sided with radical reformers who attacked the papacy, scorned scholasticism, and ridiculed the standard texts used in the schools. These brothers were perhaps no longer true representatives of the great movement originated by Groote and Cele; they may be called "Biblical humanists," or possibly "Christian humanists," although in some respects the terms "Biblical" and "Christian" on the one hand and "humanism" on the other seem mutually exclusive.

A few words should also be said about another group of Groote's followers, namely, the Augustinian Canons Regular of the Congregation of Windesheim. In the year 1384 Groote had expressed the wish that his disciples would found a monastery where some of them could live under an established monastic rule and thus protect the brothers who chose to remain "in the world." The Augustinian rule was chosen because it was less ascetic than the others. In the year 1386 a site was selected at Windesheim, three miles southeast of Zwolle, and fourteen years later some of the Sisters of the Common Life founded their first convent at Diepenveen, three miles north of Deventer. During the course of the fifteenth century a large number of other monasteries were added and a still greater number reformed by the followers of Gerard Groote. It has been estimated that in 1475 the Congregation of Windesheim counted seventy-one monasteries and thirteen convents, and that under its influence more than three hundred other institutions were reformed. But it should also be noted that many houses of the Sisters of the Common Life adopted the Third Rule of St. Francis, and so joined the Franciscan order.

One prominent Roman Catholic writer in the Netherlands has recently asked the question whether this great congregation and the brotherhood which furnished many of its recruits could not have prevented the coming of Protestantism. And he answers the question in the negative, adding that during the rise of the Devotio Moderna the Church had already declined so greatly that the comparatively small number of Groote's followers could keep it no longer intact.[8] The scope attained by the combined forces of the Devotio Moderna failed to make much impression outside the Netherlands, northern France, and northwestern Germany.

It is naturally difficult to determine what were the principles or teachings of the Devotio Moderna. One is always too easily led to personify a movement, while after all intellectual and spiritual movements cannot be measured and analyzed. The names applied to them are conventional. It frequently happens that one person or one book may seem to represent different movements or to be affected almost simultaneously by different movements. Some

[8] J. de Jong, "Een Nederlandsche godsdienstige beweging: de 'Moderne Devotie,'" *Nederlandsche Katholieke Stemmen,* 1928, p. 109. The whole article (pp. 99–109 and 138–147) is worth reading.

of the Brethren of the Common Life and many members of the Congregation of Windesheim resembled Ruysbroeck and Eckhart and Suso and Tauler. They were true mystics, while other members were more didactic, more methodical, more active in a material or intellectual sense. To the first group belonged Gerlach Peters, Henry Mande, and Thomas à Kempis; to the second, Groote himself and Radewyns and Zerbolt. The principles of their movement were largely drawn from the Bible, the writings of the Church Fathers, and distinguished members of the Medieval Church. But the productions of Eckhart, Suso, and Tauler were by no means neglected by the brethren and their friends.

There was one book which most clearly reflected the spirit of the Devotio Moderna. That book is the celebrated *De Imitatione Christi*, or *Imitation of Christ*, composed at least in part by Thomas à Kempis shortly after his residence in Deventer. Much has been written about the authorship of the *Imitation*, for it was said to have been composed by Gerson, the French writer, or by a certain, or rather an uncertain, Gersen, a fictitious monk of northern Italy. In recent years, however, nearly all scholars who have devoted careful study to the subject agree that the book must have been composed in or near Deventer by Groote and his followers or by Thomas à Kempis alone. There is not the slightest doubt that the *Imitation* was the direct outcome of Groote's labors and that it is, so to speak, the Gospel of the Devotio Moderna.

"After the Gospel," writes one Catholic scholar, "the *Imitation* undoubtedly is the book that reflects with the greatest perfection the light which Jesus Christ brought us down from Heaven. It eminently contains the Christian philosophy. . . . Nowhere else do we find the same doctrine inculcated with a more persuasive eloquence and simplicity than in the unpretending little volume that all of us have a hundred times perused." [9] This view has been set forth by writers of many other denominations and creeds. Next to the Bible the *Imitation* has been for the last four hundred years the most widely read book in Europe and America. And during all these years it has spread throughout the world the

[9] A. J. Thebaud, "Who Wrote the Imitation of Christ?" *American Cath. Quart. Rev.*, 1883, p. 650.

teachings of the Devotio Moderna, or as nearly as human beings could reproduce it, the spirit of the primitive Christian Church.

The underlying thought of the *Imitation* is the fact that man is a pilgrim here, an exile. According to Groote and his followers, man is a sort of prisoner on earth; his prison is the flesh, which besets him on every turn with obstacles, blocking his way back home to the happy state before the fall in paradise. The *Imitation*, therefore, distinctly teaches the depravity of human nature: "O how great is human frailty, which is always prone to evil. For through Adam, the first man, Nature being fallen and corrupted by sin, the penalty of this stain has descended upon all mankind." [10] Man is urged to examine his inner self: "Who has a greater combat than he that labors to overcome himself? You must be lord and master of your own actions, and not a slave or hireling. The perfect victory is to triumph over ourselves." [11] "The most profitable reading is the true knowledge and consideration of ourselves." [12]

It should be noted in particular that the *Imitation* disapproves of placing too much trust in human beings and of seeking comfort from human friendship: "He enjoys great tranquillity of heart who cares for neither the praises nor dispraises of men." [13] Fame, therefore, is absolutely worthless, as are also honors and material possessions. A spirit of Christian mysticism pervades nearly the whole book. "He to whom all things are one, he who reduces all things to one and sees all things in one, may enjoy a quiet mind and remain peaceable in God. The Kingdom of God is within you, says the Lord. . . . Learn to despise outward things and to give yourself to things inward, and you shall perceive the Kingdom of God to come in you. . . . Christ will come unto you and show you his consolation, if you prepare for him a worthy mansion within you. . . . Let not Moses speak unto me, nor any of the prophets, but rather do thou speak, O Lord God, Inspirer and Enlightener of all the prophets; for thou alone without them canst

[10] Book I, Chap. 22.
[11] Book III, Chap. 53.
[12] Book I, Chap. 2.
[13] Book I, Chaps. 1, 8, 10, 20, 25; Book II, Chaps. 6, 7, 9; Book III, Chaps. 26, 45, 54, 58.

perfectly instruct me, but they without thee profit nothing." [14]
The *Imitation* does not, however, disparage the value of book learning: "Yet learning is not to be blamed, nor the mere knowledge
of anything whatsoever to be disliked, it being good in itself and
ordained by God." Empty phrases, mere style, and scholastic
disputes, on the other hand, are considered almost valueless.[15]

Unlike the works of the first Protestants, the *Imitation* does not
set forth the view of the total depravity of man nor the complete
destruction of the human will. Since man was created in God's
image, something divine is preserved in his heart: "For the small
power which remains is as it were a spark lying hid in the ashes." [16]
Grace, or the Holy Spirit, can fan this spark into a bright flame, if
man wishes it so. This inner light will then purge away sin and
finally make room for pure love, and so prepare a mansion within
the human body for Christ. Such had been Groote's view and
such was also the view of those who composed the *Imitation*.
These devout followers of Jesus believed that through love and
faith, love foremost, through coöperation between God and man,
one's soul could be sanctified and saved. Finally, great emphasis
was laid on sanctification before physical death: "And I (God)
daily read two lessons to mine elect, one in reproving their vices,
another in exhorting them to the increase of all virtues." [17]   Great
was human dependence on God, but man had not completely lost
his divine heredity. Weak he was, so weak in fact that he could
do nothing at any time without the power of the Holy Spirit,
except to stretch out a hand, so to speak, to receive salvation.
And in the last analysis even that act required a certain amount of
divine assistance. A man like Martin Luther did not venture far
beyond the limits of the Devotio Moderna when he expounded
the doctrine of justification by faith alone.

As for Erasmus, however, he remained in harmony with the
thoughts of the Brethren of the Common Life at Deventer, and
later he was impelled to write a booklet on the freedom of the
human will, attacking Luther's view. In many other respects also

---

[14] Book I, Chap. 3, Book II, Chap. 1, Book III, Chap. 2.
[15] Book III, Chaps. 3, 43, 44.
[16] Book III, Chap. 55.   [17] Book III, Chap. 3.

he was to reproduce teachings of the brethren in the Yssel valley. Even after he had left the dormitories of the pious brethren and had decided to spend a number of years in a monastery not belonging to the Devotio Moderna, he still remained in close touch with this movement, as will appear.[18]

[18] For a detailed history of the Devotio Moderna, see my book, which thus far has remained the only comprehensive history of the whole movement, namely, *The Christian Renaissance, A History of the "Devotio Moderna"* (New York, The Century Co., 1925). On the influence of this movement see A. Hyma, "The Influence of the 'Devotio Moderna,'" *Nederlandsch Archief voor Kerkgeschiedenis,* 1926, pp. 275–278. This article is an answer to the criticism of many reviewers who assert that the present writer has exaggerated the influence of this movement. It was, unfortunately, unknown to A. Renaudet when he wrote the review for the *Revue Historique,* Vol. CLV, 1927, pp. 408–409. Under no circumstances, however, was Renaudet justified in saying that, according to the present writer, the Devotio Moderna was "une Renaissance chrétienne, d'ou seraient sorties la Réforme et la Contre-Réforme." Lucien Febvre makes a similar error in misrepresenting my interpretation of the movement (*Rev. Hist.,* Vol. CLXI, 1929, p. 67).

CHAPTER IV

THE HUMANISTS

A GERMAN scholar has shown that the mind of Erasmus before the year 1500 was largely dominated by the spirit of two intellectual movements, namely, the Devotio Moderna and humanism.[1] These two movements can readily be distinguished from each other, and one is not stating a paradox in saying that men like R. Agricola, Gansfort, Hegius, and Erasmus represented both movements, though naturally in varying degrees. One could also, however, speak of still another movement, named Transalpine Renaissance, which contained elements of both the Italian Renaissance and the Devotio Moderna. P. S. Allen, for example, has made use of this term for the heading of a chapter in *The Age of Erasmus*. Erasmus has been called the prince of the humanists, but he could just as well be named the king of the Transalpine Renaissance. Movements are not like material objects; they can be grouped and classified in many ways, and often overlap each other.

One of the most interesting problems in the history of modern civilization is the relation between the Renaissance in Italy and the Transalpine Renaissance. Although a great many books and articles have dealt with various phases of this problem, no serious attempt has ever been made to treat it as a whole and on a comprehensive scale. The problem may forever remain unsolved, for nothing seems so difficult to trace as the course of ideas. One is too likely to ignore the possibilities of telepathy, intuition, and inspiration, and one usually jumps at conclusions too quickly. It

---

[1] See P. Mestwerdt, *Die Anfänge des Erasmus, Humanismus und "Devotio Moderna"* (Leipzig, 1917). No one who wishes to write an up-to-date biography of Erasmus can afford to ignore this scholarly work. Both Pineau and Mangan, for example, would have produced better contributions if they had properly consulted it.

must baffle a casual reader to peruse a multitude of conflicting opinions concerning the humanists in Italy; it certainly is bewildering to note that the moment one seeks the truth beneath dogmatic statements he becomes more and more confused until he has read practically every production of all the Italian humanists as well as those composed beyond the Alps. And who can ever say that he has done that?

Many historians have pointed out that the humanists in Italy were irreligious, that the scholars north of the Alps were naturally more religious, and that humanism gradually adopted a more serious and pious aspect as it traveled northward. But are the Germans by nature more religious than the Italians? Perhaps they are at times, but a historian takes a great deal for granted when he uses this theory as an infallible hypothesis. No one has yet answered the question why the Transalpine Renaissance differed so greatly from its parent in Italy, because a considerable number of monographs are required before the larger problem can be solved in its entirety.

Since Erasmus in a large measure personifies the Transalpine Renaissance, it will be impossible at the present time to say conclusively where he got his humanistic principles. Long before he first saw Italy he had absorbed much of the spirit of the Italian Renaissance, but just how he happened to do this is by no means clear. The same thing is true of the Brethren of the Common Life in Deventer and elsewhere. It will not do to say that the Devotio Moderna remained unaltered from generation to generation. Right in the citadel of the movement, so to speak, in the brethren-house at Deventer, some very pious souls became greatly affected by the teachings of the humanists. When Alexander Hegius wrote to his friend Rudoph Agricola that he had read Valla's dialogue *On the True Good*, he seemed not a bit shocked, although Gerard Groote would have exhorted his friends never even to touch it. Can we say then that Alexander Hegius was not true to the spirit of the Devotio Moderna, although he was intimately associated with the Brethren of the Common Life at Deventer? We may or we may not do so, according to the definition we give of the Devotio Moderna.

It is also possible to define the terms humanism and Italian Renaissance in various ways, as was indicated above. Fortunately a number of satisfactory accounts of the Italian Renaissance have been produced, of which the contributions by Burckhardt and Symonds still remain standard references. Symonds has unquestionably given a more comprehensive survey than Burckhardt; the latter's work is disappointing because of its high reputation.[2] Especially valuable for the present study is the ninth chapter of Symonds' volume which is entitled *The Revival of Learning*. It presents an admirable summary of the character of humanism in Italy during the fifteenth century, upon which the following discussion is partly based.

Now that the century of Erasmus has long since passed, it is comparatively easy to view the civilization of the Renaissance in Italy with an impartial eye. The revival of classical antiquity seems no longer so important as it did in 1475; the admiration for Cicero and Plato has given way to a fairly indifferent study by the majority of European and American scholars, who feel no longer the need of condoning vice, nor of admiring the mediocre talents and the conceited boastings of a host of stupid but elegant humanists.

Symonds draws a striking comparison between the sophists of ancient Greece and the humanists of the quattrocento. "The essence of sophism," remarks Symonds, "is the substitution of semblance for reality, indifference to truth provided a fair show be made, combined with verbal ingenuity.... The discord between his philosophy and his conduct awakes no shame in the sophist, because it is the highest triumph of his art to persuade by eloquence and to dazzle by rhetoric. Phrases and sentences supply the place of feelings and convictions. Sonorous cadences and harmonies of language are always ready to conceal the want of substance in his matter or the flimsiness of his argument."[3] In common with the sophists, the humanists in Italy as a rule contradicted themselves by praising self-control and simplicity, and

---

[2] G. J. Hoogewerff, *De ontwikkeling der Italiaansche Renaissance*, pp. xvi–xvii. The criticism expressed here deserves consideration; so does the whole book.

[3] J. A. Symonds, *The Revival of Learning*, pp. 513–514.

simultaneously quoting filthy remarks from Martial. A scholar like Guarino da Verona, who himself was upright, felt no shame in expressing admiration for worthless trash like Beccadelli's *Hermaphroditus;* and Pope Nicholas V, one of the most virtuous pontiffs in a century, spent nine days in reading the foul satires of Filelfo.

It has been said that many humanists served a good turn in ridiculing scholastic philosophy, because the Schoolmen at Paris and Cologne built huge structures of dialectics on mere hypotheses, instead of turning to the examination of the sources and of nature. But what about those numerous humanists in Italy who preferred to report imaginary, though beautifully written, speeches, and constructed histories so obviously unreliable that no modern historian can use them? We know that in order to understand the environment in which lived the most brilliant humanists, it is unsafe to trust the accounts left by humanists themselves.

Another fact which needs emphasis at the present time is the hostility of the lower clergy in Italy to humanism. Savonarola was but one among thousands of preachers who warned their flocks against the vanity, mockery, and deceit of the wandering scholars. The latter did make a great deal of noise, but were vastly outnumbered by the members of the lower clergy who opposed them and survived them. The humanists, living as they did in an isolated world of their own, did not voice the spirit of the Italian people. They did not even frame a workable school system, but catered almost exclusively to sons of princes and aristocrats. What did it matter if the pope himself sponsored humanism, except that the head of the Roman Catholic Church ceased to function as the representative of Jesus the Christ? He was so far removed from the common people that his actions were scarcely noticed by them, for they remained illiterate, neglected alike by prelates and scholars. If they were pious and the humanists irreligious, they owed their piety very largely to their pastors, while the latter cared not what the humanists declared fashionable in manners and speech. Even if the Italian people had been the most religious in Europe, as they probably were at one time, the humanists need not have felt duty-bound to drop their sophistry and imitate the early Christians.

That the majority of the humanists were grossly immoral cannot be gainsaid. Gyraldus, a distinguished professor at Ferrara, did not exaggerate when he described the general run of humanists in the following manner: "No class of human beings are more subject to anger, more puffed up with vanity, more arrogant, more insolent, more conceited, idle-minded, inconsequent, opionated, changeable, obstinate; some of them ready to believe the most incredible nonsense, others skeptical about notorious truths, some full of doubt and suspicion, others void of reasonable circumspection." [4] The humanists, as Symonds indicates, recognized no laws except those of their own taste and inclination; they accepted no authority superior to their own judgment. Their passionate admiration for pagan antiquity "undermined their Christianity without substituting the religion or the ethics of the old world. They ceased to fear God; but they did not acquire either the self-restraint of the Greek or the patriotic virtues of the Roman. It is not, therefore, a marvel that, while professing stoicism, they wallowed in sensuality, openly affected the worst habits of pagan society, and devoted their ingenuity to the explanation of foulness that might have been passed by in silence. Licentiousness became a special branch of humanistic literature. Under the thin mask of humane refinement leered the untamed savage; and an age that boasted not unreasonably of its mental progress, was at the same time notorious for the vices that disgrace mankind. These disorders of the scholars, hidden for a time beneath a learned language, ended by contaminating the genius of the nation." [5]

It is safe to say that Erasmus and most of the other humanists

---

[4] J. A. Symonds, *op. cit.*, pp. 518–519.

[5] J. A. Symonds, *op. cit.*, p. 521. Symonds is by no means the most severe critic. Burckhardt and many other authorities present similar viewpoints. Ph. Monnier, in the last chapter of *Le Quattrocento*, shows that morals became greatly corrupted in Italy toward the close of the fifteenth century, and that the higher clergy were strongly affected by the low moral standards of the humanists. He concludes the survey with the following brief summary (II, 415): "Le cri qui monte est un cri de plaisir. Plus de chaînes, plus de fausses hontes, plus d'importunes et misérables retenues! Gloire à la nature, à la raison et à la vie! Jouissons au soleil jusqu'au crime! Satisfaisons nos appétits et nos instincts! Cultivons nos gouts et nos passions!" And then, adds Monnier, came Savonarola, the antithesis of pagan humanism.

in transalpine Europe differed widely from the typical humanists just described by Symonds; and it is equally true that there were in Italy at all times a number of scholars who by their integrity, modesty, honesty, and generosity distinguished themselves from the less worthy members of their class. When Agricola, Hegius, and Erasmus extolled the virtues and the characters of the great scholars in Italy, they unquestionably referred to such men as Traversari, Guarino, Petrarch, Ficino, and Pico. The latter exerted more influence beyond the Alps, and it is therefore desirable to study in detail the views of these men if one wishes to trace the spread of humanism from Italy into the northern countries.

None of the Italian humanists seems to have affected the mind of Erasmus so much as did Lorenzo Valla. He was born in Rome in the year 1406, the son of a lawyer from Piacenza. At a rather early age he learned Greek from Giovanni Aurispa and Latin from Leonardo Bruni. In 1430 he left Rome and in a few months secured a professorship in the University of Pavia, where he immediately attracted attention through his attacks on the teachers of law. In one of his lengthy epistles he made the following statement: "Among the jurists at the present time there is not a single one who is not contemptible and ludicrous. They have been so poorly trained in every field of knowledge, . . . particularly in rhetoric, that I am sorry for civil law because of these commentators. It would have been much better if it had never been written, since it is being interpreted by these beasts." [6]

More noteworthy, however, was his treatise, composed at this time, named *On Pleasure and the True Good*. This work consists of three books; the first half of the first book contains a speech by a stoic philosopher; the second half of the first book and the whole of the second book present the views of an epicurean philosopher; and the third book gives the opinions of a Christian philosopher. Each in turn defends his own ideals, but when the third speaker has finished, the other two congratulate him, and it appears as if he has won. Nevertheless, Valla does not repudiate the scandalous suggestions of the epicurean philosopher. So the question has often been raised: How could a man like Valla present systems of

[6] M. von Wolff, *Lorenzo Valla*, p. 9.

thought which were diametrically opposed to each other, and yet were approved by him? The answer lies no doubt in the peculiar combination of the formal acceptance of the Roman Catholic creed and the views of pagan philosophers. Italy had so long been Christian that even the most flippant scholars on this peninsula scarcely dreamed of rejecting the doctrines of their church. Valla was irreligious most of the time, but a thousand years of habit on the part of his ancestors had left an indelible impress on his mind which would occasionally assert its rights. Hence it became possible for him and his friends to admire doctrines which were the opposite of those taught by their own church.

The next composition of Valla was *De Libero Arbitrio*, or *On the Free Will*, a title chosen later by Erasmus, no doubt in imitation of the Italian humanist. Then followed an important contribution, named *De Professione Religiosorum*, or *On Monastic Orders*, in which Valla attacked the clergy. The booklet is in the form of a dialogue and the situation is as follows. Valla meets a number of learned colleagues and friends on the market-place. In the church near the market they form a circle, where they discuss the discovery of a conspiracy against the king. A monk joins them who is known to most of the men present. During the conversation a remark is made by one of the scholars to the effect that priests had no doubt taken part in the conspiracy, since they were always meddling in politics. This angers the monk, who forthwith defends the clergy. When he is asked why the clergy enjoy so many privileges, he replies that the clergy have received them from God and that in heaven they are promised still greater gifts.

A lively discussion follows, in which Valla is asked by his friends to take upon himself the defense of the laity. "You clericals," Valla asserts, "act from compulsion, we from free will. You keep the fear of God, we the love of God. You would never have taken the vows if it had not been out of fear of damnation. That is the reason why the worst people, who despair of finding another occupation, come to you. One may truly name monasteries asylums in which outcasts seek shelter, such as bankrupts, slaves, criminals, wretches — in short, all those who have nothing to lose and much to gain. . . . However, I shall attack you no further lest it seem as if I were hostile to you. I will rather admit that the monks have much in their favor. It is they who in a certain sense support the Church; they preach to the people, they give alms; they sponsor the holy ceremonies of the Church; and they endeavor to write edifying and illuminating books."

Valla's treatise on the *Donation of Constantine* is usually regarded as the first example of modern criticism. From 1436 to 1447 he was in the service of King Alfonso of Naples and it was during this period that he most bitterly attacked the papal power. An excerpt from the treatise just mentioned will plainly reveal the trend of his thoughts: "One may ask me of what I accuse the popes. I declare them guilty of the grossest obscurantism, the most shameless greed, with which they serve the demons. . . . Of our own free will, oh pope, have we come to you that you might rule over us. And now we are equally free to withdraw from your rule. You want to rule over us against our will, as if we were minor children. By God, the injustice we have suffered impels us to rise in rebellion against you. Have you not exhausted our city, robbed our churches, dishonored our women and virgins, and drenched our streets with the blood of our citizens?"

Very important is Valla's work *On the Elegance of the Latin Language*, in which he condemns the brand of Latin used by nearly all his contemporaries. "Present conditions are such," he argues, "that every true friend of [classic] literature can scarcely restrain his tears. The Latin language is now in no better plight than the city of Rome after its capture by the Goths. For centuries the philosophers, jurists, and orators have been using a language which does not show any longer a trace of pure Latin and with which they can barely make themselves understood." Few readers read these words with so much approbation as did the Dutch scholar Erasmus, who could not look back with pride, as did Valla, to a time when his native country was the center of European civilization; and yet it was Erasmus who even surpassed his Italian teacher in the services rendered by him to the restoration of classic Greek and Latin.

In 1447 Pope Eugene IV passed away and was succeeded by Nicholas V, a patron of the humanists. Valla received an invita-tion to enter the papal service. He stayed for half a year with a brother-in-law in Rome, where he had a curious love-affair. When he was accused by his relatives of being too cold to arouse the love of women and therefore unfit for married life, he decided to show them the contrary by seducing a servant of his brother-in-law, who bore him three children in two years. But when his friends urged him to marry her, he refused, adding that he planned to enter holy orders and become a priest![7]

When Valla was advanced in Rome, Poggio, a scholar of inferior caliber, became envious and started a quarrel which caused many harsh words on both sides. But Poggio was not wrong in accusing Valla of offensive vanity, nor in pointing out the frequent use made by Valla of flattery. Nevertheless, Erasmus, who later heard of the quarrel, rightly remarked how immoral and mean and ignorant Poggio appeared by the side of Valla. For the latter retained at least a goodly portion of gratitude and respectability. Whereas Poggio threw his mistress aside as soon as he grew tired of her, his rival supported his concubine and at one time even tried to marry her.

Valla is sometimes called the incarnation of the spirit of humanism; many historians and critics consider him the most important humanist in Italy. Hence it may not seem out of place to devote so much space to him as he has received here, particularly on account of his influence on Erasmus. One should be very cautious, however, not to give credence to the supposition that Valla aimed to restore Christianity, notably the apostolic Christian church.[8]

---

[7] L. Valla, *Opera* (Basel, 1540), p. 362.

[8] P. Mestwerdt, *Die Anfänge des Erasmus*, pp. 30–31. The writer, who is a keen critic, maintains that Valla fought for the triumph of Christianity, not the Christianity of his day which had absorbed many pagan rituals, but a purified form: "Er hat auch in 'De libero arbitrio' den christlichen Glauben gegen die heidnisch-stoische Philosophie verteidigen wollen. Freilich ein gereinigtes Christentum. . . . Es ist wohl zu merken, dass Valla nicht die kirchliche Lehre, die er vielmehr bekämpft, sondern das Christentum der Apostel und Väter zum Maßstab des von einem Christen zu fordernden Glaubens erhebt." Reference is made here to two clauses in the *Opera* (p. 999) of Valla, namely, "apostolorum imitatores" and "piissima antiquitas," but what are these except empty words? Does Valla anywhere show a real desire to have the pope imitate St. Peter and does not Valla, under Pope Callixtus III, a member of the notorious house of Borgia, accept several benefices? Imagine a man trying to imitate the apostles by refusing to marry a concubine because he wants to become a priest!

He may, in his dialogue on pleasure, have placed Christian philosophy above epicurean teachings, although sufficient evidence is lacking,[9] and he may have been a good Catholic, which seems rather doubtful, but to maintain that he actually attempted to resuscitate the spirit of the primitive church is to misrepresent the whole character of the latter institution. Valla himself in all probability never fully comprehended the aims and ideals of the apostles, and he certainly did not strive very hard to imitate them. Nor is there any reason left why one should any longer repeat the legends which were spun in the age of Erasmus. Even Valla's *Notes on the New Testament* are no more than a piece of philological work, just as were his translations of Herodotus and Thucydides. Valla wanted to go back to the earliest sources, but he did not reach the living word which proceeded directly from the souls of the apostles.

Another Italian humanist who is said to have done a great deal for the restoration of primitive Christianity was Marsiglio Ficino of Padua. But this great scholar also has been frequently misunderstood. He was a leading member of the Platonic Academy in Florence and translated the works of Plato for Cosmo de' Medici. About the year 1475 he composed a work entitled *De Christiana Religione*, or *On the Christian Religion*, in which he sought to harmonize Platonism with Christianity. Although he fairly worshiped Plato, he never comprehended Platonic philoso-

---

[9] J. Vahlen, *L. Valla*, p. 186. Vahlen does not succeed in convincing every reader. On the other hand it is not fair to interpret the remarks of the epicurean philosopher in the dialogue *On Pleasure* as representative of Valla's own convictions. Ph. Monnier makes this error in Vol. I of his celebrated *Le Quattrocento* (p. 276), where he says: "Ici encore Valla arrive, et, dans son dialogue *De Voluptate*, en face de cette phraséologie creuse, il met la fin de la vie dans la volupté." Monnier's interpretation has been accepted and repeated by numerous American and European historians, wherefore attention is called to it here. More trustworthy is the analysis of the dialogue by G. Mancini in his *Vita di Lorenzo Valla* (Florence, 1891), where a careful distinction is made between the original edition, printed at Louvain, and the subsequent edition of 1540 (Basel), and where, on page 61, it is explained that Valla did not attack the Christian religion. The following statement is worth quoting: "Il Fiorentino addebita ai nemici del Valla la opinione invalsa che il *Dialogo* combatte il Cristianesimo. . . . Infatti Lorenzo repudia senza sottintesi o ambagi la morale pagana, fonda i propri criteri sull' etica cristiana purgata dalle superstizioni, dal reale o finto orrore degli ascetici contro i piaceri della vita."

phy, and as for the Platonic Academy, it has been pointed out by
P. Villari, a very competent critic, that here an attempt was made
to combine paganism with Christianity so as to form a system of
philosophy identical with Platonism.   This attempt naturally resulted in much confusion.[10]   To Ficino and his associates everything said by Plato and Aristotle, as well as by Confucius and
Zoroaster, seemed sacred.   Christianity was based on the Platonic
doctrines, and it was argued that the teachings of Socrates were
the same as those of Christ.

The Platonic Academy attracted many foreigners to Florence.
Englishmen, Frenchmen, and Germans returned from Italy and
spread in their countries the Hellenism of the humanists.   Reuchlin, in particular, became more than ever converted to the new
idea, which found favor in many circles.   We are told that in this
way the Renaissance of Christianity developed in Europe, starting
in Florence and spreading into transalpine countries.   In Germany it is said to have resulted in the individual interpretation
of the Scriptures.

It will not be amiss to quote here a few sentences from the new
biography of Erasmus by Mangan, who has clearly perceived how
befogged was the mind of Ficino and how misleading are the
interpretations of those who seek the revival of the apostolic
church in the Platonic Academy or in the teachings of Ficino's
disciples.   Mangan gives the following extract from Drummond's
biography and adds a remark which merits serious study.   "'Man,'
says Erasmus in the *Enchiridion*, 'consists of soul and body,
which at first acted together in perfect harmony, and would have
continued to do so, had not the serpent sown the seeds of contention between them.   Since that time there has been perpetual warfare between the two, the spirit striving against the flesh and the

---

[10] P. Villari, *Niccolò Machiavelli e i suoi tempi*, p. 170: "Ciò che risulta di più
chiaro in mezzo a tanta confusione, si è che per gli accademici, Cristianesimo e
Paganesimo debbono formare una sola e medesima cosa col Platonismo."   A
similar conclusion is drawn by Ph. Monnier in *Le Quattrocento*, II, 128: "La pensée
de l'Académie platonicienne, élaborant des œuvres de ce caractère, était con-
damnée à n'avoir pas de lendemain.   Son herméneutique échoue dans la puérilité
comme l'ontologie métaphysique qu'elle dessine se résout dans un syncrétisme
incohérent."

flesh against the spirit.' But the consequences of the first sin would not seem, in the estimation of Erasmus, to have affected the essential nature of the soul, which is still spoken of as divine, and as retaining a consciousness of its heavenly origin. 'But that divine principle, which, bearing sovereign sway within us, ever counsels us to our good, remembering the source whence it has come, admits no baseness nor impurity.' Drummond's comment on the above is a most surprising statement, viz., 'his [Erasmus'] idea of human nature is almost wholly Platonic.' It is nothing of the sort; it is simply the third chapter of Genesis paraphrased." [11]

And so one could mention scores of instances of modern critics joining the humanists in their failure to make a clear distinction between Platonism and Christianity, and in crediting the Platonic Academy with reproducing theories from Plato's works which were in fact composed long before the time of Plato — not in Greece, but in Palestine. The Greek classics were very important, but they did not render the Bible obsolete or superfluous, nor were they an adequate substitute for Christianity any more than the latter could fill the place of the classics.

In analyzing the views of Ficino's most illustrious successor in Italy, the celebrated John Pico of Mirandola (1463–94), one will meet much the same problems. Pico was a member of the nobility and received an excellent education. He studied not only in Bologna, Ferrara, and Florence, but also at the Sorbonne in Paris. He somewhat startled the professors at the latter institution by stating that Aristotle taught the same doctrines as did Plato, and Avicenna (980–1038) the same as Averroës (1126–98). Shortly after his return from Paris in 1486 he formulated nine hundred theses which he intended to defend publicly, but the authorities of the Church prevented the debate, because thirteen of the theses were considered heretical. In one of them, for example, he asserted that no source of knowledge convinces us more of the divinity of Christ than magic and the cabala, the latter being a Hebrew work which contained fantastic theories about creation and the cosmic elements. In 1488 Pico was imprisoned in France,

[11] J. J. Mangan, *The Life, Character, and Influence of Desiderius Erasmus of Rotterdam,* I, 172.

but shortly after that he returned to Italy, where Lorenzo de'
Medici protected him. In his youth he was light-hearted and ca-
pricious, but about the year 1490 the sermons of Savonarola
strongly affected him. He now turned from the worshipful study
of oriental philosophy to Christian mysticism. He believed that
every word in the Bible had a hidden meaning. He never attacked
the doctrines of the Roman Catholic Church and particularly in
his letter to Giovanfrancesco, his nephew, he showed himself a
true Christian.[12]

It is extremely difficult to say how much of the thought of
Valla, Ficino, and Pico was absorbed by the leading humanists
north of the Alps. Some scholars became personally acquainted
with Italian humanists, as did Colet; others read their works and
had to be content with the reports of friends and acquaintances,
as did Erasmus for a time. A halo of almost supernatural learning
seemed to surround those favored beings who told with rapture
how they had actually heard the voice of the great Ficino or of the
famous Pico. When ambitious boys of twelve or thirteen saw such
a scholar, freshly arrived from the land of intellectual giants, they
were nearly struck dumb with awe. This happened one day to
Erasmus when he beheld the beaming features of Rudolph Agricola,
"who was one of the first to bring a breath of the new learning
from Italy."

[12] A. Liebert, *Giovanni Pico della Mirandola*, pp. 122–123. See also p. 220,
where Pico says: "I believe that the world crucified Jesus for my sake." Shortly
before his death Savonarola dressed him in the garb of a Dominican friar.

PART II

CHILDHOOD

CHAPTER V

BIRTH AND PARENTAGE

ERASMUS was born in the night of October 27–28,[1] but the
year of his birth is not certain. Although most biographers
have agreed on the year 1466, the available evidence at the present time points to the year 1469 as being more nearly correct.

Not only have Preserved Smith and P. Mestwerdt observed
that Erasmus showed a tendency as he grew older to place the
date of his birth back farther and farther,[2] but other writers have
also accepted the year 1469.[3]

Even the birth-place of Erasmus has long been in doubt. It is
true he called himself "Roterodamus," and in his autobiography
he said he was born in Rotterdam, but since his parents were
living in or very near Gouda both before and after his birth, it
has been thought possible by several biographers that the son
was born in the latter city.[4]

[1] According to Melanchthon his birth occurred four hours before sunrise, or
at about 3 A.M. (see *Corpus Reformatorum*, XII, 266). Erasmus himself mentioned the "eve of Oct. 28"; hence it is safe to say that the event took place
during the night.

[2] P. Smith, *Erasmus*, pp. 7–8, 445–446; P. Mestwerdt, *Die Anfänge des Erasmus*, p. 177, note 1.

[3] Cornelius Loos of Gouda, *Illustrium Germaniae Scriptorum Catalogus*, under
the heading Erasmus: "Prodiit in lucem anno 1469." See also H. Kronenberg,
Wanneer is Hegius te Deventer gekomen, pp. 1–3. It is worth noting that Cornelius
Loos was for many years a prominent citizen of Gouda. In 1555, when the
"Oude Mannen Huis" ("Home for old men") was founded, he became one of
the three regents (see I. Walvis, *Beschrijving van der Goude*, I, 180, where his name
appears as Jan Cornelisz Loos). In 1603 Cornelius A. Diephorst, the only surviving monk of Steyn, where Erasmus was a monk, bought a place for himself
in the Oude Mannen Huis. According to him Erasmus was taken on a boat from
Gouda to Rotterdam the same night he was born (see J. Walvis, *op. cit.*, I, 269).
Loos, however, maintains that the guilty father, who lived near Gouda, sent his
servant to a neighboring city, which city must have been Rotterdam.

[4] Reynerus Snoy, a magistrate in Gouda and a learned writer, is said to have
maintained that Erasmus was born at Gouda (see M. A. G. Vorstman, "De

The autobiography of Erasmus (*Compendium Vitae*) is not entirely reliable; nevertheless it is a very important source. Says Erasmus, "He was born in Rotterdam on the eve of the festival of Simon and Jude, 57 years ago.[5] His mother was named Margaret, the daughter of a certain physician in Zevenbergen.[6] His father's name was Gerard. The latter was secretly united with Margaret, in the hope of marriage. And there are some who say that the expectation was mutual, which greatly displeased the parents and brothers of Gerard, for they hoped to make of him a priest. . . . When Gerard learned that they would not permit him to marry he left and sent them a letter written with his own hand, saying, 'I shall never see you any more.' Margaret had in the meantime become pregnant. The child she bore was brought up in the home of its grandmother. As for Gerard, he went to Rome. His parents, when they heard where he was, wrote to him that the mother of his child had passed away; whereupon Gerard, believing the report to be true, returned home. He had become a priest. When he discovered the fraud, he nevertheless did not marry her, nor did he ever touch her again." [7]

It is difficult to say how much of Erasmus' account is true. In the first place, Rotterdam may claim Erasmus as its native son, for not only did he himself honor that city in his own name, but all available evidence confirms the theory. In the Nauwe Kerkstraat at Rotterdam there is a house bearing an inscription to the effect that on the spot where this house stands the great scholar was born. A smaller house used to stand here which as early as

---

Geboorteplaats van Erasmus," in *Ned. Arch. voor Kerkgesch.*, 1845, pp. 236–238). The note printed here is from Ms. 924, City Library Gouda, fol. 33ª–36ª. The writer of this note had just copied an extract from the book by Loos mentioned above, and asserted that he knew more about Erasmus than did Loos. But it is doubtful whether Snoy was a reliable witness any more than the anonymous writer of the note. Loos, on the other hand, appears to have had access to the most trustworthy sources.

[5] The *Compendium Vitae* was composed in the year 1524. On its value as a source, see P. S. Allen, *Opus Ep. Er.*, I, 46, 575–578. It should be noted that Allen undoubtedly takes the first part of the biography too seriously. It is an exaggeration to say that the statements given here "are correct even in small points."

[6] This town was located in North-Brabant, about six miles northwest of Breda.

[7] *Opus Ep. Er.*, edited by P. S. Allen, I, 47–48.

PLATE II

Front wall of a house in Rotterdam built on the site of the
house in which tradition says Erasmus was born

1540 was being shown to visitors as the birth-place of Erasmus.[8] In 1549 there was already a wooden statue in Rotterdam which proclaimed Erasmus as a native of this city.[9] This wooden statue was later torn down by Spanish soldiers and replaced by a more substantial one.

Fruin [10] and Mangan [11] are of the opinion that Erasmus' father was already a priest when the boy was born. The present writer holds the same view, for Erasmus was preceded by another child, his brother Peter, about whom enough is known to exclude him from the realm of fiction.[12] For Erasmus the illegitimacy of his birth was a constant annoyance; nay, more than that, a source of ceaseless worry. He felt bound to cast a heavy veil over the facts connected with the birth, particularly when he sought to obtain benefices in the Church. In 1506, when he was asking Pope Julius II for a dispensation, he was by no means ready to admit the facts, wherefore the pope expressed the belief that Erasmus was the off-spring of "a bachelor and a widow." [13] Eleven years later, however, when the need of a benefice impelled him to reveal more of the truth, Pope Leo X, his friend, granted him a dispensation which officially removed the disabilities resulting from the illegitimate birth. On January 26, 1517, Leo X pronounced the fact, no doubt supplied by the applicant himself, that Erasmus was the child of "an illegitimate, and even, as I fear, of a damnable union." [14] In other words, Pope Leo X feared that the father of Erasmus was a priest when his son was conceived.

It was by no means an uncommon occurrence in the Middle Ages for a priest to have a concubine. Gerard Groote had preached

---

[8] P. Smith, *Erasmus*, p. 7.

[9] R. Fruin, "Erasmiana," *Bijdragen voor Vaderlandsche Geschiedenis en Oudheidkunde*, Nieuwe Reeks, x, 267.

[10] *Ibid.*

[11] J. J. Mangan, *The Life, Character, and Influence of Desiderius Erasmus of Rotterdam*, I, 5: "Gerard, the father of Erasmus, fell in love with his housekeeper, Margaret, but, being in Holy Orders, could not marry her."

[12] J. B. Pineau, *Érasme*, pp. 2–3.

[13] The words used were "de soluto genitus et vidua." See P. S. Allen, *op. cit.*, II, 434, first footnote; also III, xxix.

[14] P. S. Allen, *op. cit.*, Ep. 517, II, 434: "Et deinde, licet defectum natalium patiatur, ex illicito et, ut timet, incesto damnatoque coitu genitus."

a sermon in 1383 in the ecclesiastical capital of the Netherlands (Utrecht) against such members of the clergy, who seem to have been rather numerous in that district. Gouda is not far from Utrecht and the year 1469 less than a century removed from 1383. Since the days of Groote the clergy had not greatly improved. Mangan, a Roman Catholic scholar, does not mince matters when he discusses conditions in the Middle Ages and explains how Gerard made love to Margaret in his own home. We may therefore assume that the housekeeper remained in that home until the end of her pregnancy. Many people in Gouda believed afterward that the little boy was transported with his mother on a boat from Gouda to Rotterdam on the night of the delivery.[15] This belief may well have been based on facts, but it is most probable that Margaret left her master's home shortly before the birth of her infant, and that it first saw the light of day in the city of Rotterdam. The father was then called to do penance, as Mangan surmises, "and be relieved of his ecclesiastical censures, which could be accomplished only after he had solemnly promised to give up the connection, and to avoid giving scandal in the future." [16] Hence we may believe Erasmus when he says that after this Gerard touched Margaret no more.

One would like to know whether Margaret actually dreaded the birth of her second child as much as is often suspected. She already had a son who was at least two years old. Nevertheless the scandal attached to the birth of another must often have preyed on her mind. She could naturally take very little exercise out of doors during the summer and early fall of the year 1469. Since she does not appear to have returned to Gouda for several years after the birth of Erasmus, it may be observed that the people of her parish must have criticized her severely for her second breach of a moral law. Just where Gerard, her lover, had his home, is not known, but it does not seem to have been within the walls of Gouda; it was probably in a village near this city.[17] At any rate, her anxiety must have left its mark upon her second son. Caution should be taken, however, not to exaggerate the physical and

[15] See p. 51, note 3.
[16] J. J. Mangan, *op. cit.*, I, 6.
[17] R. Fruin, *op. cit.*, p. 267.

mental ills caused by her condition, since no definite information can be found.

The name given to the little boy was from the very beginning Erasmus, or rather Herasmus, and not a Dutch equivalent,[18] as is often wrongly assumed. The father was no doubt a scholar, for Erasmus tells of him that in Rome he diligently applied himself to the study of Latin and Greek.[19] So he chose the Greek name Erasmus, while the additional name Desiderius was supplied by Erasmus himself at a subsequent date, when he was making good progress himself in Greek, that is, about the year 1497, for in a poem addressed to Gaguin, dated January 20, 1497, he named himself Desyderius Herasmus Rotterodamensis. He retained the form Herasmus until 1503; the name Roterodamus was first employed in 1506.[20]

It is interesting to speculate on the name Erasmus Rogerii of Rotterdam, or the complete title, *Erasmo Rogerii Roterodamensi clerico*, used by Pope Leo X in the dispensation granted to Erasmus on January 26, 1517.[21] Erasmus had decided to name himself Erasmus Rogerii, instead of Erasmus Gerardi, although in his autobiography he plainly stated that his father was called Gerard. In this connection Mangan makes the following suggestion, which appears to be the logical solution. "Erasmus knew that he had no claim to any name but that of his mother, and accordingly signed himself Erasmus Rogerii of Rotterdam, Rogerius presumably being his mother's family name. His brother Peter never made any request for a dispensation and continued to bear his father's name of Gerard."[22] It has been suggested, notably by Fruin, that the papal scribe, Sadoleto, made a clerical error, but Allen has pointed out that in Sadoleto's beautiful handwriting it would be very difficult to read or write Rogerii for Gerardi.[23] The solution presented by Allen, however, namely, that Erasmus' father

[18] *Ibid.*, p. 269.
[19] *Compendium Vitae*, ed. by P. S. Allen, pp. 47–48: "Mox applicuit animum ad honesta studia. Graece et Latine pulchre calluit. . . . Omnes auctores sua manu descripserat."
[20] P. S. Allen, *op. cit.*, I, 73, first footnote.
[21] *Ibid.*, II, Ep. 518, p. 437, line 44.   [23] P. S. Allen, *op. cit.*, I, 578.
[22] J. J. Mangan, *op. cit.*, II, 63.

was named Rogerius Gerardus,[24] is unsatisfactory, for Erasmus could not very well sign his father's name to a petition to Pope Leo X for a dispensation which concerned chiefly the removal of disabilities caused by the illegal union of his father. A name he needed; his father could no longer supply it; therefore he chose that of his mother.

Now the question may be raised why Erasmus said in his autobiography that he was brought up in the home of his grandmother at Rotterdam. His mother no doubt went to seek shelter with dear friends or rather relatives, and since Erasmus mentions a grandmother, probably with her own mother. About twenty years later Erasmus became intimately acquainted in his monastery with a certain Servatius Rogerii, or Servatius, the son of Rogerius, of Rotterdam. The terms of affection applied to this young man by Erasmus make one wonder whether he was a cousin, particularly so since Erasmus' first prose composition, *De Contemptu Mundi*, was in the form of a long letter to a nephew or cousin whom he tried to persuade to enter his monastery. About this whole matter a good deal will be said below, but for the present it is desirable to bear in mind the likelihood of the name Rogerius having been derived from that of Margaret's father.[25]

There must have been many reasons why Erasmus was often chagrined because of his illegitimate birth. It is impossible to say how many times contemporaries reminded him of his father's crime. In our age the stigma of such a birth is no doubt greater than in the fifteenth century and it is likely that Erasmus suffered comparatively little from the abuse of his associates. The celebrated Rudolph Agricola, whom Erasmus so greatly admired and whose career was so eminently successful, was the son of an abbot, but he does not appear to have experienced many drawbacks from his birth, although it must be added that at the time of his birth the father was probably not yet a priest. Then there was the master-mind of Italy, the peerless Leonardo da Vinci, also a natural son, but he too could rise above the handicap of his birth. However, there are cases on record of scholars who hated or envied

[24] P. S. Allen, *op. cit.*, I, 578.
[25] See J. J. Mangan, *op. cit.*, II, 63.

Erasmus, stooping to fling the unpleasant circumstances into his face and made him writhe with shame. Even so brilliant a man as J. C. Scaliger used the terms "concubinage, sordid parents, prostitution," and implied that his father had frequently been punished by the pope for his misdemeanors.[26]

Much can be said for the argument employed by Preserved Smith when he endeavors to prove that Erasmus put the year of his birth earlier as he grew older, because he wished "to save the reputation of his father and to make it easier to get for himself certain ecclesiastical dispensations. At that time the union of a priest with a woman was considered a greater sin than the union of two unmarried lay persons, and the illegitimate child suffered under a heavier stigma. If Erasmus could make himself and his contemporaries believe that he had been born before his father took orders, he would have a powerful motive to do so. When he selected the year 1466 he may have appropriated the birth year of his brother, who was just three years older than himself." [27]

In one important respect Erasmus differed from Rudolph Agricola. Whereas the latter bore his burden manfully and returned to his countrymen after having made an enviable reputation in Italy; whereas he continued to cultivate friendships with the companions of his youth and early manhood, Erasmus began to drift farther and farther away from the little circle of friends in Holland as he grew more famous abroad. Apparently he could not bear reproach or criticism; he welcomed flattery and sought the favors of rich and influential patrons, but the burghers of Gouda and the monks of Steyn, near Gouda, he avoided as much as possible, partly because they knew more about his parents than he could bear. There were also other reasons, as will appear shortly. But the fact remains that the illegitimate birth threw a blight on the early career of Erasmus. Whether the serious defects in his character observed by his contemporaries and by later biographers were caused by the anxiety of his mother and the re-

[26] J. C. Scaliger, *Epistola 15:* "Nunc populares tui, aliquot etiam vicini, viri boni, nobiles, te aiunt ex incesto natus concubitu, sordibus parentibus, altero sacrificulo, altera prostituta, qui pater tuus semel atque iterum a pontifice castigatus." Quoted by J. J. Mangan, *op. cit.*, I, 4. The reference is not clear.

[27] P. Smith, *Erasmus*, p. 8.

bukes of acquaintances is a question which cannot easily be answered. Perhaps the reply should be partly affirmative and partly negative. Erasmus might have overcome his physical and moral disabilities, since all the world knew that he himself was not to blame.

CHAPTER VI

SCHOOLDAYS AT GOUDA

IN ERASMUS' autobiography we read that his father "provided a liberal education for his boy, and sent him to school when scarcely four years old; but in his early years he made little progress in vernacular studies." [1] We have no definite knowledge about the school attended by Erasmus, except that a certain Peter Winckel taught at Gouda and that Winckel was his teacher.[2] The latter was vice-pastor of St. John's Church at Gouda for many years. On February 13, 1505, he was one of the witnesses for the making of the will of G. W. Raet at Gouda. In an authenticated document of that date his name appeared as "Magister Petrus Johannes Winkel, ecclesiae Goudensis pro tunc vice-curato." [3] In another document of the year 1505 he is named "magistro Petro Winkel." [4] Four years earlier he was also living at Gouda; [5] between 1492 and 1501 his residence was in the same city.[6] More important, however, are the treasury accounts

[1] F. M. Nichols, *The Epistles of Erasmus*, I, 7. For vernacular studies Nichols has "that unattractive sort of learning for which he was not born." The original is "litteris inamoenis," about which phrase Ch. Ruelens writes: "Nous croyons qu'il s'agit tout simplement . . . de l'enseignement primaire de la langue maternelle d'Érasme" (see his Preface to *Erasmi Rot. Silvi Carminum*, p. v).

[2] At least, this is what Erasmus reports in his *Compendium Vitae* (ed. Allen, lines 47–48: "Petrus Winckel, tum ludi litterarii magister Gaudae"). All that this means is that about the year 1484 Winckel taught school at Gouda and this information is probably correct, for the principal school at Gouda was controlled by the chapter of St. John's Church, of which he was most certainly vice-pastor. In another place Erasmus tells that Winckel was his teacher, namely, in the well-known letter addressed to the fictitious person Grunnius (ed. Allen, Ep. 447, II, 295, lines 80–87): ". . . praesertim unum, sub quo ludi literarii magistro in prima puericia grammatices prima rudimenta didicerant. . . ."

[3] H. A. G. Vorstman, *De Broeders des Gemeenen Levens te Gouda*, p. 147.

[4] *Ibid.*, p. 140.

[5] H. F. Van Heussen, *Historia Episc. Foed. Belgi*, I, 305.

[6] *Tresoriersrekening*, 1496, of the City of Gouda, fol. 12a, where we are told that Winckel went to Mechlin for nine days. In the same accounts for the year 1491–92 under the heading *Reizen*, or Trips, fol. 2b, we read that he went to Louvain in the service of the city.

of the city of Gouda in earlier years, although the accounts for the years 1487, 1488, and 1489, under the heading of *Uitgaven en Scencken* ("Expenditures and Donations"), fol. 2, recto, present the following memorandum: "... die vicecureyt 1 stede canne wiins, meester Pieter een canne wiins, meester Jacob een canne, meester Damiaen 1 stede canne." From this we gather that Winckel had not yet become vice-pastor of St. John's Church and that he was the principal teacher. In the accounts for the year 1485, on fol. 14 recto, or the third folio recto of the heading *Uitgeven en Scencken*, we read: "... meester Anthonus ende meester Pieter scoelmeesters elck een canne wiins." In 1485, therefore, Winckel was the second teacher. The treasury accounts for 1483, on fol. 2 recto, mention the following fact: "Item vercoft meester Pieter, priester, vier pont groot tsiaers liifrenten." This reference also applies most probably to Peter Winckel and shows that in 1483 he was already a priest.

According to the letter to Grunnius, both Erasmus and his brother Peter were educated at a tender age by Peter Winckel. A great deal has been written about this letter and Mangan has finally given a translation of the whole composition, which has great value, for, although Erasmus names himself Florentius here and his brother Antonius, and although he purposely misrepresents the motives of his guardians as well as the characters of his teachers, it will be fairly simple to discover just where Erasmus deviated from the truth. The letter was composed by Erasmus in August, 1516, for the purpose of securing from Pope Leo X the dispensations referred to above.[7] Nearly all authorities agree that the name Grunnius must be considered a figment. Moreover, Cardinal Ehrle, former librarian of the Vatican Library, assured his friend Mangan recently that the papal scribe named Lambert Grunnius was a mythical personage.[8] The letter, however, is a genuine composition from the hand of Erasmus, which throws much light on his character as well as on the history of his youth.

In this letter we read the following statement about Erasmus'

---

[7] P. S. Allen, *Opus Ep. Er.*, II, 291–293.

[8] J. J. Mangan, *The Life, Character, and Influence of Desiderius Erasmus of Rotterdam*, I, xii.

teacher: "They were urged to enter a monastery by one of their guardians, an arrogant man, who enjoyed a great reputation for piety, especially because they had under him, as schoolmaster, learned in childhood the first rudiments of grammar. This man was generally regarded as a pious and righteous personage, for he was free from gambling, immorality, extravagance, drunkenness, and other infamous vices; but he actually was extremely selfish and amazingly parsimonious, not a prominent figure in public opinion, nor did he approve literary attainments, except the few which he had himself acquired with difficulty. For when Florentius, now a boy of fourteen, wrote him a somewhat elegantly couched letter, he replied severely that if he wrote him such a letter again he must add to it a commentary, for it was his own custom to write plainly. He appears to have had the idea that if he could gain any disciple for the monastic life, he was offering God a most acceptable sacrifice, and he used to relate boastfully how many youths he had induced to enter the orders of St. Francis, St. Dominic, St. Benedict, St. Augustine, and St. Brigid." [9]

The letter addressed to Winckel about the year 1484 is still extant. Here we find some of Erasmus' remarks corroborated: "I am very much afraid the close of the short current period will find our affairs not yet placed in safety, but still at that late hour requiring to be so placed. I think therefore that every contrivance, every care and every effort should be used to prevent any loss occurring. You will say perhaps that I am one of those who are anxious the sky should not tumble down. I admit it might be so said, if the amount were waiting in the cash-box. But your prudence will press on with due caution the settlement of our accounts. The books are still to be offered for sale, still to look out for a purchaser, still to find a bidder. See how far they are from being disposed of." [10]

There is a bare possibility that Peter Winckel first taught in Rotterdam and later at Gouda, as Mestwerdt suggests,[11] but since Erasmus' brother, who was three years older than Erasmus, was

---

[9] *Ibid.*, I, 11–12; P. S. Allen, *op. cit.*, II, Ep. 447, lines 80–95.

[10] F. M. Nichols, *op. cit.*, I, 41.

[11] P. Mestwerdt, *Die Anfänge des Erasmus*, p. 179.

also taught by Winckel and since it was practically certain that Erasmus' father was a priest in the vicinity of Gouda at the time Erasmus was born, one may safely assume that Winckel taught at Gouda when Erasmus was four years old. Erasmus probably was reared in the home of his grandmother at Rotterdam until he was two or three years old, whereupon his father returned from Rome, penitent for his moral transgression, and now ceased to live with his former housekeeper Margaret. She, however, did not lose interest in her children, for, as we shall see later, she accompanied Erasmus to Deventer when the city of Gouda could no longer provide the education demanded by his parents.

The schools of Gouda did not enjoy much prosperity during the latter half of the fifteenth century. At that time the city did not own the principal school, which was in charge of a "church patron," formerly the count of Blois, and since 1397 the count of Holland. Hence it happened that Emperor Charles V, who was also ruler of the former county of Holland, was the patron of this school. A letter of the year 1469 shows that the rector of the principal school was officially named "Rector scolarius ecclesiae Goudanae." In other words, the school was controlled by the church, that is, St. John's Church. At the opening of the fifteenth century the school was situated near the church, but in 1407 a new building was constructed, facing the market-square, on which in 1450 the beautiful city hall of Gouda was erected. On the site of the school built in 1407 there is standing today a very interesting building, called Arti Legi. In this school there was room for three hundred pupils. About the year 1450 the wooden schoolhouse was torn down and replaced by a new building constructed of stone (1453–54).

Unfortunately, in the *stadsrekeningen*, or accounts of the city, in the period from 1463 to 1491 not one reference is made to the school. We do know, however, that in 1487 the city paid 21 guilders to a teacher named William, which proves that the magistrates had some interest in the local school. Just how much control the city government exercised over the principal school the sources do not reveal.[12] There were also other schools in Gouda during the latter half of the fifteenth century, but since Erasmus

[12] For further details see L. A. Kesper, *Geschiedenis van het Gymnasium te Gouda*.

names Winckel his schoolmaster and since the latter was one of
the pastors of St. John's Church, it is unlikely that Erasmus attended any one of the smaller schools.   When little Erasmus
trotted down the streets of Gouda in the years 1474 and 1475 he
used to see several buildings which are still standing today.   Moreover, the older part of Gouda has roughly retained for centuries
the same topography as seen by Erasmus in 1474, and afterward
when he was a monk in Steyn.

Gouda has a long and eventful history.   On the spot where the
rivers Gouwe and Hollandsche Yssel[13] met, settlers built homes in
the twelfth century and named their settlement De Gouwe, ter
Goude, Ter Gouw, Golda (Latin), or Gouda.   Traffic on the two
rivers was heavy and the little town developed rapidly.   The
great highway from Leiden and Amsterdam to the river Meuse, or
Maas, also passed Gouda.   The rising tide of commerce, therefore,
could not fail to make Gouda one of the largest cities in the county
of Holland.   Early in the thirteenth century a magnificent castle
was constructed for the count of Holland near the mouth of the
river Gouwe, which must have inspired Erasmus with awe.   But
when in 1577 the municipal government of Gouda feared that
hostile armies might endanger the safety of the city by seizing the
castle,[14] they gave orders to have it demolished.   Only the tower
was left standing, until in 1808 that also fell beneath the hammer.
A grain mill, which now occupies the spot where once the bulky
castle stood, is therefore called "the Castle."

In the fourteenth century the city received many privileges
from the counts of Blois, who from 1305 to 1397 were its suze-
rains.   After the year 1397 the counts of Holland exercised im-
mediate overlordship over the city.   Large numbers of Flemings,
driven from their homes in Flanders, came to settle in Gouda.
They introduced there a flourishing textile industry, and production of beer also grew by leaps and bounds.   Ships used to ply between Gouda and Flanders, bringing grain to Gouda and shipping
beer to Flanders.   As a result of the growing industries, the city

[13] In the eastern provinces of the Netherlands there is a river which is called
simply the Yssel.
[14] Spanish forces were seeking to suppress rebellion in Holland.

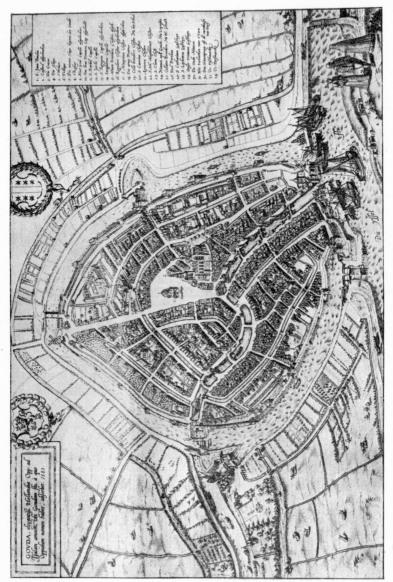

MAP 1. Plan of the city of Gouda (1585)

expanded westward. Though two disastrous fires in 1361 and 1438 retarded progress, Gouda rose each time from the ashes. Gradually its trade extended to the shores of the Baltic. By the year 1475 its population reached the 20,000 mark. It seemed as if Gouda might surpass Dordrecht and Leiden and Rotterdam. But a change in the principal routes of commerce spelled evil for Gouda. Amsterdam and Rotterdam drew much of its commerce away, so that by the year 1800 its population had dwindled to 11,000.[15]

Although the city of Gouda enjoyed a comparatively high degree of prosperity when Erasmus lived in or near its walls, the schools in this city experienced a period of decline. Whereas in 1407 the magistrates had made provision for a school with three hundred pupils, at the end of the century the number did not exceed two hundred, in spite of the fact that the population of the city had increased considerably. Another curious fact was that the Brethren of the Common Life, who in other places were building large dormitories for schoolboys, suffered at Gouda from an extreme degree of poverty.

The home of the brethren at Gouda used to belong to the Franciscan monks, who in 1419 moved outside the walls to a spot near the Yssel, located less than a mile from the city and on the same bank of the river. Here they founded a new monastery, not under the rule of St. Francis but that of St. Augustine. They named their monastery Emmaus, but since it was located in the principality of Steyn, it was later generally called Steyn. The monks sold all their property in town, and every bit of it was turned over to secular hands with the exception of a small house in the Spieringstraat, where lived a priest named Dirk Florisse. In 1425 he transferred this property to the chapter of Sion, of which Steyn was a member, on condition that on holidays the monks of this chapter would "hold collations," that is, give short addresses or sermons. The monastery of Emmaus, or Steyn, supplied these sermons in this home until in 1438 nearly the entire city was destroyed by a fire, including the "collation-house." The chapter of Sion, however, had the house rebuilt and for five years sermons

---

[15] G. J. J. Pot, *Geïllustreerde Gids voor Gouda* (Gouda, 1923), pp. 1–11.

were preached there by its monks. Shortly after the year 1443 the Brethren of the Common Life at Delft were invited to found a house of their own at Gouda. The rector complied with the request (1445), but without asking the permission of the rectors at Deventer and Zwolle, so that he eventually lost his position. It was not until the year 1456 that the house at Gouda was recognized by the rectors at Deventer and Zwolle. The burghers of Gouda named the Brethren of the Common Life "collation brethren" because of the fact that they had been asked to supply the sermons preached formerly by the Augustinian monks of Steyn. The house was dedicated to St. Paul.[16]

The real founder of the house was a certain Henry of Arnhem, who wrote a history of it, in which he stated that "at first, before we had a school and thereby gained the favor of the public, rector Henry (the chronicler) and the other brethren suffered great poverty." [17] The brethren used to receive alms from the people, and partly because of their poverty their house was not accorded recognition for several years. They also put up a printing-press, but somehow their community failed to develop properly. It certainly cannot be said that the town was too small. At any rate the school conducted by them was not considered good enough by Erasmus' parents for their sons. Master Winckel may not have met their demands either. Whatever was lacking, however, seemed to be possessed by the city of Deventer, for Gerard and Margaret, the parents of Peter and Erasmus, decided to send their boys to Deventer, where the Brethren of the Common Life provided satisfactory quarters for the pupils attending the school attached to the Church of St. Lebwin, while some of their members belonged to the teaching staff of that school. The brethren at Deventer were famed for their piety and sober learning. They also had a good library and were honored by bishops and cardinals. Surely, there was a better future for Erasmus at Deventer than at Gouda!

[16] A. H. L. Hensen, *Henric van Arnhem's Kronyk*, pp. 1–7.
[17] *Ibid.*, p. 40.

CHAPTER VII

IN THE CITY OF DEVENTER

NOT many years ago a very interesting volume was published in The Hague, which gives a description of Deventer in the second half of the fourteenth century.[1] In the present chapter an attempt will be made to reproduce the essential features of this description and to modify them so as to fit conditions in the year 1475, when Erasmus, accompanied by his mother, removed to this city from another metropolis on the river Yssel in Holland.

When one imagines oneself standing about the year 1475 on the right bank of the Yssel opposite the city of Deventer, one notes a striking contrast between the peaceful meadows and the thriving Hansa town across the water. Deventer has become a wealthy center of commerce. Its merchants have enabled the populace to build several stately churches, roomy monasteries, and splendid homes; and massive walls surmounted by heavy towers enhance the beauty of the scene as from a distance one gazes in admiration at the city. Along the bank of the river one sees a busy traffic, and numerous are the ships that are arriving and departing each day. Some of them are bringing wood from German forests and grain from Polish farms; others are loaded with stones hewn in the mountainous districts to the south. Some are carrying fish and some have a cargo of merchandise.

After crossing the river we enter the city and pass a number of workshops, where in a simple and rather primitive manner (from the viewpoint of a sophisticated inhabitant of a twentieth-century metropolis) all sorts of articles are manufactured. Everywhere the old craft guilds are still functioning, with their system of masters, journeymen, and apprentices. The streets are very narrow

[1] F. Buitenrust Hettema en A. Telting, *Een bezoek aan een Nederlandsche Stad in de XIVde Eeuw* (The Hague, 1906).

and one must use caution in passing the houses where the bakers have placed their products on "bread benches" in front of their shops, or where the manufacturers of leather goods, of furs, or of textiles have prepared similar exhibitions. The magistrates are very strict here; they take care that all articles have a proper weight. Occasionally they send an official to test the weights and measures and to weigh or examine the goods placed on sale.

In the center of the city is the market-square, named Brink. Here we can examine at leisure the architecture of the principal buildings. About one-third of them are still of wood, several with the upper story protruding over the lower. The majority have thatched roofs, but some are covered with tiles, and the number of tiled roofs is rapidly increasing, since the magistrates have warned against the danger of fire. There are also a few buildings covered with slate; these belong to the more wealthy burghers, usually merchants who have been eminently successful in various enterprises. Their homes are also distinguished by windows made of glass, but their less favored neighbors have to content themselves with panes of oiled paper, linen, or pigskin. Most houses are very low, leaving but seven or eight feet between the gutter and the street.

The color of most buildings is dark. Brown tar is commonly used, instead of paint, to protect the wood against the elements. The glaring contrast between the color of the tar and the yellow straw or the red tiles or the blue slate affects one rather unpleasantly. And so does the *ensemble* of the average group of houses on either side of the ordinary streets. They do not form a neat row, but nearly all stand apart from each other in a helter-skelter fashion. There is almost always at least a yard of space between the houses, "so that everybody can place a ladder upon his own lot."

It is evident that the knowledge of hygiene is not very widespread in the city, nor is cleanliness deemed a great virtue here. In some places the streets look most unsanitary, for many a burgher keeps a manure pile in his yard, not seldom in front of the house, where pigs, chickens, and children gleefully dig up the filthy dung. Pigs feel quite at home on the streets as well, for generally only a narrow strip in the center has been paved, while the market-square is also largely unpaved. The pavement is not smooth, since it consists of stones of all shapes and sizes. In some of the more narrow streets, named *stegen*, holes in the pavement have been filled with reeds or straw. Most lots have been inclosed by railings or fences, or they are marked off by ditches. Little poles in front of the lots indicate "how wide the street will have to remain," else greedy burghers might add part of the street to their property. The dirt which collects on the streets is taken away in little carts from time to time by officials, but the men do not come frequently. Many a time it is the rain which has to be relied upon in the cleaning of the streets.

The interior of the homes offers much food for wonder. Chimneys are few and so are stoves. In the center of each house still remains the time-honored fireplace, above which is seen a large round hole in the roof to let the smoke escape upward. This opening is covered when there is no fire, but in cold rainy weather it is sometimes difficult for the people to keep comfortable. Sleeping quarters are also rather unsanitary, particularly where beds have been placed in a room, or rather, a closet, where one sleeps all night behind closed doors without any ventilation whatsoever. As for bathing, that is a custom practically unheard of among the adult population. Children have to be bathed regularly, so the stolid burghers admit, but grown-ups merely need to change their underwear once in a fortnight; baths are entirely unnecessary.

And woe to the citizens when perchance a plague should visit the city. In the previous century such was no rare occurrence and who knows that another one is not due again in a few years? We, who know that in 1483 there will be a visitation which will once more sweep away hundreds of human lives within this city, feel duty-bound to warn the heedless burghers. But they reply that there is no remedy for contagious diseases. Nature must take its course; man is helpless against plagues and floods and earthquakes, which are sent by God, who alone knows the value of each human life.

There is much in the administration of justice, in the relation between social classes, in the municipal government, and in the realms of religion and education which we might criticize. Only we should discover to our chagrin that the burghers of Deventer could not appreciate our point of view. The possibility of social progress never seems to occur to them. It is true that in the fourteenth century Gerard Groote revealed many abuses existing in the Church and he found a warm response in the hearts of both clerics and laymen. The curriculum of the celebrated school attached to St. Lebwin's Church has also undergone a marked transformation. There is a change going on in some directions, where it may have far-reaching effects. Elsewhere conditions must remain the same for centuries.

We shall now ask Erasmus and his mother to acquaint us with the topography of Deventer, in order that we may be able to locate the more important buildings. With their assistance we shall prepare a plan of the city, showing with the aid of heavy black lines the successive expansion of the old city, which dates back to the sixth century. The numbers given below correspond to those on the accompanying map.

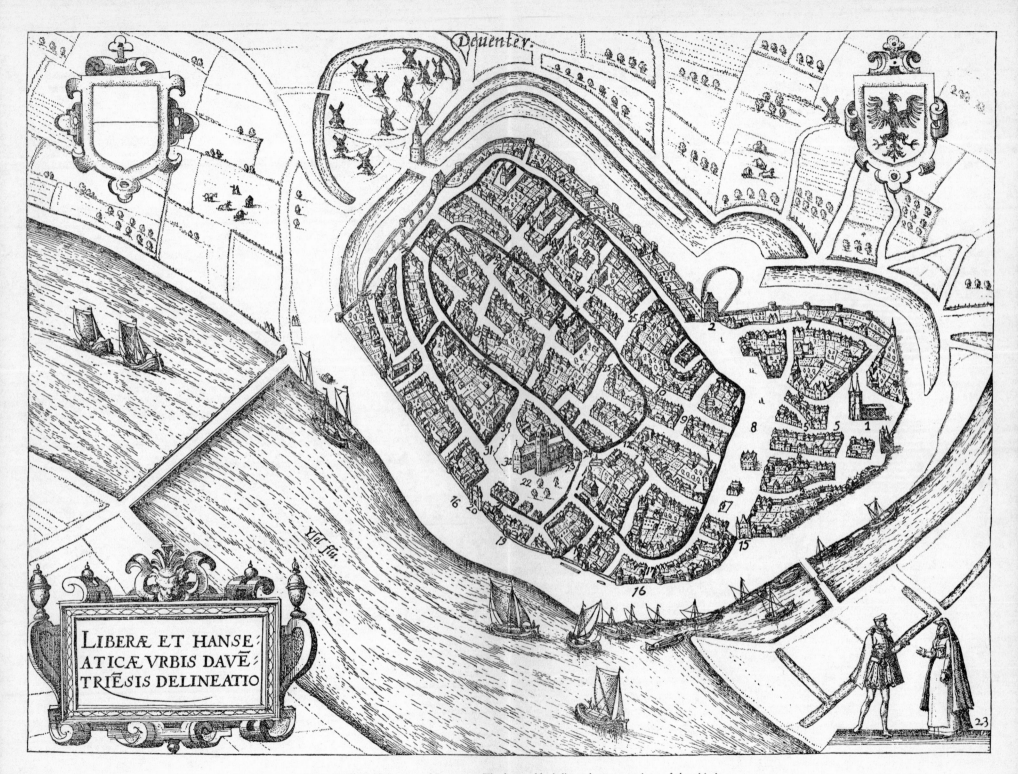

Map 2. Plan of the city of Deventer. The heavy black lines show expansions of the old city

KEY TO THE NUMBERS ON MAP II

1. *Bergkerk*, or *Ecclesia montis*, sometimes called Church of St. Nicholas, built *ca.* 1200
2. *Bergpoort*, a gate in the wall
3. *Ricmodestrate*, that is, Rich-Man Street
4. *Menstrate*
5. *Berchstrate*
6. *Roggestrate*, that is, Rye Street
7. *Walstrate*
8. *Brink*
9. *Biermanstege*
10–11. *Overstraten*
12. *Vleijschschuppestede*
13. *Assenstrate*. A very old street. St. Lebwin is said to have lived here in the eighth century.
14. *Polstraat*
15. *Zantpoert*
16. *De Welle*
17. *Malcsterstegelen*. The word *stegele*, or *steeg*, means "a narrow street."
18. *Apeldorenstegele*
19. *Duempoerte*
20. *Dijkpoorte*
21. *Waterstrate*
22. *Kerkhof*, or Cemetery
23. *St. Lebuïnuskerk*, or Church of St. Lebwin, constructed in 1040, rebuilt in 1251, and again in 1334

24. *Poot*
25. *Bisschopsstrate*, or *Platea episcopi*
26. *Pundessteghele*, or *Pontsteeg*
27. *Broerenkerk*, built in 1338
28. *Engestrate*
29. *Korenmarkt*
30. *Graven*
31. *Nieuwe Markt*
32. *Lieve Vrouwe-Kerk*, built *ca.* 1250
33. *Norenbergstrate*
34. *Papenstrate*
35. *Tibbestege*
36. *Diefsteghe*
37. *Nieuwstrate*
38. *Leusensteghe*
39. *Kuypersteghe*
40. *Bagijnestrate*
41. *Spinhuisstege*, or *Fratersteghe*, named after the *fratres*, or Brethren of the Common Life
42. *Hagensteghe*, or *Kromme Steghe* (see G. Dumbar, *Het Kerkelijk en Wereltlijk Deventer*, I, 629–630)
43. *Smedenstrate*
44. *Molenstrate*
45. *Stakeldertoren*, near the present Lindestraat

CHAPTER VIII

CHORISTER IN UTRECHT

ERASMUS tells us in his autobiography that he went with his mother to Deventer when he was nine years old,[1] but Allen has shown that Erasmus was at Deventer as early as the year 1475.[2] In the same work Erasmus says he left Deventer at the age of thirteen,[3] although he was still there at the end of the year 1483. So one must use great caution in employing this source of information. Since Erasmus removed to Deventer in or before 1475 to attend the celebrated chapter school of St Lebwin's, he probably came directly from Gouda, and remained at Deventer a few years before he removed to Utrecht.

Most authorities have assumed that Erasmus was in Utrecht before going to Deventer, but there are two circumstances which seem to disqualify this hypothesis. In the first place, Erasmus completed only six grades at Deventer between 1475 and 1484, and although, according to a tradition,[4] he made slow progress in his studies, we have no reason to believe that he failed twice in passing a grade. The only evidence supporting the tradition just

---

[1] P. S. Allen, *Opus Ep. Er.*, I, 48: "Ubi nonum ageret annum, misit Daventriam; mater sequuta est, custos et curatrix tenerae aetatis." Since he was still of such "a tender age," we may assume that he was less than nine years old.

[2] *Ibid.*, p. 579. Here a quotation is given from the *Exomologesis* of Erasmus, where he says: "Olim quum admodum puer agerem Daventriae, audiebam [a sermon] . . . erat autem iubilaeum." In other words, it was in the year 1475, when Pope Pius IV proclaimed a jubilee, although it was not due until the year 1500.

[3] *Ibid.*, p. 48: "Tum pestis vehementer ibi saeviens sustulit matrem, relicto filio iam annum decimum tertium agente. Quum pestis in dies magis ac magis incrudesceret, tota domo in qua agebat desolata, reversus est in patriam."

[4] P. Smith, *Erasmus*, p. 12: "Erasmus' later observation that he was a dull pupil is to some extent borne out by the fact that he took eight years to cover at Deventer the curriculum passed by Butzbach in two years." P. Mestwerdt, *Die Anfänge des Erasmus*, p. 202: "Es hat sich eine Tradition erhalten, dass ihm anfangs das Lernen schwer gefallen sei."

mentioned is a remark made by Erasmus in his autobiography about his poor showing "in the vernacular studies, for which he was not born." There may have been various reasons for his slow advancement under Peter Winckel's guidance, but it cannot be shown that he was a dull pupil at Deventer. The sources reveal on the contrary that Erasmus made excellent progress in his studies, for not only did he know the whole of Terence by heart before he left Deventer, but when he removed to 's-Hertogenbosch he was conscious of greater intellectual capacity than some of his own teachers possessed. Again, his friend Beatus Rhenanus testified that at Deventer Erasmus was for the most part self-taught, which can never be said of a stupid boy.

Another reason why Erasmus did not go directly to Utrecht from Gouda is the fact that no boys were allowed to enter the school conducted for choristers in the cathedral at Utrecht unless they were at least six years old.[5] Erasmus says that his mother accompanied him to Deventer because of his tender age. If he was born in 1469, as is most likely, he was only six when he resided at Deventer during the papal jubilee of 1475. He probably remained two or three years at Deventer, whereupon his father and mother decided to have him sing under Obrecht in Utrecht. Should his voice prove satisfactory, he would secure free education in the cathedral school, and afterward a prebend in the Church. Although the Brethren of the Common Life at Deventer were very charitable, they did not provide boys with all their needs. Hence the advisability for Erasmus of trying the career of chorister.

It might be argued that Erasmus was perhaps permitted to sing in the cathedral at Utrecht before attending the school attached to that cathedral; but this assumption is obviously incorrect, because it was not the organist of the cathedral who had charge of the choristers, but the *scholaster*, who supervised the work of the rector of the school. A chorister in the cathedral in Utrecht was much more closely associated with the clergy than are the boys who sing in the choirs of various American churches. The conclusion is, therefore, justified that boys were not permitted to sing in the choir of the cathedral in Utrecht who did not attend the cathe-

[5] M. Schoengen, *Geschiedenis van het Onderwijs in Nederland*, p. 373.

dral school. There had been a time when boys under the age of six were sent to this school, but the regulation mentioned above was drawn up to prevent recurrence of such cases.

Very little is known about Erasmus' activities in Utrecht, except that he sang under the celebrated Obrecht,[6] one of the outstanding musicians of all Europe. During the second half of the fifteenth century the Dutch possessed some of the ablest teachers of music to be found anywhere, not excluding Italy. It became a custom to employ Dutch and Flemish musicians in such cities as Rome and Florence. One of the greatest of all these artists was Obrecht, who graced the cathedral of St. Salvator in Utrecht. The parents of Erasmus must have been anxious to provide for him the best of everything in the field of education. When he was only four they had him instructed by a learned pastor at Gouda, and when he grew older they considered the schools of Gouda too mediocre for him. Hence they selected the most famous school in the northern Netherlands, located at Deventer.

As for the musician in Utrecht who was to train Erasmus' voice, no better guide could have been selected by Gerard and Margaret, the parents of Erasmus, than James Obrecht, whose name was also spelled Obrech, Hobrecht, Oberti, and Hoberti. He has been called the greatest master of counterpoint of the fifteenth century. He was born probably about the year 1430 in Utrecht, and by 1465 he had become choir master of the chapter of the cathedral in his native city.[7] Glareanus said of him that in one evening he could compose a mass worthy of admiration by the most accom-

---

[6] P. S. Allen, *op. cit.*, I, 56: "Proximam sibi laudem vendicat Daventria, quae puellum adhuc ex aede sacra Traiectensi cantorculum deductum, ubi praecentiunculas obire solitus phonascis etiam tenuissimae vocis gratia pro more templorum cathedralium inservierat, instituendum suscepit." This quotation is from a biography by Beatus Rhenanus. An English translation is found in Nichols' edition of Erasmus' letters, I, 23 ff. Rhenanus claims that Erasmus first went to Utrecht . . . , "having been before a choir-boy in Utrecht Cathedral." Another contemporary of Erasmus referred to this period in Utrecht, namely, Glareanus. See *Nederlandsch Archief voor Kergesch.*, X, 340; Glareanus, *Dodecachordon* (Basel, 1547), pp. 120–134.

[7] It is possible, however, that Obrecht, like several other skilled artists, had been engaged by David of Burgundy, the bishop of Utrecht, to grace his episcopal court, and that he was born elsewhere. The archives of the cathedral and the city archives contain no data which the standard works have not given.

plished musicians. He remained in Utrecht until 1483. From 1483 to 1485 he held a position in the cathedral at Cambray; from 1489 to 1490 he served in Bruges; from 1491 to 1504 he was employed in Antwerp. In the latter city he was in charge of a choir counting sixty-seven voices, exclusive of children. He prepared new hymnals for the choristers. His reputation was such that hundreds of visitors came from long distances to listen to his choir. In 1493, for example, the choir of St. John's cathedral at 's-Hertogenbosch visited him in Antwerp. But even in Utrecht he had attracted attention and received much merited praise.[8]

The cathedral of Utrecht, named Church of St. Salvator, or Church of St. Martin, was the oldest Gothic structure in the northern Netherlands. It was constructed between 1254 and 1288; various additions were made until 1517, and the tower was built in the years 1321-82. It was erected on the spot where in 1023 a Romanesque cathedral had been dedicated by Bishop Adelbold. This building had been damaged several times by fire, and was practically destroyed in 1253. The stones of the older cathedral were used for its construction. Five periods of active building between 1254 and 1517 may be differentiated. In 1492 David of Burgundy, bishop of Utrecht, officially dedicated the whole structure, but further construction did not cease until 1517. It was, however, nearly completed when Erasmus was a boy.[9]

The cathedral chapter enjoyed an honored position, for Utrecht had for centuries been the ecclesiastical metropolis of the Low Countries north of the Rhine. That the most capable musicians of the northern Netherlands should have happened to be located here was not surprising. One can easily imagine how eager the boys in Erasmus' native country must have been to secure a prebend in the church of St. Salvator. The documents prove that boys who sang in the choir received a sort of scholarship, or endow-

---

[8] F. J. Fetis, *Biographie universelle des musiciens*, VI (Paris, 1875), 343-346.

[9] A useful history of the cathedral is a booklet entitled *De Dom van Utrecht*, by G. van Klaveren, Utrecht, 1926. It mentions a storm which in 1674 destroyed almost the whole church except the tower, and tells how the ruins remained a formless mass for a century and a half. During the past twenty years the tower has been restored, and at the present time it is the tallest and finest church tower in the Netherlands.

ment, or prebend. They were entitled to free board, lodging, clothes, and education in the chapter school. The rector of such a school received a fixed salary for educating the *chorales*, so that he could find no excuse for asking tuition.

The cathedral supported ten choir-boys,[10] as did also the churches of St. Peter,[11] St. John,[12] and St. Mary.[13] The choir-boys lived in a house situated near the cathedral, named *choralenhuis*. They formed the nucleus of the chapter school, where they received instruction in grammar, logic, and music. Their school was patterned after the schools attached to the English cathedrals.

A document drawn up in the year 1468 throws welcome light on the duties of the rector of the chapter school where Erasmus received instruction shortly afterward. In this document it was stated that the *scholaster* of the cathedral would be expected to appoint a rector who had secured a Master's degree, or else an educator equally capable. Among other things, the rector was not to permit the boys to beg for alms.[14]

The school of St. Salvator's was undoubtedly the best school in Utrecht at the time Erasmus sang under Obrecht. In 1476 the Brethren of the Common Life had founded a home in this city, and a few years later they opened a school in their own house, after having asked permission of the *scholaster* of the cathedral. By the opening of the fifteenth century their school attracted large numbers of pupils from various districts and, if Erasmus had arrived after 1500, he might have remained in Utrecht to finish his elementary education. Even the chapter school might have furnished such an education, for it was customary for choir-boys to remain till they were eighteen or twenty-one, whereupon they could obtain a benefice.

The instruction given in the cathedral school differed little from that provided elsewhere by similar schools. It was what Erasmus later called "barbarous." The scholastic methods, the old medi-

---

[10] M. Schoengen, *op. cit.*, p. 372.

[11] *Ibid.*, p. 204.

[12] *Ibid.*, p. 206.

[13] *Ibid.*, p. 207.

[14] *Ibid.*, pp. 352, 360–364. It should also be noted that the *scholaster*, and not the organist, was placed in charge of the choristers.

PLATE III

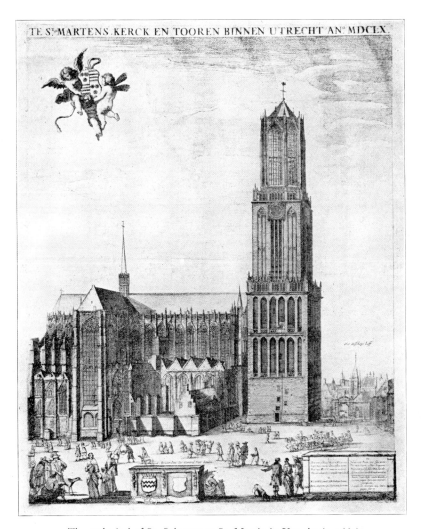

The cathedral of St. Salvator or St. Martin in Utrecht (*c.* 1660)

eval grammars, the lack of classical knowledge — all this was afterward severely criticized by Erasmus and by other humanists. But it was not so much the chapter school as Obrecht, the famous organist, that had attracted the attention of Erasmus' parents.

Beatus Rhenanus, a friend of Erasmus, tells that the latter was a chorister in the cathedral in Utrecht, "where after the fashion of such churches he had been employed for the sake of his small, high-pitched voice." [15] It may well be that his parents had taken a certain amount of pride in his voice and may have reasoned that it might enable him to procure a good education, and later a benefice in the Church. His father seems to have retained his position and wished no doubt to see the son enter the ecclesiastical service. But for some reason unknown to us the stay in Utrecht was rather short. Else Erasmus would have alluded to it in one or more of his writings. He evinced practically no interest in music at later periods in his life. Anecdotes were told about his attitude toward musicians, but none of these have much value. It seems that the visit to Utrecht bore little fruit.

There is a possibility that Erasmus remained in Utrecht two years, for in the eight years between 1475 and 1484 he passed through only six grades in the school at Deventer. He probably covered one grade each year, as was customary for the majority of pupils. Even though he had not made rapid progress in the vernacular studies at Gouda, the curriculum at Deventer must have appealed fairly well to him, since the study of Latin was emphasized there. Erasmus may have had a very good reason for never referring to his experiences as chorister in Utrecht. One might surmise that his teachers were disappointed with his voice, for otherwise he would certainly have wanted to remain. What could have pleased his father more than to see him safely established in the choristers' house attached to the cathedral in Utrecht? And what would have been pleasanter for the son than a life of comparative leisure in a comfortable home? Utrecht possessed far wealthier churches than either Gouda or Deventer. Here lived David of Burgundy, the opulent bishop who was placed above all other members of the clergy in the Netherlands north of the

[15] See p. 74, note 6.

Rhine. It must have been a disappointment for Erasmus' parents, if not for the boy as well, that he could not find a suitable place in the cathedral chapter in Utrecht. This was probably the reason why Erasmus preferred to ignore his work under Obrecht in all his writings. Neither parents nor guardians nor teachers could be held responsible for his failure, wherefore he felt constrained to pass over in silence the stay in Utrecht.

There may have been other reasons, however, why Erasmus left Utrecht so soon. His father may have lacked sufficient influence to enable his boy to get a good start. A number of circumstances unknown to him or his parents may have conspired against him. Perhaps his brother Peter was instrumental in having him removed to Deventer. It is also possible that Erasmus was a rather dull pupil at first at Deventer, wherefore it may have taken him two years to pass the lowest grade in the school. In that case he must have spent only one year or less in Utrecht. But it is much more likely that his voice proved disappointing in Utrecht, and that between 1475 and 1484 he resided at Deventer for a period of six years, and also that two years were consumed in various attempts to find some ecclesiastical post for him in Utrecht and possibly in one or more other cities. The sources which inform us about Erasmus' experiences in Utrecht are extremely scanty, so that the biographer will have to content himself with speculation, which is always an unsatisfactory way of arriving at the truth. Suffice it to say here that Erasmus missed a chance to obtain a desirable prebend and that it was not the fault of Obrecht nor of his teachers nor of his parents, at least not directly, for he would have been certain to inform posterity about their shortcomings.

PART III

WITH THE BRETHREN OF THE COMMON LIFE

CHAPTER IX

THE SCHOOL OF ST. LEBWIN

ON ERASMUS' stay at Deventer the sources throw considerable light. Says Beatus Rhenanus, "His apprenticeship in
letters was begun at Deventer, where he imbibed the rudiments
of Latin and Greek. . . . As a boy Erasmus knew the Comedies of
Terence as familiarly as his own fingers, having a most tenacious
memory and clear head. . . .[1] The ability of Erasmus was soon
shown by the quickness with which he understood and the fidelity
with which he retained whatever he was taught, surpassing all
the other boys of his age." [2] These remarks seem to disprove the
tradition according to which Erasmus was dull in his early school
years.

Rhenanus continues in the same strain when he remarks that
"among the Brothers of the Common Life was John Sintheim, a
man of good learning for that time, as is shown by the Gram-
matical Commentaries which he published, and who attained a
great name in the schools of Germany. This class of long-cloaked
cenobites are employed in the work of education; and Sintheim
was so delighted with the progress of Erasmus that on one occasion
he embraced the boy, exclaiming, 'Well done, Erasmus, the day
will come when thou wilt reach the highest summit of erudition';
and having said this, dismissed him with a kiss."

In the autobiography of Erasmus we read: "That school was
still barbarous. The *Pater Meus* was read over, and the boys had
to say their tenses; *Ebrardus* and *Joannes de Garlandia* were read
aloud. But Alexander Hegius and Zinthius [Sintheim] were beginning to introduce some better literature; and at last from his
elder playmates who were in Zinthius' class, he first got scent of
the better learning. . . . In this school he reached the third class." [3]

---

[1] F. M. Nichols, *The Epistles of Erasmus*, I, 23.
[2] *Ibid.*, p. 25.   [3] *Ibid.*, I, 7.

"The education which Erasmus received at Deventer," asserts Allen, "was still in thraldom to the medieval ideal. Greek was practically unknown, and in Latin all that was required of the student was a sufficient mastery of the rudiments of grammar to enable him to express somehow the distinctions and refinements of thought for which he was being trained. Niceties of scholarship and amplitude of vocabulary were unnecessary to him and were disregarded." [4]

The *Pater Meus* referred to by Erasmus was a series of declensions, and the *Tempora*, or *Tenses*, a collection of conjugations. In addition to these the boys at Deventer employed the metrical grammar of Ebrardus of Bethune in Artois, who flourished in the twelfth century, and the grammar of John Garland, who taught in Toulouse in the thirteenth century. These works were exceedingly dry and rather impractical, at least uninteresting. They are described at length by Allen, who, as a true classical scholar, takes considerable pains to point out their bad features,[5] and adds elsewhere that "if Deventer school in 1475 was fed upon the monstrosities we have seen, it is not likely that Winchester and Eton had any better fare." [6] It may, therefore, seem somewhat surprising that this school of St. Lebwin at Deventer produced so many capable teachers of Latin Grammar. But before the arrival of Hegius in 1483 the rectors do not appear to have attracted many promising students. It was Hegius who actually made Deventer famous.

There seems to be little need in this our twentieth century to bewail the fate of Erasmus, who arrived at Deventer eight years before Hegius became rector of the school of St. Lebwin. Our schools at the present time certainly do not emphasize the study of Latin and Greek, wherefore it is somewhat difficult for the average student to appreciate the biting criticism hurled by Erasmus at the teachers of his youth. When we read the Dutch or German or English chronicles of the fifteenth century we meet with an astonishing array of strangely spelled words. It would not look right for us to spell Dutch, German, or English as did the

[4] P. S. Allen, *The Age of Erasmus*, pp. 7–8.
[5] *Ibid.*, pp. 36–49.   [6] *Ibid.*, p. 120.

contemporaries of Erasmus. But somehow we cannot lament the way in which living languages comport themselves. Medieval Latin was also a living language and as such it nobly served its purpose. Those who read the *Imitation of Christ* in its original form do not regret the curious expressions used by Thomas à Kempis. If transposed into classical Latin this priceless jewel of Christian mysticism would lose much of its unique value. And so it was with other compositions of the fifteenth century.

On the other hand, it would be grossly unfair to find fault with Erasmus for having condemned the methods of his teachers at Deventer. From his standpoint he was absolutely justified. Before the year 1480 the school attached to St. Lebwin's was still "barbarous," for classical Latin and Greek were neglected here. If Erasmus had arrived at Deventer but ten years later than he did, he would have had much less cause for complaint, inasmuch as the Brethren of the Common Life after the year 1485 allied themselves closely with the humanists in the interest of the classical scholarship. From their schools in Utrecht, 's-Hertogenbosch, and Liège were to issue forth many of the most enthusiastic champions of humanism. For us the important questions, however, remain, first: What were the subjects taught in the school of St. Lebwin before 1483 and how were they taught? and secondly, What were the ideals of Alexander Hegius, who caused a considerable change in the years 1483–84? Did Erasmus perhaps get his love for the classics at Deventer in spite of his verdict to the contrary?

It is a well-known fact that in the Middle Ages the schools conducted by the clergy were for a long time superior in quality and quantity to all other schools. During the fifteenth century, however, public schools were founded in many cities. Particularly in Italy, secular schools, both public and private, emulated ecclesiastical institutions. In the Low Countries a similar phenomenon occurred. Zwolle, for example, had an excellent school at the end of the fourteenth century, which was controlled by the municipal government. At Deventer, however, as at Gouda and Utrecht, the principal school was that which belonged to the chapter of the church.

Some writers speak of eight grades in the school at Deventer; others mention the number nine. There must indeed have been one preparatory grade and eight real grades, making a total of nine.[7] Erasmus may first have been placed in the former class; and if so he actually passed seven grades in as many years. In some respects the first grade, which was called eighth grade, was also preparatory. In the five lowest grades (ninth to fifth) grammar and etymology were taught. In the next two rhetoric was emphasized; in the two highest classes (second and first) such subjects as philosophy and logic were propounded. These two grades were what we would call high-school grades; the first two years in the university would also be called high-school grades.

The school of St. Lebwin had been greatly affected by the reforms inaugurated by Gerard Groote. From 1378 to 1381 the rector of this school was William Vroede, an intimate friend of Groote. He was succeeded by John Lubberts (1381-85)[8] and not by Radewyns, the rector of the brethren at Deventer, although many writers have assumed this because it was believed at one time that the school was conducted by the Brethren of the Common Life. It is also wrong, therefore, to assert that Egbert ter Beek, the rector of the brethren in Erasmus' time, was rector of the school. The name of the rector of the school preceding Hegius has not come down to posterity. All we can say is that some of the *lectors*, or teachers, in the school were connected with the brotherhood, and that a large percentage of the pupils were housed in dormitories of this brotherhood. Godfried Toorn, who was rector of the brethren-house from 1410 to 1450, had been a teacher in the school.[9] Erasmus himself mentions the name of Sinthius, teacher in this school and a member of the brotherhood. As said above, after the invention of printing the brethren were compelled to rely on other sources of income besides the copying of books.

Through the influence of Groote and his followers the methods of John Cele, rector of the public school of Zwolle from 1374 to

[7] Such, for example, was the case with the school at 's-Hertogenbosch. See A. F. O. Van Sasse van Ysselt, *De voorname Huizen en Gebouwen te 's-Hertogenbosch*, III, 125.

[8] G. Dumbar, *Analecta Daventria*, I, 114.

[9] M. Schoengen, *Die Schule von Zwolle*, pp. 17-18.

PLATE IV

The church of St. Lebwin at Deventer

1417, were largely materialized in the school of St. Lebwin. A description of these methods, therefore, will give a quite accurate account of what Erasmus was taught in the "barbarous" school at Deventer. Cele's principles were also perpetuated by Dringenberg at Schlettstadt, by Murmellius in Münster, and by Sturm in Strassburg, and even Calvin and the Jesuits were greatly indebted to them.[10]

In the lower grades the trivium was taught in accordance with a universal custom in the Middle Ages. Added to this was the quadrivium, part of which was not as a rule given in elementary schools, but only in the universities. Moreover, in the two highest grades specialists were employed; hence Erasmus' remark about Sinthius, who taught only in these grades. Besides grammar, rhetoric, logic, and philosophy, the pupils also learned something about arithmetic, music, and astronomy, while ethics was not wholly neglected, and the elementary principles of medicine were also taught.

Cele and the teachers at Deventer did not break with scholastic philosophy, nor did they cast aside the old medieval grammar. They strongly emphasized the value of practical religion, however, and they did criticize the impractical scholastic disputes engaged in by the learned doctors in Paris and Cologne. Cele's maxim was, "The kingdom of heaven consisteth not in knowledge and speech, but in work and virtue." Cele taught his pupils the value of humility, modesty, and obedience, and urged them to study the Bible and the Fathers.

Such was the "barbarous" program initiated by Cele at Zwolle and by his followers at Deventer and many other cities. Cele was a practical teacher. He saw that no two boys were exactly alike, nor were they equally well supplied with funds. With the Brethren of the Common Life at Zwolle he made arrangements to house them in a suitable manner. Those who could afford it were expected to pay the brethren for their room and board, while Cele asked tuition. The poorer class of boys, of whom there was a great number, instead of being compelled to beg for alms, were kindly taken care of by the brethren, and Cele even gave them money

[10] A. Hyma, *The Christian Renaissance*, pp. 97–98, 122–135, 288–299.

for the books, ink, and paper they needed in school. In order to take care of each pupil's individual needs, he divided his school into eight classes, which was something like pioneer work, and was imitated everywhere. One of his pupils wrote about his chief aim: "Although he took great pains in teaching the trivium and quadrivium with effect, nevertheless he did not thereby diminish his interest — nay, he ever increased his zeal in instructing his pupils in the sacred writings, good manners, a saintly and Christian life, and the fear and love of God. For in the morning he would explain an Epistle and in the evening some other part of the Scriptures, addressing the whole school."

One feature of Cele's method was the *rapiarium*, or collection of excerpts, later also called *farrago*, which every pupil had to make. From the Gospels and other books of the New Testament he selected the plainest and most helpful sayings. These he dictated in a loud voice to the whole school. "For," says John Busch, his pupil, "he wanted his boys to have the leading events and the most striking passages found in the Epistles and the Gospels collected in one copy-book, a theological excerpt-book, in which the most useful thoughts found in the sacred writings were gathered in brief extracts. This would enable them more easily to commit such passages to memory."

John Cele was a friend and admirer of the Brethren of the Common Life, and in a certain respect was a member of their house at Zwolle, although he did not live in this house. The brethren had a custom of granting membership to men who were of service to their order. Cele was actually more than a member, for he served as a guardian of the new house at Zwolle. Furthermore, he conformed in manners and speech to the habits of Groote and Radewyns, and "in all things made himself like unto their congregation. . . . He exhorted his pupils to do likewise." [11]

Cele is mentioned here at length because his ideals were transmitted to his successors at Zwolle, who also remained on friendly terms with the brethren. Among the many hundreds of pupils educated at Zwolle during the course of the fifteenth century were two men who exerted great influence on Erasmus and who were

[11] A. Hyma, *op. cit.*, p. 379, note 298.

closely in touch with Groote's brotherhood. These men were Wessel Gansfort and Alexander Hegius. Their mutual friend was Rudolph Agricola. The three scholars formed a sort of triumvirate amidst the rising power of humanism in the Netherlands when Erasmus was being educated at Deventer. To them he owed many of his pet ideals, although he only reluctantly admitted it in later years.

The school of St. Lebwin was equally indebted to these three humanists. It may be that this school, before the arrival of Hegius at Deventer,[12] was but slightly affected by the influence of the humanists. Nevertheless the chapter of St. Lebwin's must have been willing to have their school managed by a man who, as rector of the school at Emmerich, not only was continuing the policies of John Cele but made further advances. Much good work had already been done before the year 1483, contrary to Erasmus' remarks. More was done by Hegius, and still more after his death in 1498. It certainly is a curious fact that at the very time Erasmus subjected the Brethren of the Common Life and Alexander Hegius to a sweeping condemnation, that is, between 1520 and 1530, the brotherhood was more than ever inclined to carry out the reforms recommended by the humanists. Fortunately the sources tell us a great deal about the brethren in Deventer during the latter half of the fifteenth century. They show that a careful distinction must be made between the vast majority of the brethren and those who before 1485 were actuated by humanistic principles, wherefore Erasmus was partly justified in his criticism.

[12] He moved from Emmerich to Deventer.

CHAPTER X

THE BRETHREN OF THE COMMON LIFE
AT DEVENTER

THE first group of brethren at Deventer lived with Florentius Radewyns in his vicarage in the *Enghe Strate*. But as their number increased, it was deemed necessary to obtain more spacious quarters. These were secured in the year 1391, when a large house was constructed for them in the *Pont-steghe*, named "House of Florentius." Most of the brethren now moved to this building, but a few continued to live in the old home until 1402. Two years before the death of Radewyns (1398) another home was founded, namely, the *Nova Domus*, or *Domus Pauperum*, where poor pupils of the church school were housed. "Behold," wrote Radewyns in 1398, "we take these youths into our house, inexperienced as they are, changeable, having as yet no definite aims or exerting much will-power, but they are tractable and pliable. Oh what would happen if one or two or three of us would persuade these boys to work, and teach them discipline and humility?"

Radewyns was succeeded in 1400 by Amilius van Buren, who one day made the following significant remark: "There is one thing which we must adhere to and observe, namely, our status as Brethren of the Common Life; for although the monastic state is preferable in the opinion of the Church, nevertheless he who lives a saintly life outside a monastery will receive the reward of saintliness." Van Buren enjoyed a prosperous reign of four years, during which the brethren founded houses in Münster and Delft. The next rector was John of Haarlem (1404–10) and the following one Godfried Toorn (1410–50). The latter, as was noted above, had been a teacher in the school of St. Lebwin, but a real scholar he was not. He counseled his associates not to read Thomas Aquinas, because this writer was too subtle for simple-minded folk. During Toorn's rectorate the house at Deventer was greatly surpassed in every way by the house at Zwolle.

When Erasmus arrived at Deventer, the brethren were ruled by Egbert ter Beek (1450–83), who during the first year of his rectorate was honored by a visit from Cardinal Cusa. He is said to have been educated at Deventer, but concrete proof is lacking. At any rate, he was greatly pleased by the work of the pious brethren, and offered them a number of prebends and similar advantages, but the modest rector declined them, for he was unwilling to depart from the ways of the simplicity and humility taught by the first members of the brotherhood.

The activities of this rector seem to disprove some of the remarks made afterward by Erasmus, who asserted that the brethren-houses were simply seminaries of monasticism. Ter Beek cautiously guarded the various institutions of his order against the powerful monasteries. One of these houses, located in the city of Doesburg, was nearly transformed into an Augustinian monastery. But the rector of Deventer hurried to the scene of operations to prevent the prior of Windesheim from incorporating the brethren-house into his congregation. When the prior expressed amazement at Ter Beek's stubbornness, saying that monasticism was superior to the status of a mere brethren-house, the rector plainly told him to leave. "For those brethren," he remarked, "who wish to become monks are free to leave us at any time, but this house is ours and shall remain ours."

The following buildings were used by the brethren during Erasmus' stay at Deventer, in addition to the two mentioned above. The principal building was constructed in 1441, and there were also two additional homes for boys attending the school, namely, the *Hieronymenhuis*, or House of Jerome, and the *Juffer Wibbenhuis*, or House of Lady Wibben.

There are no sources left to tell where Erasmus lived when his mother was with him at Deventer. One might easily guess that Margaret helped to support her son and that they lived together in rather modest quarters. It is also possible that the mother was a domestic servant somewhere in the city, so that she could provide no home for her boy. However this may be, Erasmus was coming more and more under the influence of the Brethren of the Common Life, and after his mother's death in 1483 he certainly lived in one of their houses, as he probably had done long before 1483. His brother Peter should not be entirely forgotten. He was probably nine years old in 1475. Shortly after his mother's death he returned with Erasmus to Gouda. Does it not appear likely that both boys were given board and lodging by the brethren while the mother worked to supply them with tuition and a few necessities? What else could she have done in her circumstances but become a maid in the home of a well-to-do family? The chief reason why so many boys were sent to Deventer and Zwolle was the presence of the Brethren of the Common Life in these cities, since their dormitories were famous. The rector of the school of St. Lebwin's who preceded Hegius was not very popular. Neither was the rector who taught in the same school when Thomas à Kempis arrived at Deventer. The latter was attracted by the pious brethren who were known to be interested in schoolboys.

For our present purpose, therefore, it is important to know what the brethren at Deventer were doing and what their ideals were from about the year 1450 to 1485. Their business was to extend the kingdom of heaven upon earth. Their chief task was to draw boys to God. They preached sermons for adults too, but they expected more results from the proper training of boys.

Egbert ter Beek, the rector, was most assuredly a "barbarous" person. In a short biography written about him in the brethren-house shortly after his death it is said that when still a boy he had his hair shaved short according to the habit of the pupils who feared the Lord. He avoided plays, games, and other vanities of this world, living a simple life, although among his friends and relatives there were some of the most prominent personages in the city who were living in worldly homes. Even when walking along the street he was so careful about what he let himself see that he did not notice persons passing by. One day when he had a dish in his hands he met one of his relatives, whom he did not notice at all. The latter knocked the dish with its contents out of his hands and shouted: "What sort of Lollard is this walking by?" But he picked up the dish with composure and continued his way.

"When his father," so reads the biography, "heard that he was getting along very well with his studies, he determined to send him to Cologne, in order that he might be advanced to the rank of teacher or even higher, so that he might obtain an ecclesiastical benefice, or a secular sinecure. But God advanced the well-being of his soul, and as he grew up he yearned more deeply for the things that are of God." In Cologne he was by no means edified by the irreligious habits of the laymen he saw and heard; so he left Cologne and secretly came to us. After many prayers and much procrastination, because he had many friends in the city, and they were among the most influential classes, he was permitted to enter our house as a novice in the year 1438, when he was nineteen years old. On the very first day of his novitiate, when he was sitting at the dinner-table, he saw one of the brethren with bent knees sitting on the floor before the table and asking forgiveness for having done something amiss. Rector Godfried, hitting him hard on the jaw, reprimanded him sharply, saying, "How long shall we be harmed by thee?" And then he allowed the brother to remain in a kneeling position before the table. When Egbert saw this he could not eat for fear. The brother finally seated himself at the table, and, as if he had suffered nothing, began quickly to cut bread, and bewailing his error, recovered rapidly. When the novice saw this, he thought: "What is the use of being afraid, when this brother enjoys suffering?"

"When Egbert's father, himself a worldly man, heard that his son had entered the House of Florentius, he grew very sad and came to him, attempting with many entreaties and promises to get his son away, and said, 'If you have decided to be a priest at all costs, I will found a new vicarage in the village of Wye and will have thee installed there.' But the son replied, 'Please observe, dear father, since thou art a prudent man, the lives of the secular priests, and thou wilt note that, in opposition to the precepts of the Gospel, their hearts and bodies are given to drunkenness and, a thing which is worse and which results from this, they transgress in the lusts of the flesh, and thou must consider the fact that I

with my nature cannot possibly live with them and not conform
to their lives.'

"Now the father retorted, 'I will give thee a room in my own
house, where thou canst live apart from the conversation of all
whom thou fearest and devote thyself at pleasure to prayer, reading,
and other spiritual exercises, with the result that by thy example
other priests will be induced to live better lives.' The boy re-
sponded, 'It will be far easier, beloved father, for me to be perverted
by them than that one of them will be converted by me. For I do
not underestimate my own weakness nor the struggle with the
devil, and it is much better for me to battle with many associates
in this saintly and praiseworthy congregation, where there are as
many allies as companions, who, thanks to long training in spiritual
warfare, know the ruses of the enemy and because of their bravery
are terrible to the devil, the flesh, and the world, so that the ranks
of the fortress when drawn up with wisdom cry out: 'Woe to the
solitary fighter, since when he falls he has no one to aid him.'

"When the father heard these words he thought he could not
resist the spirit which spoke thus, and acquiesced and allowed his
son to serve the Lord, and always remained a supporter and friend
of our house. He even gave his son a part of his property. When
the devil discerned that through Egbert's carnal father he could
gain nothing, he began to attack him with suggestions. . . ." [1]

Another important official among the brethren in the days of
Erasmus was John Hatten, the procurator. He was confessor of
the schoolboys and is said to have labored diligently in their be-
half. He also spent much time in preaching to them. A biography
prepared in the brethren-house gives the following details. "He
instructed the schoolboys with his short addresses and exhorted
them to study the sacred writings, the lives of the saints, and the
Quatuor Novissima,[2] which taught chastity and the contempt of
the world. And he used to give examples of what was happening
to saintly people, through which he induced many to confess their
sins and to enter monasteries.[3]

[1] G. Dumbar, *Analecta Daventria*, I, 162–166, *passim*.
[2] A lengthy treatise prepared by Gerardus Vliederhoven.
[3] The term *religio* in the phrase *religionis ingressum* of the original Latin may
simply mean piety, but *religio* is usually synonymous with monasticism.

Schoolboys and also younger and older people he used to accost after confession or on other occasions, with a pleasant mien, as was always his custom, saying, "How are you, beloved? Are you going to be a servant of our Lord Jesus?" He also would exhort them to salute holy Mary, saying "Hail Mary, who has labored much in you." His love of his fellow-men burned with such ardor that every one, rich and poor, and of either sex, he sought to draw to God. He was so zealous and so compassionate that when he saw some one sinning or comporting himself in an unseemly fashion, he sympathized with his brother in spirit and began to admonish him, as a doctor does to a sick person.

When in his official capacity or out of necessity he talked with women, he always did so with his face averted and his eyes closed, and his words, in accordance with the counsel of Jerome, were few and to the point. No one ever heard him utter sensual speech. He always insisted on the practice of manual labor, so as to avoid the necessity of begging for alms.

He rose to great heights of humility, regarding himself as dust and ashes, and like an earthly worm, blaming himself in everything, and desiring that others might do likewise. To those who used to extol monasticism above our order, he used to reply, "In the halls of our Lord there are not only exalted and noble ministers. These, such as God makes them, I congratulate rather than envy, but it is well with me if I merit the place of a dishwasher." [4]

In one of the manuscripts written in the brethren-house at Deventer [5] a large number of sayings of various brethren were jotted down which give the reader a clear insight into the atmosphere breathed by Erasmus at Deventer. First in order are remarks made by John Hatten, for they follow immediately the biography of this brother. The title is, *Here follow some sayings and exhortations of this same Hatten.* A few excerpts are freely paraphrased and condensed here.

He said that one's passions should be revealed to the spiritual

---

[4] The last three paragraphs are based on G. Dumbar, *op. cit.*, I, 185–186, 190, 192–193, 196–197, 212, 215.

[5] Mr. 128 G 16, Royal Library, The Hague, fol. 156b–177b.

father, instructor, or brother, for it is not possible to withstand the devil. He used to tell the story of a mechanic of this city who had the habit of saying to the devil: "Let me alone or else I'll go to the brethren and confound thee." If the passion was stubborn and would not leave, he would put on his coat as if he were ready to go and then he was liberated. During hard labor we must think, he said, that soon our life will end [6] and presently this body with which we labor will be devoured by worms; and nothing will harm him who works faithfully. And tomorrow we may die. And Jesus will say, "Call my servants and give them their reward." He also said that we should not be too worried about our shortcomings, but should think about improving ourselves. He told us about a certain William of Doesburg who used to say to Mary: "O Mary, I have laughed and joked too much and have sinned much in similar fashion; I flee to thee. I propose to do better. I shall read an 'Ave Maria' once, twice, or three times when I must needs be greatly disturbed." This brother was always happy and fervent, . . . and he looked forward to death with rejoicing.

He said to a schoolboy after confession that if he wished to make progress in the spiritual life he should keep before his eyes four beings: first, God, who sees everything; second, his guardian angel, who is always present; third, his superior, whose presence he should perhaps fear; fourth, one of the saints, whose life pleases him, or someone still living whose life seems worth imitating, and he should always bear in mind how this person comports himself in manner, words, and deeds.

When he felt himself getting excited or vehement in reproaching or criticizing, he would say to himself: "I will sleep on it." [7] When brothers or novices were accepted he used to consider which were their besetting sins and he would continually remind them of these until he felt that they had been corrected, and then he would single out some other defect for correction. On the acceptance of

[6] The original has: "Quod valde cito erit nobiscum hic factum." This may have been literally translated from the Dutch: "Dat zeer spoedig zal het hier met ons gedaan zijn."

[7] Quando se sensit fervidum aut vehementem ad ammonendum vel corripiendum, dicebat sibiipsi: "Ick wilt beslapen" (fol. 159a). On this page and elsewhere Dutch phrases occur frequently.

a novice he would say, "Thank the Lord," and then in Dutch, "I have acquired a new assistant who will help me to scour my rusty conscience."

Next we are told how humble he was at times when the evening address was given to the boys on holy days (fol. 160a), how he read only simple books (fol. 160b), how he emphasized the value of prayer, what he thought were good antidotes for dejection (fol. 161a), pride (fol. 162a), inconstancy (fol. 162a), temptations (fol. 162b), procrastination (fol. 163a), and vanity (fol. 163b).

One day he was asked whether the dead brothers living in heaven remembered the brothers who were still alive. He replied that they prayed to God for their safety as long as they saw that the latter were striving to follow in their footsteps; and they gave aid to them through their prayers when the latter were seriously battling against their insufficiency and negligence. But when they saw their brothers slothful and seeking only after temporal things and following after fleshly lusts, and walking without a bridle upon the broad way which leads to perdition, and not imitating their fathers, then they detested them as degenerates.

In the same manuscript appear some sayings of various brothers who lived in the brethren-house shortly before the year 1460. The selection begins as follows: "One day the brothers assembled and Rector Godfried said: 'Let us not seek many privileges for our brotherhood.' Rudolph (Dier of Muiden) [8] said: 'There are two things we must look out for in accepting novices; in the first place, whether they are fit and strong physically, and in the second place, whether they are mentally sound, that is, inclined toward our status of humility and the teaching of boys, and desirous of improving their character.'

"On another occasion Rodolphus said: 'O what do you think, brethren, is menacing the House of Florentius, when the brethren are proceeding to cast aside the *Profectus Religiosorum*,[9] the *Horologium Eternae Sapientiae*,[10] the *Meditations* of St. Bernard and similar devotional books, and start to read sermons or similar intellectual works?' And Otgerus Hoern said: 'When I have studied a little I am ready to talk to the boys or other people about some

---

[8] He was librarian of the brethren-house.

[9] By David of Augsburg.   [10] By Suso, a German mystic.

spiritual matters. But when I have weighed down my mind with much reading and long studies, I am not fit for prayer or some other form of devotion; I scarcely know what to say.' And Godfried said: 'Nothing retards our spiritual progress so much as our not being fit for receiving the Holy Supper, since we have not properly prepared ourselves for it.'

"There came to the House of Florentius Theodore Herxen [11] and Henry, rector in Albergen, and Henry Heusden; [12] and as they gathered with us, the question was put, 'What is the perfect mortification?' . . . And among other things, Henry of Albergen said: 'This seems to me the perfect mortification, that one wishes to live and die as a person base and despised, who is reputed to be worth nothing.' And he added: 'I wish to find four such persons here; I hope, however, that you all are such. But alas, in congregations and monasteries I find very few.'

"Henry of Gouda said: 'This is the true custodian of chastity, that one never feels secure, but is always suspicious of danger. And although for a long time he has not experienced temptation, he nevertheless keeps close watch over his interior and exterior senses.' Godfried, our rector, used to say he did not care if between the confessionals of the brethren he slept, as long as he found these two virtues intact, namely, chastity and brotherly love."

In the same manuscript (fol. 175a–177b) a letter was reproduced which had been written by Henry of Edam, procurator in the House of Florentius at Deventer and addressed to a novice in the brethren-house at Emmerich. The letter is of some importance, for Erasmus must have known Henry of Edam, who was in the brethren-house at Deventer in the year 1479,[13] and remained there several years; moreover he was a friend of Hegius, Agricola, and other Dutch humanists.[14]

---

[11] Rector of the brethren at Zwolle.
[12] Henry of Heusden, prior of Windesheim.
[13] G. Dumbar, *op. cit.*, I, 236.
[14] M. van Rhijn, "Wie was Hendrik van Edam?" *Ned. Arch. voor Kerkgesch.*, 1927, p. 157. Van Rhijn mentions the fact that Henry of Edam was prior of the brethren-house at the end of the fifteenth century. The term prior, however, is never appropriate for a leader of a group of Brethren of the Common Life. The

"Beloved brother," wrote the procurator, "if you desire to please God and the brethren, endeavor diligently to keep the following precepts, and you will find real peace of heart and the grace of God. . . .

"In the first place, you must strive to show all the brethren respect and obedience with simple heart and willing soul, because of the great merit of simple obedience, as the obedience actuated by love which we show toward one another is often greater than that which we show to prelates.

"In the second place, apply your whole heart to the things that are to be done in your house, and you ought to learn carefully the daily exercises to be performed, for in that way you will always delight in your work and be most contented. For he who does his work carelessly and imperfectly will find no pleasure in his labors; and, besides, he will be reprimanded by the brethren. Thus he often wavers in his good intentions and does not stand firm; nor can such a man make any progress in virtue.

"In the third place, beware of haste in your work, namely, in your writing and reading, but do everything wisely and attentively, and pray often between tasks. Never in your life argue against any brother, but submit yourself always to another and humble yourself before him. . . . Be respectful and circumspect in your words and ask the brethren about the difficulties you meet in the Scriptures, and nowhere feel free to invent explanations. You had better learn than teach. You ought often to come and bewail your passions and defects and take counsel in regard to them. You should gladly hear your defects so that you may make progress. You ought always to read books which teach man to know his vices and contain remedies against the latter, books which can arouse your mind to love of God. . . . Do not read books which whet the intellect on strange themes not pertaining to salvation.

"Whatever the brethren teach you, consider that important

---

man who governed the principal building was invariably named *rector*, the officials placed in charge of less important buildings were called *procurators*, and the official in the Heer Florenshuis at Deventer who ranked next to the rector also received the title of *procurator*. On fol. 175a of the manuscript under discussion, Henry of Edam is termed "procurator Daventriensis in domo domini Florencii."

and be grateful for it and apply it to your work, or strive to the utmost to avoid what they counsel you must be avoided or renounced, and even though you do not now grasp the reason for it, nevertheless you will understand it later. You can never advance if you wish to decide according to your own discretion and choice what is good or bad and not believe the brethren with simple heart."

This letter by Henry of Edam is of interest to the student who wishes to understand what passed through Erasmus' mind at Deventer when his mother had died and he was considering whether it would be advisable for him to become a novice and afterward a member in the House of Florentius. When another plague finally compelled him to return to Gouda and continue his studies elsewhere, he was advised to live in one of the dormitories of the Brethren of the Common Life at 's-Hertogenbosch. He said many years later that he wished he had become a member of the brotherhood, for the brethren exacted no irrevocable vows. He did assert, however, that the brethren almost compelled the boys to become monks. Did the brethren at Deventer perhaps do those things, or was Erasmus lying again?

A very important description of the atmosphere in the school and dormitory at Deventer was left by a German monk named John Butzbach, who studied under Hegius and was supported by the Brethren of the Common Life at Deventer. Butzbach was a much more reliable witness than Erasmus; at least he did not deliberately tell lies about the brotherhood. He left two separate accounts: one in his *Hodoeporicon*, or "Book of Wanderings," [15] the other in his *Auctarium*, a large collection of biographies of men he had met.[16]

In the first of these works Butzbach tells how he went to Deventer with a letter of recommendation from an abbot and was placed in the seventh class. But he stayed only a short time. His

---

[15] Published by D. J. Becker, in *Chronika eines fahrenden Schülers oder Wanderbüchlein des Johannes Butzbach*, Regensburg, 1869.

[16] Published in part by K. Krafft and W. Crecelius in *Zeitschrift des Bergischen Geschichtsvereins*, VII (Bonn, 1871), 213–288. The title of the article is "Mitteilungen über Alexander Hegius und seine Schüler, aus den Werken des Johannes Butzbach."

mother, however, prevailed upon him to return to school and he went back to Deventer in the fall of 1498. "The rector of the school," says Butzbach, "examined me again and placed me in the eighth class, where seven other adults sat, who had come to this school out of fear, for 7,000 men had been defeated before a besieged city by the bishop of Utrecht and the duke of Gelderland, and 100 had been condemned to death, whom I saw lying on the wheel during my first three days at Deventer. My adult associates learned slowly, because fear had induced them to come, while I labored hard by day and by night to overcome the handicap of my age. So I remained but a short time in the eighth class; my associates were dismissed. One of them sat for four years in the eighth class, and learned to read with difficulty, although he was living with one of the teachers of his class. I skipped the seventh class and by Easter I was in the fifth.

"When I was in the fifth class I secured a room in the *Domus Pauperum*, the home for poor pupils maintained by the Brethren of the Common Life, in which at that time no one was admitted who had not yet reached the fifth class and had no intention of becoming a monk. I suffered many illnesses, for it seems to me that I have never been in such an unhealthful climate as at Deventer."

After an account of the school of St. Lebwin, which will be reproduced below, Butzbach tells how he was sitting in the third class and had decided to remain until the spring of 1501, when the reverend Father Oeconomus arrived at Deventer from the monastery of Niederwerth near Coblenz, with the object of taking back with him some pupils to the monastery of Laach, where they were to become monks under the abbot. "He showed his letter to the rector of the school and also told the Brethren of the Common Life about it. Then he left town on some other business. In the meantime diligent search was made in the school and the dormitories for such 'clerks' or 'clerics,' as they are usually called, young men who had already made much progress in their studies and had decided to exchange worldly wisdom for monasticism. Three weeks passed and the messenger returned to Deventer. When he learned that not a single boy had shown any desire to go back with him to the monastery, he appealed to John Oostendorp, rector of the school.

"Oostendorp had succeeded Hegius as rector and was a capable and learned man. He immediately went to the third and fourth classes and attempted in an eloquent address to win some of the pupils to monasticism. He praised in particular the Benedictine order and the monastery of Laach and the eminence of the abbot of Laach. But all his efforts seemed in vain. The pupils had just begun the school year, had paid their teachers tuition for half a year, and did not like to ask the money back. They had found suitable quarters for themselves, and they did not wish to leave them so soon. Furthermore, it happened to be very cold and the journey would be long." Finally, says Butzbach, he determined to go himself and, accompanied by another pupil, he arrived at Laach on December 18, 1500.

According to Butzbach, the *Domus Pauperum* maintained by the brethren at Deventer was intended only for boys who expected to become monks. This statement by Butzbach has caused much surprise to scholars who believe that the brotherhood founded by Groote was not friendly to the monastic orders. Generalizations are always dangerous. One cannot do justice to a living organization by stating facts which are true of only a certain period and frequently in only a certain locality. Shortly after the death of Groote the mendicant monks were hostile to the brethren, and it was a mendicant monk who attacked them at the Council of Constance. But before the year 1415 the Augustinian Canons Regular as well as other monastic orders maintained friendly relations with the brethren. The latter had founded the monastery of Windesheim, and this institution in turn had sought to protect the brethren in 1395. All that the brethren asked for was to keep their houses intact and to be allowed to live the common life without monastic vows. They supported hundreds of boys, regardless of the purpose which impelled them to seek an education. They did not unduly urge any boy to become a monk, but certain kinds of pupils who seemed particularly fit for the monastic life they exhorted to follow their calling.

In the year 1500, says Butzbach, only prospective monks were

allowed to live in the *Domus Pauperum*. Is this assertion correct?
The phrase used by Butzbach is *intencione monachandi*, and probably includes the status of the brethren themselves. They were
often named monks, for their institution resembled closely the
Augustinian Canons Regular. They were not bound by the three
monastic vows of poverty, chastity, and obedience, but in practice
they maintained these virtues more carefully than did the average
monks. Butzbach merely implies that the younger boys could not
secure a place in the dormitory where he was living, and since the
brethren agreed to pay a large part of their expenses, they made
the boys promise to devote themselves later to the service of God
in a home for brethren or monks. They were not to join the secular
clergy, nor were they to seek other secular positions. If they
wished to contiuue their studies at some university, they would be
expected to remember their promises. Erasmus, for example, was
permitted to leave his monastery and study at the University of
Paris, on condition that he return to Steyn after he had secured his
degree. He, however, was compelled to return, but Butzbach and
his companions merely promised to practice religion.

The constitution of the brethren-house in Deventer [17] also throws
light on the way in which novices were treated there. A person
who applies for a place in the house should be virtuous, teachable,
a competent student of literature, pleasant, sound of head and
breast, able to write; his previous habits should be satisfactory,
and he must be adaptable to the common life. Care should be
taken that he be not accepted because of his temporal possessions
but rather for God's sake. After proper inquiry has been made he
may be accepted for a period of two or three months. If during
that time he does not seem to agree with the atmosphere of the
house, he is to leave again; perhaps he may be promoted to a
better place with the assistance of the brethren. If, however, his
manners please the brethren, he will not be accepted as a member of the house until he has remained another ten or twelve
months. During this period he is to be watched closely by the
brethren, who are to note whether his resolution to join is firm,

---

[17] Published in A. Hyma, *The Christian Renaissance*, pp. 441–474. Several
chapters of this constitution are not found in any other constitution known to us.

whether he can take criticism and correction and humiliation, whether he obeys promptly when asked to do mean and humble things, and whether he frankly confesses his temptations.

During the period of trial he is to be told what it means to become a Brother of the Common Life. One of the brethren becomes his master, or guardian, who will instruct and examine him. The master will frequently exhort him to leave behind him the ways of the world, to mortify his own will and his own reasoning powers, to embrace gladly humble and base things, to become dead to the world and to his own nature, to devote himself wholly to God, to seek his cell and to remain quiet, to read and pray, to perform manual labor in his cell or elsewhere and to follow the rules of the house. His master must each day observe his habits and correct him secretly and urge him to confess his sins as much as is proper.

When the novice has passed his trial and wishes to obtain a membership in the house, he must in private kneel before the rector and each one of the brethren in turn, and ask for a place, saying humbly that, although he does not merit one yet, he promises with the aid of God to become more worthy. Then the brethren will at an opportune time assemble and they will be asked whether they are ready to accept the novice, and if so, he will be asked to appear before them upon his knees. Then the rector will say, "What is it, brother, that you ask?" And he will answer, "I beg the grace of God and membership here." After that he will be told that in accordance with the precepts of the primitive Christian Church he can have no property of his own and must live chastely and virtuously. The rector will then ask him whether he is a free man or a serf, whether he has left any home or monastery, whether he has promised to marry, whether he is bound by any vow or afflicted with some hidden or incurable disease, whether he is of legitimate birth and whether he can be promoted to the priesthood. He will then be informed that if he is accepted he shall renounce all private property before a notary-public and witness within one month after his acceptance, and if he leaves the house or is expelled for legitimate reasons, he cannot recover his property and may take nothing with him out of the house except his daily clothes. He will also be told that laymen have no vote in this house, so that he cannot expect to have one unless he be ordained.

When he accepts all the conditions, the brethren will kneel and sing some hymns. A formula of acceptance will be pronounced, whereupon the rector, while the brethren still remain in a kneeling position, will say: "In the honor of the Almighty God, the blessed Virgin Mary, the most holy Paul, our patron, and all the saints, we accept thee as a member of this house and give thee a place therein and the use of all our temporal and spiritual possessions."

The constitution used by the Brethren of the Common Life at Deventer differs from later constitutions, notably that used at Zwolle, in that it is more elaborate and less practical. The older document contains features which must have seemed rather silly to men who were widely read and wished to win the respect of influential people. For example, at the end of Chapter XXXVII, which is the final chapter, a list of punishments is given for a variety of misdemeanors, which undoubtedly aroused the mirth of many a proud humanist. Only a few can be given here.

He who arrives late at the table or at the devotional services asks for forgiveness, kissing the floor. He who has been admonished or corrected and excuses himself throws himself upon his knees with his head bent on the floor and confesses his guilt. He who falls asleep beside his candle brings his candle and asks forgiveness. He who has offended a brother in word or deed asks forgiveness on the same day before the offended brother on bent knees, and before those also who were present when he perpetrated the offense. He who sings badly, or causes confusion in other ways by laughing or joking or similar actions, particularly in church, asks forgiveness. He who has, out of negligence, kept schoolboys or other youths in his cell after the outside doors have been locked asks forgiveness.

This constitution, the accounts given by John Butzbach, the letter by Henry of Edam, the sayings of various brothers living in the brethren-house, the biographies of Henry Hatten and Egbert ter Beek, and Erasmus' own story prove that the Brethren of the Common Life at Deventer during the latter half of the fifteenth century were still as simple-minded as the followers of Florentius

Radewyns, who taught Thomas à Kempis to imitate Christ. For wealth, fame, and honor they cared not; the world, the devil, and the flesh were their enemies. The interest displayed by most of them was not the interest of educators in our sense of the word. They had no desire to make the schoolboys learned in worldly ways, but to draw them to God, that is, to make them pray much, read the Bible and other devotional books, meditate in their private rooms — in short, to practice the Christian religion in imitation of the Apostles. Their aim was to restore primitive Christianity, not by mere talk, as many humanists are supposed to have done, but in reality. If they can be said to have inaugurated a renaissance, they certainly had a right to call it a Christian renaissance!

CHAPTER XI

HEGIUS, AGRICOLA, AND GANSFORT

AMONG the pioneers of humanism in the Netherlands, Hegius, Agricola, and Gansfort occupied the front rank. Each of these three humanists was closely in touch with the Brethren of the Common Life and also exerted considerable influence upon Erasmus. Hegius has been mentioned first, because he was rector of the school of St. Lebwin at Deventer during the last year of Erasmus' stay at Deventer. Erasmus called Hegius his teacher and until he had become world-famous praised Hegius in no uncertain terms.

Alexander Hegius was born in 1433, in the village of Heek in Westphalia; hence his name, Hegius. He attended the school at Zwolle and shortly afterward commenced a clerical career; he taught at Wesel from 1469 to 1474 and at Emmerich from 1475 to 1483. In both of the latter places the Brethren of the Common Life had dormitories where pupils of the local schools resided. In Emmerich, Hegius was visited by Rudolph Agricola, who taught him a little Greek, and Hegius was also an intimate friend of Wessel Gansfort.

John Butzbach attended the school of St. Lebwin just at the end of Hegius' career and left the following description of this pedagogue and of his school. "The city of Deventer possesses in addition to its fairs, which are held several times a year, an institution of learning which has made this city famous far above all other cities in these districts. This school has for a long time been conducted by very learned rectors, but I hear to my sorrow that since the death of Hegius in 1498 it has greatly declined. Yes, this man was worthy of the highest praise. I greatly love this man, who granted me a place in his school.

"Formerly this school was of great service to the reformed

monastic orders, for it sent to their monasteries highly trained
young men, since everybody exerted himself to secure suitable candidates as long as the school enjoyed a good reputation. At that
time [1] one could obtain more desirable pupils in the fifth class at
Deventer and Zwolle than at the present time in the first and
second class, although now better writers are studied than in the
past. A generation ago, as I have often heard, they used to read
little more than the *Parables* of Alanus, the *Moralia* of Cato, the
Fables of Aesop, and a few other compositions which at present are
heartily despised.

"In those days one had the habit of conquering the greatest
difficulties through diligence and one's own ability; now the best
writings are read, but the pupils treat them as the ass felt toward
the lyre (according to the Greek proverb ὄνος πρὸς χελώνην).
And so every excellent institution declines in the course of time,
including our monastic orders, the latter largely because the school
at Deventer has deteriorated.

"Alexander Hegius was most learned in the sacred writings as
well as in the secular philosophy; he was well trained in both
Latin and Greek; a man of sharp intellect and eloquent, of
righteous habits and conversation, and a truly Christian philosopher, a lover of the poor, the simple, and the humble, not stylish
in dressing, of plain speech, kind to the virtuous and the industrious, but harsh to the depraved. He was a friend of our monastic
order,[2] and also of others, particularly of the Franciscans and the
Augustinian Canons Regular.[3] He ceaselessly endeavored to persuade people to imitate Christ. This is proved by various monastic
orders who today still count many of his former pupils. This man,
greatly loved by God, died amidst the lamentations of the poor,
for he had spent all his substance on alms, so that at his death he
left nothing except his books and his clothes."

Butzbach remained at Deventer for two years after the death
of Hegius and afterward [4] described the school of St. Lebwin in

---

[1] From 1475 to 1500.

[2] The Benedictines. The words used here (p. 238) are: "religionis nostre."

[3] The words used here are: "et maxime de observantia minorum et regularium
specialissimus fautor."   [4] About the year 1520.

the following words. "In the fifth class I sat for half a year under Godfried, who had a bachelor's degree in both canon and civil law and a master's degree in arts. Then, after an examination, I passed into the fourth class, where I was instructed for one year by John of Venray, a highly learned man. At the end of that year I was promoted to the third class, which was in charge of Bartholomew of Cologne, a very industrious and scholarly man, whose poems and prose writings are admired by the greatest scholars. He is in fact a man of lofty spirit and well instructed in many subjects. He favored the diligent pupils and gladly aided them in many ways, with the result that such enthusiasm was aroused by him among his pupils that they were extremely loath to leave him. Notwithstanding his eminence, he never received a master's degree from any university, wherefore many despise him as a pedant. He, on the other hand, being a true philosopher, sets more store by real knowledge than an empty title. For many, and almost all whom we now call masters and doctors, possess scarcely enough knowledge in any one of the lower subjects. When a student at the present time has the patience to remain in school without working hard, he can get his degree by means of a present, regardless of his knowledge or ignorance."

It is obvious from what viewpoint Butzbach regarded the methods and habits of Alexander Hegius and of the other teachers at Deventer. He was pleased with the instruction received there and remembered gratefully the extraordinary kindness exhibited by many affluent burghers of the prosperous Hansa town on the Yssel. His interpretations cannot satisfy all readers, for he was not an impartial observer; but the facts given by him are very largely correct. Hegius was not the kind of man to imitate the typical Italian humanists. He was in perfect accord with the Brethren of the Common Life at Deventer. Worldly things had very little value in his eyes. Personal property he did not accumulate, nor did he seek the name of a great scholar. Character, not book-learning, was for him the highest gift. He was, however, a humanist, which cannot be said of the vast majority of the Brethren of the Common Life.

Hegius was determined to reform his school after the humanistic pattern. Sinthius, one of his subordinates in the school and also a member of the brethren-house at Deventer, published a new edition of the grammar of Alexander de Villedieu, which was substituted by him for the more complicated grammars. Hegius reasoned that the *Medulla*, the *Disciplina Scholarium*, the *Gemma Gemmarum*, the lexica of Hugutio Brito and John Januensis, and the *Catholicon* be cast aside as no longer worthy of serious study.[5]

"The current grammars," reasoned Hegius," are barbarous. This the Italians know best; they love their children too much to impose on them such useless, harmful trash. As a matter of fact, if grammar, which is the art of speaking, could talk itself, it would turn with vehemence against those educators who treat it in such manner that it can no longer be called grammar.

"Grammar is a fine art, but not that which at present is being studied at great expense by the boys. The grammarians of our time sin heavily against their pupils, since they compel them to learn barbarous Latin. He who improperly writes or accentuates German words is ridiculed by everybody, but those who corrupt our Latin language (and they are legion) and elevate their 'art' to heaven with eulogies, are not condemned. The Church Fathers, like Augustine, Jerome, Gregory, Ambrose, and Cyprian wrote correct Latin, for their models were the best writers among the ancients, such as Cicero, Sallust, Livy, and Virgil." [6]

Like the Brethren of the Common Life at Deventer, however, Hegius did not despise the language of the people about him.[7] In his *Dialogi*,[8] published in 1503 at Deventer, by his pupil James Faber, he wrote down many statements in the dialect of his native Westphalia. In his *Farrago*, on the other hand, published at the end of the *Dialogi*, he asserted that one should appropriate the diction of Cicero, Virgil, and Sallust, and imitate the Italian

[5] A. Hegius, *Dialogi*, fol. O⁴ verso; D. Reichling, *Murmellius*, p. 13. The *Catholicon* mentioned here by Hegius was a dictionary.

[6] A. Hegius, *op. cit.*, fol. O² verso.

[7] It is true that Groote and the first group of brethren at Deventer placed a penalty on the use of the vernacular (see G. Dumbar, *Analecta Daventria*, I, 8), but the preceding chapter proves conclusively that, at the time when Erasmus was in Deventer, even the leading officials used Dutch.

[8] An excellent analysis of the *Dialogi* is presented in J. Wiese, *Der Pädagog Alexander Hegius*, pp. 19–35.

humanists. Here he did not speak as a true medievalist, but appeared to have absorbed some of the ideas of the Italian Renaissance. It would, therefore, be misleading to say that Hegius represented the Devotio Moderna in all its aspects, unless the movement itself had become subject to change.

The Brethren of the Common Life were very slow to evince much interest in classical scholarship. The printing-press of the brethren in Brussels, for example, did not turn out a single classical or humanistic production.[9] And when Erasmus was at Deventer, the library of the brethren-house counted only three such works in a total of forty-two titles known to us.[10] The presses at Deventer, on the other hand, printed a very large number of them between 1480 and 1500, namely, productions of Plautus, Persius, Virgil, Terence, Hesiod, Tibullus, Ovid, Cicero, Seneca, Plutarch, Plato, Barzizzi, Valla, Vegius, Filelfo, Aeneas Sylvio, Dathus, and Petrarch.[11] The reason is simple. Hegius and his colleagues were almost entirely responsible for it.

In the minds of these modest humanists two widely different currents of thought were represented side by side. There was in the first place the powerful effect produced upon them by the Devotio Moderna, and Hegius felt it strongly when, for example, he was writing the following statement in a letter to Gansfort: "I have followed your counsel. The knowledge of literature is pernicious which is conducive to the suppression of virtue."[12] In an epistle addressed to Agricola, on the other hand, he remarked: "I have read Valla's *On the True Good*, where Vegius defends epicurean ideals and Cato the part of virtue. Vegius makes me an epicurean. He persuades me to think that something is good in so far as it brings pleasure, and that opposed to each virtue there is a vice."[13]

---

[9] P. Mestwerdt, *Die Anfänge des Erasmus*, p. 144.

[10] M. E. Kronenberg, *De bibliotheek van het Heer-Florenshuis te Deventer*. Here 294 titles are given, of which 42 were printed before 1485. Of these, 35 deal with theological subjects and 4 are devoted to law. None of the manuscripts possessed by the brethren appear to have contained classical productions. A few additional titles are found in A. Hulshof, *De bibliotheek van het Heer-Florenshuis te Deventer*

[11] P. Mestwerdt, *op. cit.*, p. 144.

[12] A. Hegius, *op. cit.*, fol. O⁵ verso.

[13] *Ibid.*, fol. O⁵ recto: "Legi librum Valle *De vero bono*, apud quem Vegius

Those who carefully peruse the poems and dialogues of Hegius will conclude with Professor Lindeboom "that considering the great reputation of the author, they are very disappointing. Compared with other humanists, Hegius makes a poor showing." [14] His *Dialogues* are indeed very dry reading. The chapter "On the Soul," for example, is simply a scholastic discourse, based on Aristotle and Averroës. What shall we say of the following question and answer? "Will the horse exist forever? No, because there will not always be men to ride on it, and the horse merely exists for them." [15] Hegius' knowledge of Greek was still very elementary, as appears in the following question and answer. "Why do the Greeks name the soul ψυχή? Because ψῦχος means cold, and the Ancients regarded the soul as something cold."[16] Hegius seems to have grasped the Platonic philosophy fairly well, but was not enough of a humanist to rise above scholasticism.[17]

Although his knowledge of Greek was very elementary, his burning ambition to teach classical Greek produced marked results. In a poem entitled *On the Utility of the Greek Language* he strongly emphasized the importance of Greek, for in his opinion the knowledge of this language was indispensable for an understanding of grammar, rhetoric, poetry, mathematics, art, and medicine.

It is worth noting, however, that Hegius frequently employed the term "barbarous," usually with reference to persons or books which do not teach good grammar.[18] "Let those grammars be cast away," says Hegius, "and let those teachers take their leave

---

voluptatis partes tuetur, Cato honestatis. Fecit me Vegius Epicurim. Persuasit enim mihi eatenus bonum aliquid esse, quatenus voluptatem afferat. . . . Persuasit idem mihi singulis virtutibus singula vicia esse contraria."

[14] J. Lindeboom, *Het Bijbelsch humanisme in Nederland*, p. 70. This excellent work contains much useful material on the background of Erasmus.

[15] Hegius, *op. cit.*, fol. C[6] recto: "Utrum genus equinum semper duraturum est. Non, cum enim nullus erit eques, nullus erit equus. Nam equus propter equitem factus est."

[16] *Ibid.*, fol. B[1] verso: "Quare anima a Gracis [for Graecis] ψυχή vocatur? Quia ψῦχος apud Graecos frigus vel refrigeratio dicitur."

[17] J. Lindeboom, *op. cit.*, p. 78.

[18] A. Hegius, *op. cit.*, fol. O[3] recto: "Neque turpe dicunt, barbare loqui." On the same page the phrase "barbare loqui" occurs again. On the next page is the term "barbarissimo," and on fol. O[4] verso we read about people who defend the "barbarous cause."

who adhere to the barbarous and corrupt vocabularies." [19]   Hegius
wants his pupils to read Varro, Festus, and Tortellius, and he
calls their attention to Italian educators, who teach grammar
correctly.[20]   In common with the other humanists of his day,
Hegius wrote poetry, which also makes disappointing reading.
But one should not criticize him too severely, for he merely shared
the follies and self-deceptions of humanism.   He wrote no true
poetry, but merely meter and a collection of classic phrases, as
did nearly all other humanists.   His Latin was fair; for his time
it was good, and he surpassed the majority of European educators.

One might well ask now what Erasmus had to say about his
former teacher, and one will discover that Erasmus first admired
and praised him, then referred to him indifferently, and still later
despised him.   In his *Adages* (no. 339) of the year 1508 he speaks
at length about Agricola and Hegius, and makes the following
remarks about the latter.   "One of Agricola's pupils was Alexander
Hegius of Westphalia, who some time ago [21] was rector of the
school at Deventer, where I was his pupil and learned the first
essentials of Latin and Greek.   He was similar to his teacher, of
blameless morals and more than ordinary knowledge."   In the
Ciceronianus we read: "I think we must not pass by Westphalia,
which gave us Alexander Hegius, a learned, holy, and eloquent
man, but one who because of his contempt for glory accomplished
nothing great." [22]   In 1540 Beatus Rhenanus, who had acquired

---

[19] *Ibid.*, fol. O⁴ verso.

[20] *Ibid.*, fol. O² verso.

[21] The first edition of the *Adages* was completed in 1499 or 1500, and printed in 1500 at Paris by John Philippi, who gave the title as follows: *Desyderii Herasmi Roterdami . . . Adagiorum Collectanea.* In this edition the proverbs are not numbered; there are only 838 altogether, while the edition of 1508 has 3260. The *Canis in balneo* is the twenty-fifth of the first edition, and is much shorter than no. 339 of the later editions. Here Erasmus merely says this about Hegius, after having mentioned Agricola: "Nominoque hoc libentius quod puellus huius [the original has *huis*] discipulo sum usus praeceptore Alexandro Westphalo [the original has *Vesphlao*]: ut huic pietatem illi tanquam nepotis debeam charitatem." See fol. A⁴ recto of this edition.

[22] Erasmus, *Opera*, vol. I, col. 1014⁶: "Haud transeundam censeo Westphaliam quae nobis dedit Alexandrum Hegium." *No.* "Virum eruditum, sanctum et facundum nominas, sed qui gloriae contemptu nihil magni molitus sit." This statement was written in 1528.

the information from Erasmus, wrote: "The headmaster of the school of Deventer at that time was Alexander Hegius of Westphalia, a man not deficient in scholarship, with some knowledge of Greek." [23]

About the school at Deventer Erasmus expressed himself in no terms of gratitude. In his *De Pueris Instituendis*, published in 1529, he said: "Heavens, what an age was that, when with so much ceremony the couplets of John of Garland were read to the boys accompanied by a complicated commentary, and a large part of the time in school was consumed in dictating, repeating, and committing to memory some silly verses." [24]

Turning to an earlier period, we read a very different account of Hegius and his school. Not only did Erasmus send some of his earliest poems to his former teacher,[25] but in a letter composed about the year 1490 and addressed to Cornelius Gerard, he said: "I see a great many most learned men of our own time who make no slight approach to the ancient eloquence. The first that occurs to me is Rodolphus Agricola, the preceptor of my schoolmaster, Alexander Hegius. . . . Alexander is himself no degenerate disciple of such a master, and represents with so much elegance the style of the Ancients, that if his verse were before you without a title, you might easily mistake the author. He too is not altogether ignorant of Greek." [26]

Finally, in his *De Contemptu Mundi* he refers to Hegius as *noster Hegius,* or "our Hegius." [27] The booklet just mentioned was written between 1487 and 1492 and, as will be explained below, expressed the ideals of the Devotio Moderna even more faithfully than did Hegius himself. Other compositions of the same period by Erasmus prove conclusively that he followed the precepts of Hegius for at least ten years after he left Deventer.

It has been observed that Erasmus considered Rudolph Agricola the preceptor of Hegius, and he was right, so far as the former

---

[23] F. M. Nichols, *The Epistles of Erasmus,* I, 25.

[24] Erasmus, *Opera,* I, 514.

[25] F. M. Nichols, *op. cit.,* I, 61: "Whatever there was besides had been partly sent to Alexander Hegius, the Schoolmaster, formerly my teacher, and Bartholomew of Cologne, a man of erudition, some of whose poems I have."

[26] *Ibid.,* I, 66.   [27] Chap. IX: "Porro ut scite noster scripsit Hegius."

induced the latter to study Greek, in which he assisted him. Hegius also studied Hebrew, but in this language he made very little progress. In the edition of Hegius' *Carmina*, James Faber, the editor, included a letter addressed by Hegius to Agricola, where the writer says "that he is starting Hebrew." [28] Furthermore, the pedagogue at Deventer was deeply conscious of his friend's superior learning. He reported to Agricola from time to time what he was reading and continually asked him for advice. This greatly pleased Agricola, who wrote in answer to one of Hegius' letters: "I cannot easily tell you how much pleasure your epistle has given me, partly because it was from you, my dearest friend, and partly because I notice that you grow daily more careful and tasteful in your language, and I cherish the fond hope that through your guidance and your exhortations . . . the refined letters will penetrate into German lands and will some day capture that fortress." [29]

In another letter by Agricola to Hegius we read: "You know that I cannot bear the corruption of language by the barbarians who are everywhere in power— that terrible Latin of theirs! But you also know their disposition: how they rage and fume and denounce whenever someone dares attack their opinions and dares assert that they as boys learned superfluous, corrupted rules, which they now, at an advanced age, will have to unlearn. They may do what they can to force me, but they cannot compel me to give up mine." [30]

Rudolph Agricola was often called the Frisian, because he was born in the extreme north of the Netherlands. His father was Hendrik Huysman (hence the name Agricola), abbot in Selwert, but not a priest when his son was born on February 17, 1444. The latter was educated in the city of Groningen, and in the universities of Erfurt, Cologne, and Louvain. He also spent many years in Italy. When in 1474 he returned from his first trip to Italy, he remained some time at Emmerich, where both he and Hegius were guests of the Brethren of the Common Life and slept in the

---

[28] Fol. A ⁵ recto.

[29] H. E. J. M. van der Velden, *Rodolphus Agricola*, p. 242.

[30] *Ibid.*, p. 232.

brethren-house in one room. It was at this time that he taught
Hegius Greek and preached humanism to him.

In 1476 Agricola was back in Italy, where he gave the com-
mencement speech in the University of Ferrara. He had musical
talent and made a great impression on his audience, for here was
one of the barbarians from the north who actually spoke better
Latin than most Italian humanists! When he left Italy in 1479 he
had become the Petrarch of Germany. He even wrote a biography
of Petrarch which was published in Holland a few years ago.[31]

About Petrarch and humanism he said: "Petrarch, the cham-
pion and restorer of letters, who resuscitated literature from its
death-slumber and brought light and lustre into the realm of
darkness— Petrarch has taught us through his grand and memorable example that nature made none of the noble things inaccessi-
ble, and that for the best men reward is not withheld for seeking
their object with all their might." [32]

"Agricola," says a capable Dutch biographer, "in common with
the Italians, is the patron of that form of education which is based
upon the Ancients. He pleads for *eloquentia*, as Cicero had understood it and Quintilian had formulated it. Not *eloquentia* as mere
eloquence, as oratory or rhetoric, but the comprehensive development of intellectual and moral properties, which make man both
sapiens and *eloquens*. Agricola is the first of German blood who
clearly and with moderation grasps and reproduces these ideas. . . .
Erasmus and Melanchthon may be more profound, but he is the
pioneer." [33]

Agricola was not ashamed of his native country, as may appear
from the following remark: "What is more wonderful than that
you, O Frisia, have produced men the like of which Liguria scarcely
knows? No, Frisia, no longer does the name of 'barbarian'
disgrace you, now that the Attic elegance and the language of
Latium temper the harshness of your pronunciation and the mellow
sound of poetry refines your uncouth manners." [34]

[31] J. Lindeboom, "Petrarca's Leven, beschreven door Rudolf Agricola," *Ned.
Arch. voor Kerkgesch.*, 1924, pp. 81–107. The biography was composed in 1477
(see p. 93 of the article).
[32] H. E. J. M. van der Velden, *Rodolphus Agricola*, p. 111.
[33] *Ibid.*, pp. 206–207.   [34] *Ibid.*, p. 125.

The principal composition of Agricola is the *De Inventione Dialectica;* at least this work was more widely read than any other. It was especially in the University of Paris that it became popular, so that it largely supplanted Aristotle's work on rhetoric. Another important production was the *De Formando Studio*, a booklet devoted to the reform of curricula. It is indeed a very readable composition and must have exerted much wholesome influence on the contemporaries of Erasmus. The true method of study, according to Agricola, has three aims: (1) to understand the subject-matter, (2) to remember it, and (3) to assimilate and reproduce it. Erasmus himself profited much by the work of this inspiring master, as can be seen in his *De Ratione Studii.*

It should be noted, however, that the influence of Agricola on Erasmus before 1490 was almost entirely indirect. Erasmus says that at the age of twelve he saw Agricola at Deventer.[35] But for many years he merely knew that Agricola was the instructor of Hegius. There is no need to reproduce here all the praise bestowed on Agricola by Erasmus. The latter could not sympathize with a man like Hegius. But Agricola was different! He was a typical humanist, a friend of influential magistrates and prelates, a roving Bohemian who loved to indulge in feasting, who disliked the cultivation of homely virtues, who hankered after fame and glory, who passionately loved classical literature, but did not devote much time to the study of Christian letters. Agricola was magnanimous, but not altruistic. He probably would have refused to die for any cause.

The last year of Agricola's life was mostly spent in Heidelberg, where he gave lectures and where he died in the year 1485. He had been asked by Maximilian, the archduke of Austria and the future emperor, to become a tutor in his home, but he refused, because he did not wish to be burdened with a regular position. But when John of Dalberg, bishop of Worms, in 1484 invited him to become his "court-humanist," he gladly accepted. In an address before the assembly of clerics of the Synod of Worms he expressed some views which are worth repeating.[36] The speech

---

[35] P. S. Allen, *Opus Ep. Er.*, I, 2.

[36] This address is found in MSS no. 36 of the *Cod. Poet. et Philol.*, State Library of Württemberg, Stuttgart.

betrays the overpowering ambition of Agricola to make a good
impression by using a choice vocabulary at the expense of content.

It is interesting to compare this speech with a sermon delivered
by Gerard Groote before the clergy of the bishopric of Utrecht.
Groote spoke as a reformer who loved the Church so much that
he did not mind the anger of the pastors whom he accused of
neglecting their duties. Agricola, on the other hand, endeavored to
please his audience, which was a very easy and enjoyable task.
"The priests," said Agricola, "rule our souls not only because of
their inherent power as priests, but also because of their profound
knowledge. So they can sail on the seas of the ancient letters and
bring us treasures." The speaker describes in pleasing tones the
important tasks of the clergy. "Their days are not spent in over-
eating, nor their nights in carousing; all their time is devoted to
prayer, song-services, the reading of edifying books, and the serious
preparation for pastoral work." [37]

Agricola differed considerably from the Brethren of the Common Life at Emmerich and Deventer and Zwolle. He was a man of
the world. He knew the great humanists of Italy; he had gazed
with admiration at the architecture of several prosperous Italian
cities, he had seen the papal curia at work in Rome, and, instead of
regarding the pomp and splendor of Italy with cool indifference, as
did Gansfort, his friend, he enjoyed the atmosphere and acclimated
himself. But at the same time he did not forget his native Frisia,
where many "barbarians" still flourished; nor did he fail to remember the friendships of his youth, in which respects he differed
from Erasmus. His task was to help his country and his countrymen. He did not fret and fume about his illegitimate birth,
because he had no reason for it. Perhaps Erasmus himself did not
feel nearly so many pangs about his own birth as is often surmised.

Since Agricola was a typical humanist, it might be asked whether
he was irreligious and stood quite apart from the men who cham-
pioned the ideals of the Devotio Moderna. It will be seen that he
remained a true friend of the brethren. Some of his poems testify

---

[37] J. Lindeboom, *Bijb. Hum.*, pp. 63–65. It is doubtful whether P. Mestwerdt
understands Agricola's attitude toward the priesthood (see his *Erasmus*, pp. 159–
161). Lindeboom's view is sounder.

to his interest in the Christian religion. There are, for example, his *Hymn of the Saints* and the long poem devoted to St. Anna, which are more than mere form.[38] Furthermore, he left a copy of a speech delivered at Christmas, 1484, in Heidelberg, which gives evidence of warm religious feeling.[39] And here again he resembled many of the Italian humanists who could not easily break with their environment and with the force of heredity. Agricola may have been superficial in his remarks about the Church and religion, but he was not irreligious.

Much could be said about Agricola's attitude toward the scholastic philosophers, but a few remarks will suffice here. In common with Hegius, he displayed a wholesome respect for the works of Aristotle, wherein he differed from the Italian humanists. He was neither a realist nor a nominalist, but favored the Thomistic philosophy above Scotism. He was less interested in theology and philosophy than in rhetoric. The range of subjects which attracted his undivided attention was very narrow, and that was the reason why he could excel in a few things. Else he would have remained unknown to posterity and Erasmus would not have called him "among Greeks the most Greek, among Latins, the most Latin." [40]

Another "Frisian" from the district named Groningen who made a favorable impression on Erasmus was Wessel Gansfort. He was born in the city of Groningen in the year 1419 or 1420. After having attended an elementary school in that city for a few years, he removed in 1432 to Zwolle, where he remained for seventeen years in succession. It is not likely that he needed eight years to pass the higher grades of the public school at Zwolle, but he did spend a dozen or more years in the *parva domus* of the Brethren of the Common Life, where for a long time he gave instruction. He became an intimate friend of the procurator [41] of this building, which was intended for school boys. At Zwolle there were separate dormitories for poor boys, for boys with a little means, and for

---

[38] R. Agricola, *Lucubrationes* (ed. by Alardus, Cologne, 1539), pp. 296–306.
[39] *Ibid.*, pp. 118–125.
[40] *Opera*, II, col. 166 ᴰ.
[41] The official in charge of each dormitory was named *procurator*.

well-to-do boys.[42] In addition to these the brethren maintained
the *parva domus*, in which Gansfort lived, "inspiring the boys to
love virtue and to hate vice," as one chronicler reports.

The instruction given by Gansfort in the "Little House" of the
pious brethren must have been very largely along religious lines
and the books he knew best were no doubt the productions by
Groote, Zerbolt, Thomas à Kempis, the Church Fathers, and
other leaders in the Christian Church, but he must often have
read the Bible, which Thomas à Kempis, his friend, had copied
four times. The productions of the scholastic philosophers, on the
other hand, were not eagerly read at Zwolle, because it was felt by
the brethren that they were lacking in personal religion.

The following statement in the *Imitation of Christ* neatly expressed the views of the humble colleagues of Gansfort at Zwolle:
"Tell me now, where are all those Doctors and Masters with whom
thou wert well acquainted whilst they lived and flourished in
learning? In their lifetime they seemed something, but now they
are not spoken of. . . . What availeth it to cavil and dispute
much about dark and hidden things? It is a great folly to neglect
the things that are profitable and necessary, and to give our minds
to that which is curious and hurtful." [43]

Had Gansfort remained with the Brethren of the Common Life
after 1449, he would undoubtedly have failed to acquire much
learning, for at the time none of the brethren had the ambition to
become a great scholar. But Gansfort left for Cologne, where he
secured a Master of Arts degree in 1452. A part of the year 1453
he spent at Louvain and in 1454 and 1455 he was in Paris. In the
year 1455–56 he taught in the University of Cologne and the
next year in Heidelberg. After that he returned to the brethren at
Zwolle, but merely stayed a few months, whereupon he traveled
once more to Paris, and now he stopped his wanderings. For
nearly eleven years he remained in this great city, which was still
the theological metropolis of western Europe.

Gansfort established friendly relationships here with many
prominent men. He liked the Occamists, not because he supported

[42] M. Schoengen, *Jacobus Traiecti . . . Narratio*, p. 125.
[43] Book I, Chap. 3.

their philosophy, but because their views seemed in harmony with the teachings of the apostles and the Church Fathers, while they also distinguished themselves for exposing the abuses in the Church. He frequently discussed various doctrines and customs which to him seemed wrong, and because of his subtle arguments he was called "master of contradictions." In 1469 he made a trip to Rome and saw much which displeased him, but his friends counseled him to keep quiet. The next year he returned to Paris for another long stay (1470–73), and this time he was honored by many scholars.

In February, 1473, he received a letter from David of Burgundy, the bishop of Utrecht, which throws some light on the genesis of Gansfort's views. "I have many about me," said the bishop, "who esteem you greatly for your learning and character; but I do not hear them teach the truths that long ago you were accustomed to declare so faithfully. I have long been aware of your brilliancy as a teacher and yet I know that there are many who are seeking to destroy you. This shall never be so long as I am alive to protect you."

The bishop avers that Gansfort had long been holding views on the Church and its doctrines which were considered heretical by more orthodox scholars. These views he had probably acquired through independent reading and thinking. Contact with the Brethren of the Common Life at Zwolle had no doubt prepared his mind for the critical attitude adopted by him later toward the higher clergy. The brethren at Zwolle frankly reproached members of the clergy for sins of omission and commission. Mystics in their institutions and in the Congregation of Windesheim, such as Henry Mande and Thomas à Kempis, had attacked scholastic philosophy, although for a very different reason than did the humanists. Gansfort went beyond their mild criticism and actually questioned some of the doctrines of the Roman Catholic Church. In this respect he deviated from the principles of the Devotio Moderna, but to a considerable degree he owed his critical attitude to the brethren at Zwolle.

In 1474 Gansfort paid a second and last visit to Italy. During this visit he revealed the influence of the Brethren of the Common Life. Whereas Agricola had always stood more or less aloof from the circle of Groote's followers and had immensely enjoyed the splendors of Italian city life, his friend evinced a spirit of indifference and, occasionally, of disgust. Not even magnificent Florence, the seat of the celebrated Platonic Academy, could attract him, for well he knew that Ficino, notwithstanding his great fame, did not understand Christianity. Had St. Augustine or St. Bernard lived there, Gansfort would have lingered for years. As it was, he said the simple brethren at Zwolle pleased him more than the vain philosophers of Florence. So he soon left Italy for the Netherlands, where he spent the last fourteen years of his life.

Shortly after his arrival at Zwolle, he wrote a very interesting treatise, *On the Sacrament of Penance*, in which he said a number of things which sharply differentiated him from the typical human- ists; hence one can call him a humanist only because he cultivated the study of classical Latin, of Greek, and of Hebrew. "Knowl- edge," remarked he, "is the interpreter of truth; wisdom is concerned with our welfare. Hence knowledge may be useless and vain. Such is all knowledge which follows truth out of curiosity. Just as the garrulousness of women is foolish because it seeks satisfaction in mere talk, so knowledge seeks merely the truth. But wisdom seeks the benefit from the truth. . . . There is a strong and weighty argument against universities to be drawn from the fact that Paul secured but little fruit at Athens; accom- plishing more in the neighboring city of Corinth and in Thessaly, which was then almost barbarous, than in the Attic city, at that time the fountain of Greek philosophy. It goes to show that liberal studies are not very pleasing to God. In fact what I saw when I lived in Cologne and Paris is certainly hateful to God — not the study of sacred literature, but the moral corruption existing in the midst of such studies. . . . 'Many publicans and sinners sat down with Jesus; for there were many, and they followed him.' This word points to the great corruption of the Pharisees and scribes of that time. For although from childhood they had received holy training in the Law, they practised it for gain rather than for piety, and they neither heeded nor followed piety, even when it displayed itself incarnate. Instead they scoffed, they mocked, they persecuted. . . . Today, we have good reason to fear that there is a still worse plague in the corruption of our preachers and pastors. Publicans and harlots will be converted to righteousness more easily in the great day of the Lord than men of this sort, who know the will of God and yet scoff at it."

Gansfort exerted a wholesome influence on Hegius, as appears in the following remark by Hegius: "You ask to be informed about my tutoring. I have followed your counsel. For all learning is pernicious that is attended with the loss of virtue." [44] When Gansfort studied Greek and Hebrew he was chiefly motivated by a desire to read the Bible and the Church Fathers in the original. He was not anxious to acquire linguistic knowledge as an end in itself, but merely to make use of it as a tool.

Erasmus was not directly influenced by Gansfort when he was at Deventer, but he was no doubt strongly affected by Gansfort's views, though afterward he read his works and revealed the effect of his opinions. Gansfort had a tendency to interpret passages in the Bible and also doctrines of the Church in a way which differed greatly from the usual method. He was accustomed to apply a spiritual meaning to concrete statements. This was particularly true of the doctrine of transubstantiation, which he did not reject, but interpreted in a rather striking fashion. "Necessarily it must be admitted," he wrote, "that when Jesus says, 'Except ye eat the flesh of the Son of man and drink his blood,' we are to understand that it is an inward eating and drinking, that is, of the inner man. . . . He who thus eats already has the benefit of outward sacramental eating, just as Paul, the first hermit, and very many after him had it even without the outward sacramental eating. To eat therefore is to remember, to esteem, to love." But a few pages farther on he writes: "This opinion of mine, in which I maintain that in commemorating Christ we not only have him present with us in the body to strengthen us, but that we even corporeally eat of him, is strongly confirmed by the words of Ambrose in his *De Verbis Dei.*"

Gansfort's views on providence and predestination are also worth noting. He believed "with Plato that nature is nothing else

[44] W. Gansfort, *Opera*, p. xxxi.

than the will of God acting with regularity, while a miracle is an extraordinary operation of the divine will." He agreed with Groote that every man has a part of divinity within his breast, and that this spark of divinity unites him with God and may induce God to act on and with it, thus causing man to believe in Christ, his Savior. Groote and Gansfort believed in a complete system of predestination, which to them appeared to be perfectly in harmony with the Scriptures: "Are not five sparrows sold for two farthings," quotes Gansfort from the Gospels, "and not one of them is forgotten before your Father in Heaven?" "Indeed not a leaf falls from a tree without his will," he continues. "Therefore in the greater works of salvation believers coöperate with God in his operations. In this life by believing, fixing our gaze upon him, loving him, we may truly coöperate with God. And in this God makes us coöperate, because without him we can do nothing; but we can do all things in him that strengthens us. For through him it is given us both to will and to do. In that coöperation on our part lie our sin and our piety."

Is there then any difference between the faith without works referred to by Paul and the works without which faith is dead, as mentioned by James? Not at all, in Gansfort's opinion. As for the reward of good works, Christ taught in the Beatitudes that every act of Christian service would bring its reward, which promise was repeated by him in the parable of the last judgment, where even a cup of cold water presented in love to some needy Christian is promised its reward. Not mere faith, therefore, but love also would be required; a love without which faith could not exist.

Gansfort, accordingly, writes: "For when he bade us be pure, perfect, holy and worthy of God, what else does he seem to promise to the sinner who turns to him in faith but that, if he has but the desire to acquire virtue, all these blessed commands will be completely fulfilled — if not in this life of trouble and misery, at any rate, some time in the land of the living? Spiritual weakness is sin, because we are enjoined to be brave in faith and resist the lion that goeth about, roaring, seeking whom he may devour. For it is a lifelong war to which God has appointed all who are in the flesh, and not a mere battle, which is occasional and is only for the hour.

All weakness, however, such as folly, ignorance, lack of wisdom, is sin. These compel one to go defenseless into battle. Hence it is to some degree clear why we 'ought always to pray and not faint, to watch and be sober, to withstand steadfast in our faith . . .' Faith is not the cause of our justification, but its proof. . . . 'The just shall live by faith. . . .' Hence in unbelievers, their unbelief separates them from life. But 'he that believeth on him hath eternal life.' Therefore our good works nourish and strengthen our faith, but do not make it alive, yet they strengthen the bond of life, namely our faith. For only Christ and the Spirit quicken us, and Christ's sacrifice sanctifies us, and we are more strongly bound to this life by the stronger bond of our faith. But nothing strengthens this bond more than love; for love is strong as death. When indeed faith works through love, it is firm and the beginning of our confidence is firm. . . . By the works of the law shall no flesh be justified before him; even if one fulfil the chief commandment by his work, he will not because of this be righteous in God's sight. . . . Hence it is not our faith — whether it be in Christ or in God who delivered Christ over to be a sacrifice — nor is it the sacrifice of Christ that constitutes our righteousness; but it is the purpose of God, who accepteth the sacrifice of Christ, and who through Christ accepteth the sacrifice of Christians."

On the sacrament of penance Gansfort makes the following remarks. "I do not believe that Peter possessed the right either to loose whomsoever he pleased from the bond of Satan or to bind him therewith. For just as there is but one that baptizes in the Holy Spirit, so there is but one that binds and looses—binds, I say, and looses with authority. For with what authority can the pope loose, when he does not know whether the person he has loosed has been loosed from the bond of Satan or not?" This is exactly what Groote used to remark. Speaking about the duties of a priest in connection with the forgiveness of sins, Groote had said: "Of what use will it be to introduce an unworthy sinner to the inner circle of true believers, if this group of believers closes their doors upon him?" Gansfort argues in one of his letters: "You, therefore, cautiously take refuge behind a condition as though behind an impregnable wall, declaring that only that will stand unshaken

which the pope in matters of this sort shall decide, 'if his key is
not in error and Christ does not reject it.' What, I ask, is the
meaning of this indispensable condition, 'if his key is not in error'?
What is this key of the kingdom of heaven? And what is the
error of this key? You are obviously assuming a key that may
err and at the same time be the effectual and lawful key of the
kingdom of heaven. O dreadful kingdom, if its gates, bars, bolts,
and keys are such that through them error, falsehood, and ignorance can creep stealthily within! The key, as Augustine explains,
is love diffused through the Holy Spirit in the hearts of the children
of the kingdom. The Lord Jesus before his resurrection promised
these two keys to Peter when he said: 'I will give unto thee the
keys of the kingdom of heaven: and whatsoever thou shalt loose
on earth shall be loosed in heaven.' In like manner he presented
these keys after the Resurrection — not to one — but to all
unitedly, when he breathed on them, saying: 'Receive ye the Holy
Spirit: whosesoever sins ye forgive, they are forgiven unto them;
whosesoever sins ye retain, they are retained.' These two keys,
in Augustine's opinion, are never rejected by Christ, nor does it
ever happen that they are in error. For he defines the keys of the
kingdom as being: (1) love diffused through the Holy Spirit in
the hearts of the children of God and (2) the Holy Spirit. And he
says that to loose and to bind is to receive into fellowship because of
the similitude of love or to exclude from fellowship because of
dissimilitude. . . . When the Lord Jesus promised Peter the keys
of the kingdom of heaven so that whatsoever he bound on earth
would be bound in heaven, he promised nothing else than the
Holy Spirit, and through the Holy Spirit the diffusion of love in the
heart of Peter."

Significant also is Gansfort's attitude toward the higher clergy.
Laymen and the lower clergy only had to obey their superiors, so
reasoned he, under certain conditions, that is, when these superiors
were more faithfully obeying Christ's commandments than they
themselves. The more responsible the position one was occupying
in the Church, the better follower of Christ one ought to be. To
deny that would be so blasphemous, says Gansfort, "that it is
actually more pernicious than any heresy whatever." Peter was

allowed by God to err, he continues, in order that people may know "what to do with salt that has lost its savor."

Gansfort, following Groote's example, compared the impious clergy of his time with the Pharisees of old, who used to ask why Christ allowed his disciples to transgress the laws of the elders. Gansfort, in accord with this, protested against the sale of benefices by the higher clergy for personal gain, and for other reasons: "Nor may even the pope give them away or sell them. And when he commits God's interests in remote provinces to mere fortune, as it were — as if he had no concern for them — then alas, what evils ensue — as one cannot but see about him!" No wonder that when Gansfort had been arguing one day with a certain Rabineus at Angers, the latter had to admit: "If these things are so, our entire foundation is false." And that is exactly what many scholars and clerics must have said about Groote's views. The state of affairs witnessed by Groote and Gansfort was leading to a general catastrophe. A reformation was needed; the Yssel country was demanding one, but Rome paid no heed: no one among Groote's followers had ever broken openly with Rome.

In returning to the influence exerted by Gansfort on Erasmus and to their connection with the Brethren of the Common Life, it will be noted that Erasmus was a child of the Devotio Moderna and, although he never quite appreciated the source from which he received many of his ideas, there were times when he was not sorry that he cherished them, as will appear. Like Groote, he attacked energetically the bad monks of his time, and fought the abuses in the Church. He eagerly studied the Scriptures and the Fathers in the original texts, and corrected them. It is generally supposed that he received his ideals from Italy but it is far more likely that he received them from Groote's followers. The monks at Windesheim had corrected the texts of the Bible and of the Fathers, and Gansfort had studied Greek and Hebrew for the purpose of getting a better understanding of them. Besides, the constitutions of the brethren-houses insisted on pure texts, "lest one's conscience might be hurt by some improper version." It was Gansfort who urged Agricola to study Hebrew, and it was he who persuaded this wandering Bohemian to devote a considerable share of his leisure time to the study of the Scriptures. Now Erasmus distinguished himself by his work on the Church Fathers. He was the first to find the pure humanity and the sublime divinity of the ancients in Christianity. The love-ethics of the Gospel, especially of the Sermon on the Mount, loosed from ascetic idealism and from that sort of piety which flees the world, was to Erasmus the purest expression of the humanity found in the classics. While many others were concentrating their whole attention on the classics of pagan Greece and Rome, Erasmus extended the services of humanism to a more liberal study of the Bible and the Fathers.

One English scholar says it was Colet who urged Erasmus in 1499 "to turn his attention to theology, and to help him in breaking through the web of dialectical sophistry that had been woven round it." Many other writers have shared this view, which they could not have done had they been acquainted with the history of the "New Devotion." When a boy, Erasmus preferred Seneca to Cicero, partly because the Brethren of the Common Life, his teachers at Deventer, had learned from Groote to value practical advice on moral questions above mere rhetoric. It was the brethren, not Colet, who led him to study Paul and Augustine, the authors whom they had studied long before Colet appeared in the field. They also aroused in him an interest in Jerome, to whom their house at Deventer was dedicated, and it might be noted here that in their original constitution the house was dedicated to Paul, something which has long escaped the attention of modern scholars. The brethren taught him to regard the chief element in Christianity as faith working through love, a return to the faith taught by Christ himself. That Erasmus knew Gansfort is plain from his own remark: "Doctor Wessel has much in common with Luther, but how much more modestly and like Christ did he propagate his ideas than most of those [Lutherans] at Strassburg." Erasmus' own thinking was colored with the opinions of Wessel Gansfort; he spiritualized the meaning of purgatory in imitation of Gansfort, and he also spiritualized the Eucharist. It was from him that Zwingli derived new views on Christ's spiritual presence in the Eucharist, as Zwingli told Melanchthon afterward.

There is one other fact about Erasmus' life that deserves attention here. It is his very unusual spirit of toleration and his constant efforts to preserve peace. Although he instinctively felt that Luther was the direct cause of his own declining fame, he nevertheless sought to befriend Luther as long as he could. This attitude seems natural in a follower of Gansfort and of the Brethren of the Common Life. Gansfort had often been suspected of heresy, as he himself stated, and Erasmus had had the same experience. Both men resented and ridiculed the attacks on their way of preaching reform. On one occasion Gansfort wrote: "I hear from my most faithful friends that John of Wesel has been convicted to die by fire. I think the methods of his judges ought to be laughed to scorn. . . . Besides, from the same friends I learn that as soon as the inquisitor has disposed of him, he will descend with an investigation upon me." Erasmus wrote in a similar vein about Luther before the breach came in 1521. In October, 1519, he insisted that Luther should not "be suppressed, but rather be brought to a right frame of mind." Luther had "an admirable insight into the Gospel," he asserted. He had asked for a discussion and received only insult; his thoughts were distorted, argued Erasmus, and his writings falsified.

One should be very careful, however, not to overestimate the influence of Gansfort on Erasmus. The latter was affected by the opinions of many scholars. From Hegius he learned something, but he also rejected much of Hegius' system of thought; from Agricola he acquired much, and again, he differed much; from Gansfort also he differed. Besides, wherever he agreed with the Brethren of the Common Life or with the three humanists just mentioned, he was not necessarily dependent on them for his opinions. All that one can say with assurance is that when his mind was absorbing knowledge and was plastic, he was subjected for several years to a course of training which reflected the ideas and methods of the Brethren of the Common Life and their friends, of whom the most eminent in the Netherlands were unquestionably Hegius, Agricola, and Gansfort.

CHAPTER XII

THE BRETHREN OF THE COMMON LIFE
AT 'S-HERTOGENBOSCH

ERASMUS wrote two important accounts of his experiences
with the brethren at 's-Hertogenbosch. The first is found in
his *Compendium Vitae*, or his autobiography; the second, which
is still more valuable than the other, is in the Grunnius letter
mentioned above. Both narratives prove that Erasmus did not
sympathize with the methods employed by the Brethren of the
Common Life. Whether his criticism is justified is quite another
matter. Opinions of recent authorities seem agreed on a negative
answer, but a solution must be preceded by a careful study of the
complete reports.

In his autobiography, in which he speaks of himself in the third
person, Erasmus makes these remarks: "When the plague at
Deventer became worse and worse every day so that the whole
house where he lived was ravaged by it, he returned home.
Gerard, on receiving the sad news, fell ill, and died soon after.
Both [parents] died not much over forty years of age. He [Gerard]
appointed three guardians, in whom he had the greatest confidence, the chief of them being Peter Winckel, then schoolmaster
at Gouda; and he left a moderate fortune, if it had been faithfully
administered. The boy was now sent to 's-Hertogenbosch when he
was already ripe for a University; but they were afraid of a
University, because they had decided to bring him up to Religion.
There he lived, that is to say he lost, nearly three years at the
Brothers' House, as they call it, in which Rombold then taught.
This class of teachers is now widely spread through the world, a
destruction to good intellects, and seminaries of monasticism.
Rombold, who was much pleased with the capacity of the boy,
began to solicit him to become one of his flock. The boy excused
himself on the score of youth. A plague having arisen in the place,

after he had suffered some time with a quartan fever, he returned to his guardians; having acquired by this time a sufficiently fluent style out of some good authors."[1]

The Grunnius letter presents a similar account: "While they were still boys they lost their mother; and their father, dying soon after, left a property, small indeed, but which would have abundantly sufficed for finishing their education, had not the rapacity of their relations, who surrounded the dying man, made that little less.

"Hence, when they were ready for the schools, which they call universities (for they were now sufficiently versed in grammar, and had learned the greater part of the *Dialectics* of Peter Hispanus), yet fearing that they might there drink in something of a worldly spirit and refuse the yoke, he [Winckel] saw to it that they were put out of the way into a company of those who are commonly called *Fratres Collationarii*, who, having nested themselves in everywhere, make a regular business of hunting up boys to be trained. Their chief care, should they see any youth of unusually high spirit and quick disposition (of which nature are almost all very fertile minds), is to break his spirit and humble him by blows, threats, scoldings, and other devices, which they call 'breaking in'; and thus to fit him for the monastic life. For this reason they are much esteemed by the Dominicans and Franciscans; for these latter admit that their Orders would very soon perish, did not some such seminary as the above feed them. For it is from such cohorts that they select their young soldiers. True, I think, they have among them some not ill-disposed men; but since they suffer from a lack of the best authors and live in their own obscurity, spending their lives in the observance of rites and ceremonies; and since they measure themselves by themselves and not by others, compelled as they are to spend a good part of the day in prayer and their customary tasks, I do not see how it is possible for them thoroughly to instruct youth. Certainly the fact speaks for itself, since nowhere else are young men sent forth worse taught or worse trained. The boys lost more than two years with them: at least it was loss of time for the younger, who was somewhat more learned than his teachers in those very branches which they professed to teach. One of the

[1] F. M. Nichols, *The Epistles of Erasmus*, I, 7–9.

instructors was such that Florentius declares he never saw a more
ignorant or a more vainglorious monster.   And such as he are the
men who are often set over boys; for they are not chosen by the
vote of the learned, but at the pleasure of the head of the order,
who frequently is uneducated.   There was one, however, who
always seemed to be delighted with the character of Florentius;
and when it became a question of his return home, this monk
began in private conversations to urge him to join their order,
mentioning many of the advantages by which boys are wont to be
attracted.   Would that the thing had been done; for either the
love of piety would have detained him willingly among them or,
if the affair had so shaped itself, it would have been lawful for him
to return to his former state of freedom.   For this body of men,
who are motivated by an individual sense of virtue and a vestige
of early religion, are not bound by irrevocable vows." [2]

The Grunnius letter deserves careful analysis, but it is not the
only important reference to the followers of Groote.   One should
not rely too much on the study of letters written by Erasmus, since
he wrote so many books which are equally valuable for the biographer.[3]   Whereas the authenticity of the Grunnius letter is not
altogether beyond doubt, there is a source in which Erasmus
speaks about the brethren in the very same vein, and which is
more reliable than the Grunnius letter.   In the dialogue *On the
Correct Pronunciation of Latin and Greek*, the author presents a
conversation carried on by Leo and Ursus.   The latter tells about
his experiences with the Brethren of the Common Life, by whom he
was educated at Deventer when he was about fifteen.   Leclerc,
the editor of the *Opera* published at Leiden, expressed the opinion
in a footnote (Vol. I, col. 922) that Erasmus was speaking of his
own experience, which is probably true.

Leo says that there is a certain brotherhood, half-way between

----

[2] J. J. Mangan, *The Life, Character, and Influence of Desiderius Erasmus of
Rotterdam*, I, 11–13.

[3] The present writer heartily agrees with J. Pusino who, in reviewing Preserved
Smith's work on Erasmus for the *Zeitschr. für Kirchengesch.* (XLIV, 626),
observed that it has become too customary to treat Erasmus' letters as the chief
source of information about Erasmus.   Huizinga's book on Erasmus is also an
example of this tendency.

monks and laymen, which teaches boys in their own houses. Ursus remarks, "I dislike the darkness in which they grope their way; I love the light. Scholars of this kind are practically self-taught, and not seldom poorly taught. . . . Among them native intellectual vigor and alacrity of mind are crushed and suppressed in a pharisaical manner. A liberal, innate talent is corrupted, and a servile, narrow character is imposed upon the young, plastic minds. Hence we do not seldom see that those who emerge from such nests exceed others in insolence, are less sincere, more false, less liberal-minded."

Leo then asks whether it is not desirable that the minds be turned to piety at a tender age, whereupon Ursus replies that it is folly to make a boy miserable and dejected and to destroy his inborn talent. And he adds, "I was educated by these brethren at Deventer, when I had not yet finished my fifteenth year. The procurator of their house tried everything to induce me to join the order. And I was a boy inclined toward piety. When this excellent man noticed that his work availed nothing, he took down an exorcism." "What did he do, I pray?" asked the bewildered Leo. "He took down a crucifix, and entreated me, as I was crying. 'Don't you know,' he said, 'what has been suffered for you?' 'I don't know,' I replied. 'I testify that through this,' he continued, 'you will not do something to render this death in vain, but you will follow my counsel lest you die eternal death with the world.'" [4]

From what has been said about the Brethren of the Common Life at Deventer it will appear that Erasmus was not far wrong in his

[4] Erasmus, *Opera*, I, 921: "*Leo.* Laudantur in hoc genere quidam, qui non ita pridem exorti, medium genus inter Monachos et Laicos, domi suae docendis pueris quaestum uberem facere dicuntur, quanquam hoc aucupium et a Monachis quibusdam affectari coepit. *Ursus.* Sua cuique sententia est, mihi displicent in hisce rebus latebrae, lucem amo. Tum id genus Doctores fere sunt αὐτοδίδακτοι, nonnunquam indocte docti, nec sui juris, et illiberaliter educati. . . . Quibus rebus fit, ut apud hos nativus ille vigor et alacritas ingeniorum frangatur, ac dejiciatur ad habitum quendam Pharisaicum, qui liberalem et ingenuam indolem corrumpit, servile quiddam et illiberale inserens teneris animis. Quin et illud non raro videmus, eos qui ex talibus nidis emergunt, evadere caeteris insolentiores, minus sinceros, magis fucatos, minusque liberales. . . . Educabar apud hos Deventurii, nondum egressus annum decimum quintum. . . . Et eram alioqui puer ad pietatem propensius."

criticism. After the year 1510 his standards of intellectual and moral values differed greatly from those of his former teachers. He was not justified in making no allowance for the possibility of two opposite views being both reasonable, but the information he gave about the attitude of the brethren toward monasticism and higher education are not nearly so far from the truth as has been surmised in recent years.[5]

The following facts presented by Erasmus are undoubtedly correct. A plague compelled Erasmus and his brother to leave Deventer, which probably happened in the summer of 1484 [6]; they departed for Gouda, where Peter Winckel was still teaching school, as contemporary documents prove.[7] Gerard, their father, died soon after the news reached him that the mother had passed away, and probably before the boys returned to Gouda. In 1484 Erasmus was fifteen years old and his brother eighteen. He purposely ignored his brother's existence in the autobiography in order to save his father's reputation, for he himself was the younger son and gave the year of his brother's birth as his own. In the Grunnius letter, facts are told intended only for the friendly ear of Pope Leo X, and here Erasmus could speak more freely.

In 1484 both boys were old enough for the universities and even Erasmus had covered the required preparatory curricula, since the last two years in the schools at Deventer and Zwolle provided courses commonly taught in the universities. Peter Winckel, the teacher at Gouda, knew that in his city the schools could offer the two boys no satisfactory training. He is depicted by Erasmus as a poorly educated pedagogue and although Erasmus should have expressed himself a little less bitterly, since Winckel showed an interest in classical learning,[8] nevertheless he must have seemed a

---

[5] P. Mestwerdt (*Die Anfänge des Erasmus*, p. 184) goes too far in saying that the brethren in 1485 were the enemies of the Franciscans and the Dominicans. One must not confuse the period after 1485 with that before 1418. Care should also be taken not to impute to the brethren who flourished in 1485 the thirst for classical learning which characterized a host of well-trained pedagogues who were connected with the brotherhood after 1500.

[6] P. S. Allen, *Opus Ep. Er.*, I, 582.

[7] See p. 60.

[8] He was anxious to secure a manuscript of Juvenal (P. S. Allen, *op. cit.*, I, Ep. 3, note to line 40), and he may have induced Erasmus to prepare an abridged edition of Valla's *Elegantiae* (C. Ruelens, *Érasme*, p. xxx).

mediocre scholar to Erasmus between 1516 and 1521, when the latter composed the autobiographies mentioned above. Why did Winckel not send them to a university? Probably because their father had expressed the wish that his sons be educated for positions in the Church. The fact that Erasmus sang for a time in the cathedral in Utrecht, which implied an expectation of a future benefice, seems to confirm this supposition. Why the school conducted by the Brethren of the Common Life was selected is not known.

Whereas the brethren-house at Gouda was founded by the brethren of Delft, and the home of the latter by the brethren of Deventer, the institution at Zwolle was the parent of the house at 's-Hertogenbosch. There was for that reason no intimate connection between the houses of Gouda and 's-Hertogenbosch. Master Winckel taught in the school attached to the church of St. John, and was afterward assistant pastor of the same church, which must have been an added reason why the boys were asked to affiliate themselves more closely with the Church. Winckel used to take trips to Louvain and Mechlin for the magistrates of Gouda. It seems probable that he was acquainted with some curates at 's-Hertogenbosch. In this city there was also a St. John's church, even more magnificent than the edifice of Gouda. In a document issued on August 2, 1485, by the magistrates of 's-Hertogenbosch,[9] three members of the clergy in that city are said to have been the executives of a will, namely, a dean of the church of St. John, the prior of a monastery, and John of Breda, rector of the Brethren of the Common Life in the same city. One may at least infer from these facts that the brethren in this place were on friendly terms with the Chapter of St. John's and that Winckel probably had acquaintances there. Erasmus happens to single out Winckel for special criticism, since he does not name the other guardians. Winckel was no doubt largely responsible for the final decision which brought Erasmus and his brother to 's-Hertogenbosch.

The brethren-house of St. Gregory at 's-Hertogenbosch had been founded in 1424 or 1425 by the brethren of Zwolle, whose house

[9] See *Schepenprotokollen*, 1485, fol. 197a. The manuscript is preserved in the *Rijksarchief* at 's-Hertogenbosch.

was also named after St. Gregory. The local institution was far
more prosperous than the house at Gouda, a fact which Winckel
certainly knew. It was responsible for the foundation of houses at
Nijmegen (1470) and in Liège (1496).[10] Like the institution at
Zwolle, it supported separate dormitories for three classes of pupils,
namely, poor, moderately wealthy, and wealthy boys.[11] The
principal building, named *Fraterhuis*, was situated on a street
named Hinthamereinde.[12] Behind this edifice was located the
Rijke Fraterhuis, or the home for rich boys; and in the Schilder-
straat was the *Arme Fraterhuis*.[13] Then there was the *Mediocris
Huis*, for boys of moderate means.[14]

It must not be imagined, however, that the boys who were
staying in the home for poor pupils received all their needs from
the brethren. They were partly supported by their friends and
relatives. All the boys who lived in the dormitories of the brethren
wore uniform clothes, like those worn in the New Brethren-House
and the Bursa Cusana, a dormitory founded by Cardinal Cusa at
Deventer.[15] The clothes of the boys of 's-Hertogenbosch are
described in a document of December 5, 1561, where it is stated
that they were "patterned after the ancient usage of the brethren." [16] They were dressed in gray, and some of them wore a
hood.

The brethren of 's-Hertogenbosch conducted a school of their
own, where at the end of the fifteenth century Latin and Greek
were taught. They also had a printing-press, like the brethren at
Gouda. Before 1500 none of their teachers had made much of a
reputation. It is very doubtful whether they had progressed as
far on the road toward pure humanism as had Hegius at Deventer.

---

[10] A. Hyma, *The Christian Renaissance*, p. 111.

[11] M. Schoengen, *Jacobus Traiecti . . . Narratio*, p. 125.

[12] L. H. C. Schutjes, *Geschiedenis van het Bisdom 's-Hertogenbosch*, IV, 404.

[13] A. F. O. Van Sasse van Ysselt, *De voorname Huizen en Gebouwen van 's-Hertogenbosch*, III, 105.

[14] *Ibid.*, p. 106.

[15] M. Schoengen, *op. cit.*, p. 124, note 4.

[16] A. F. O. Van Sasse van Ysselt, *op. cit.*, III, 124, where the clothes are described: "Cleyn grauw tabbartken, streckende ter halver schenen desselven
scholiers, beneden toegenayt ende gemaekt sijnde nae de oude usantie van de
fraters."

PLATE V

The cathedral of St. John's at 's-Hertogenbosch

So from the viewpoint of Erasmus in 1517 and 1521 the educators in Deventer were more advanced and better in every way.

The school conducted by the brethren of 's-Hertogenbosch was named *de groote school*, or "the large school," and seems to have been the only school of fairly large size in the city.[17] During the sixteenth century it ranked with the finest secondary schools on the Continent, but Erasmus left before 1488, and therefore the period after 1488 cannot explain his criticism. He was undoubtedly disappointed with this school when he entered it in 1484. Erasmus mentions a certain Romboldus, whom he probably regarded as the chief educator. There is no reason to doubt his word. The name Romboldus was very rare, but it occurs about five times in the *Schepenprotokollen* of the year 1485, a very large volume, in which the name Reymboldus appears also. Unfortunately the Romboldus mentioned by Erasmus acquired so little fame that it has thus far been impossible to identify him. The other teachers cannot have taught Erasmus much.

The constitution of the brethren-house at 's-Hertogenbosch differed very slightly from that of its parent at Zwolle.[18] It was a trifle shorter, but the variations are not worth noting. The caliber of the men in the respective institutions cannot have differed much. Since Zwolle was the intellectual center of the Devotio Moderna when the institution at 's-Hertogenbosch was founded, one may say that the latter institution was not more hostile to the pursuit of secular learning than the house at Deventer. Its library was similar to that of the *Heer Florens-Huis* at Deventer. The books were turned over to the Abbey of Berne, located a few miles west of 's-Hertogenbosch, when the brethren left the institution in 1623. They were sold in 1887 at Leiden, and in the catalogue of the sale they are properly enumerated. Some of the books may have disappeared before this sale, but the remaining titles give a fairly accurate idea of the interests of the Brethren of

---

[17] A. van der Does de Willebois, *Studiebeurzen*, III, 249. There is no evidence of begging on the part of poor pupils, but they often received alms, as also happened in Deventer.

[18] The former was printed in M. Schoengen, *op. cit.*, pp. 239–273; the latter, in G. Coeverincx, *Analecta*, II, 99–114; but the whole constitution has not been reproduced in the *Analecta*.

the Common Life.[19]   The amazing thing is that in 1623 the brethren of 's-Hertogenbosch had been conducting a school which trained boys after the humanistic pattern, but the brethren themselves remained as simple-minded as ever.   The list of the books left by them will speak for itself.

1. Albert of Strassburg, *Sermones* (manuscript).
2. Bonaventura, *Speculum Disciplinarum* (manuscript).
3. Thomas Aquinas, *De Puritate Conscientiae et de Modo Confitendi* (manuscript).
4. Henricus Diest, *Exercitium pro Novellis* (manuscript).
5. *Graduale Romanum* (manuscript).
6. Richard of St. Victor and Thomas Aquinas, *Tractatus Theologici* (manuscript).
7. *Vitae Sanctorum* (manuscript).
8. St. Ambrose, *Opera Omnia*.
9. St. Anthony, *Opus Historiarum*.
10. St. Augustine, *Retractio de Consensu quatuor Evangelistarum*.
11. Boethius, *De Consolatione Philosophiae*, with commentary by Thomas Aquinas.
12. Bonaventura, *Quaestiones super 2*[am] *Sententiarum*.
13. Bonaventura, *Profectus Religiosorum*.
14. Caesarius Cisterciensis, *Dialogus Miraculorum*.
15. Aurelius Cassiodorus, *Expositio in Psalterium*.
16. Eusebius and Beda, *Historia Ecclesiastica*.
17. Guillelmus Parisiensis Episcopus, *Opera*.
18. Guillelmus Altissiodorensis, *Summa Aurea in quatuor Libros Sententiarum*.
19. Henricus Herpf, *Sermones de Tempore et de Sanctis*.
20. St. Jerome, *Vita S. Patrum*.
21. St. Hilarius, *Opera complura*, with commentaries by John Gerson and John de Fabrica.
22. *Itinerarius sive Peregrinarius B. V. M.*
23. Jacobus Phil. Bergomensis, *Supplementum Chronicarum*.
24. Jacobus de Voragine, *Sermones de Sanctis*.
25. Joannes Caldrinus, *Auctoritatum et Sententiarum Tabula*.
26. St. Chrysostom, *Sermones*.
27. Joannes de Cuba, *Hortus Sanitatis*.
28. Joannes Salesberiensis (John of Salisbury), *Policraticus*.
29. *Libellus de Modo Confitendi et Poenitendi*.
30. Franciscus de Marone, *Sermones de Tempore*.
31. *Paradisus Conscientiae*.
32. Petrus de Herenthals, *Expositio super Psalmos*.
33. Petrus de Palude, *Thesaurus novus Sermonum*.
34. *Pharetra, Auctoritates, et Dicta Doctorum*.
35. Richard of St. Victor, *De Superdivina Trinitate*.
36. Seneca, *Opera Philosophica et Epistolae*.

[19] See G. Coeverincx, *Analecta*, II, 167–168.

37. Thomas Aquinas, *Summa Theologiae.*
38. Thomas Cantipratensis, *Bonum Universale sive De Proprietatibus Apum.*
39. Albertus Magnus, *Postilla super Evang. Lucae et Super Evang. Matthei.*
40. J. Altestaig, *Vocabularius Theologiae.*
41. Angelus de Clavasio, *Summa Angelica.*
42. Bonaventura, *Opuscula quamplurima.*
43. Duns Scotus, *Super quatuor Sententiarum.*
44. Hugo of St. Victor, *De Sacramentis.*
45. Hugo of St. Victor, *Allegoriarum libri decem.*
46. L. Valla, *Adnotationes in Novum Testamentum.*
47. Vincentius de Valentia, *Sermones de Tempore.*

Another fact which will explain the criticism of Erasmus is the very friendly relations between the Brethren of the Common Life of 's-Hertogenbosch and Gouda, and the clergy, both secular and regular. Whereas the brethren at Zwolle felt it their duty to find fault with the pastors, their friends of 's-Hertogenbosch, as well as of Gouda, affiliated their interests with those of the clergy. As a means of increasing their sources of income they read masses in both churches of St. John. In a manuscript dated March 24, 1480, "the rectors and priests of the House of St. Gregory agree to read masses in the chapel near the tower of St. John's at 's-Hertogenbosch." They were to receive 45 pounds, or 15 pounds for each of the three masses. On fol. 5ᵃ of the manuscript the names of three church wardens are given, namely, Amelis, Gerit, and Claes; and also that of Herman Pietszoon of Dordrecht, the assistant pastor.[20] When the local institution of the brethren was dissolved (1623), most of the movable property was left to the chapter of St. John's, while at Gouda the library of the brethren was turned over to the church of St. John, although Gouda had become Protestant, unlike 's-Hertogenbosch.

When Erasmus wrote the Grunnius letter in 1517 he was disgusted with the mendicant monks and thought he could not say anything much worse about the Brethren of the Common Life than that their dormitories were seminaries of the mendicant orders, particularly of the Franciscans and the Dominicans. He referred to the period from 1484 to 1486, but at the same time he spoke in the

[20] This manuscript is the property of the Provinciaal Genootschap van Kunsten en Wetenschappen van Noord-Brabant at 's-Hertogenbosch.

present tense, or about conditions in 1517. After the year 1486 he had become acquainted in Paris with John Standonck, principal of the College of Montaigu, and a former pupil of the brethren at Gouda. He also met John Mombaer, who had come to France on a mission from the Congregation of Windesheim. It was Mombaer's hope to reform the famous Abbey of St. Victor in Paris. Both he and Standonck were on friendly terms with the Dominicans (1490–1500). Together with the so-called Holland Dominicans, they earnestly strove to bring about a thoroughgoing reform in the Gallican Church. Erasmus himself at one time (1497–99) expressed a personal interest in this work, but afterward he drifted away from the ideals of Standonck and Mombaer, who both represented the principles of the Devotio Moderna. Is it surprising, therefore, that Erasmus associated the work of the Brethren of the Common Life with the mendicant monks? He was quite justified in saying that around the year 1500 many recruits were furnished for the mendicant orders by the Brethren of the Common Life.

But was Erasmus also right in assailing the intellectual standards of the brethren? He was, to a considerable extent, if he referred only to the period before 1486. The average rector of a local institution before that year could not be called a scholar, and even after 1500 the majority of the rectors were still narrow-minded men, if judged from the standpoint of Erasmus, who in 1517 was the intellectual king of Europe. Generalizations, however, are often dangerous, wherefore it will be best for us to mention a few specific cases.

One of the most important sources for the study of the question just raised is a narrative, or chronicle, written about the year 1503 in the brethren-house at Zwolle by James Voecht of Utrecht, who was born about 1423 and became a member of the house in 1450. Afterward he was procurator of the Domus Pauperum, or House for Poor Students at Zwolle, and he occupied the highest office in the local institution next to the rector and the procurator of the principal building. Fortunately his chronicle was most ably edited by M. Schoengen, the archivist at Zwolle, who added a mass of welcome data.

Of the house at 's-Hertogenbosch we read: "It was founded about the year 1424 by one of our brothers, named Gerard Scadde of Calcar, the brother of our first rector. He came to our house from the University of Prague on a visit to his brother, who earnestly argued with him about the superiority of heavenly things. But the student replied: 'We cannot all leave the world and embrace poverty.' 'Very well,' said the rector, 'if all things are distributed and I receive the heavenly gifts while you get the earthly things, I shall be content with my share.' These words struck home and a little later the student returned. He became a very good man, adopting our humble and abject clothes and mode of living. Although his parents were wealthy and he was highly respected in the world he despised all worldly things and dedicated himself to eternal treasures. His mother was a devout lady and, attracted by the fragrance of his virtues, removed to Zwolle. . . . He founded a good institution at 's-Hertogenbosch, where he died in 1435."[21]

"John of Calcar, a devout member of our house, lived here for more than twenty years, quiet and obedient, and efficient in all the spiritual exercises; he became at the death of Gerard Scadde the second rector in the house at 's-Hertogenbosch. He ruled this house well and was beloved of God and men, and helped to increase the number of the brothers and their temporal possessions; and he ably instructed the brothers according to the rules which he had learned and followed in our house."[22]

This rector was still ruling the house at 's-Hertogenbosch in 1470, as appears from a letter written in or after 1470 at Nijmegen and addressed to him by John Brugman,[23] the most celebrated preacher in the history of the Netherlands, and at that time a mendicant monk. The latter used to attack the brethren at Deventer and Zwolle, but by the year 1470 he had become a warm friend of Egbert ter Beek, the rector at Deventer, and of John of Calcar. He now praised the brethren in the highest terms for

---

[21] M. Schoengen, *op. cit.*, pp. 78–80.

[22] *Ibid.*, pp. 98–99.

[23] Brugman removed to Nijmegen in 1470 and may have written it one or two years later.

"drawing boys into the service of God." In the letter written to John of Calcar he said: "To the devout and venerable men in Christ, John of Calcar, and the other brethren at 's-Hertogen-bosch. . . . The merciful Samaritan who poured oil into the wounds of the robbed Jew and gave him wine to drink prepared your status in the Christian Church, in order that your virtues and discipline might fertilize the field and produce a luxurious vineyard. Al-though you do not bear the titles of prelates and possess the degrees of the scholars, nevertheless you are the true pastors and instruc-tors of the young. I have not been able nor am I able at present to believe otherwise than that the merciful Father has sent you to cherish these regions, so that you should implant goodness, disci-pline, and a knowledge of salvation in the children, about whom the Truth says: 'Suffer the little ones to come unto me.' Not only do you permit but by your life and doctrine you compel the chil-dren and youths to come to Christ, who is the fountain of life and truth." [24]

In the year 1460 Brugman preached a sermon in the brethren-house at Deventer, taking for his text the well-known saying of Jesus reported in Mark, Chapter X: "Suffer the children to come unto me, for of such is the kingdom of heaven." He mentioned in the first place a treatise by John Gerson, entitled *On the Drawing of Children to Christ*, which the brethren loved to read. Then he referred to Gerard Groote, who had tried to reform the immoral clergy in the Netherlands and afterward concentrated his efforts on the training of boys who might become reformers in turn. "I like no order more than yours," he continued, "except my own, namely, the Franciscan order, and if there were no Franciscans, I would fall on my knees before you and beg for a place in your house. . . . I wish I had spent the time which I devoted to study in Paris, at Deventer instead, for here knowledge and man-ners and virtues are taught which are more valuable than pure learning." Turning to the pupils of the brethren, he remarked:

---

[24] This letter was printed for the first time in an article entitled "Een Onuitge-geven Sermoen van Johannes Brugman," by A. W. Wybrands, printed in *Arch. voor Ned. Kerkgesch.*, I (1885), 208–228. The letter is printed on pp. 226–228. Brugman was a Franciscan monk.

"I exhort you to listen attentively to your teachers in order that you may remember their precepts. But I also admonish you children always to keep God before your eyes in your studies, so that it may be your intention, when your studies have been completed, to serve God, according to the counsel of the brethren of the Heer Florens-Huis, who know which monasteries are good and which are bad." [25]

At the end of the letter mentioned, Brugman asked the brethren at 's-Hertogenbosch to "accept this young boy, and teach him the rules of your house." He, a Franciscan monk, was sending a boy to the Brethren of the Common Life with the purpose, no doubt, of having him prepared for the monastic life. He also told the boys at Deventer to trust the Brethren of the Common Life, because they knew which monasteries would suit them best. He confirmed the verdict of Erasmus further by describing the labors of the brethren, whose aim, as he well knew, was not to instil classical learning but to teach them to follow Jesus and to imitate the Apostles. And in a letter addressed to the brethren at Deventer he pointed out that they followed no monastic rule, "neither the rule of Basil, nor of Augustine, nor of Benedict, nor of our father Francis, nor do they have strict vows, but simply the rule laid down in the first Epistle of St. Peter, the first chapter, where he said: 'Ye have purified your souls in obeying the truth through the Spirit unto unfeigned love of the brethren, see that ye love one another with a pure heart fervently. . . .' Now that for many the day is drawing to a close, our mother the Church calls for her sons who, having no patron, are content to imitate the Fathers and the members of the primitive Church by taking care of boys and by drawing the people to Christ." [26]

[25] This sermon has been printed in the article mentioned above.

[26] W. Moll, *Joh. Brugman*, I, 207–208. Brugman had traveled a great deal, and near the end of his life expressed the opinion that in the Netherlands there was an unusual amount of piety. Says Moll (p. 13): "Is het een wonder dat de bereisde Brugman, toen ook hij eene halve eeuw later zijne omzwervingen en hervormings-werk in onze gewesten had aangevangen, reden vond om zich te verblijden in het nieuw en beter leven, dat hij ontwaakt zag? 'Het is een land,' dus schreef hij in die dagen, terwijl hij bepaaldelijk het oog op Holland had, ofschoon hij elders dierge-lijke lofspraken ook aan andere gewesten heeft gegeven: 'het is een land, waarvan de inwoners schoon van gelaat zijn, maar schooner nog en eerlijker en rijper van

Brugman knew human nature. He had carefully inspected the institutions controlled by the Brethren of the Common Life and realized that here were men whose chief aim was to reform the Church through a return to the standards set by Jesus and the Apostles. When Lorenzo Valla told his friends in Italy to revive the primitive Church he merely talked without comprehending the issues at stake. But when the brotherhood founded by Groote embarked on a Christian renaissance, they accomplished something. Erasmus could not appreciate their ideals. He loved to talk and to write with elegance. His mind was devoted to the restoration of scholarship, and even after his visits to England, where Colet exerted considerable influence on him, he never seriously endeavored to imitate the lowly Jesus. He thought there was no need of that and despised the Brethren of the Common Life for their humble ways. Such was his privilege, but notwithstanding his unwarranted condemnation of the Brethren of the Common Life, the facts given by him are very largely correct. All that the modern reader has to do is to remember what seemed to Erasmus the greatest thing in life.

---

zeden. Dit volk is over het algemeen zeer godsdienstig, zeer getrouw in den omgang, minder begeerig naar buit en roof, barmhartig jegens de overwonnenen woest slechts jegens zijn vijanden. Het is wel een klein deel van de wereld, maar, geenszins het minste onder de duizenden van Duitschland; want terwijl de overige deelen der kerk krank zijn, is dit vooral een moeder van veel godsdienstigheid, vruchtbaar aan deugden en deugdzamen, eene ijveraarster voor alle hervormde menschen, eene bevorderaarster van gasthuizen en armenhuizen, een spiegel voor maagden en in onthouding levende weduwen, eene beschermster des geregelden levens van alle kloosterorden., ' Dit land,' dus vervolgde hij iets later, ' is onvermoeid in het bouwen en rijkelijk in het sieren van kerken, zeer gevuld boven vele natiën en landen met christelijk leven en vereenigingen van contemplatieve menschen.'"

PART IV
IN THE MONASTERY

CHAPTER XIII

THE MONASTERY OF STEYN

IF ERASMUS remained at 's-Hertogenbosch for two years and
a half, as seems probable, he must have returned to Gouda at
the end of 1486. He tells in his autobiography that one of his
three guardians had died of the plague, and the other two began
to look for a place in some monastery. They obtained one in
the monastery of the Augustinian Canons Regular at Sion, near
Delft, which was the principal house of the small chapter or
congregation of Sion, but instead of compelling Erasmus to enter
it, they gave him time for consideration. He had been suffering
from a serious fever for a year and had to be treated with for-
bearance.

"When the day of reckoning came," continues Erasmus, "the
youth answered prudently that he did not yet know what the
world was, nor what a monastery was, nor yet what he was himself; consequently it seemed wiser that he should pass some years
in the Schools, until he was better known to himself. When he
found the lad firmly saying this, he [Peter] fell foul of him at once.
'It is all in vain then,' said he, 'that I have taken the pains to get
such a place for you by great solicitations. You are a scoundrel
and under no good influence. I renounce my guardianship of you.
Look out for yourself how to get your living.' The youth answered
that he accepted the renunciation, and was old enough not to require
guardians. When he [Erasmus] saw that he made no way by blus-
ter, he put forward his brother, who was also a guardian, to conduct
the business. His [Peter's] plan was cajolery; and there were further promptings from all quarters. A partner he [Erasmus] had,
who betrayed his friends. The fever was pressing. Nevertheless, no
monastery was acceptable to him [Erasmus] until by mere chance
he was making a visit to one of the same order at Emmaus or Steyn,

145

near Gouda. There he fell in with Cornelius, formerly his chamber-fellow at Deventer, who had not yet put on the religious habit; he had seen Italy, but had come back without having learnt much. This young man, for a purpose of his own, began to depict with marvelous fluency that holy sort of life, the abundance of books, the ease, the quiet, the angelic companionship, and what not? A child-ish affection drew Erasmus toward his old school-fellow. Some friends enticed and some pushed him on. The fever weighed upon him. He chose this spot, having no taste for the other. He was tenderly treated for a time, until he should put on the sacred robe. Meanwhile, young as he was, he felt the absence of real piety there. And yet the whole flock were led by his influence to study. Before profession he was preparing to go away, but was detained partly by human shame, partly by threats, and partly by necessity." [1]

The Grunnius letter also presents an interesting narrative, which corroborates the *Compendium Vitae*, or autobiography. It will be recalled that here Erasmus has much to say about his brother and that he names himself Florentius. "When, therefore," so reads this letter, "Antonius and Florentius had returned home, the guardians, who had not used the best of judgment with regard to their inheritance, small as it was, began to treat about their entering a monastery, partly that they might the more quickly be relieved of their care, and partly that the schoolmaster, who alone was administering the estate (for one, seized by the plague, had died quite suddenly, without giving any account of his stewardship, and the third, who was a banker, took very little interest in their care), considered that he would make a most pleas-ing offering to God, were he to present these two lambs. Softened by these means, the elder brother began to weaken, evidently forgetful of the oath which he had more than once taken to be firm. None the less did the younger persist in his determination. In a word, the faithless Antonius, after betraying his brother, accepted the yoke, having first stolen all their ready money — no new habit of his. For him the affair turned out well; for he was a man of dull mind, but lusty body; selfish, cunning, and artful; a

---

[1] F. M. Nichols, *The Epistles of Erasmus*, I, 7–9. Minor modifications have been made in the translation for the sake of clarity.

thief, a drunkard, and a voluptuary; in short, so different from his younger brother, that one might imagine him to be a changeling. He was always his brother's evil genius. Not long afterward he played the part among his companions that Iscariot played among the Apostles. When, however, he saw his brother miserably entrapped, his conscience stung him, and he deplored bitterly that he had ruined him by drawing him into the snare. You have here the confession of a Judas; would that he had followed his example and hanged himself before he had committed such an unfraternal deed! Florentius, like all who are apt of study, was unsophisticated and careless about everyday matters, and displayed a wonderful simplicity in these things. You will find many with beardless chins who are mature in cunning; but he had a mind for nothing but his studies. His whole bent was in that direction; and by the force of his nature he was borne thither, having lived in school from his early childhood. Of delicate constitution, yet not unfit for mental activity, he had just entered on his sixteenth year.

"While he thus stood uncertain, looking everywhere for some divinity to appear and point out a way of safety, he happened to visit a certain community near the town where he lived, and found there one Cantelius with whom he had been brought up from infancy. This man was older by some years, having a cunning mind, ever bent on self, yet of high spirit. It was not so much piety as good eating and a love of ease that had allured him to a monastic life.

"When Cantelius perceived from his conversation what remarkable progress in learning Florentius had made, thinking at once of his own interests, he began with incredible affection (for his nature was mercurial) to exhort him to follow the same kind of life that he himself did, sketching in words a beautiful picture of his own Order, emphasizing its blessed tranquillity, liberty, and concord. But why should I go on? It was a brotherhood of angels. He repeatedly dwelt on the abundance of books that were to be had there, and what opportunity for study; for he well knew the bait by which the mind of the boy might be caught. In short, if you had heard this man, you would have said that the place was not a monastery, but the mead of the Muses. Florentius loved this

Cantelius with intense boyish ardor, due to the candor of his nature (especially since he had found him again beyond his expectation after so long a time), as is customary with those of his years, who are likely to conceive violent affections for certain acquaintances. For he had not yet learned to judge men's minds, but from his own feelings estimated others. . . .

"He betook himself to the monastery, which was not the one intended for him by his guardian, but the one where he had accidentally found his old associate. Now this place was so unsanitary and unhealthy that it was scarcely fit for raising cattle, much less for his delicate little body; but such tender years as his had not yet learned to discriminate in matters of food, climate, or locality. Besides, he had not betaken himself thither with the intention of joining the Order, but only that he might for a little while escape the clacking tongues until time itself might bring forth something better. Meanwhile Cantelius eagerly enjoyed his good fortune, taking advantage of the good nature and simplicity of his companion. For Florentius frequently and secretly by night would read to him a whole comedy of Terence, so that in a few months, as a result of their secret nocturnal sessions, they had finished the principal authors, but with a great risk to the boy's delicate constitution."[2]

Few readers of this second account by Erasmus, which was composed in the year 1517, will be able to keep from their minds a certain amount of suspicion; they are inclined to doubt the sincerity of Erasmus. In the year 1517 he was trying to obtain a dispensation which would free him for ever from the monastic vows and from the monastic habit. It was to his interest to describe his entrance in the monastery of Steyn in such a way as to prove that he had been fairly compelled to enter against his will. He thereby displays a trait in his character which removes him entirely from the principles of the Devotio Moderna, for selfishness and duplicity were extremely rare habits among the followers of Gerard Groote.

If the Grunnius letter were completely ignored, however, we should lose a very important source, and once again it becomes

[2] J. J. Mangan, *The Life, Character, and Influence of Desiderius Erasmus of Rotterdam*, I, 13–18.

necessary to search for facts which will reveal how far Erasmus
went in slandering others in order to save himself. Unfortunately
the sources do not flow freely. A chronicle giving the history of the
monastery of Steyn seems never to have been written, and the
obituaries have been lost, together with the charters and official
documents. Nevertheless there is enough left to tell what sort of
life Erasmus lived there, and what his fellow-monks were doing
most of the time.

The monastery of Steyn, as indicated above,[3] was founded in the
year 1419. It was frequently called Emmaus, because of its prox-
imity to Gouda, which was compared, though not very aptly, to
Jerusalem. Among its priors were the following: Joannes Nicolae
(1439–64), Joannes Christiani (1464–96), and Nicholaus Werneri
(1496–1504).[4] It belonged to the chapter of Sion, as Erasmus
stated, and ranked second to the monastery of Sion, according to a
document of the year 1444, in which a list of the members of this
chapter is given.[5] This chapter was formed early in the fifteenth
century.[6] The membership grew to fourteen, but internal conditions were far from satisfactory. By the year 1440 it looked as if
the congregation were nearing dissolution, but in 1444 the chapter
was founded anew. In the Act of Reunion of this year we read:
"Henceforth no convent of this chapter may accept or rescind
any privilege without general consent of the chapter, in order that
distrust and suspicion may be barred and internal peace restored." [7] Now followed a period of prosperity, and the number
of monasteries and convents affiliated with it grew to twenty-five.[8]
Cardinal Cusa in 1451 granted the chapter important privileges,
of which the most valuable was the one dated September 20, 1451,

---

[3] See p. 65. Cf. H. A. G. Vorstman, *Het Klooster Steyn of Emmaus bij Gouda*,
p. 329.

[4] H. F. van Heussen, *Historia Episc. Foed. Belgii*, I, 194. On p. 193 is a statement to the effect that Erasmus entered Steyn in 1487, which is undoubtedly
correct.

[5] MS no. 70 H 76, Royal Library, The Hague, fol. 6a.

[6] J. G. R. Acquoy, *Het Klooster te Windesheim en zijn Invloed* II, 35. The exact
date is not known.

[7] *Ibid.*, p. 37.

[8] R. C. H. Römer, *Kloosters en Abdijen van Holland en Zeeland* (Leiden, 1854),
I, 369–438.

whereby Pope Martin V placed the Chapter of Sion on the same footing with the great Congregation of Windesheim.[9]

It has often been stated, though without any justification, that the chapter of Sion used to belong to the chapter of Windesheim and later withdrew from it, or at least shaped its rules after those of Windesheim.[10] None of these assumptions is correct. Both chapters had much in common; Windesheim was older than Sion, and when in the year 1462 a constitution was framed for the chapter of Sion, the rules of Windesheim were consulted, just as Windesheim had examined the rules of other chapters. It should surprise no one that several chapters in the constitution of Sion are identical with those of Windesheim, for both had common origins. Both were subdivisions of the order of the Augustinian Canons Regular; Windesheim and Sion were sisters. They each led an independent existence, and none of the sources give any clue to intimate relationship, nor to substantial dependence of Sion on Windesheim.

Erasmus himself throws much light on conditions in the monastery of Steyn. The letters written by him in this monastery prove conclusively that he was reconciled for the time being with monasticism. His most important contribution to the subject is a treatise devoted to the praise of monasticism, which requires a separate chapter in the present work. A careful study of these sources shows that after Erasmus left the monastery, he developed an ever-increasing antagonism to the monastic life. Furthermore, it appears that flattery, fame, and honor deteriorated his character. Again, remarks made by him in 1517 about his brother Peter are sadly at variance with a letter addressed by him to this same brother when he was still in Steyn.

Even if we grant that Peter was a rascal and had not taken proper care of his younger brother, it is no credit to Erasmus when in 1517 he said to the head of the Roman Catholic Church that it

---

[9] MS 70 H 76, Royal Library, The Hague, fol. 7b–16a. The lesser privileges are mentioned on fol. 16a–20b.

[10] H. F. van Heussen was largely responsible for these erroneous reports, which, although fully exploded by Acquoy (*Het Klooster te Wind.*, II, 38–43), are still being copied. Even Allen, who is usually very careful, ignores the masterful work of Acquoy and repeats the view of Van Heussen (P. S. Allen, *Opus Ep. Er.*, I, 583).

were better if Peter had hanged himself. Shortly after Erasmus'
entry in Steyn, consequently after the so-called betrayal of
Erasmus by a modern Judas Iscariot, Erasmus wrote to him as
follows: "Have you quite thrown off the character of a brother?
Have you ceased altogether to care for your Erasmus? I write,
send, and send again. I expostulate, I enquire of those of your
house that come here, and find they have no letter and no message;
only they say you are safe and sound. Nothing is more cheering
for me to hear than that, but your part still remains unperformed.
You seem to be so resolved, that I think it would be an easier thing
to draw milk from a grindstone than anything like a letter from
you. But what has become, my Peter, of that original kindness of
yours, and of that love which was no ordinary love, but worthy of a
brother? Have you so soon passed from Mitio to Demeas? But
if your affection be estranged, I do not say by any fault of mine,
but by any suspicion of fault, I beseech you to accept my apology
at once; and as you never failed me in the hardest times, stick to
me now that Fortune, though not favorable, is less cruel.

"If you want to hear what I am doing, I love you greatly, as you
deserve, carry you on my lips and in my mind, think of you, dream
of you, have frequent talk about you with friends, and with none
more frequent, more familiar, or more pleasant than with our
countryman, Servatius, a young man of the brightest character,
and sweetest temper, and devoted to those studies which have
chiefly delighted both you and me from our boyhood. He wants
very much to see you." [11]

Further evidence of Erasmus' duplicity is found in the title of a
poem composed by William Herman of Gouda, an intimate friend
of Erasmus. The poem in question has the following superscription: "To the very accomplished and most learned gentleman,
Peter Gerard of Rotterdam, brother of Erasmus, On the Praise of
Friendship." This poem was edited by Erasmus himself, as
appears from the dedication by Erasmus to the bishop of Cambray,
dated Paris, November 7, 1496. There were altogether eighteen
poems by William Herman,[12] which he had intrusted to Erasmus

[11] F. M. Nichols, *op. cit.*, I, 42–43.
[12] The poem dedicated to Erasmus' brother is the seventeenth in the series. It

in 1496, when the latter visited Steyn. They were printed in
Paris in 1497 under the title of *Sylva Odarum* and were introduced
by a prefatory letter of Gaguin, the celebrated French humanist.
So in 1496 Erasmus was content to have his brother called "very
accomplished and most learned." Apparently Peter had not done
his younger brother much harm before 1496. The latter was furthermore still a friend of the Augustinian Canons Regular.

We may now proceed to examine a more important factor,
namely, the reasons why Erasmus became a monk. It will not do
to deprive the account of 1517 of all biographical value. Erasmus'
description of the ideals of the Brethren of the Common Life has
been shown to be largely true, wherefore it is likely that his narrative of subsequent events will contain many incontestable facts.
Emerton has justly remarked that "the biographers have not
tried in any consistent fashion to measure the character of Erasmus
as affecting the value of our sources of knowledge. If we should
reject, for example, the letter to Grunnius as a source of Erasmus'
early life, we should have very little left. If we should accept it as
history, we should be mingling fact and fancy in altogether uncertain proportions. The only safe method is, therefore, to try in each
case to weigh the value of the text before us with fullest reference
to all the circumstances." [13]

A great deal of pressure was unquestionably exerted upon Erasmus by Peter Winckel, the teacher at Gouda. Erasmus' brother
yielded early and went to Sion, but Erasmus hesitated for a long
time, probably during the whole winter of 1486–87. When the
period of grace was ended, Winckel and a banker were anxious to
have Erasmus take care of himself. His father's property had
largely disappeared and a prebend was not easily secured. Gerard,

---

was also included in a volume of poems by William Herman and Erasmus, printed
at Louvain in 1512, and edited by Adrian Barlandus (see fol. D⁴ verso to E¹ verso).
The title of the poem addressed by Herman to the brother of Erasmus reads here as
follows: "Carmen Saphicum ad Petrum Girardum Rotterdamum Erasmi germanum:
virum tum perhumanum: tum eruditissimum." Although the title is of some importance to the conscientious biographer, the opening lines of the poem, although
ignored as a rule, also have considerable significance, for they confirm the regard
felt by Herman for Peter: "Petre non paucis tua singularis Plurimum virtus:
placidique mores: Iure te gratum faciunt: amari Vis: et amare."

[13] E. Emerton, *Desiderius Erasmus of Rotterdam*, pp. xv–xvi.

the father, had disgraced himself and Winckel was not yet an influential person. Erasmus was weak physically. He did not like to work for a living. Begging was out of the question. What other course was open to him except a monastic career? In the monastery he would have leisure for study, he would be freed from financial worry, he would be safe from marauding soldiers. The country was torn by civil strife, but the monasteries were scarcely affected by the miseries which were spreading throughout Holland and Zeeland.

When Erasmus asserted that he was practically compelled to enter a monastery he was absolutely right. But by whom? By Winckel or the banker or the monks? No, only by a combination of circumstances. In 1487 he was at least eighteen years old; he knew very well what he was doing, and for several years after 1487 he was not sorry he had taken the decisive step. But when the monastery had given him all he asked and he was ready to leave, he saw to his chagrin that the monastic vows held him fast. They could not be broken, and that was the reason why in 1517 he remarked that it would have been far better for him if he had joined the Brethren of the Common Life at 's-Hertogenbosch.

Another factor which must be considered is the period of probation through which Erasmus passed; he had an opportunity to try monasticism for at least one year before he took the three vows. During that period he was on trial himself, and the monks of Steyn would have been very stupid if they had compelled him to remain among them against his will. What incentive could they have had to make him a monk if he disliked them, unless he was rich or of noble blood? But to make room for the illegitimate son of a priest without means was charitable on their part. Erasmus does not, therefore, blame them so much as his two guardians and a former schoolmate, named Cornelius of Woerden, whose native town was located a few miles west of Gouda. They influenced him, to be sure, but Erasmus was a coward to ascribe to them the responsibility for the step which he took in 1488 when he had finished the year of probation, or the novitiate.

Once a monk, Erasmus began to make the most of his opportunities. He had acquired a deep love for the classics before he returned to Gouda in 1486. Whether the example of Agricola and Hegius led to his study of Latin and Greek masters cannot be stated definitely, but he had undoubtedly acquired the habit at Deventer, wherefore he was disappointed with his teachers at 's-Hertogenbosch. In the letter to Grunnius he reports that "he did what imprisoned captives are wont to do: he solaced himself with his studies as far as this was allowed, for it had to be done secretly, though it was allowable to get drunk openly. Accordingly he relieved the tedium of his captivity with literature until some unlooked for chance — some god from the machine — should show him a hope of deliverance.

"The boy's tender body was so little inured to fasting that, if he deferred eating beyond his usual time, he was frequently in danger from atrocious pains in the stomach and fainting spells. Perchance greasy louts will laugh at this, fellows like sheep who will frisk if you feed them hay. But skilled physicans are well aware that this is peculiar to some constitutions, some refined organizations; hence they prescribe for them foods easily cooked, frequently and sparingly taken; although you may find others who, having once filled their bellies, can go without food longer than the vultures. Physicians tell us, too, that such constitutions are particularly sensitive to cold, winds, and dampness, and are more quickly affected by the weather around them than by food within them. The boy had another discomfort peculiar to his constitution, which had clung to him from childhood on, and which he could not overcome: he could not sleep until well into the night; and if he were once disturbed he could not go to sleep again for several hours. How often used he to deplore, in conversations with his friends, that he was prevented from enjoying those golden hours, and was compelled to lose the pleasantest part of the day in sleep! How often did he try to overcome his nature in this regard, but in vain! Occasionally he tried the plan of staying up all night supperless, but not without detriment to his health. Fish he so loathed that merely the smell of it would give him a severe headache and fever." [14]

In perusing these remarks of Erasmus one should try to be as

[14] J. J. Mangan, *op. cit.*, I, 19–20.

lenient with him as possible, for he was no match physically for the average monk at Steyn. How it must have annoyed him to see some of his fellow-monks enjoying a hearty meal, and how their phlegmatic natures must have enraged him! He was neurasthenic, as Mangan correctly observes: "Surely never was any boy more exposed to the causes which make for neurasthenia — the prenatal anxiety of his mother, due to her uncertain relations with his father, the early loss of his parents, mental overwork, lack of exercise from sedentary occupation, unfavorable psychic influences due to the uncertainty of his future — all these were well calculated to undermine his nervous poise and lessen his emotional control. Hence his intense likes and dislikes, his morbid sensitiveness, his selfishness, his constant demands for sympathy, his self-centred attitude, his egotism, his readiness to speak ill of his nearest and dearest for some real or imaginary injury, all these and other defects not here mentioned point to the fact that he was a victim of chronic nerve exhaustion, which has been so often the curse of men of genius." [15]

Be this as it may, Erasmus had much reason in 1517 to feel dissatisfied with some phases of monasticism. The monastery was a terrible place for a young man who was not suited for a monastic career. It was not always possible for a youth of eighteen who was attracted by the leisure offered to him in a monastery to discover in one year whether it would meet his needs for a lifetime. Erasmus often read for hours at night, for he dared not be seen devouring the classics. Very few of the monks in Steyn shared his love for classical literature, wherefore Erasmus thought them stupid. He was bright, and many of them were dull. They enjoyed their duties for the most part, but he had not come to perform duties. They had a vocation, namely, the monastic career, a life devoted to spiritual exercises; Erasmus, on the other hand, wanted time for study. They spent many hours in reading, singing, and praying, which he thought mostly a waste of time. They misunderstood Erasmus and he was not broad-minded enough to admit that they had as much right to go their way as he had to follow his own.

[15] *Ibid.*, p. 38.

The letters written by Erasmus between 1486 and 1493 reveal a fact which requires a little emphasis. Contrary to the narrative of 1517 or of 1521, Erasmus did not find the monastery a very bad place. He had obtained an opportunity of studying the ancients and was able to improve his Latin style. Occasionally he was actually merry, for he afterward wrote to William Herman of Gouda: "What was there at Steyn so dear to me, that it has not among these mischances been lost in oblivion? You have yourself seen me at times playing the youngster, and have often laughed." [16] This friend of Erasmus was a great comfort to him in Steyn. He was a native of Gouda and had studied at Deventer under Hegius, as is proved by the title of a hitherto unpublished poem in MS 1323 of the City Library at Gouda.[17]

That Erasmus was fond of William Herman appears from the following remark in a letter to the bishop of Cambray, introducing the *Sylva Odarum* of Herman, which was printed in Paris in 1497: "William of Gouda, who from my earliest youth has been my Patroclus or my Pirithoüs, my one sweetest companion in everything and especially in liberal studies, is now the first and highest hope of our country of Holland; which formerly, neglected and untilled, grew nothing but briars and thistles and weeds, but has begun at last to produce a harvest worthy of Italy. A train of circumstances has led to the first fruits of this harvest being offered in sacrifice to your name. When some time ago I was staying several days with this friend in order to complete the recovery of my health, among many subjects of familiar and delightful conversation he discovered and brought out some Odes which had been the amusement of his youth, but only to submit them to my censure with a view to their destruction." [18]

William Herman was of the same age as Erasmus; at least a composition entitled *Certamen Erasmi et Guielmi* states that it was composed when they were both nineteen.[19] Their friendship lasted several years, but after the year 1500, when Erasmus was

---

[16] F. M. Nichols, *op. cit.*, I, 179.

[17] The poem begins on fol. 10 verso and the title is: "Carmen Guielmi Hermani agentis gratias praeceptori suo Alexandro Hegio: Praecantisque illi leta et prospera omnia."

[18] F. M. Nichols, *op. cit.*, I, 119.   [19] Erasmus, *Opera*, VIII, 565.

rapidly advancing to the position of intellectual dictator of Europe, and Herman failed to keep pace with him, Erasmus grew indifferent. For the period of about one year he was transferred to a monastery in Haarlem, but returned to Steyn in or after 1490.[20]

Another friend of Erasmus who had been brought up at Gouda was Cornelius Gerard, a more learned monk than William Herman, whose correspondence with Erasmus forms the most important source of information on Erasmus' stay in Gouda next to the two prose writings which will be analyzed below. Cornelius Gerard (also named Cornelius Aurelius, because he was from Gouda, and the Dutch word *goud* means "gold") was a cousin of William Herman, for they addressed each other as *nepos* in their letters. Cornelius was probably educated at Deventer although not under Hegius, since he appears to have been older than Erasmus.[21] He was not an inmate of Steyn, but between 1488 and 1497 he was residing in an Augustinian monastery at Lopsen, near Leiden, which was a member of the Congregation of Windesheim.[22]

No monk at Steyn appreciated Erasmus' literary tastes so much as did Cornelius Aurelius. It is even possible that he taught Erasmus a good deal, since he was Erasmus' senior and was called the tutor of Erasmus by Alardus of Amsterdam in the latter's Preface to the *Batavia* of Aurelius. His correspondence with William Herman sounds not a bit monkish; it is almost entirely devoted to classical studies. And although he did not so enthusiastically laud the works of Lorenzo Valla as did his friend Erasmus, nevertheless a letter of his was printed in Cologne with Erasmus' Paraphrase on Valla's *Elegantiae*.[23] He says on one occasion to Erasmus: "I hope you will not be angry with me for having altered here and there a very few words in your verses, and changed the metre toward the end." [24]

To Cornelius Aurelius Erasmus could freely express his love for the classics. He had as yet risen very little above the level of the

[20] P. S. Allen, *Opus Ep. Er.*, I, 128.
[21] *Ibid.*, p. 92.
[22] P. C. Molhuysen, *Cornelius Aurelius* (1903), pp. 4–22.
[23] This was the edition of 1529 printed by Gymnich. The letter by Aurelius was addressed to John Berius, a teacher at Rotterdam.
[24] F. M. Nichols, *op. cit.*, I, 63.

other pupils of Hegius and still spoke of them in terms of the highest praise. But at the same time he added: "If we come to Italy, where do you find more observance of ancient elegance than in Laurentius Valla or Philelphus; where more eloquence than in Aeneas Silvius, Augustinus Dathus, Guarino, Poggio, or Gasperino? Our Thalia was well-nigh extinct when Laurentius and Philelphus by their admirable erudition saved her from perishing." [25] In another letter he wrote: "My authorities in poetry are Maro, Horace, Naso, Juvenal, Statius, Martial, Claudian, Persius, Lucan, Tibullus, and Propertius; in prose, Tully, Quintilian, Sallust, Terence. Then for the observation of elegances, there is no one in whom I have so much confidence as Laurentius Valla, who is unrivalled both in the sharpness of his intelligence and the tenacity of his memory." [26]

A very interesting dispute broke out relative to the prestige and merits of Valla. When Erasmus urged his friend to read this celebrated humanist, Aurelius replied at first: "In begging me so urgently to read L. Valla, you amuse as well as edify me. . . . Are you right then in committing me to one who is denounced by the whole world as a defamer? So far in jest. How much I have in fact profited by his books . . . you may judge . . . by the fluent style I now write." [27] But Erasmus doubted whether Aurelius was appreciating Valla, for he wrote next: "Upon what you say about our Valla, I put this interpretation, that you do not express your real opinion, but write either to practice the facility of your pen in defending a paradox, or to supply me with a subject to write about. . . . To Valla's guidance you will safely commit yourself. When you do so, you will find that your writings will acquire no little polish, — unless perhaps you are preparing to write for Dutchmen only." [28]

A little later it appeared that Aurelius showed little respect for Valla, wherefore Erasmus said: "You describe Valla as 'a Croaking Crow,' a jester and not an orator. . . . Lastly you will put at my disposal your books, of which you have a good store, and over

---

[25] F. M. Nichols, *op. cit.* I, 66–67.
[26] *Ibid.*, p. 64.
[27] *Ibid.*, p. 69.
[28] *Ibid.*, pp. 70–71.

which you sit like some Hesperian dragon." [29]   It should be observed that the books recommended by Erasmus were not found in the libraries of the chapters of Sion and Windesheim.   Hence the budding humanist in the monasteries at Steyn and Lopsen had to resort to clandestine methods.

The ecclesiastical authorities were especially bitter against Valla, who was accused of immorality.   When Aurelius pointed this out to Erasmus and added that Poggio, one of Valla's adversaries, was deemed a better man than Valla, Erasmus took up the cudgels for the latter in writing: "Poggio — a brawler so illiterate, who even if he lacked obscenity would not be worth reading, but so obscene that, even if he were most learned, yet ought to be rejected by all good men — he, I say, just as if he were a noble fellow, and popular, is in everybody's hands and, translated into every language, is read and re-read.   Valla, who is not obscene and is a hundredfold more learned, rests under the imputation of being mordant and sarcastic, and is avoided as a dangerous fellow, even by those who have never read the writings of the man." [30]

The question has been asked by some biographers whether Erasmus in 1490 or 1491, when he was defending Valla so warmly, was actually acquainted with the writings and the character of Lorenzo Valla.   It is unlikely that he had read all of Valla's writings; he referred frequently to the *Elegantiae*, and this may have been all he knew, but Hegius had read the notorious dialogue, *On Pleasure*, with approval, wherefore it may very easily have been accessible to Erasmus.   As for Valla's private life, this cannot have been known to his defender in the Netherlands, else his admiration would have moderated considerably.   If one grants that the speaker in the dialogue *On Pleasure*, who recommended that all women should appear on the streets undressed so that men might enjoy the scenery, and asserted that prostitutes were more useful than nuns — if this speaker did not represent Valla's point of view, which is still an open question, then Valla was nevertheless showing considerable interest in the speaker's propositions.   After the year

[29] *Ibid.*, pp. 72–73.
[30] J. J. Mangan, *op. cit.*, I, 196–197: for the Latin, see Allen, *op. cit.*, I, 409, no. 182, lines 87–94.

1500 Erasmus still supported Valla and in some of his *Colloquies* followed a method similar to that of Valla. Many of the editions of Erasmus' *Colloquies* do not, therefore, reproduce the obscene selections.

In order to understand fully to how great a degree Erasmus was drifting away from the principles of the Devotio Moderna before he left Steyn, it will be necessary to examine his correspondence with Servatius Rogerius of Rotterdam, a fellow-monk at Steyn, and afterward prior of that monastery. The name of this young monk has been mentioned before in a quotation from a letter by Erasmus to his brother Peter.[31] In the same letter Erasmus remarked: "If you will, as I hope, come to see us before long, you will not only esteem him worthy of your friendship, but will easily like him better than your brother; he is a person that no one can help loving. For this reason I am more disposed to ask you to lend him that small copy you have of Juvenal's *Satires*. Do not fear, my Peter; you will never confer a favor on a better object. You will find him grateful, and he will not forget it."

Erasmus conceived for Servatius a curious fancy which is very puzzling, for if one takes the letters seriously which Erasmus addressed to Servatius, one must conclude that Erasmus was extremely neurotic at the time. Contrary to the advice of the Brethren of the Common Life, who warned against sentimentality and frowned on very intimate friendship; contrary also to the teachings of the *Imitation of Christ* and of the Devotio Moderna as a whole, he indulged in a form of literature which cannot have failed to repulse the person to whom it was dedicated. We shall never know how much of it was mere letter writing, but it will be advisable to accept the verdict of Allen and Pineau and Mangan to the effect that Erasmus was giving expression to affection. He felt the need of confiding in someone, since most of his associates did not understand him. So he composed a series of epistles which throw light on his character. Erasmus was ashamed of them afterward and never published them.

"I should write more frequently to you," says Erasmus on one occasion, "very dearest Servatius, if I knew for certain that you

[31] See p. 151.

would not be more fatigued by reading my letters than I by writing them. And your comfort is so dear to me, that I had rather be tortured by what gives you rest, than fatigue you by what gives me pleasure. But since lovers find nothing so distressing as not to be allowed to meet one another, and we very rarely have that in our power, I cannot forego the opportunity of bidding this letter find its way to you in my stead. How I wish it may be some time our fortune to have no further need of letters, but to be able to meet face to face as often as we please. That joy is denied us; I cannot think of it without tears; but am I therefore to be deprived of all intercourse with you?" [32]

In another letter we find the following statements: "When my love for you, my dearest Servatius, has always been and still is so great, that you are dearer to me than these eyes, than this soul, than this self, what is it that has made you so inexorable that you not only do not love, but have no regard at all for him who loves you best? Are you so inhuman as to love those that hate, and hate those that love you? When you are away, nothing is sweet to me; in your presence I care for nothing else. When I see you happy, I forget my own sorrows; if anything painful has occurred to you, so help me Heaven, if my pain is not greater than your own. Has this crime deserved so much hatred as you show me? But now, my Servatius, I am not unaware what reply you will make to me. It is what you often answer. You will say, 'What on earth do you require me to do for you? Do I hate you? What is it you want?' Can you ask this question? I demand no costly presents. Only let your feeling for me be as mine is for you, and you will make me happy.

"Farewell, my soul, and if there is anything human in you, return the love of him who loves you." [33]

That Erasmus was doing more than exercising his pen is clear from these words: "I left nothing untried by which a young mind might be affected, but harder than adamant you still persist in your resolve.

"Yesterday, my Servatius, I should have come to you to offer you some comfort, if I had not known that my very presence is

---

[32] F. M. Nichols, *op. cit.*, I, 46–47. [33] *Ibid.*, pp. 47–48.

disagreeable to you. I saw your looks were altered, your eyes cast
down, your complexion sad, and all your gestures portended some
sorrow. . . . My William, since you shrink from me, will be in
everything an assistance and comfort to you. I shall remind him
without fail to take pains to be so. Farewell." [34]

There is one letter, however, which proves that style was an
important element in this peculiar correspondence. "Do not
write in your own way," says Erasmus here, "with borrowed
sentences, or even what is worse, heaping up expressions, here
out of Bernard and there out of Claudian, and fitting them or
rather unfitly sewing them on to your own, as a crow might do
with a peacock's feathers. . . . You need not be ashamed of
barbarisms, if any such should occur; you shall have from us
correction, and not ridicule." [35] The tone adopted here by
Erasmus is that of a tutor, and the surmise is justified that Servatius was younger than he and had not been in the monastery
as long as had Erasmus. These facts will be mentioned again
in connection with the discussion of Erasmus' *De Contemptu
Mundi*.

In the year 1514, when Servatius was prior at Steyn and com-
manded Erasmus to return to his monastery, the latter wrote a
memorable epistle, containing autobiographical notes similar to
those in the letter to Grunnius, but also different.[36] In this letter
Erasmus could not very well resort to a fanciful tale, wherefore its
value as a source of Erasmus' stay in the monastery is considerable. Erasmus is more careful here in his criticism of the monks
at Steyn. About his entrance in the monastery he remarks: "But
someone will say, 'What about the year of probation (as they call
it), and the age of maturity?' that is ridiculous. As if one should
demand that a boy in his seventeenth year, especially educated
to literature, should know himself, which is a great thing in an old
man; or as if he could learn in one year what many grey-haired
men do not yet understand."

Erasmus' attack on the habits of some of the monks at Steyn is

[34] F. M. Nichols, *op. cit.*, I, 48–49.
[35] *Ibid.*, p. 51.
[36] See P. S. Allen, *op. cit.*, I, no. 296.

very significant. "The desire for money," he continues, "never attracted me, nor am I affected by the wish for glory. Although formerly I was inclined to pleasures, I never was a slave to them. Wine-bibbing and drunkenness I always detested and avoided. As often as I meditated on associating myself once more with you, there recurred to my mind the envy of many of you, and the contempt of everybody, how dull, how tasteless, and how far from savoring of Christ was the conversation and how unmonastic the meals; in a word, the entire routine of the life, from which if you take away the ceremonial, I fail to see what you have left that is desirable. Finally, there recurred to my mind the frailness of my health, so increased by age, sickness, and hard work, that I could no longer satisfy you, and would only destroy myself. For some years past I am subject to gravel, a surely severe and mortal disease. For some years past also I drink only wine, and this only of certain kinds, compelled thereto by my malady. I cannot bear every sort of food, nor even every kind of climate, for this disease of mine recurs very easily, and demands the greatest moderation in my mode of living; and I know the Dutch climate, and I know too how you eat, not to say anything at all about your customs. So that if I were to return to you I would have accomplished nothing except to cause trouble to you and death to myself." [37]

How different is the appeal to Pope Leo X in the letter to Grunnius: "In this way Florentius, the victim of so many machinations, was forced into the religious state, ever struggling and loudly protesting against it still; but his conscience was free; and it seems to me, that he is no more held by his vow than if he were to give his word to pirates threatening him with death. Nor do I doubt but that, with his usual sense of justice, the Sovereign Pontiff will be as indignant with these kidnappers as he will be favorably inclined towards the case of their victim."

It is clear that Erasmus was not happy in the monastery of Steyn after he had spent a few years there. Since he arrived during the winter of 1486–87 and left about six years later, one may assume that from 1487 to 1490 he was fairly content with monasticism, but became more and more dissatisfied with every passing

[37] J. J. Mangan, *op. cit.*, I, 362.

month. The library had many good books, but not the kind in which he was interested. He wanted to read classical writers, not patristic literature. There had been a time when he enjoyed reading Augustine and Jerome. At Deventer and 's-Hertogenbosch he was exhorted to study the Bible, the *Imitation of Christ*, and the Church Fathers. For many years Christian literature had seemed to him the finest flower of the human intellect, but between 1490 and 1493, as well as during the six following years, his chief interest lay in the revival of classical scholarship.

The more Erasmus was estranged from the ideals of the Devotio Moderna, the more discontented he grew in the monastery. What cared he now for self-denial, obedience, discipline, fasting, brotherly love, poverty, chastity, and humility? He wanted a polished style, time for study, freedom from mental and physical restraint, good food, pleasant surroundings, travel, refined and elegant society, and fame.

Many biographers of Erasmus have wondered what sort of library the monastery of Steyn possessed. Erasmus frequently complained about the dullness of his fellow-monks. He alleged that one could study only secretly, while it was permitted to gorge oneself at the table and get drunk. Fortunately an inventory was made of the books in the library at Steyn by the magistrates of Gouda after the monastery had been dissolved. The list was drawn up in a slovenly and chaotic fashion, and has never been published. It is too long to be given here, but a few notes will be sufficient to show why Erasmus in 1492 was dissatisfied with the library of his monastery.

In the year 1549 the monastery of Steyn was destroyed by fire and its occupants removed to Gouda. The city surrendered in 1572 to the forces of William of Orange, whereupon much ecclesiastic property was confiscated. But the monks of Steyn were allowed to keep their books. In 1599 only two survivors were left, namely, H. J. Blij and C. A. Diephorst. When Blij passed away in 1599 the magistrates had a list drawn up of the books found in his home. In 1631 Diephorst died and ten years later a catalogue of his books was made at the order of the magistrates. It appeared that a part of these books had formerly belonged to the Brethren of the Common Life at Gouda, and the others to the monks of Steyn.[38]

Although some of the books listed as having come from the library at Steyn were added after Erasmus' departure, one can at least form an estimate of the spirit which permeated the house in his time. From the writings of Erasmus himself the monastery selected those which expressed congenial views, for example, the *Handbook of the Christian Knight*, a work entitled *On the Mercy of God*, the *Annotations on the New Testament*, the *Commentary on the Gospel of Mark*, and the *De Ratione Concionandi*. (There was a period in Erasmus' life when the old ideals formed at Deventer returned, augmented by the stimulus received from newly won friends.) There were also, naturally, several copies of the Bible. Works by St. Augustine were listed thirteen times, by Chrysostom nine times, and by Jerome two times; there were compositions by Origen, Bede, Basil, Gregory, Anthony, Boethius, and Bernard; also a large number by ecclesiastical writers of lesser note. As for the classics, these were not nearly so numerous, though not altogether neglected. Terence was mentioned three times, and productions by Euripides, Aesop, Cicero, Sallust, Pliny the Younger, Valerius Maximus, Justinus, and Aulus Gellius were also included; furthermore, a number of contributions were cited by such humanists as Politiano, Ficino, Angelo, Reuchlin, Clichtow, Despauterius, and John de Monte-Regio. The name of Lorenzo Valla, however, does not appear any more than that of Poggio or Benvenuto Cellini, or any other humanist who was considered irreligious or hostile to the Church. It is rather surprising that Reuchlin was read at Steyn, for he was at one time regarded as an enemy of the higher ecclesiastical authorities. Otherwise the list of books is exactly what one would have expected of an Augustinian monastery. It was similar to the list given by John Busch concerning the library of the monastery of Windesheim.[39] The latter mentioned no classical productions because it was drawn up shortly

---

[38] L. A. Kesper, *De Oorsprong der Librye*, in *Dagblad van Gouda*, August 12, 13, 14, 1912.

[39] See K. O. Meinsma, *Middeleeuwsche Bibliotheken* (Amsterdam, 1902), pp. 284–288.

before 1460. It will be safe to say, therefore, that the monastery of Steyn, at the time Erasmus resided there, contained not more than one half of the classical and humanistic works listed in the catalogue prepared for the municipal government of Gouda. It confirms much of Erasmus' criticism.

One more phase of Erasmus' activity in Steyn requires mention here, namely, the pictures he drew. In a letter addressed to a friend named Sasboud, Erasmus remarked: "I do not see what flowers you mean, unless it may be that little book, in which I painted some flowers for you when we were together." [40] For many decades there was a tradition in the city of Delft according to which Erasmus had painted a picture of Christ on the Cross, with Mary and St. John. In the seventeenth century several writers at Delft referred to this picture, asserting that it had been on exhibition there for some time. [41] It should be noted, however, that in the letter to Sasboud, Erasmus had also said this: "But I beg you, Sasboud, to beware of so devoting yourself to this art of Painting as to give up your interest in Letters. . . . If I were not prevented by the limits of time and of this letter, I could mention a great number of persons, and those of our own body, who having seen what glory is gained by Letters and what shame by ignorance, feel the deepest regret when they see too late that the season of youth, which is adapted to study, has slipped between their fingers." Again this insistence on the study of classical literature. No, Erasmus cannot have devoted much of his time to painting. For him it was a mere diversion, and as such it should be regarded by his biographers, who will testify that all the writings produced by Erasmus in his youth revealed his devotion, first to religion and then to classical scholarship.

[40] F. M. Nichols, *op. cit.*, I, p. 55.
[41] M. Brockwell, *Erasmus, Humanist and Painter.*

CHAPTER XIV

ERASMUS PRAISES MONASTICISM

THERE was a time in Erasmus' life when he was pleased with monasticism. This period fell between his return to Gouda at the end of 1486 and the year 1489 or 1490, or perhaps even a trifle later. We would know very little about this period had it not been for a treatise composed by Erasmus, entitled *On the Contempt of the World*, which has been practically ignored by nearly all his biographers, although as a source it outranks all the letters written at Steyn that have survived.[1]

In the catalogue of his writings addressed to J. Botzheim in the year 1523, Erasmus asserted that he had written the treatise *On the Contempt of the World* when he was barely twenty years old,[2] but in the Preface of the earlier editions he put his age at twenty-four years. From the content it appears that it was composed shortly after the author had become a monk at Steyn, hence in 1488 or 1489, when he was, as he admitted to Botzheim in 1523, barely twenty years old, and before experience had disillusioned him.

The treatise in question resembled Erasmus' letters to Servatius Rogerius in that their author was extremely sorry afterward that he had written it. In the year 1521, when the more zealous friends of Erasmus reminded him of the fact that he had not always been hostile to monasticism, and pointed out to him that copies of the treatise written at Steyn were being put into circulation, he decided to publish the work himself. He added a most interesting Preface, which the earlier copies naturally did not contain. For this reason not all the printed editions have this Preface. There

---

[1] One very rare exception is Pineau, in whose *Érasme* a whole chapter is devoted to the *De Contemptu Mundi*.

[2] P. S. Allen, *Opus Ep. Er.*, I, 18, lines 16–19.

is one, for example, printed at Leiden in 1641 by John Maire, which opens directly with the first chapter. Furthermore, the twelfth or last chapter of the treatise is so different in tone from all the others that it was unquestionably added by Erasmus at the time the treatise was published by him. The only part of the treatise written at Steyn was, therefore, the text of the first eleven chapters. The other parts are extraneous matter.

It was a most common thing for a young monk at the end of the Middle Ages to write on the contempt of the world. Dozens of compositions with such a title had already issued from the pens of other monks. St. Bernard and Pope Innocent III had written such treatises, and so had Petrarch and Richard de Ryckel. Thomas à Kempis had composed a dialogue by that name and the first chapter of the *Imitation* was entitled, "Of the Imitation of Christ, and Contempt of all the Vanities of the World." The Brethren of the Common Life emphasized the folly of seeking happiness in earthly things. Nothing was more natural, therefore, for Erasmus than to compose a work in praise of the monastic life, in which he expressed some of the ideals of the Devotio Moderna. It was just as logical for him to laud monasticism in 1488 as it was to write some poems in praise of classical antiquity. During his last year at Deventer he had been strongly affected by the teachings of the Brethren of the Common Life. When he lived at 's-Hertogenbosch, his mind was still very plastic. It imbibed for two years and a half the principles enunciated in the *Imitation of Christ*, so that, when he returned to Gouda, he was fully prepared to renounce worldly ambitions and to seek a retreat in the monastery.

Although the Augustinian Canons Regular were not noted for ascetic tendencies, since they appreciated the value of good meals and rest, they nevertheless professed to devote their lives to spiritual exercises. In Steyn also the monks had a real vocation, namely, the cultivation of such virtues as chastity, obedience, self-abnegation, humility, brotherly love, and honesty. They did not strive after personal property, fame, and honor. In other words, their business was to despise the world and to seek heavenly things. Contempt of the world was their motto, at least in theory.

When Erasmus discovered after 1487 that some of his associates did love the flesh and were indolent, his ardor cooled. But before 1488 his dreams had not yet been shattered.

The treatise by Erasmus seems to have been addressed to a certain Jodocus, whom Erasmus names cousin or nephew only at the beginning and the end of the composition. Since the final chapter was not found in the original draft, the end of that chapter is of no importance. Moreover, in the edition of 1641 by Maire the usual title is lacking above the first chapter. Here the word *nepos* does not occur at all, and it is safe to presume that Jodocus was no cousin or nephew of Erasmus.

By the year 1521 Erasmus had already told a great many deliberate lies. His chief concern had become to safeguard his own interests. He did not want his enemies to know that at one time he had favored monasticism. So he had to practice a little more deception. He hit upon a scheme which, although not clever, misled some of his adversaries. Anyone who compares the twelfth chapter of the treatise in question, which is an attack on monasticism, with the preceding chapters can at once detect a striking contradiction.[3] Erasmus must have thought his readers very stupid if he imagined they would fail to discover his duplicity. Then he added another trick. He claimed to have written the treatise at the request of an individual, named Theodore of Haarlem, who wished to induce his nephew, Jodocus, to enter a monastery. So the treatise was intended for his nephew and Erasmus did not express in it his own views, but those of Theodore of Haarlem, who was trying to make a proselyte for the monks. Poor, innocent Erasmus had been the tool of a wicked man.

The superscription of the printed edition of Erasmus is, therefore, "Theodore of Haarlem to his Nephew Jodocus," but, as was mentioned above, the edition by Maire, of 1641, does not have either this title or the Preface. In the catalogue of 1523, also alluded to above, Erasmus alleges that he wrote the treatise for a friend who wanted to make his nephew a monk. Perhaps some readers might suggest that one has no right to doubt the truthful-

---

[3] J. L. de Burigni, *Vie d'Érasme*, I, 44. Many other writers since de Burigni have noted this discrepancy.

ness of Erasmus' statements.   Might not Erasmus have written it
when he had returned to Gouda at the end of 1486? [4] It is not
fair to suspect Erasmus of telling lies until one finds repeated
evidence of such actions.   This evidence is unfortunately found on
every hand after Erasmus left the monastery of Steyn.   Tem-
porarily at least his character was suffering from his great ambitions. He loved no one but himself; he felt no scruples whatsoever
about deliberately deceiving his own friends, as may be gathered
from two letters written by him on the same day (January 27,
1501), one to an intimate friend named James Batt,[5] the other to
Anna of Borselen, Lady of Veere, whose protégé he was.[6]

In the epistle directed to the affluent lady, Erasmus graciously
wrote: "Three Annas were known to the ancients; the sister of
Dido, whom the Muses of the Romans have consecrated to
immortality; the wife of Elkanah, with whose praises Jewish
records resound; and the mother of the Virgin, who is the object
of Christian worship. Would that my poor talents might avail,
that posterity may know of your piety and snow-white purity,
and count you the fourth member of this glorious band. It was no
mere chance that conferred upon you this name, making your
likeness to them complete. Were they noble? So are you. Did
they excel in piety? Yours, too, redounds to heaven. Were they
steadfast in affliction? Alas that here, too, you are constrained to
resemble them. Yet in my sorrow comfort comes from this
thought, that God sends suffering to bring strength. Affliction it
was that made the courage of Hercules, of Aeneas, of Ulysses
shine forth, that proved the patience of Job." After a great deal
more in this strain, he concludes: "I send you a poem to St. Anne
and some prayers to address the Virgin. She is ever ready to hear
the prayers of virgins, and you I count not a widow, but a virgin.
That when only a child you consented to marry, was mere defer-
ence to the bidding of your parents and the future of your race;
and your wedded life was a model of patience. That now, when
still no more than a girl, you repel so many suitors is further proof

---

[4] P. S. Allen (*Opus*, IV, introd. to Ep. 1194) suggests, for example, the time
before Erasmus entered the monastery.

[5] P. S. Allen, *op. cit.*, Ep. 146, I, 346–349.   [6] *Ibid.*, Ep. 145, I, 342–346.

of your maiden heart. If, as I confidently presage, you persevere in this high course, I shall count you not amongst the eighty concubines of Solomon, but, with (I am sure) the approval of Jerome, among the fifty queens." [7]

Contrasted with this brazen flattery is the following remark found in the letter to Batt: "If she neglects her affairs, need you feel solicitous? If she dallies and trifles with her friend N., need you be angry? Has she nothing left to give? I see this one thing plainly, that, if she gives nothing now for such reasons as these, she will never give anything in future, because such excuses are never lacking to the great. Were she to give me the trifling sum of two hundred francs, to be counted in with the immense amount that she is dissipating, I suppose it would be a matter of great moment? She has the wherewithal to support those cowled leeches, those scoundrelly idlers — you know whom I mean — and has she not enough to maintain in leisure a man who may write books worthy of posterity, if I may be permitted to boast a little about myself? She has fallen into many difficulties, no doubt, but by her own fault, since she preferred to attach to her skirts that handsome popinjay rather than some grave and sedate personage, as was becoming to her sex and age." [8]

It may not seem kind to reveal the double-dealings of a neurasthenic mind, but the truth is that Erasmus was too much of a humanist to adhere to the simple tenets of the Christian faith. He is said to have been greatly affected by Colet, who as a man was far superior to Erasmus, but neither Colet nor any other friend could restore to Erasmus' mind the homely virtues once acquired at Deventer. This is the reason why one must weigh so carefully his statements about the years spent in the monastery. Almost everything connected with the period of his childhood and youth seemed revulsive to him after the year 1514. The Dutch people, the Dutch climate, the Brethren of the Common Life, and the monks at Steyn were all held responsible for the experiences which afterward annoyed him.

[7] P. S. Allen, *The Age of Erasmus*, pp. 131–132.

[8] J. J. Mangan, *The Life, Character, and Influence of Desiderius Erasmus of Rotterdam*, I, 156.

One fact remains; there is the person addressed constantly as Jodocus in the treatise *On the Contempt of the World*. Who was this individual, and was his real name Jodocus? A French writer has recently suggested that he was probably William Herman of Gouda, who seems to have entered Steyn later than Erasmus.[9] An American author, on the other hand, has thought of Servatius Rogerius.[10] The arguments produced by both biographers seem plausible and it is very difficult to choose between them. Servatius came from Rotterdam, and William from Gouda; so did Erasmus. Both were of about the same age. Servatius, as suggested in an earlier chapter,[11] may have been a relative of Erasmus, because Erasmus' surname was given by Pope Leo X as Rogerii, or Rogerius in the nominative case, exactly the same as that of Servatius. Leo X called the subject of our study "Erasmus Rogerius of Rotterdam," while the young monk on whom Erasmus bestowed so much affection in the monastery was named Servatius Rogerius of Rotterdam. The two monks may, therefore, have been cousins. But the difficulty encountered in this argument is that, when Erasmus introduced Servatius to his brother Peter, he did not hint at any relationship by blood. He simply said that Servatius was from their native Rotterdam. Peter may on the other hand have been unaware of the existence of cousins in Rotterdam. After all the two brothers were of natural birth and therefore could hardly claim to have any cousins. Since Erasmus does speak of a *nepos*, which word sometimes meant cousin, although usually it stood for nephew, there seems more likelihood of Servatius having been the person addressed in the treatise.[12]

Perhaps a detailed analysis of this composition will throw further light on the relation between the author and the recipient. The Preface, added in 1521, may be translated as follows: "I have often complained, dear reader, of being the victim of the zeal of my friends. While I am still living and in spite of my protests, they circulate among the public some trifling pieces with which I amused myself while a mere boy in practicing the art of composition, never

---

[9] J. B. Pineau, *Érasme*, p. 31, note 5.
[10] J. J. Mangan, *op. cit.*, II, 63.
[11] See p. 56.
[12] See pp. 160–162.

dreaming that they would fall into the hands of men. I am, therefore, more concerned over this situation in this happy age because
they would have been less liable to the ridicule of the people had
they been printed at the time they were first composed.

"A long time ago — I was scarcely twenty [13] — at the malicious
request of a man who is still in this world, I wrote a letter through
which he expected to persuade his nephew Jodocus to embrace the
same mode of life as his own. Many copies of this letter have been
made, and it is circulated under my name, although I have no
nephew named Jodocus. I wrote it indifferently and with negligence, as one can readily see; it is a collection of common sayings;
I had not yet read good authors. The printers were threatening
to publish it if I did not do it myself. So I have just read it over
again, making a few slight revisions, and I have permitted it to
go to the printer. In doing this I hope that some day people will
cease being so passionately interested in the trifles of my youth.
Farewell, dear reader; if you read these things, do so with indul-
gence and in the spirit in which they were written, that is, in a
bad humor."

On the title-page of the early editions there is a statement to the
effect that Theodore of Haarlem, for whom Erasmus was said to
have composed the letter, or treatise, happened to belong to the
Augustinian Canons Regular.[14] It is certain, therefore, that the
young man addressed in the letter was exhorted to join the order
to which Erasmus himself belonged. But whether this Theodore of
Haarlem was a real person is by no means clearly proved by remarks of Erasmus. If he had mentioned this monk in the body of
the treatise, it would have been quite another matter. Even the
name Jodocus is probably fictitious. All we know is that Erasmus
praised monasticism to a young man with whom he had been
intimately acquainted for some time. It is impossible to determine who he was.

The tone of the treatise is serious, not like that of a mere exercise

[13] In the text (Chap. VII) he says that he is about 24 years old. It is possible
that in 1488 or 1489 he thought he was born in 1465.

[14] The Cologne edition of 1523 has this statement: "Theodoria Harlemei Canonia
ordinis divi Augustini." Allen (*Opus Ep. Er.*, IV, 457) thinks that "Theodore of
Haarlem was no doubt a real person."

in rhetoric. It is scholarly, but convincing withal. If Erasmus himself had not been convinced of the advantage offered by a monastic career, it is difficult to understand why he wrote so earnestly. Only a consummate actor could have simulated the conviction expressed in every one of the eleven chapters. The first chapter is a sort of introduction. "For quite a while," writes Erasmus, "I have been thinking of writing you about so delicate a subject as the monastic life, but I hesitated, not so much because of negligence as of fear. But finally I chose to act, for is it not right that your well-being should be as near to my heart as is my own?" In the year 1488 or 1489 this question seemed to him of the utmost importance. The monastery was a place where his friend could live a pious life and so help to save his soul. Afterward this composition may well have seemed a trifle to the sophisticated Erasmus, but in the first months at Steyn he expected much from monasticism.

Erasmus appears to feel much affection for Jodocus. It might seem arrogant, he says, to urge his friend to join him, but love impels him to act. He talks as he does in the letters to Servatius and one wonders whether Jodocus was Servatius. On the other hand, Erasmus adds that he and Jodocus used to study together.[15] He cannot have said this to Servatius, for his brother did not know Servatius until introduced to him by Erasmus, unless Erasmus and Peter did not study together in Deventer. We know that William Herman was a native of Gouda and a former pupil of Hegius. Erasmus could remind him of their school days. They were of the same age and Erasmus was indebted to Herman's father for kindness shown to him.[16] When still at Steyn, Erasmus spoke affectionately about Herman, as was noted above.[17] After 1490 Erasmus and Servatius were not on very friendly terms, but Erasmus and Herman wrote poems together. However, it is also possible that the person exhorted by Erasmus never came to Steyn. He may have remained "in the world."

[15] "Mutuus a pueris convictus, mira quaedam animorum consensio, communia optimarum artium studia." Would an uncle talk that way to a nephew? Erasmus was unkind to his readers in assuming so much stupidity on their part.

[16] P. S. Allen, *Opus Ep. Er.*, I, Ep. 28, lines 6–8.

[17] See p. 156.

At any rate, Jodocus is dearly beloved by Erasmus.[18] His well-being is Erasmus' greatest concern. "I am writing this letter," he says, "in order to draw you away from the clamor of the world and into the monastery, that is, into a life of solitude and quiet." There Jodocus will be safe from the perils of the world. Even David and Solomon, continues Erasmus, were not safe. The only way to evade worldly evil is to flee from it. Ulysses, according to Homer, also had his troubles, although he was a virtuous man. The world is like a tempestuous sea, upon which the frail boat of sinful man is tossed about. The monastery, on the other hand, resembles *terra firma;* here one is at ease.

The second chapter is entitled, "It is dangerous to remain in the world." It sounds very much like thousands of other arguments produced in medieval monasteries. In the third chapter temporal possessions are said to be of little or no value. All such things are fleeting. Quotations are reproduced from Virgil, Ovid, Horace, and Juvenal, showing that riches are nothing but vanity. Patristic literature also furnishes a few arguments, and a brief text from the New Testament [19] represents the Bible. It is evident that Erasmus had already read many classical productions and was beginning to feel indifferent toward the Bible. This attitude was not to be lasting, however.

In the fourth chapter we are told what evils fleshly lust has in its train, namely, poverty, dishonor, shameful maladies, spiritual blindness, divine displeasure, and eternal damnation. Marriage is an asylum for the feeble; it is a state of servitude and full of disgrace. "Celibacy is far better and infinitely more happy." As for honors, these are, according to the fifth chapter, as ephemeral as temporal goods. There was Alexander the Great, but what good did all his fame do him when he died in the midst of the highest earthly glory? And what of Xerxes and Hannibal and Caesar? They are all dead and their great empires have long since fallen to pieces.

Then follows a discussion about the certainty of death, for which preparation must be made by young and old, for it often

---

[18] "Quando autem te aeque atque meipsum diligo."
[19] Mark vi. 19–20.

comes when least expected. At the hour of death the great issue will be whether the soul has been saved for eternity. What of the vain and ambitious? Death will come suddenly and who will get their possessions? "Behold, Death stands at your door and will cast you down from the pinnacle of prosperity to the ground, and like a swift storm will sweep away you and all your things. Our Rudolphus [Agricola] wrote to this effect. Death takes everybody; he who is born must die, but virtue has no end and good works are lasting."

The next topic is the misery of the world. What, with incessant civil war, famine, pestilence, and widespread poverty, can one expect of life in the world? "We are now both twenty-four years old and have not yet in all these years seen a cessation of hostilities." [20] Erasmus was right, his youth was spent in a country torn by incessant social wars. These wars had been one of the causes of his removal from Gouda to the monastery of Steyn. William Herman of Gouda wrote an Ode on "Holland disturbed by War, Want, Death, and Factions," which was among the poems published by Erasmus in 1497.

The eighth chapter of the treatise, "On the Contempt of the World," is devoted to the happiness of the solitary life. The picture of beatitude drawn by Erasmus seems all the more alluring because he himself had come to Steyn in search of solitude. The burden of the argument is to exchange perishable riches for eternal life and heavenly possessions. "Do you want to gain eternal life? Live a good life. Do you wish to enter paradise? Leave the world behind you as most polluted and afflicted. . . . Do you love true riches? Cast aside false ones." And solitude enables one to do all these things. To those who remain in the world, life is miserable, death more miserable, and the life after death most miserable. To the religious inmates of monasteries life is blessed and life after death most blessed. The yoke of Jesus is easy and his burden is light. In heaven we shall share in his victory and joy and splendor.

In view of the terrible hardships which Erasmus afterward

---

[20] This must also seem a surprising statement for an uncle to make to a nephew who is much younger than he.

(1517) said he had suffered, it is instructive to read the description of his duties prepared in or before the year 1490. "I am ready to swear," he wrote, "that there is no duty here which is not filled with happiness.[21] There is nothing more lucrative than our poverty, nothing more free than our servitude, nothing more carefree than our labors, nothing more filled than our emptiness, nothing more broad than our narrowness, nothing more joyful than our sorrow." Those who cannot believe these statements are compared with cattle, who, being devoid of reason, obtain knowledge only through their corporeal senses.

This subject is continued in the ninth chapter, where Erasmus tries to prove that the highest liberty is found not in the world but in the monastic retreat. Outside the walls of the monastery men are in bondage to a multitude of cares and worries. There are the relations with various members of the family, with neighbors, with enemies. Worse than that, in the world one is a slave to one's passions. But in the monastery nothing is permitted except that which is pleasant, and nothing is prohibited except that which is not pleasant.

The tenth and eleventh chapters are devoted to tranquillity and happiness respectively. It is of course easy to prove that one can find tranquillity in the monastery. "Elsewhere," says Erasmus, "the noise of the world is disturbing. One person weeps, the other laughs; this one utters complaints, that one quarrels; there is shouting, running to and fro; wherever you turn, nowhere do you find quietude. How can anybody compose his mind amidst so much turmoil? Not in the city but in the mountain, not in the court but in the cave, not in commotion nor in the fire but in the soft whisper of the wind did Elijah find God. And the sacred histories reveal that not in the tumult of the crowds but in retreat most miracles were performed. Where did the prophets live? In the cities? No, on the banks of the Jordan. And where did John the Baptist spend most of his time? In the desert. Jesus our Lord also was wont to flee from the crowds, and went to the mountain, the desert, the sea, or the river, where he taught, healed, and

[21] Erasmus used the word *voluptatis*, instead of *felicitatis*. Perhaps he had read Valla's *De Voluptate*.

fed his followers. It was on a mountain that the transfiguration took place. In the desert he fasted and prayed."

The solitary life, reasons Erasmus, brings great happiness. It is in fact an epicurean life. The monks have a peaceful conscience; they cherish the expectation of eternal life. "It is true," he admits, "we watch, fast, and maintain silence lest greater griefs befall us. We do not dance, and we refrain from licentiousness. But do you think we miss happiness? We exchange, we do not lose; for a few and small things we receive many and great ones. The monks do not choose to become like cattle; they know there is something sublime and divine within man which they prefer to develop rather than cater to the body. Man's nature is more dignified than that of the beast. Our body, except in a few slight details, differs not from an animal's body, but our soul reaches out after things divine and eternal. The body is earthly, wild, slow, mortal, diseased, ignoble; the soul, on the other hand, is heavenly, subtle, divine, immortal, noble. Who is so blind that he cannot tell the difference between body and soul? And so the happiness of the soul far surpasses that of the body."

Furthermore, there is the pleasure of reading books, the Old and New Testament, the Church Fathers, or, if one prefers simpler reading, the scholastic theologians like Thomas Aquinas and Albertus Magnus. The works of classical antiquity may also be included if one knows how to distinguish between harmful and salutary plants. At the close of the treatise Erasmus paints an engaging view of the monastic grounds, describing the flowers in the garden and the orchard. The heavy foliage shades one in hot weather. The meadows are spacious; here one can romp, but one cannot get lost. The monastery is indeed the best place for study and friendship.

The eleventh chapter concludes the treatise as it was written at Steyn. In 1521 Erasmus added a chapter without a title, which he named the twelfth chapter. Here he makes statements like the following: "Formerly monasteries were nothing else than retreats of good men, whose lives were angelical. No one at that time was a monk who did not happen to be a real Christian. There were no monasteries which were not groups of men who practiced pure

Christianity. . . . But now! Many monasteries are worldly; here discipline has relaxed; they are nothing but seminaries of impiety, where it is impossible to be pure and upright. . . . The majority of candidates now enter the monasteries to have an easy time and to administer to the wants of the belly, not of the soul. Those who have lived frugally in the world and were industrious become extravagant and indolent in the monastery."

Simulation must have become a habit of Erasmus by the year 1521, for if he had indulged in it sparingly, he would have been a little more cautious. One may well ask what good Erasmus could could do for himself in adding such contradictory remarks to the original treatise? Could he expect any intelligent reader to believe that the treatise was written for an uncle to send to a young nephew, when the treatise plainly says that the writer and the person addressed had studied together and were of the same age? This Theodore of Haarlem was certainly not a real person. Again, the twelfth chapter was certainly no part of the original treatise. The Preface was no credit to Erasmus, and the Appendix could not possibly have caused respect in the mind of a single thinking person.

To return to the treatise itself, Erasmus had no reason to be ashamed of it, for it contained more than seventy quotations from the classics (Virgil, Horace, Ovid, Terence, and Lucan), as against but five from the Bible (Matthew vi. 20; Job xxi. 13; Luke xii. 20; John v. 19; Matthew xi. 29–30).[22] These texts from the Bible were frequently quoted in sermons, so they do not prove that he was familiar with the Scriptures. Classical antiquity was his treasure and there rested his heart with contentment. The whole treatise showed how strongly he had already been affected by the humanists. It was well written and its vocabulary was much more extensive than that of various productions of the Brethren of the Common Life. He had praised monasticism as a dispassionate critic who employed his reason far more than his feelings. At the time of its composition Erasmus did not comprehend the true meaning of monasticism, and it is doubtful whether he ever did. Had he been a true monk, he would have omitted the

[22] J. B. Pineau, *Érasme*, p. 39.

quotations from classical writers, for they knew nothing about Christianity. Furthermore, he would have told his friends about Jesus Christ, who was not regarded as a mere person, but a miracle. When he did mention Christ, he spoke of him with scarcely more reverence than of Cicero or Virgil. More than that, he gave no expression to any amount of love for Christ, and so betrayed his ignorance of the monastic vocation. When he says that "our whole life is epicurean," and employs the word *voluptas*, he gives further evidence of misunderstanding monasticism. That thousands of other monks also shared in this misunderstanding is true, but that is not a point to be considered here. We want to discover what monasticism meant to Erasmus before he left Steyn and why he afterward attacked it.

A true monk loved Christ with all his heart and mind and soul. He thought and spoke of Christ every day and tried to imitate him every hour. He strove to deny himself, to efface his own personality, to subordinate his will to that of Christ, and to suffer for Christ. Erasmus on the other hand thought only about himself. He completely missed the mark when he described the advantages of monasticism. The monastery was intended for men who wished to destroy all selfishness. Erasmus, on the other hand, always spoke about gain. True, it was spiritual gain, but it was never surrender, resignation, self-denial, self-depreciation. What Erasmus said was reasonable and prudent; perhaps it was wise. But he did not resemble the author of the *Imitation of Christ*; he did not know why St. Benedict and St. Francis had founded monastic orders.

What did Erasmus renounce when he entered Steyn? Parental affection, love of brothers and sisters, friendship, temporal possessions? How did he try to offer sacrifices? Not a single letter written by him at Steyn reveals real love of God or Christ. Instead of speaking about the cross of Christ, he enumerates advantages gained for oneself. The cross, which saves through pain and death, seems to have had practically no significance for Erasmus at Steyn. Humanism had obscured the real meaning of Christianity for him. The Italian humanists, although they outwardly accepted the tenets of the Christian faith, tried to harmonize this faith with the teachings of Greek, Roman, and even Oriental philosophers. We see Erasmus under the influence of humanism and drifting rapidly away from the principles of the Devotio Moderna. Perhaps we can now understand why Erasmus experienced such a sad fate after Luther grew famous. It may have been his selfishness that caused him so much bitter disappointment in the end. He wanted always to serve his own interests, never to suffer for a great cause. Perhaps this explains much in his later life which otherwise must seem an unsolved puzzle.

CHAPTER XV

THE "BOOK AGAINST THE BARBARIANS"

SHORTLY after the year 1490 Erasmus conceived the idea of writing a book on the "barbarism" of the scholastic philosophers and theologians as contrasted with the polished learning of the humanists. He was entering on a period in his life during which he, for the time being, subordinated his inborn religious inclinations to a devotion to classical scholarship. He was becoming disappointed with monasticism. The message of the *Imitation of Christ* to the effect that one should love to remain unknown and to be considered worthless had made very little impression on him. Although he was by no means irreligious, he thirsted for fame and honor. Groote's disciples desired to imitate Christ and to despise worldly things; Erasmus had made an effort to conform to their ideals and after the year 1495 he would return to some of them; from 1490 to 1495, however, he traveled along the road to the humanistic paradise.

It is not known when Erasmus left the monastery of Steyn, nor is it clear why he left it. He said in the letter to Grunnius that he was disgusted with his fellow-monks, and to Servatius he complained about the unhealthful climate and the coarse food, adding that the majority of the monks at Steyn were not leading exemplary lives. But the real cause of his departure must be sought in his own mind. The causes listed by himself were contributing factors; they influenced his mind. He was expected to mortify and crucify his own will and personality; that he refused to do. Had all the monks led saintly lives, Erasmus would no doubt have lingered longer at Steyn. Had his constitution been stronger, he could have enjoyed himself after the year 1490.

An opportunity to escape presented itself in 1492 or 1493, when Henry of Bergen, bishop of Cambray, in the southern Netherlands, invited him to become his secretary. He accepted the position and left Steyn. It must not be imagined, however, that he ceased to be a monk, or that he was not expected to return to Steyn in due time. He continued to wear the monastic garb for several years. But the secrecy surrounding his departure showed that the step he took was bold and could not please his superiors. Even William Herman of Gouda was not told about the trip, as appears from the following remarks: "I should like to have been with you in that journey. It would have given me a great deal of pleasure and perhaps some to you, and would have been advantageous to both of us. When I had received your message, I begged and entreated the man to allow it; and after your departure he was most bitterly reproached for his unkindness. I look after your business here as our friendship may fairly lead me to do, and you to expect. Theoderick will be of service to you. I have never ceased to wonder, my Erasmus, at your not only taking no advice about your going, but not even communicating to me the resolution you had formed. It cannot be expressed how much I desire to see you back again (for with whom can I live so pleasantly?), but so that your return may be to your advantage, and no less at the same time to your credit. The trouble you have escaped no one knows better than I, who am even now tossed about in the same storms. I often congratulate you, and think how happy you are to have swum out of the billows." [1]

On his way south Erasmus carried with him a rough draft of a book he had decided to write, namely, the *Book against the Barbarians*, which he completed in the village of Halsteren, where Bishop Henry had a summer residence. The book was begun, according to the Preface of the printed editions, when Erasmus was twenty years old, or about the year 1489. In the letter to Botzheim (1523), Erasmus said he was a youth.[2] It was completed by the spring of 1494. In a letter to Cornelius Aurelius he wrote at the time of its completion: "I am working on this book in the country. It is my intention to compose two parts: the first

---

[1] F. M. Nichols, *The Epistles of Erasmus*, I, 94–95.

[2] P. S. Allen, *Opus Ep. Er.*, I, 19, line 16: "Admodum adolescens aggressus sum Antibarbaros."

will be an attack on the barbarians and a refutation of their arguments, the second will be a eulogy of Letters." [3] Only the first part has survived, namely, the *Book against the Barbarians.* In 1495 Erasmus submitted this composition to Robert Gaguin, the celebrated Parisian humanist, who advised him not to publish it, since in his opinion it would create much hostility. Erasmus was in no position, he argued, to make many enemies, particularly among the authorities in the Church and in the universities. The booklet, therefore, remained unpublished. It was revised and enlarged when Erasmus was staying at Bologna in the winter of 1506–7, and it was first published in 1520, accompanied by a letter to Sapidus. [4]

 The printed editions of the *Book against the Barbarians* do not, therefore, reproduce the original version. This has been unfortunate in a way because it would have been interesting to discover what Erasmus had to say when he was leaving Steyn. He was still a friend of monasticism, but not devoted to it as were many of his acquaintances. For years he had been affected to an ever increasing degree by the influence of the humanists. We have evidence which makes it seem probable that the booklet mentioned above was nearly completed when Erasmus left Steyn. It followed immediately upon the treatise *On the Contempt of the World.* In the first place, there is a letter addressed about the year 1489 to Cornelius Aurelius, in which Erasmus says he is working on it. In the second place, his correspondence between 1490 and 1495

[3] P. S. Allen, *op. cit.,* Ep. 37, lines 9–14. It is worth noting that the original has the phrase "in refellendis ineptis barbarorum rationibus." The title of the book in the manuscript version at Gouda reads: "Liber. . . in quo refelluntur rationes inepte Barbarorum. . . ." There is a very striking similarity between these two phrases, which seems to prove that the title in the Gouda manuscript is the original one intended for the book by Erasmus at the time of its composition. In the opinion of the author himself before the year 1495 the composition was "a book in which the arguments of the barbarians are refuted." Many years later Erasmus referred to this book as the *Antibarbari* or *Liber Antibarbarorum,* and that is the reason why later writers have always used these titles. Nevertheless the earlier description is the better one, for Erasmus did not write a "Book of the Opponents of the Barbarians," as the contents clearly show. It was, on the other hand, a book in which the barbarians were attacked, not by all the speakers, but by some of them. The burgomaster, or mayor, certainly is not an opponent of the barbarians.

[4] The first edition was printed at Basel by Froben, and not at Cologne. See Allen, *op. cit.,* I, 121.

expresses the same attitude toward the "barbarians" as does the book itself. The revisions and additions made by Erasmus in Italy must have been rather slight.[5] Such at least has been the contention of the authorities.

Instead of having to rely on surmises, however, we gain certitude with the discovery of a draft of the book written in the back of a volume of Jerome's works, reposing at present in the City Library at Gouda. The volume in question is a beautifully preserved copy of the ninth volume of the *Opera*, printed at Basel in 1516. The manuscript written in this volume was the work of a Brother of the Common Life in Gouda, who completed it in 1519. A comparison with the printed editions will immediately prove that here we have the earliest known draft of the *Book against the Barbarians*. In analyzing this composition, therefore, it behooves us to follow throughout the manuscript copy, which is printed for the first time at the end of the present volume.

First of all, however, it should be noted what Erasmus told Sapidus in the Preface to the edition of 1520: "That there is a certain marvelous force and energy inherent in us, dear Sapidus, I gather from my own experience. In my childhood polite letters were wholly banished from our schools of learning. Not only was assistance from books and teachers lacking, but there was no reward to stimulate my ability. Moreover, the whole world tried to frighten me away from the study of polite letters and to push me in the other direction. In spite of all this, a certain native impulse — it was not judgment, for I was too young to have any at that age — seized me and carried me off to the haunts of the Muses, just as if I had been inspired. I began to hate all those who I knew were insensible to the humanities; I fell in love with those who delighted in them. As for the men who had acquired a reputation in these pursuits, I looked up to them and venerated them as if they were divine. Even now in my old age I do not repent of this attitude. Not that I would condemn studies which have not been as agreeable to me as to others, but that I know how cold, imperfect and blind erudition becomes if the support of the Muses is withdrawn.

[5] J. B. Pineau, *Érasme*, pp. 75–76.

"Nevertheless, I am really ashamed to say how some individuals stupidly denounce what is by far the noblest part of learning, condemning by the name 'poetastry' all that belongs to the ancient and more refined literature. As these people tormented me shamefully during my childhood and tried to drive me from my beloved studies, I began to avenge myself with my pen, without, however, attacking anyone by name. I had not yet reached my twentieth year when I began this composition."

"During my youth," he continues in the work itself, "I had retired to a little village in Brabant, [6] to escape an epidemic which was then raging violently in our district. The place, healthful and pleasant as it was, seemed especially suitable, not only for safeguarding health but also for the secluded pursuit of studies. In this respect, moreover, it was better than the Academy of Plato. . . . [7] In addition to the recommendation of healthful air it had also the advantage of perfect silence, pleasant enough even for a philosopher, and perhaps for the Muses, who are said to delight in limpid springs, and emerald river banks, and the shady depths of groves. While hiding in this retreat and enjoying the country, I received an unexpected visit from William Herman, the dearest of all my friends, who from early childhood had been attached to me by ties of unusual sympathy as well as by a pleasant companionship in the pursuit of studies. . . . Not to enjoy so great a pleasure jealously alone, I immediately had our friend James Batt summoned, who was then secretary of the neighboring city of Bergen." [8]

When the three friends were assembled, they took a walk and met Jodocus, a physician, and William Conrad, the mayor of the village. A lively conversation ensued, which was recorded in the *Book against the Barbarians*. Erasmus was careful not to inject his own personality, so that no one could accuse him of sponsoring views pronounced by the characters he introduced. Presently Batt became the principal speaker. Erasmus probably was imitat-

[6] This is Halsteren.

[7] This sentence is not found in the Gouda copy. The same thing is true of other parts of this paragraph.

[8] Bergen-op-Zoom is about three miles south of Halsteren and approximately ten miles north of the present boundary between Holland and Belgium.

ing the method employed by Valla in the treatise *On Pleasure*, where three speakers defend three totally divergent views. At any rate, Erasmus was never more strongly influenced by Valla than at the time he composed the booklet under discussion.

It has already been noted that in the letters written at Steyn, Erasmus expressed the highest respect for Valla, but that he probably did not know Valla's character very well. Even before he went to Steyn, his admiration for Valla had impelled him to prepare an abridged edition of Valla's *Elegances*. He said that a schoolteacher had suggested this work to him. Perhaps it was Peter Winckel who did, for Erasmus was eighteen years old at the time; so he had just returned from 's-Hertogenbosch and was living in Gouda. The work was done very hurriedly, said Erasmus. He gave the extracts from the *Elegances* to the pedgaogue, and did not even keep a copy for himself. Later it was printed without his permission or his knowledge. It was accompanied by notes which neither Erasmus nor Valla had made, and printed under the title of *Epitome by Des. Erasmus of the "Elegances" of L. Valla*.[9]

The *Book against the Barbarians* was composed a few years later. It shows that Valla's campaign against scholasticism had attracted the attention of scholars north of the Rhine and that Erasmus had grasped the meaning of Valla's war-cry. In the monastery at Steyn, Erasmus had studied Valla with the utmost enthusiasm. He felt it his sacred duty to oppose the "authorities," the stubborn, old-fashioned dignitaries in church and school who clung to the hallowed standards in religion and education. Gaguin was a good counselor when he urged Erasmus in 1495 not to publish his bold composition. When at last it was printed for the first time in 1520, Erasmus had reached the zenith of European fame and cared little whether the old fogies would be angered or not. By that time, however, the campaign of the older humanists had nearly spent its force. Luther was now the man of the hour and humanism became for the most part a dead issue. Erasmus' book was not widely read and for that reason most of his biog-

[9] *Epit. Des. Erasmi in Elegantiarum Libros Laur. Vallae.* The first edition was printed in 1529 at Cologne. In the same year an edition appeared in Paris; in 1531 a revised edition was published at Freiburg. See P. S. Allen, *op. cit.*, I, 108–109.

raphers have paid scarcely any attention to it. Nevertheless a detailed analysis of the work proves its historical value.

The copy made in the house of the Brethren of the Common Life at Gouda was completed one year before the first edition was printed. It has interesting variations from the printed copies, and adds weight to the contention so often expressed by conscientious scholars that if one wants to understand the development of Erasmus' mind, one should not consult the later editions of his works but, as far as possible, the earliest drafts or editions. Erasmus has long ceased to be the intellectual dictator of Europe, or even of a single country; and his compositions cannot any longer enjoy a wide circulation because people's interests are different from those of Erasmus' contemporaries; the crude drafts are more important for most of us than the polished revisions printed at a later date.

Few books of Erasmus were subject to such significant and interesting changes (at least from the viewpoint of the biographer) as the *Book against the Barbarians*. This is particularly true of the first ten pages. Whereas in the printed editions the rustic retreat is compared with the Platonic Academy, the Gouda copy has simply the word Academy. Here Erasmus says he is going to found some sort of academy. The first visitor is William Herman, as in the other editions, but how differently is he described. Instead of coming as an unexpected visitor, he simply arrives, but is accorded a much longer description of his virtues. Both versions have the phrase from Cicero *qui mihi a teneris unguiculis*, which Cicero borrowed from the Greek, as he himself said; but the Gouda copy adds in parentheses the phrase "as in the Greek proverb," while the printed editions have "as they say." Then the Gouda version informs us that this expected visit of William made Erasmus very happy. So he did not come unexpected.

As for James Batt, we learn that a boy sent for him, which information is not given in the printed version. Batt is described plainly as not unlearned but most upright, while later editions say nothing about his learning, but state that he was upright, well-mannered, and well instructed in doctrine. There are besides innumerable minor variations which naturally cannot be recorded here. It is sufficient for our purpose to note that the copy made in 1519 at Gouda preceded all the printed editions and must have been based either on the original version completed before 1495 (which is almost certain), or at least very much like it. Hence it alone can give us the correct information about Erasmus' views at the time of its composition. In the present analysis it will be followed throughout, and only those variations in the printed editions will be given which throw important light on the genesis of Erasmus' mind.

The five speakers are having a pleasant time. They all take part in the lively conversation. Batt seems to be a jolly person and occasionally makes the whole group smile. After some casual remarks of no particular importance, they agree that the philosophers of their time have ruined the cause of Polite Letters, and that the classics must be restored again. The current Latin is abominable, they argue, in conscious imitation of Valla, the humanist whom Erasmus adores above all other humanists. The "old writers" alone knew how to express themselves with elegance and propriety. Away with the atrocious language of the philosophers, for they have defiled the pure Latin of the ancients.

They discuss various topics, nature, the sun, the heavens, and in the printed editions also "the calamities of our Holland," which are not mentioned in the Gouda copy. It is curious that Erasmus added this phrase, since three of the five speakers were natives of Brabant, and could not very well say "our Holland." In the nineteenth or twentieth century the inhabitants of Bergen-op-Zoom can use this phrase, because the term Holland now includes all the Netherlands north of Belgium. The Gouda copy is, therefore, the best version. After various trips to France, England, and Italy, Erasmus may have forgotten the distinction between Holland and Brabant.

Presently the speakers take up the relation between Christians and pagans. It is here that Erasmus afterward made an extremely important change. He inserted the following passage: "The Christian religion was not founded by philosophers, nor by orators, nor by dialecticians, nor by mathematicians, but by the simple Christ, and propagated by the Apostles. Afterward worldly customs corrupted the pure creed of the primitive Church, Polite Letters were neglected, the philosophy of Aristotle and Plato was forgotten, 'liberal studies' perished."

But what does the Gouda copy have? It is much briefer here. "Formerly the Christians," asserts Erasmus, "did not know pagan literature. They condemned beautiful things as vile, partly because they were moved by a zeal of faith more vehement than wise. Because of their hatred for their adversaries they wanted to have nothing in common with them, partly because they abhorred human nature, partly because they avoided labor. Their indolence was disguised under the name of religion." All of this, except the first sentence, is also found in the printed editions. The Gouda copy says nothing here about the origin of Christianity. Before 1495 Erasmus had not noticed a deplorable decline in the Church. Abuses in the Church had not yet attracted his attention. Formalism, the invocation of saints, relics, and the like, had not yet disturbed him.

Then follows a long passage, not found in the Gouda copy, telling how tyrants closed the schools to the Christians, assuming that, if the people were deprived of knowledge, they could be dominated more easily. Monasticism is bitterly attacked, but none of this is found in the Gouda version. The monks are ignorant, says Erasmus, and the average abbot fears nothing more than that his monks should improve their discipline. The monks neglect good literature and antiquity. This concludes a speech by the magistrate of Bergen-op-Zoom, and now William Herman, according to all versions, remarks that the whole world is getting old and worse.

The fact that in the original version nothing is said about the monks is significant, for it takes away the last prop from beneath the edifice so carefully reared by Erasmus and so faithfully maintained by most of his biographers, namely, the theory that he was thoroughly disgusted with monasticism when still residing at Steyn. It confirms the testimony presented in the treatise, *On the Contempt of the World*, and in all the contemporary letters. That even those biographers who presented extensive analyses of the colloquy did not hold a later revision responsible for the startling remarks about the monks is rather surprising,[10] since Erasmus plainly speaks of revisions.

Another interesting fact worth noting is the spelling of Erasmus' name on the fourth page of the Gouda version. Here it appears first as Hierasmus and then as Herasmus, and nowhere does the manuscript have Erasmus, which is further evidence of its resemblance to the original draft. On this fourth page Erasmus makes a few remarks himself. The question has been raised why the literature, science, and the arts which flourished in ancient Greece and Rome have suffered ignominious deterioration. While the physician holds the stars responsible, the magistrate believes that the opposition of Christianity in particular and religion in general to secular learning has been the principal cause. Then follows the view of William Herman just mentioned. He voices the feeling of many mystics who believed that the end of the world was near. Even Gerard Groote had repeatedly expressed such a belief, and the Brethren of the Common Life accepted it. William Herman supports his theory with arguments adduced by the mystics, according to our dialogue.

After a brief statement by Batt, Erasmus expresses a view, held also by Batt, which differs greatly from the opinions enunciated by the three other speakers. He asserts that the bad schoolteachers are responsible for the decline in sound scholarship. Incidentally he does not wholly reject the explanation given by the magistrate, who said that the Christians who were moved by deep religious fervor showed little interest in learning. But he does say this, "You all judge wrongly, at least in my opinion. Why do you seek the cause of men's failures in objects or in the actions of others, instead of blaming the persons themselves, for they have caused their own misfortunes?" And a little farther on Erasmus remarks that there are plenty of propitious stars and enough good brains, and if people fail, it is not the fault of fate, nor of some evil spirits, but of will-power. Batt supports this

---

[10] See P. Mestwerdt, *Die Anfänge des Erasmus*, p. 257. The author tries to find another explanation here, and had he known the Gouda version he would have thoroughly revised the lengthy chapter devoted to the *Book against the Barbarians*.

view and grows excited when he compares the glory of the ancients
with the puny accomplishments of his contemporaries.

The fifth page of the Gouda copy is again free from the numerous derogatory remarks about the ignorant monks found in the
printed editions. At the bottom of the page is an important
reference to the grammars which should be thrown out of the
schools. Whereas Alexander of Ville-Dieu, and the so-called
Graecista, or the grammar of Ebrardus of Bethune, are listed,
the printed versions add the grammar by Michael Modista, the
Breviloquum, the *Mammetreptum*, and the *Catholicon*, the last of
which is a dictionary. It is likely that Erasmus did not know some
of the latter works before the year 1495. The grammar by
Modista was also mentioned in the *Conflict between Thalia and
Barbarism*, which is one of the reasons why the present writer
believes that, if this poem was actually composed by Erasmus, it
dates from the period after 1495.

It has been generally understood that when Erasmus revised
his *Book against the Barbarians*, he rendered his criticism of the
"barbarians" less severe.[11] Now we may judge his method most
advantageously by examining three of the more important passages of the printed editions and comparing them with the statement found on page 5 of the Gouda copy. In the printed versions
we read: "Nowhere does the tyranny of the barbarians reign so
unmolested as among us. They think it a privilege to censure
things, and their activities are preferably carried on among women
who have no spirit, and no feeling of shame, and also among im-
beciles. These sycophantic leaders tell them that it is a heresy
to know Greek, a heresy to speak the language of Cicero. . . .
Nothing is more despicable, more hostile to the Muses than these
people who speak through a mask of religion; thanks to their
venerable garments and their saintly appearances, they have acquired an authority over the simple and effeminate, they take
advantage of the folly of the people, they zealously foster their
caprice. These are the men whom one generally consults and who
interfere in family affairs. One might as well ask a camel to

---

[11] P. Mestwerdt, *op. cit.*, p. 248: "So ist anzunehmen, dass er die ursprünglichen
Gedanken eher gemildert als verschärft hat."

dance or a donkey to sing. If one consults a Franciscan, a Jacobite or a Carmelite about methods of education for one's children . . ., these counselors, with amazing severity, advise against the study of the poets. For these blind leaders, the poets are Quintilian, Pliny, Aulus Gellius, and Livy. . . . They show the steps by which they have advanced, being men born amid outright barbarism and so reared. One of them orders pupils to learn the Psalter, another advises them to study Latin in the Proverbs of Solomon, still another recommends the insipid Michael Modista, or the *Mammetreptum*, or the *Catholicon*. . . . Such is the advice that they incessantly pour into peoples' ears; in the confessional chair, where they maintain the folly of the world; in the celebrated auricular confessions, where they feel that they are among the gods."

This is not a mild statement and if the original version had been still more severe, it certainly must have contradicted all the other compositions written by Erasmus before 1495. But such is by no means the case. The Gouda version begins in the same manner as the later copies, but it is not suggested that "nowhere is there such tyranny as among us." Erasmus was in no position to make such a statement, since he had never left the Netherlands. The term *ptochotyranni* is not yet used to describe the barbarians. Nothing is said about heresy. "To know Greek is heresy," was a phrase coined many years after 1495. All that the Gouda version has is the statement to the effect that "nothing is more odious and sickening than those people who are devoid of religion and, when consulted by parents about their children, deter the latter from studying poetry." It should be specially noted that nothing is said about people with "venerable garments and saintly appearances," nor about Franciscans, Jacobites, and Carmelites. There is not even a hint at any members of the clergy, either secular or regular. No one is criticized for recommending the Psalter or the Proverbs of Solomon. And certainly there is no reference to the auricular confession. It is strange that biographers have not expressed doubts about the authenticity of these accusations presumably made by Erasmus before 1495.[12] For how could he possibly

[12] J. B. Pineau, *op. cit.*, p. 49, arrives at the same conclusions as did Mestwerdt. These two biographers have thus far given the most extensive analyses of the treatise

have said such things when he was still in the monastery or else just after he had left it? It is known that as late as the year 1497 he took a vital interest in the reforms attempted in France by the Congregation of Windesheim, of which he strongly approved. How then could he have accused the monks of ignorance, deception, and all sorts of crimes when he knew only the Augustinian Canons Regular, of whom he was one and whom he earnestly praised?

After the fifth page of the Gouda version of the *Book against the Barbarians*, the variations in the different drafts are much less numerous and less significant, and from this point it becomes possible to follow both versions without much interruption. Presently it appears that the booklet is not merely a humanistic attack on the methods of contemporary educators, but presents very interesting views on the Christian religion, scholastic philosophy, politics, and ecclesiastical affairs.

First of all, there is a significant speech by the mayor. Accosting Batt, he says: "Your authors are — I shall not speak falsely — in the first place pagans, a point, however, on which some defence could be made; secondly, they are extremely difficult to learn, a fact which in itself arouses dislike in not a few; finally, the most serious objection, they are lascivious, nay, even obscene. Now, here is the case: you are throwing out Christian authors and introducing pagan authors; you discard the known and substitute the unknown; you crowd out the old and bring forward the new; you remove the easy and place before us the obscure; finally — which is the chief point — you ban the chaste authors and put lascivious ones before our youth. What countenance do you think I shall assume whenever the burghers ask me, a magistrate, whether the public school in the town exists for the purpose of teaching young men the amours of courtesans, just as if they are not naturally inclined toward such studies, that they may learn to conduct stratagems skilfully, to trick their parents slyly, to be shameless, to lie, to put on a bold face, to steal — for these things they learn from your comedies. . . ."

The next speaker is Erasmus, who remarks that the five friends

---

On the Contempt of the World and of the *Book against the Barbarians*. They both show enough skepticism, except in the case now under discussion.

have assembled to form an academy patterned after that of Plato. If the Platonic or Ciceronian plantain tree is wanting, he will show them an apple tree, in whose shade they will discuss and dispute various important topics. So they seat themselves under the tree, where the real dialogue commences with a few remarks by Batt. The latter, it should be remembered, had become intimately acquainted with Erasmus in the year 1493. It seems that Batt proved a more congenial friend to Erasmus than William Herman. At any rate, Batt from now on is the principal speaker, whose views Erasmus plainly supports.

Fixing his gaze upon the mayor, Batt spoke as follows: "Deservedly I am now being stabbed with my own sword, for I who bade you merely trifle with the subject in a grand manner am reduced through your efforts to such a position that today nothing will be more foolish or trifling than I. * * * We shall offer, therefore, to defend classic literature against its new enemies. I see that three groups of foes especially are causing trouble. The first wants to have the republic of letters utterly destroyed; the second does not toil to destroy it completely, but to confine it within too narrow limits; the last group wishes the republic to be safe though afflicted, since they themselves shall hold the ruling power and after abolishing its native laws, introduce foreign magistrates and customs. And the first group seem to me to be those who are simply ignorant — I know not whether their hatred or their stupidity is the greater — and detest all literature under the name of poetry on some religious pretext or other. The second group I know are those who, poorly taught, accept other studies, that is, their own kind, but hate worse than a snake the humanities, [13] without which all learning is blind. Finally, now, what others shall I say there are except those who admire and approve any kind of literature, especially poetry and rhetoric, but on the condition that they themselves be considered the greatest poets and rhetoricians, since they are nothing less? Nor will it be easy to say, meanwhile, from which of these enemies the republic of letters suffers the greatest harm, or by which it must confess the greater part of its disasters have been received."

[13] The Latin is "humanitatis literas."

This last class Batt represents as believing that classical literature is pernicious. And here he meets the objection raised by the magistrate.

Batt asserts that pristine philosophy and theology have deteriorated. The barbarians have also corrupted these branches of learning. They do not know how to write good Latin or good Greek; their commentaries do not illuminate, but degenerate, they do not decorate, but contaminate. So the youth of the land are improperly instructed and for that reason Batt, Erasmus, and their friends have taken up their arms. It will be recalled that Erasmus warmly defended Valla, who had been accused of immorality. Erasmus held Valla blameless, largely because he did not know the real Valla. So, too, Batt defends the classical comedies without stopping to analyze those compositions which actually were pernicious and did tend to corrupt the morals of the pupils who studied them. Batt condemns the enemies of the classics, but does not fully meet their arguments. He does, however, point out to the magistrate that it is unwise to criticize poetry which one has never read. He correctly talks about the blind leading the blind, for contemporary teachers knew very little about classical literature, while their style, from the humanistic standpoint, was generally very poor. He gives expression to a viewpoint held by Erasmus between 1490 and 1500, but greatly modified afterward, when many scholars had been doing exactly what the magistrate had feared, namely, overemphasizing the value of style and underestimating the importance of high ideals and of character.

On the tenth page of the Gouda version, Batt proceeds to explain the "barbarism" of the scholastic philosophers. There is indeed much that should be condemned, he argues, just as there is much that is unjustly condemned. "O servile cattle," he says to those who attack classical literature, "tell me, I beg, of what does that new magnanimity of yours consist? What strange kind of condemnation is this? You cannot despise money, can you, and glory in your contempt for true erudition? * * * You must first study literature before you condemn it." It should be noted here that in the printed versions a very long passage precedes the statement just quoted. It is a bitter attack on the monks. Since the enemies of classical scholarship had pointed out the questionable value of some of the Latin comedies, Erasmus thought he could meet their argument by exposing the immorality, ignorance, and other vices of the regular clergy. Once again therefore the Gouda version helps to correct the old view that even before 1495 Erasmus was disgusted with monasticism.

On the next page we reach a passage where Erasmus cites Augustine and Jerome as champions of enlightened scholarship. They also claimed that Cicero and Plato were well worth studying and that pagan literature had much in common with Christian writings. The printed versions add that Basil and Chrysostom, likewise, had not neglected to read Cicero and Plato, or rather, the great rhetorical and philosophical lights, including these two. In 1494 Erasmus apparently was not yet fully acquainted with these two Church Fathers.

Then follows a chapter in defense of writers like Cicero, Virgil, and Horace, where the reader is informed how foolish it is to make a distinction between these and Christian authors. "If we are forbidden to use pagan productions, what then, I beseech you, will be left in the fields, in the cities, in the churches, in the houses, in the workshops, at home, in war, in private or in public life? So far is it true that we Christians have nothing not handed down by pagans. That which we write, whatever we speak in Latin, we have received from pagans; by them were the letters of the alphabet discovered, by them was the use of speech invented. . . . I shall not here enter upon that quarrelsome debate about the pagans, which is not worthy even of women; it is not ours to discuss the damnation of the pagans, of those, I say, who preceded our faith. Then, if we should wish to follow conjectures, I shall easily convince you either that those pagan men were saved or that no one at all is saved. * * * Let us leave their evils to them, but why should we not make use of good things? This is a course worthy of a Christian, of a wise man, of a scholarly man. * * * [Jesus said,] 'When I have been lifted up from the earth, I shall draw all unto me.'"

Here Batt, who expresses Erasmus' views, speaks as a true

humanist. Scholars like Valla, Poggio, and Ficino (Pico also for a time) tried to make the Christian faith seem closely akin to the beliefs held by the great thinkers of Greece, Rome, and even of the Near East. "What then of the whole Mosaic law," continues Batt, "so many rites, so many ceremonies, so many kinds of sacrifices, so many promises, so many oracles? Did not all these things, as Paul bears witness, seem to them like phantoms? . . . It is not surprising that the Christian religion, once born, easily spread to every part of the earth, if, so to speak, it flowed from one head to the members of the same body. . . . All the brave deeds of the pagans, all their clever words, ingenious thoughts, careful teachings, Christ had prepared for the coming of his kingdom."

After a brief interruption by Erasmus (his name is given here only in the Gouda version), Batt continues his lengthy oration. "I think," he said, "that there is no learning except that which is secular (for that is what ancient learning is called), or at any rate that is based on secular literature and trained in it. . . . 'What does it matter,' people say, 'if we are not theologians? If one knows Christ well, it is sufficient, even if one knows nothing else. Eternal life was promised, not to the learned, but to the pure. Shall my soul be damned, then, if I do not have enough insight into divine Paul's writings? What of it if I do not comprehend Jerome's language, or if I do not even read the works of Augustine and Ambrose? Suppose I do not understand even the Gospel?'"

This is the way some of the mystics reasoned among the Brethren of the Common Life, and Erasmus had no doubt heard this argument. His answer is this: "Stupid, what indeed if you should not know your own self, if you be a camel and not a man? Have faith, even cattle will enter heaven." It can hardly be said that this answer is convincing. Perhaps Erasmus thought it a clever piece of juggling with words, but this form of humanistic sophistry was certainly no credit to his intellect.

On the fifteenth page of the Gouda version an interesting discussion commences on the educators. Once more a number of bad grammars are listed. Then follows a significant attack on the scholastic philosophers and theologians. "There are some who call their works *Summae* and *Summarum Summae*. . . . When they boast of their own saintly teachers, irresistible teachers, most subtle teachers, seraphic teachers, then they seem to attribute to themselves an importance to which the very majesty of the Gospel ought to yield. . . . Out of these volumes are ecclesiastical addresses woven, from them are gathered the doctrines by which the world is ruled, from these are we judged Christians or otherwise. Also, in their teachings they never hesitate, they doubt nothing, they are sure of everything, they command everything. One would think that they were lawgivers, not teachers." Here again Erasmus is consciously imitating the Italian humanists, and like them, he makes very bold statements about the greatest thinkers of the medieval Church, but without rejecting their dogma. Whether Erasmus knew the scholastic productions himself is doubtful. He was falling into the same error of which many enemies of classical scholarship were guilty, namely, of condemning things they had failed to examine properly.

Erasmus here enunciates his predilection for skepticism and rationalism. In common with many other sharp intellects he thought that it took more intelligence to doubt than to believe. "Behold," he made Batt say, "the modesty that supine ignorance brings with it; how much better it was to imitate the caution of the philosophers of the Academy, with whom they [the ignorant] are not even to be compared." According to Erasmus, the great Church Fathers were far nobler than all the theologians who succeeded them. Jerome and Augustine in particular used their intellectual gifts; they employed good Latin, were not credulous, and yet were deeply religious. But contemporary theologians were simply intellectually indolent.

The eighteenth page of the Gouda version gives a speech by the physician, which does not necessarily express Erasmus' own viewpoints any more than the three speakers in Valla's dialogue *On Pleasure* all reflect Valla's views. For how could Valla support simultaneously three totally divergent views? So in the present case biographers should be careful not to set down all the remarks by all the speakers as representative of Erasmus' views.[14] He employs Batt as his mouthpiece, but not the mayor and the

[14] Mestwerdt makes this error repeatedly, particularly on p. 260 of his biography.

physician. The latter asks several questions: "Are only literary men going to inherit heaven? . . . What will become of the uneducated masses? What of the simple brethren who, walking in the footsteps of the Apostles, did not learn the snares of Aristotle, nor the thorny subtleties of Chrysippus, nor Attic wit, nor Plautine eloquence? Is not this that simplicity which alone Christ seems to have chosen for himself when he wished to enter Jerusalem riding on a donkey? And his exhortation was: 'Learn of me, for I am meek and humble of heart.' He did not say: 'Learn to speak fluently, to measure the heavens, to weave a syllogism,' but 'learn humility.'"

Batt was at once ready with an appropriate answer, that the use of the word 'donkey' must apply to character, not to intellectual standards. In other words, Christ did not ride on a donkey to indicate how poorly educated he was. Batt concludes his oration, which again expresses Erasmus' view, with an attack on the ignorant monks which is naturally missing in the Gouda version. The printed copies add the following words: "Nobody exercises such tryanny as those very imitators of apostolic simplicity. The uneducated abbots do not permit the monks to become familiar with polite literature." Here again Erasmus, who in 1520 had shaken off the obnoxious monastic vows, was anxious to justify his action by an exposure of illiteracy in the monastery. But whether he succeeded in answering the physician's question is doubtful. His reply is as evasive as those which were to have met the arguments advanced by the magistrate.

Batt also makes an interesting speech about the respective merits of martyrs and heretics, which plainly foretells the later attitude of Erasmus toward the Protestants. "The man whose life is pure," argues Batt, "has done nobly. But in doing nobly he serves merely his own interests, or at the most his influence is exerted on only the few individuals with whom he lives. But if to his upright character erudition is allied, how much more beautifully and widely will his virtue flourish, as if a torch had been lighted? If one is a member of that group who are able to commit to letters the finest reflections of the mind, that is, if he is not only learned but eloquent, necessarily the influence of such a man is most widely

spread, not merely to his intimate friends, not only to his contemporaries and to his neighbors, but also to foreigners, to posterity, to the most distant inhabitants of the earth. Untaught
virtue dies with its author unless it is handed down to posterity in
writings. Not the lands, nor the seas, nor the long succession of
ages prevent trained erudition from reaching all humanity in its
flight. I do not wish to raise here the invidious comparison
whether the blood of the martyrs or the pen of scholars did more
to advance the cause of our religion. I do not disparage the glory
of the martyrs, which no one can reach even by the greatest eloquence. But so far as our advantage is concerned, we owe almost
more to some heretics than to our martyrs themselves. And while
there have been a great number of martyrs, scholars have been
few. The martyrs in dying diminished the number of Christians;
the learned writers by their persuasiveness have increased it."

Then follows a lengthy argument by Batt, in which he quotes
many authorities to prove that learning is not to be despised nor
condemned, since it certainly is most useful. This speech is excellent. The references to Augustine and Jerome show how well acquainted Erasmus was with these Fathers even before 1495. He
also makes judicious use of Biblical quotations, while he reveals
more familiarity with Plato than he is commonly supposed to
have had.

After a brief interruption by Erasmus and Herman, who both
approved the speaker's arguments, Batt quotes the opponents of
pure book-learning as saying something worth noting here: "You
see that the Christian faith was not founded by physicians, nor
by dialecticians, nor by poets, nor by rhetoricians, but by rustic
men, uneducated, crude, in short, fishermen. We know that the
Apostles were called, not from the Academy of Plato, not from the
porticoes of the Stoics, not from the schools of the Peripatetics,
but from ship and net; nor did Christ open rhetorical or dialectical
schools, but merely handed down his precepts of living." It is
plain, is it not, that the view of the opponents does not represent
Erasmus' own opinion, and should therefore not be quoted as such?
Batt's reply, however, expresses the verdict of Erasmus.

"O sacrilegious impudence," continues Batt, "they dare to

speak of the Apostles as untutored in order that they may defend
their own rusticity. . . . Tell me, slanderous mouth, fit for the
branding iron, do you say that the Apostles were untutored fellows?
I say, on the contrary: In what school did they learn when from
their fishing they were suddenly sent out to make converts? Did
they turn straight from steering ships to guiding the world? What
did it matter that they did not hear the lectures of Plato or of
Chrysippus or of some other philosopher when they followed the
very parent of philosophy himself as a teacher for so long a time,
saw him performing miracles, lived with him continually, talked
with him constantly? . . . After Christ rose from the grave, he
remained on earth for forty days, he appeared then to his disciples,
advised them, taught them. Nor was even this enough, for after
he ascended to heaven he sent down a Comforter who was not to
suffer them to remain in ignorance any longer. . . . Since it
pleases you to revile the Apostles, is Paul untutored? . . . For,
being not only learned but eloquent, he of all men seemed to be
fitted to bear arms against the learned schools of Athens, to endure
the disdain of philosophers, to subject Roman eloquence to the
sway of Christ. Is John untutored? If so, whence came that
sublime voice, 'In the beginning was the Word, and the Word
was with God, and the Word was God?' Or is Peter untutored?
His letters, though unpolished in style, nevertheless are certainly
not without knowledge. Was James untutored?"

Once more Erasmus fails to refute the arguments of his opponents. He usually evades the issue, as he does here. The
arguments produced by the great mystics were lost on Erasmus,
for he did not comprehend mysticism. The point completely escaped him when he tried to meet the assertions of men like Ruysbroeck, Tauler, Suso, Eckhardt, and Thomas à Kempis. They
reasoned that book-learning was not necessary, since one could be
instructed by the Holy Spirit through infusion of ideas. Whether
they were right or wrong is not for us to determine here. Our task
is to discover what Erasmus had learned when he left the monastery of Steyn, and we observe that the mysticism of the Brethren of the Common Life and of the Augustinian Canons Regular
had passed over his head.

It is also worth while to follow Erasmus' line of thought when Batt praises the Church Fathers and then states that since their time philosophy and theology have degenerated. Not that during the intervening seven or eight centuries scholarship remained totally extinguished, but educated men were rare, and industry was at a discount. Thomas Aquinas was a most noble writer, however, for he published commentaries on Aristotle, the pagan philosopher, and also on theological questions, where he discussed creation and The Trinity and quoted from Cicero and the poets. Scotus, although not acquainted with the Muses, is nevertheless educated. And as for more recent and contemporary philosophers, who are much less learned, he excels among them who has been fully instructed in secular learning.

"By the immortal God," continued the mayor, "suppose I become changed from a magistrate into a philosopher?" "This I will permit," said Batt. And then he continued as follows: "Peter was the first of the Apostles and Jerome the first of the (Christian) scholars. Peter possessed the greatest ardor of faith; Jerome, the greatest erudition. Imitate the spirit of the one and the learning of the other. But you prefer to have me rank the Apostles rather than the scholars. Foremost of those in the first rank I place Peter and Paul. Paul was very well versed in all kinds of literature. When reproved by Paul, Peter though superior in authority both believed and obeyed the more learned Apostle."

Once more the magistrate interrupts Batt with a brief remark. "In this discussion," he says, "which is more spirited than pertinent, you seem to me to make two errors. For we had proposed to consider profane literature, not divine learning, which it is clear the Apostles received; and this divine learning they acquired, not through human studies, but by the gift of heaven." Batt now replies that this is true. All our studies will be in vain, our magnificent libraries useless, if we are not aided by the Holy Spirit. "Unless we prefer to wait until in the manner of Paul we are carried either into Paradise or into the third heaven itself, to hear secrets which man may not reveal to man. But we must decide whether we want everything revealed to us at once, or whether we prefer that the spirit be present as often as it is needed. I think that the latter is by far the more convenient, for if the whole revelation comes at once, we shall have the labor of remembering. Wherefore, in order to relieve the memory of this burden, it will be better to intrust everything to the Holy Spirit, that it may be present only when called and invoked as the situation demands, as much of it as will offer enough, no more. If a book is to be written, let the Spirit fly to us, and while we remain passive, let it rule the pen. If a sermon is to be delivered, let it descend to our ears in the form of a dove and shape our language, and let us merely remember to open our mouths, that we may sing with the royal psalmist: 'I have opened my mouth and I have attracted the Spirit.'"

This is indeed a strange way of treating the subject of divine inspiration. It confirms very plainly the impression gained previously that Erasmus knew almost nothing about mysticism. He spoke most carelessly about the vocation of the Holy Spirit, considering his position in the years 1490–95. He, an Augustinian monk, was prating about the holiest things in the universe (for him and his associates) in a bantering, jesting fashion, as if it were a matter of little consequence. We can see now why he became restless in the monastery and later derided monasticism. For him research counted more than faith and inspiration. Asceticism grew repugnant to him. Primitive Christianity lost its charm for him. Not charity, but learning he sought, not self-denial, but fame, not humility, but honor. His *Book against the Barbarians*, which for more than four hundred years has been wrongly judged in its historical setting, becomes a most valuable source of information when properly interpreted. It helps to explain a number of puzzling problems in the youth of Erasmus, and it throws new light on his later life.

CHAPTER XVI

POEMS AND ORATIONS

IT IS rather difficult to determine the time of composition of the poems and orations produced by Erasmus before the year 1495. Several of them mention Erasmus' age, however; others are referred to in his letters. The rest give no definite clue. Finally, there are four short pieces of poetry of which only one copy is known, since they have not been published before. The latter will be found at the end of the present volume.

Nearly all the poetical writings of the period under discussion reveal the influence of Alexander Hegius. Erasmus as a rule selects the same subject-matter as his former teacher. Like Hegius, he and his two intimate friends, William Herman and Cornelius Aurelius, write about Biblical subjects, saints, the Virgin Mary, and classical personages. One of the very earliest of Erasmus' writings is the *Carmen Bucolicum*, also named *Pamphilus*, because in the printed edition it begins with the word *Pamphilus*. It is supposed to have been composed at Deventer.[1] A manuscript at Gouda appears to contain the poem in its original form, with the name Rosphamus instead of Pamphilus, showing Erasmus' lack of classical learning when residing at Deventer. This earliest known version is also printed at the end of the present work.

Erasmus was afterward by no means proud of the poems he had composed in his youth. "We were wholly given to a dry, weak, bloodless, and colorless form of poetry, partly out of mental poverty, partly in blind imitation. . . . We wrote as boys, not for sensitive, but for Dutch, that is, very dull ears, and since we tried

---

[1] The title in the *Opera* (VIII, 561) is: "Carmen Bucolicum, quod lusit natus annos quatuordecim, quum adhuc Daventriae sub Alexandro Hegio litteris operam daret." This would place it in the year 1483 and is further proof that Erasmus was born in 1469.

piously to conform to their tastes, we pleased neither them, nor the educated." [2]

One poem ascribed to Erasmus is entitled *Conflict between Thalia and Barbarism*. It is supposed to have been written by him when he was at Steyn, but although the name Thalia appears in a contemporary letter,[3] that name is not necessarily a reference to the poem in question. If Erasmus was its author, he must have written it after 1492, but it is most probably the production of another author. The subject discussed is the barbarous condition in the school at Zwolle. The poem is in the form of a dialogue between Thalia and Barbarism; the latter defends the school at Zwolle. It is clear that if Erasmus in a letter to Cornelius Aurelius, who was interested in the school at Deventer and praised that school for many years after 1492,[4] mentioned the name Thalia he could not have thought of the school at Zwolle, in which he had never been interested himself.[5]

In the letter to Botzheim (1523) he gives some information about his poems. "But you have long been awaiting a list of them, not an apology. Well, you shall have it; and first I shall enumerate those things which I wrote in verse, a pursuit for which I had such a propensity in my youth that I could only with difficulty make myself write prose. . . . It was in Paris that our bold efforts first began to be made known to the world; it was there that my friends published a piece in hexameters, mixed with tetrameters, addressed to Faustus Andrelinus. . . . But many years before that I had written a Sapphic poem in honor of the archangel Michael, not of my own accord, but impelled by the prayers of a great man, who was in charge of a church of which St. Michael was the patron saint. Although I restrained my pen, so that my poem might seem a prose work, yet the prelate dared not appropriate it on the ground that it was so poetical that, as he said, it might have been written in Greek. Such was the unhappiness of those times." [6]

[2] P. S. Allen, *Opus Ep. Er.*, I, Ep. 113.
[3] See p. 158.
[4] See p. 207.
[5] The poem is printed in the *Opera*, I, 890. The author condemns a textbook by Michael Modista. It is doubtful whether Erasmus knew that work before 1493.
[6] P. S. Allen, *op. cit.*, I, 3, lines 15–35.

The poem referred to has survived and was published in the Leiden edition of the *Opera* (vol. V, 1321). It is entitled *Ode in Praise of Michael and the Angels,* and resembles some of Hegius' poems. It might be noticed in this connection that Cornelius Aurelius, who assisted Erasmus in composing poetry, wrote an extremely long poem in honor of the Virgin Mary, a copy of which is found in a manuscript in the Athenaeum Library at Deventer. In the Preface to this poem he says that at one time he had decided to drop the work on it, but "a certain Augustinian Canon Regular named Herasmus exhorted me to continue it." [7] The poem was composed between 1494 and 1497 in the monastery of Lopsen near Leiden.[8] There are repeated references in the Preface to the Brethren of the Common Life at Deventer,[9] for it is addressed to James Faber, a member of the brotherhood and a teacher at Deventer, who in 1503 published Hegius' poems. Cornelius Aurelius always remained true to his order and cannot have ridiculed the Brethren of the Common Life, wherefore Erasmus certainly did not join him in making fun of the brethren at Zwolle.

Since Erasmus was not anxious to see his early poems in print, the majority did not appear in that form during his lifetime. One of them, however, was published with a number of poems of William Herman in Paris by Erasmus himself (1497). It was entitled *Hendecasyllabum Herasmi ad Studiosos* and, as it was little better than the other poems written before 1497, it was never reprinted during the lifetime of Erasmus, nor does it seem to have been published after his death.

In 1513 Reyner Snoy, a noted physician and magistrate of Gouda, published there a number of poems by Erasmus, Corne-

---

[7] Ms. 101 B5, fol. 4b: "Iam enim prime decadis libris absolutis mihi prae animi pusillanimitate in tanto opere pene labenti piae exhortationis manum porrexit quidam canonicus regularis, Herasmus nomine, etate floridus, religione compositus et omnium facile nostri evi tam prosa quam metro praestantissimus."

[8] P. C. Molhuysen, *Cornelius Aurelius,* p. 22.

[9] See, for example, fol. 1b: "Didicissem poetridas (ut Persius ait) picas tum devotorum fratrum domus Florentii dispendio tum animarum periculo Daventriensis oppidi scholis advolasse et iam incipere labora simplicium fonte prolui (ne dicam pollui) caballino, inflammatus zelo domus Dei. . . ." Another example is found on fol. 4a: "O, inquit, tandem inveni quod devotis illis patribus domus Florentii pro instruendis iuvenibus non minime conducat."

lius Aurelius, and William Herman. In 1864 they were repub-
lished in facsimile by Ch. Ruelens, who added an essay on the
youth of Erasmus. It was Snoy who maintained that Erasmus was
born at Gouda, although transported to Rotterdam soon after his
birth. In the preface of the volume of poems edited by him,[10] he
stated that Erasmus and William Herman lived together in Steyn
for nearly ten years and here composed the poems mentioned.[11]
At that time, continues Snoy, Erasmus was not yet twenty years
old.[12]

There followed in the first place three so-called satires by
Erasmus, which are not found in the *Opera* of Erasmus. The first
describes the errors of those foolish men who pursue, as the highest good, objects with only transitory value.[13] The theme is similar to that covered in some of the chapters in the treatise *On the
Contempt of the World*. Men are deemed mistaken in their quest
after earthly things. The poem is simpler and less tinged with a
classical atmosphere than the treatise. Erasmus had no intention
of impressing his readers with his learning. The second "satire"
is addressed to a dissipated young man, who is admonished to think
of approaching death.[14] This poem is also a purer expression of the
monastic ideal than the treatise. It might easily have been written
by a man like Thomas à Kempis. The third piece is entitled *The
Rich Miser*.[15] It is very similar to the other two. Perhaps they
were all written during Erasmus' first year at Steyn.

[10] They were printed by Allardus Gauter.

[11] "Guielmus noster Goudanus ut alter Theseus cum Herasmo suo in Steynico
rure annis ferme decem convixit." Although Snoy had much reason to speak with
authority, Erasmus cannot have arrived in Steyn before the autumn of 1486 and
left not later than 1493. We may say that he spent about six years in Steyn.

[12] "Nondum annum agebat vigesimum." Cornelius Loos of Gouda claimed
that Erasmus was born in 1469. The monk who wrote a criticism about Loos'
biographical remarks (see p. 51, note 4) did not, however, dispute the date given
as Erasmus' birth-year. Snoy probably accepted the year 1469 also. The poem
he edited had therefore been composed before 1490.

[13] The title is "Herasmi Roterodami Satyr prima in Errores Hominum degene-
rantium et pro summo celistique bono varias falsorum bonorum species amplecten-
cium."

[14] The title is "Satyr secunda in Juvenum luxuria defluentem atque Mortis
Admonitio."

[15] The Latin title is "Satyr tercia in Divitem Avarum."

Following these three poems is a production named *Apology*, arranged in the form of a dialogue between Erasmus and Cornelius Aurelius. It was reprinted by Leclerc in the *Opera* (Vol. VIII, 567) from a manuscript copy formerly owned by Scriverius. Cornelius made reference to it in one of his letters to Erasmus,[16] where it appears that Erasmus wrote the whole poem, but Cornelius put it into the shape of a dialogue. It discusses the familiar theme of "barbarism," and attacks the old-fashioned scribes who fail to appreciate classical antiquity. The date of its composition may be placed between 1489 and 1492. The next piece is another poem of Erasmus which was not published in the *Opera*. It is entitled *To Lesbius, About Money*.[17] This brief poem differs from the first three in that it is entirely based on classical literature. Erasmus testified in his letter to Servatius of the year 1514 that he had never desired to amass temporal possessions. The poems mentioned thus far seem to corroborate that statement. Erasmus could find many arguments in pagan and Christian writings to show how foolish it was to set his heart on the acquisition of money or its equivalent.

The last poem in the collection edited by Snoy is a contribution by William Herman of Gouda, describing the terrible conditions caused by civil war in Holland.[18] It forcibly reminds the reader of a number of statements found in Erasmus' treatise *On the Contempt of the World* and it helps explain why Erasmus, after lengthy deliberation and at least a year of probation, chose to become a monk at Steyn.

More important than Snoy's selections are the poems published in the *Opera* by Leclerc at Leiden. In the eighth volume appeared the *Carmen Bucolicum*, or *Pamphilus*, mentioned above, and the *Apology*, also referred to above, besides thirteen other poetical productions. The first of these is an *Ode on Love* (*Oda Amatoria*), which is brief and colorless. The second is an *Elegy on the Muta-*

---

[16] See p. 157, note 24.

[17] The Latin title is "Ad Lesbium Metrum phalenticum hendecasyllabum. De Nummo."

[18] The title is "Guielmi Goudani Canonici divi Augustini in Steyn Theologi ac Poete Clarissimi. Prosopopeia Hollandie bello, penuria, morbo, factionibus, tamdiu vexate de suorum calamitate lamentantis."

bility of the Seasons,[19] a neo-classical piece. Then follows a much longer poem, named *Elegy on Patience, which alone conquers everything, and on the Affliction of Mortals, not so much to be escaped in whatever way possible as to be bravely conquered by Patience*.[20] The next contribution was composed by Erasmus and William Herman of Gouda when they were both nineteen years old. It is entitled *Contest between Erasmus and William about Spring*.[21] It makes pleasant reading. Since the title of the poem itself mentions the age of Erasmus and of Herman, we may place the date of composition in the year 1488, when both writers had just been professed in Steyn and were busily engaged in studying the classics and in perusing the works of the leading humanists. The poem evinces an appreciation of the beauties of nature and a marked interest in plant life, which is remarkable for Erasmus, who afterward did not even describe the majestic scenery witnessed by him in visiting Italy from beyond the Alps.

The poem following the *Apology* is a short *Eulogy on Pope Gregory*,[22] written in a respectful vein. The next piece is an *Epigram on the Four Last Things*.[23] A book had been written by that name in the Netherlands, whose author is probably Gerardus de Vliederhoven; it was widely read in the Augustinian monasteries and Erasmus seems influenced by it. The subject is the Last Judgment, but Erasmus' poem of only ten lines does not do justice to the theme. Then follows another insignificant piece of poetry with the title *The Book Speaks*.[24] This is followed in turn by a *Poem addressed to a Friend*,[25] similar to the dialogue on spring, for it describes the forces of nature, something which left Erasmus indifferent afterward.

A rather important poem is the *Ode on Mary and the Incarnation*

---

[19] *Elegia de Mutabilitate Temporum, ad Amicum* (col. 563).

[20] *Elegia de Patientia, qua Sola vincuntur Omnia, atque de Dolore Mortalium, quomodo non tam fugiendus, quam fortiter Patientia vincendus sit* (cols. 563-565).

[21] *Certamen Erasmi atque Guielmi de Tempore Vernali, quod per Viridantia Prata alternis ex tempore luserunt, anno eorum decimo nono* (cols. 565-567).

[22] *In Laudem beatissimi Gregorii Papa* (cols. 570-571).

[23] *Epigramma de Quatuor Novissimis* (col. 571).

[24] *Libellus loquitur* (col. 571).

[25] *Carmen Asclepiadeum Choriambicum, quarto Glyconico. Ad amicum suum* (cols. 571-572).

of the Word,[26] very probably written at Steyn. It consists of one
hundred and one stanzas, and is a curious mixture of Biblical and
classic phrases. Erasmus' friend, Aurelius, as was observed above,
a few years later composed a poem with a similar title (*Mariados*),
in which task he was spurred on by Erasmus. The two poems are
somewhat different, however, for Erasmus was mostly exercising
his pen, while Aurelius was motivated by deep religious ardor.

Another fairly long poem, resembling the preceding one, is
named *Poem on the Marvelous Signs made by the Dying Christ*.[27]
Here Erasmus wisely refrains from dragging in characters and
scenes from classical literature, which he used copiously at the
beginning of the poem on Mary. It seems that Erasmus actually
became animated by the scene he described. Well he might, for
the crucified Christ was the topic uppermost in the minds of all
true monks and nuns in western Europe.

Longer still, but not more convincing, is the following selection,
entitled *Heroic Poem on the Solemnity of Easter and the Triumphal
Glory of the Risen Christ and his Descent into Hell*.[28] Erasmus talks
about Styx, the Underworld, and Cocytus, the river which flows
there. The burning river Phlegethon is also mentioned. Even the
Eumenides, or the furies of the nether regions, confront Christ
before his resurrection, and Lake Avernus, situated near Cumae in
Italy, a pestiferous place, is duly mentioned. The name Phoebus
occurs here as well as in the poem on Mary; in the latter piece one
also reads about the lake and rivers just given, which must strike
even a casual reader as being out of place. What did the Virgin
Mary have to do with those malodorous rivers and Lake Avernus?
A deeply religious monk would have spoken more exclusively about
sin and spiritual suffering. Apparently Erasmus had not yet come
to the conclusion that hell-fire was not a real fire, but denoted a
spiritual or mental condition.[29]

[26] *Ode dicolos tetrastrophos Hendecasyllaba Sapphica, Paean divae Mariae, atque de
Incarnatione Verbi* (cols. 572–577).
[27] *Carmen de Monstrosis Signis Christo moriente factis* (col. 577–579).
[28] *Carmen heroicum de Solemnitate Paschali, atque de triumphali Christi resurgentis
Pompa et Descensu ejus ad inferos* (cols. 579–584).
[29] Although a statement in *De Contemptu Mundi* (see *Opera*, V, 1356A) seems
to express the view later held by Erasmus, Mestwerdt is wrong in overemphasizing

Two short poems conclude the collection; they are odes commemorating the good work of Galter of Gouda. The first is named *Ode Lamenting the Death of Galter of Gouda*,[30] the other, *Funeral Sermon on Galter*.[31] This man is described as the dearest friend Erasmus had; no one was a better man or more worthy of a longer life. One may well ask why Erasmus never mentions this dearest of friends in his correspondence. It has been suggested that Galter was the same person as Gauter, the printer. Erasmus was acquainted with only a few men in Gouda. One of these was Gerard Leeuw, a well-known printer. What is more natural than that he should also know Gauter, the other printer? On the other hand the second is not named Galter, but Allardus Gauter; so it is likely that these two poems were written in Steyn, where he learned one day of the death of Galter. After the year 1513 it made very little difference to Erasmus who died in Gouda. Finally, it seems impossible that the two mediocre pieces listed were composed by Erasmus when he had advanced far in the art of writing.

In Steyn, therefore, we see Erasmus already becoming a typical humanist. Galter of Gouda, whom he scarcely knew, was dearer to him than his most intimate friends. He was doing very well indeed for a beginner. Every true humanist had at least a dozen friends who were each the most learned and the most virtuous and the most beloved of all the men he knew. Erasmus had begun nobly; within six years he would praise Anna of Borselen, Lady of Veere, above all other ladies named Anna, not excluding Biblical characters; and simultaneously denounce her behind her back to one of her acquaintances as a frivolous flirt. Afterward he would publish these letters side by side to show how clever he was. He would blame others for his misfortunes, call his brother a criminal who should have hanged himself; he would flatter the rich, and despise the simple. Such were in parts the fruits of Italian humanism.

Before analyzing the orations prepared at Steyn, it will be well

---

a detached statement. He seems to ignore the poems, which are clear enough. (See P. Mestwerdt, *Die Anfänge des Erasmus*, p. 231.)

[30] *Ode Ubi deplorat mortem Galteri Goudani* (col. 584).

[31] *Epitaphium ejusdem Galteri.*

to describe briefly the four poems found in a manuscript at Gouda, which are printed for the first time in the present volume. The first is dedicated to Master Engelbert of Leiden, who was a friend of Wessel Gansfort.[32] It is interesting to contrast the flattery of this poem with the remarks made about this scholar by Erasmus after he had risen to fame. In this poem he frankly tells Engelbert that the firmament and the fields are harbingers of his rising fame. Although Engelbert remains in the same place, his reputation spreads everywhere. The day will presently arrive when "barbarism" will fall and poetry, under Engelbert's leadership, will ascend to sublime heights, up to the stars. This is a pretty speech, a piece of rather innocent flattery. But when one reads Erasmus' remarks about this "leader of sublime poetry" in the *De Conscribendis Epistolis*, a textbook on letter-writing, one sees a great change. Engelbert has misled the youth of the land by making them write in a bad style. He had written a simple text in rhetoric and showed a deplorable lack of knowledge, according to Erasmus.[33]

The second poem in the Gouda manuscript is *An Elegy on the Comparison between Sorrow and Joy*. The first part describes the miseries of sinful man; then follow a few remarks about joy. One could scarcely call this tasteless piece poetical. Erasmus must have been glad that it was never published during his lifetime. The following selection is *An Elegy on the Overwhelming Power of the Quivered Cupid*. In it Erasmus says that finally he knows what love is. It is a fire in the breast hotter than Etna. . . . It enters the eyes, penetrates the bones, and with its silent flames consumes one within. It takes away sleep. It never rests. If it is unable to unite the bodies of the lovers, it nevertheless joins their hearts. Here Erasmus says something which may seem interesting. The preceding poem was little more than a few platitudes badly grouped together. Erasmus tells further how Samson was ruined by love,

[32] M. Van Rhijn, "Engelbert van Leiden," *Ned. Arch. voor Kerkgesch.*, 1927, p. 295. Engelbert was rector of the principal school in Leiden from 1458 to about 1464, but continued to teach there after 1464.

[33] In the edition of 1533, printed at Cologne, Erasmus says on p. 21: "Apud Hollandos orbis lumen habebatur Engelbertus quidam, qui suis epistolis nihil aliud docebat pueros quam inepte scribere."

how Solomon was troubled by it, how it extinguishes the light of
reason, and how even great Babylon was destroyed by it. The
author shows the effect of the asceticism taught by the Brethren
of the Common Life and by the monks about him. Other sources
he also knew., Patristic literature is full of it, he says, and St. Paul
himself speaks plainly enough.

The fourth poem is a plaintive elegy on sorrow, which does not
appear to have much meaning. It is followed by an important
poem of William Herman of Gouda, describing Alexander Hegius
as a poet who encourages his pupils to write verses. As a source
for the study of Erasmus' youth it has considerable value, particularly since it has never been published before. One need not read
it attentively to discover why Herman and Erasmus and Aurelius
loved to write poetry and why their verses resembled so closely
the poetical productions of their former teachers. A few pages
farther is found the earliest known draft of Erasmus' *Carmen
Bucolicum*.

Other sources of information about Erasmus' literary activity in
Steyn are two orations composed by him about the year 1490.
The first is a funeral oration in honor of Bertha de Heyen of Gouda,
a widow, who left two daughters.[34] This widow was very charitable, spending a large part of her handsome income in caring for sick
and poor people.[35] The monks of Steyn were frequently invited to
her house, and Erasmus seems to have been a favorite of hers. He
says: "She had a daughter named Margaret, who was very beautiful and whom she dearly loved. This daughter was married, and
her wedding was celebrated with splendor. After six weeks of
married life she contracted a fatal illness. I was called to her
house and went. A large number of people were standing around
her bed; they were all weeping and sobbing. The mother alone
did not weep. When the poor daughter had surrendered her soul
to God, Bertha said to me: 'You come here to console me as if an
injustice has been done to me, something which should arouse my
indignation. But He who takes my daughter away is the same

---

[34] Published in the *Opera* (VIII, cols. 551–560).

[35] Erasmus himself had often witnessed her charitable actions, according to his
oration.

who gave her to me. What right have I to complain? She has no doubt been taken in order that I may be punished for my sins!"

This is a very impressive account and the reader is disappointed when he peruses the description of Erasmus' grief, which, if it has been depicted correctly, makes him look rather silly. But the whole narrative which follows is pure affectation. "Every time," says Erasmus, "the sweet image of Bertha was presented to my mind, my eyes immediately filled with tears, as if they were the blood of my broken heart; my sobs redoubled, groans escaped me, witnesses of my inward grief; a cold shiver ran through the marrow of my bones; a frightful paleness was drawn upon my features; my tongue stuck to my palate; my spirits fell; cruel grief overwhelmed me so that I could not bear it. I confess my weakness (although I am ashamed of it), I am overcome by my feelings, I am absorbed in sorrow, I cannot control my eyes."

True sorrow, as Ruelens observes,[36] does not seek utterance in such language, nor does it seek to pile fragments from classical authors upon each other. The two surviving daughters of Bertha, to whom the oration was addressed, could not possibly have appreciated Erasmus' learning. They would have been more pleased with a few simple, honest words.

In this funeral oration Erasmus expresses some of his views on religion in general and on monasticism in particular. "Bertha was beautiful and rich," argued Erasmus, "and devout. Why didn't she enter a convent? It would have been more prudent, I admit, but in my opinion it is far more meritorious to lead a pure and innocent life amidst the seductions of vice, to pass her existence in tranquillity in the midst of the turmoil of the world. Virtue alone enabled her to do this."

Then Erasmus proceeds to draw a highly interesting comparison between Bertha's mode of living and that of his fellow-monks at Steyn: "When we used to dine at her house, if one of us would drop a few bold words which might compromise the reputation of our neighbors, she always looked displeased and interrupted the pernicious speech, saying: 'While you are seated at my table,

---

[36] Ruelens, *Érasme*, p. xxxvi. He gives an excellent French translation of the pages here translated into English.

beware, brethren, of making derogatory remarks about people who are not present, or to report the misdemeanors of someone else, for my ears are not pleased by them!'" This quotation is sometimes reproduced to show that Erasmus had been compelled against his will to enter the monastery and revealed in the funeral oration traces of discontentment.[37] It seems to the present writer, however, that Erasmus was merely describing Bertha's virtues. He knew that her daughters would feel grateful to him; besides, he must have told the plain truth without trying to preach. He probably had trespassed himself. One would expect that from a young man who but a very few years later indulged in this habit without feeling ashamed of himself.

The funeral oration has a note at the bottom which informs the reader that Erasmus composed it at the age of twenty-one. It is a curious fact that almost every production written by Erasmus before 1495 proves the statement of Cornelius Loos of Gouda to the effect that Erasmus was born in 1469, and not in 1466. One may well wonder why even those biographers who were familiar with many important sources still accepted the year 1466. Erasmus cannot have entered Steyn before 1487. According to the oration now under discussion, he had often been entertained by Bertha, the mother of the deceased daughter. He tells about Margaret's wedding and says that six weeks later she died. Erasmus seems to imply that he has known Bertha for two or three years. If he had been born in 1466, he would have reached the age of 21 in 1487, and as a monk could not have known her for more than a few months.

In addition to the oration composed in honor of Bertha de Heyen, we have one addressed to Cornelius Aurelius of Gouda, named *Oration on Peace and Discord against the Seditious.*[38] "Although it is not at all necessary to try to persuade you, Cornelius, by any speech of mine to promote the cause of peace and love, inasmuch as by your gentle nature you have since boyhood always been foremost in desiring and cultivating peace, nevertheless, considering

---

[37] Ruelens, *Érasme*, p. xxxvi. "Il était devenu religieux malgré lui. . . . On trouve des traces de son mécontentement dans tout ce qui nous reste d'écrits de sa jeunesse."   [38] *Opera*, VIII, cols. 545E–552B.

the conditions of our times, I do not find any subject on which it can now be more useful or opportune to speak." Then he goes on to show how foolish and wicked men are to fight for temporal possessions. We are poor, he remarks, and are at peace. The human body is so constituted that it needs peace and tranquillity, else sanity cannot last. When one part of the body suffers, the whole body is ill; so in a community all are disturbed if one member is in trouble. "No man can maintain his dignity by fighting, not even a heathen, a savage, a barbarian, an idolatrous person; much less a Christian, a member of the clergy, a monk!" It is not clear whether Erasmus thinks a monk superior to a plain Christian. At any rate, monasticism was generally regarded as the most purely religious mode of life possible on earth. Erasmus seems content with his lot. He is twenty years old, according to a note appended to the bottom of the oration. He speaks as an experienced monk. Had he been born in 1466, he could not have been a monk at the age of twenty. Once again the sources point to 1469 as the birth-year of Erasmus.

The poems and orations produced by Erasmus before 1493 prove that he had read extensively; both patristic and classical literature had furnished him with many useful phrases. Like the letters written at Steyn, his minor writings just reviewed were to a considerable extent mere rhetorical exercises. Nevertheless, they throw much light on the development of his mind and of his character. Erasmus frequently reveals his inner nature, his predilections, and his ambitions. He is still fairly unsophisticated, dominated by the views of his former teachers and of the Augustinian Canons Regular. The Devotio Moderna is fighting with humanism for the first place in his mind. But other movements are also represented. Scholasticism is still present, although rapidly losing a foothold. The whole civilization of the Burgundian Netherlands is making all sorts of impressions on Erasmus' mind. Soon he will soar far above his compatriots. As he ascends higher and higher into the literary firmament, he begins to loosen the ties which have hitherto restricted the expanding forces of his intellect. The learning acquired by him in his childhood and early youth seems ever more insignificant, and the literary productions of that period are in his estimation mere trifles; some of them actually make him shudder with shame. But let him take comfort in the thought that all gifted men of his kind have had and will have such experiences.

It is impossible for the biographer to describe the relationship between the young Erasmus and the middle-aged Erasmus until he has fully analyzed both characters. Erasmus himself did not know how much he owed respectively to his parents, the Brethren of the Common Life, Hegius, Agricola, Gansfort, the monks at Steyn, the bishop of Cambray, the college of Montaigu, Gaguin, Colet, More, Reuchlin, Luther, and a host of other scholars. The things he did know were frequently distorted by him in order that his contemporaries and posterity might believe only what he wished them to believe. When still a boy he studied Augustine and Jerome. He was strongly influenced by some of the greatest mystics of the Middle Ages. Even at Deventer he became acquainted with many classical productions and with the rising tide of transalpine humanism. Those authorities, therefore, who maintain that until Erasmus met Colet he had never had an opportunity to break with scholasticism,[39] either ignore the influence of such works as the *Imitation of Christ*, or the writings composed by Erasmus before 1495. Much emphasis is usually placed upon the influence of Ficino, Pico, and the other Italian humanists. Their labors are said to have had international significance; they are held responsible for a renaissance of Christianity. But what about the *Imitation of Christ?* Were its hundreds of editions read only in the Netherlands, and could Erasmus not acquire religious fervor by following the precepts of the men who directly influenced him? One must be very careful not to destroy the proper balance between the forces which shaped the mind of Erasmus. It is hoped that the present study may lead to a more

---

[39] Recently a professor in Berlin has reiterated the old theory in the following words: "Durch die englischen Humanisten wird dann Erasmus von Rotterdam mit Picos Schriften bekannt, und diese bieten ihm zum erstenmal die Gelegenheit, das Christentum anders aufzufassen, als die Scholastiker es lehrten." The article in which this remark is found was published in the *Zeitschrift für Kirchengeschichte*, XLIV (1925), 504–543. The author is Ivan Pusino, a scholar who knows a great deal about the Italian Renaissance and unconsciously appears to slight similar movements north of the Alps.

scientific analysis of the mind of Erasmus just before he met the dean of St. Paul's Cathedral and other great and noble men. Perhaps it will be seen that what these men did for Erasmus was not so much to instil new views into his mind as to resurrect dead ideals, formulated long ago but starved to death by improper care. The youth of Erasmus requires more attention if one really wants to know where the prince of the humanists got his ideas. It will be a fascinating task for some lover of truth to lift the veil behind which the seeds of lofty ideals grew into fair plants whose flowers, sunned by propitious skies, reached full maturity and finally bore the rich fruit which amazed all Europe and still holds the attention of all truly educated men and women.

APPENDIX A

SEVEN POEMS BY ERASMUS AND
WILLIAM HERMAN OF GOUDA

These poems are all found in Manuscript 1323 of the City Library of Gouda. The manuscript has been referred to in Chapter XIV of the present volume. It has been fully described by P. S. Allen in the first volume of his edition of the letters by Erasmus (pp. 118, 609-611).

Only the last of the seven poems has been published before. The version reproduced here is probably identical with the original draft, but differs in numerous particulars from the printed copies. It reveals a lack of knowledge of classical literature on the part of Erasmus when he was still a monk. He may even have composed the *Carmen Bucolicum* before he entered the monastery.

The poems by William Herman of Gouda contain several references to Alexander Hegius, the teacher of Erasmus and Herman at Deventer. They were probably written about the year 1484, when both boys were still greatly impressed by the learning of their teacher. Herman never ceased to admire Hegius, but Erasmus, as was explained above, after the year 1495 began to despise the man whose accomplishments from the standpoint of a true humanist were indeed very mediocre.

The spelling of the manuscript, which is not always consistent, has been retained, but small initial letters of proper names have been changed to capitals.

I. *Erasmus magistro Enghelberto Leydensi*

8r   Ethere quot placidis rutilant sub noctibus ignes
        Siderei, guttas quot capit unda freti,
    Quot flavae segetes Cereri, quot pocula Bacchi,
    Et quot verna virens gramina campus habet,
    Tantas et plures vates divine salutes
    Exoptat vitae nostra Camena tuae.
    Fama loquax populos late diffusa per omnes
    Ignarum quemquam non sinit esse tui,
    Qui licet usque loco maneas immotus eodem,
    Hac tamen immenso notus in orbe volas.

Hec facit ut nil te dubitem me noscere, quamquam
Non unquam facies sit tua visa mihi.
Illa meas quoniam delapsa est nuper ad aures,
Laudis et ingenii nuncia multa tui,
Insigni virtute virum, Musis et amicum
Praedicat, ac superi tollit ad astra poli,
Ingens fama quidem, atque viro bene digna perito,
Sed longe meritis est minor ipsa tuis.
Nam (nunc suspectae dubitem ne credere linguae)
Hauserunt versus lumina nostra tuos.
In quibus oppressae lucet spaes multa Camenae,
Quae misere toto prohpudor orbe iacet.
Ergo precor ceptos fac perge vir optime calles,
8 v   Inque dies crescat haec tua cura tibi.
Barbaries indocta cadat, facunda poesis
Te duce sublime tollat in astra caput.
Iamque vale, eternos dent numina vivere in annos,
Atque immortales det tibi Parca dies.

II. *Elegia Erasmi de collatione doloris et leticiae*

Nimbus et obscurae pellantur ab aethere nubes,
Pectoribus nostris cura dolorque cadat.
Affricus aequoreos cesset sustollere fluctus,
Pectoribus nostris cura dolorque cadat.
Frondiferae boreas agitare cacumina sylvae,
Pectoribus nostris cura dolorque cadat.
Cura dolorque cadat, surgant nova gaudia, cedant
Luctus et Eumenides, cura dolorque procul.
Cura dolorque procul, viridem solet ille iuventam
Ante diem rugis conmaculare suis.
Ante diem solet ille gravem celerare senectam,
Ille solet dulces abbreviare dies.
Ille rapit vires, vorat ossibus ille medullas,
Fronte perempta perit forma dolore suo.
Pectoribus sensum furor aufert pessimus ille,
Eripit ingenium pessimus ille furor.
Ergo procul Stigias procul hinc demigret in undas,
9 r   Tartareumque cahos, cura dolorque cadant.
Adsit leticia, pulchram decet illa iuventam,

PLATE VI

Erasmus magistro enghilberto leydensi.

Ethere quot plaudis rutilat sub noctib3 ignes
Sideris: guttas quot rapit unda fiti.
Quot flauz segetes reten, qt pocula bacchi.
Et quot verna virens gummia rapus hab3:
Tatas et plures vates diuine salutes
Proptus vite nostra camena tue.
Fama loquax populos late diffusa p ones:
Ignarw quemqi no smit esse tui.
Qui licet vsqz loco maneas innotq eode:
Hac tamen menso notq T orbe volas.
Hec facit ut nil te dubite me nosce: qp
Pro vnqi facies sit tua visa mihi.
Illa meas qui delapsa est nup ad aures:
Laudis et ingenij nucia multa tui.
Insigni virtute viru, musis et amicu
Pzdicat: ac superi tollit ad astra poli.
Inges fama quide, atqz viro bn digna peito:
Sed longe mevite est minor ipsa tuis.
Ha Cnur suspecte dubite ne crede lingue :)
Hauserut versus limina nostra tuos.
In qbus oppresse lucet spes multa camene:
Quis misere toto phpudoz orbe iaret.
Ergo pror ceptos far pqe vir optie calles:

Facsimile of folio 8r, MS 1523, City Library of Gouda

Qua sine nil pulchrum, nil queat esse bonum.
Corporis illa iuvat vires, seniumque moratur
Tristius, et letos protrahit ille dies.
Leticia maior est forma, serenior est frons,
Leticia ingenium clarius esse solet.

III. *Elegia Erasmi de prepotenti virtute Cupidinis pharetrati*

Nunc scio quid sit amor: amor est insania mentis.
Ethna fervidior pectoris ignis amor.
Nutibus et signis teneri pascuntur amores,
Inter blanda oritur suavia stultus amor.
Lumina mollis amor primum subit, inde medullis
Figitur, atque potens ossa penetrat amor.
Ossa penetrat amor, tacitisque edit intima flammis,
Ima suis facibus viscera torret amor.
Viscera torret amor, mentem vetat esse quietam,
Atque adimit somnos irrequietus amor.
Non requiescit amor, sed mutua victor amantum
Corpora si nequeat, pectora iungit amor.
Sit licet unus amor, nectit duo corda duorum.
Ut duo iam non sint efficit unus amor.
Quem ferus urit amor, in amati pectore totus
9 v   Absens ipse sibi est, quem ferus urit amor.
Quem ferus urit amor nil dulce ubi desit amatum,
At qum rursus adest, nil grave sentit amor.
Omnia vincit amor, adamantea claustra relaxat,
Ferrea (ceu stipulam) vincula rumpit amor.
Omnia vincit amor sine cede et sanguine certans,
Et domat indomitos non domitandus amor.
Mollia nodosae validae pro robore clavae
Alciden trahere pensa coegit amor.
Praelia Mavortis quem non potuere cruenti
Magnanimum Eacidem vincere, vicit amor.
Denique quid vastus Sampsone valentius orbis
Edidit? Hunc potuit sternere solus amor.
Quidve tulit totus Salomone peritius orbis?
Hunc quoque quo lubuit, victor abegit amor.
Doctus amor vigiles custodum fallere curas,

Noctis et excubias ludere doctus amor.
Cardine doctus amor nullum faciente tumultum
Scit reserare fores, claudere novit amor.
Omnia vertit amor, facit insipidos sapientes,
Atque Argi cecus lumina cecat amor.
Omnia vertit amor, mutum facit esse disertum,
In puerosque senes vertit amatus amor.
Fortia frangit amor, fragiles docet esse potentes,
Audaces timidos reddere novit amor.
Vulnera dirus amor temnit crudelia, ventis
10r Turbida nymbriferis aequora temnit amor.
Quid non fortis amor? et morte valentior ipsa est.
Mortem quam trepidant omnia, vincit amor.
Didonis egit amor miserae per viscera ferrum,
Insanus laqueo Phillida strinxit amor.
Per te fortis amor moritur Babilonia Tysbe,
Pyramus et per te sub Styga pergit amor.
Singula quid memorem? Vincit puer improbus ille
Omnia, tu pueri tu quoque seva parens.
Seva parens pueri? magis an puer improbus ille?
Improbus ille puer, tu quoque seva parens.

IV. *Elegia Erasmi: Querula doloris*

Qum nondum albenti surgant mihi vertice cani,
Candeat aut pilis frons viduata suis,
Luminibusve hebet aciem numerosior aetas,
Aut dens squalenti decidat ore niger,
Atque acuant rigidae nondum mihi brachia setae, aut
Pendeat arenti corpore laxa cutis,
Denique nulla meae videam argumenta senectae,
Nescio quid misero sorsque deusque parent.
Me mala ferre senum teneris voluere sub annis,
Iamque senem esse volunt, nec senuisse sinunt.
Iam quae canicie spergant mea tempora tristi,
10v Praevenere diem cura dolorque suum.

V. *Carmen Guielmi Hermani, agentis gratias praeceptori
suo Alexandro Hegio, precantisque illi leta et prospera
omnia.   Invocat Phebum*

Tu nova Tyronis trepidantia pectora firma,
Tu quae cantabo carmina Phebe rege.
Innumeras grates dum vivam semper habebo
Et quantas poterit vis mea semper agam
Illi praedulces qui me deduxit ad amnes,
Et iunctum choreis qui dedit esse sacris,
Numine Parcarum sit ei longissima vita,
Quarum cunctorum numine vita fluit.
Abbreviant aevum, prolongant (ut lubet) illae.
Illarum arbitrio tempora cuncta fluunt.
Illi propiciae sed donent Nestoris annos,
Ter centum Nestor,[1] vivat et ille precor.
Sepe tuam miserata manum rescindere filum
Atropos incipiens (noxia namque) trahe.
Unde trahit Lachesis nunquam colus imminuatur.
Turgeat, eductum sit velut usque nihil.
Neve fatigata longo pia Clotho labore
Proiice (rumpentur parvula fila) colum.
Quamque datis (nam spero datis) longum superesse,
Non sit de nigro vellere queso colus.
11r Ut meruit vitam, meruit simul esse beatam,
Iustas in talem vos decet esse virum.
Non illi noceat tellus, non pontus et aether,
Igne suo Phebus, lumine luna suo.
Dum petet ille, suum splendorem sidera donent,
Sit cum nube polus, sit sine nube polus.
Non noceat ventus qui solis surgit ab ortu,
Indeque qui radios sol ubi condit aquis.
Non noceat ventus qui parte existit ab illa,
Qua qum sit currus, est mediata dies.
Non noceat ventus qui parte exurgit ab illa,
Quae Phaetontis equos sensit adesse semel.
Mite ipsum faciat sese, ponatque procellas,
Ille per immensum qum parat ire fretum.
Illius in patulas non intrent aequora rimas,

---

[1] The word *vixit* was written in a later hand above the word *Nestor*.

Quacunque ille vagis puppe feretur aquis.
Alma et abundanter tribuat sua munera tellus,
Et sua non teneat munera flava Ceres.
Bacche tuum laetum non desit ei quoque munus,
Et vite in cauta pendeat uva tumens.
Sint et in arboribus saepe tot poma nucesque.
Ut sint curvatae pondere queque suo.
Et pecus illius (fuerit si fors pecus illi)
Ubra domum niveo turgida lacte ferat.[2]
Nec sterilis sit si fuerit (quod non reor) uxor,
    11v Nec sit, quae tali sit male digna viro.
Sit quoque cui magnum nomen faciat sua virtus,
Qui querat mores gnatus habere patris.
Quaeque duos vultus fortuna putatur habere,
Aspiciat semper prosperiore virum.
Instabilis summos quamquam devolvet in ima,
Summus at in summa stet tamen ille vota.
Largas fundat opes impleto copia cornu,
Nec cornu vacuum sinerit esse suum.
Anulus in digitis de fulvo fulgeat auro,
Et niteat vestis, sit quoque et alta domus.
Sit domus aërias quae pulset culmine nubes,
Sit cui non tota par sit in urbe domus.
Nec famuli non sint, quod et esse decet sit in illa,
Et nunquam flammis concidat usta feris.
Sintque dies vitae (quos multos spero futuros)
Quos lapide indignos non meliore putet.
Non praeceps veniat sed nec properantius aequo
Qum mors adveniet, nec violenta ruat.[3]
Si fuerit qui forte velit furiis agitatus
Eximium stricto decutere ense caput,
Per mare si veniet (et ego quod eum rogo) cymba
Neptuni saevo fracta tridente cadat.
Vel ferat in scopulos ventus, si evaserit illos,
Innumero laceret Scylla canora cane.
    12r Aut instar montis navi se iniecerit unda,
Ut sic aequorea mole gravetur aquis.
Unda gubernaclum devolvat, cumque procellis

---

[2] The words *ubra pro ubera* were written on the margin.
[3] The words *Imprecatur mala hostibus eius* were added on the margin to the left.

Flamina de puppi te Palinure ferant.
Tum quoque non rectum rabido voret equore vortex,
Sique potest, altis sub bene currat aquis,
At scelus arripiat nihil id quo ad litora tendat,
Et frustra tumidis brachia iactet aquis.
Ne quicquam et superos votis vocitarit, et ora
Impleat, et vocis conprimat unda sonum.
Adfer opem mihi nauta precor si dixerit, oro
Quisquis eris promptus navita ne affer opem.
Quod si forte tuam nitetur scandere navem
Tu prohibe, et conto deiice sacrilegum.
Ne lachrimis moveare cave, roget attamen insta,
Nam tantum pietas est vetuisse scelus.
Quod si forte tibi munus promiserit, illud
Despice, sit melior munere vita tibi.
Ni facias, praedico tibi tua cymba peribit,
Istud erit merces nolle perisse scelus.
Illud et ut periit cum illo tute peribis,
Illud at ut pereat si sinis, ipse manes.
Adde, quod hoc monstrum cupiunt sibi monstra marina,
Dignum, quo pellat belua magna famem.
Eolus haud patitur navim quae continet illud
Salvam, sed ventis libera colla dabit.

12 v Equora motabunt illi, fluctusque ciebunt,
Ut redeant grati (hoc pereunte) deo.
Quicquid habet tellus quicquid quoque pontus et aether
Est inimicum illi, tu nec amicus ei.
Et quamvis eciam fuerit tibi sanguine iunctum,
Ne pereas, pereat, iunctior esse tibi.
Seu terra veniet qui vitam demere queret,
Qui nobis magni causa doloris erit,
Excidat e curru si curru forte vehetur,
Sive vehetur equo, deiiciatur equo.
Decidat, et fractis cervicibus (imprecor illi)
Tollere qui venit,[4] vita relinquat eum.
Aut si per sylvas iter egerit, o iugulate
Latrones (properat qui iugulare) virum.
Sin vero fuerit quis de concivibus eius
Atque intra muros cui domus urbis erit,

---

[4] A later hand added *scilicet: vitam.*

Praecipites quondam ut venti de carcere missi
Eneae naves impetiere pii,
Quaeque fuit multis gens non invisa deo,
Quaeque fuit summi sanguine creta Jovis
Disiecta est toto nimium miserabilis alto
Undis parsque eius succubuere feris,
Sic tecta Eoleis ventorum turba reclusis
Carceribus, praeceps omnis in ista ruat.

13 r Et velut inventum timidum circum leporem unum
Mille canes latrant nec fugere ille valet,
Sic domus ex omni ventorum parte furore
Impulsa, ignoret qua cadat, atque cadat.
Quod si forte sui generis venti esse sequaces
Maluerint, contra quod tulit arma deos,
Et quia sic placitum superis, hominem scelerosum
Noluerint pressum viribus esse suis,
Exeat ille quidem, nec adhuc pervenerit illo
Quo properat, sed mox cepit ut ire domo,
Iuppiter e celsa precor ut detorqueat arce
Fulmina atrocia, quae non leviora volo,
Quam quibus attacta periit Clymeneia proles,
Sive Gygantaeus dissilit unde furor.[5]
Et sic aethereis celestis ab ignibus ignis
Exeat, et corpus stet sine sanguine iners,
Aut qui de multis quibus est invisus in eius
Potantis patheram nigra venena dabit
(Ut quondam Mydas quicquid tetigisset in aurum
Transiit, atque aurum potus et esca fuit).
Ille suo tactu conmutet cuncta veneno.
Sitque venena cibus, sitque venena merum.
Vos vos ille colit Helyconia turba sorores
Et vestri curam nocte dieque gerit.[6]
Quaeque magis rara est (quamvis sit rara colentum

13 v Absque ego quod lachrymis non meminisse queo)
Illius est turbae quae vestra ad flumina ducit,
Dulcius et iuvenes nectar amare docet.
Illius et turbae reliquos excellit, in hortis
Arboreum pinus vincit ut omne genus.

---

[5] Above this word was written the word *labor*.
[6] On the margin to the right was added *Precipuus Musarum cultor Alexander*.

Eruperant cunctos ut candida lilia flores,
Utque alios ignes Lucifer ipse suo.
Luna velut stellam solis quae nunciat ortum,
Ut lunae ignivomus lumina solis equus.
Haec super [7] et Musae crebro properatis ad illum,
Confugio vobis sunt pia tecta viri.
Non tam ros pecori, nec lapsus ab aethere nymbus
Aridulo (sitit et quod tamen usque) solo.
Nec tam qui nimium solis calefactus ab igne est,
Illi grata austri lenior aura venit.
Cuique sitis magno magna est collecta sub aestu
Perspicuus vitro quae magis amnis aqua.
Cuius et iratis obiecta est cymba procellis,
Tam gratus nautae portus et esse nequit.
Litora nec mediis qui lapsus fertur in undis,
Quam gratum vobis illius hospicium.
Illius et tectis subitis, complauditis, atque
Ales, fugit avis quae rapida ora Jovis,
Aut quae de laqueo caeco sub gramine cauto
Non licet illesos extulit illa pedes.
14r Aut [8] licet excussae tergo plumae ceciderunt
Fraudavit sese que tamen (illa) plagam [9]
Aut [10] piscis (quamquam non est illesus ab hamo)
Qui cadit et repetit quas modo liquit aquas.
Aut [11] quae de rapidis pastorum forte suorum
Erepta est canibus faucibus agna lupi.

Alexandri Hegii potita domo quare Musis gaudium oriatur,
reddit causam, quadam exclamatione docendo qualibus
quantisque malis qum foris sunt afficiantur.

O quociens eius indigne vos laniatas,
Luminibus vidi tecta subire meis.
Laurea de sacris pendebat tracta capillis,
Decideratque hederis facta corona comis.
Atque quibus fulvum nunquam certaverit aurum,
Fedati, et toti nil nisi pulvis erant.
Et quod erant poteram vix perspexisse capilli,

---

[7] A later hand added *scilicet: preter.*
[8] A later hand added *sicut.*
[9] A later hand added *scilicet: rete.*
[10] A later hand added *sicut.*
[11] A later hand added *sicut.*

Namque capillorum non color ullus erat.
Tales verberibus per colla rubentia quondam
Lactea, quaeque putem vincere posse nives,
Perque humeros nimis incompti sine lege volabant
Et tectae illorum parte fuere genae.
Erutaque ipsorum manibus pars magna nephandis,
In lacera passim veste recurva iacet.
Forsan in occultis et erant quoque vulnera membris,
Quamque fuit vestis tam laniata cutis.

14v Vestibus et iacuit non copia parva cruoris,
Sive erat is vester, sive alienus erat.
Credo equidem, tantum credo? quin dicere et ausim,
Partim vester erat, partim alienus erat.

Probat prius, a maiori.

Quis rabiem illorum sola invisae quibus estis
Expletam lacera veste fuisse putet?
Imo avidi Stygios nituntur mittere in amnes.
Et facerent, modo si non vetet esse deas.

Docet posterius.

Ac velut ex alto quae decidit aethere grando
Se quatit atque premit, texit ut omne solum,
Sic homines qui non homines, quos arripuere
Tres Furiae, et si qua est addita quarta tribus.
Ut caedant cuncti numerus qum non sinat ingens,
A se (quis credat?) vulnera multa ferunt.
Arcent namque imos primi, primi feriuntur
Ut cedant imis, aequus enim ardor eis.
Dumque cruentatis surgunt ad verbera palmis,
Et vos commaculat vester et ille cruor.

Docet vultum Musarum fuisse maculatum quammaxime.

Deformatus erat crudeli vulnere vultus,
Quodque foret vultus non bene cernere erat.

15r Ah scelus indignum quae illo nituere colore
Candida quem pariunt lilia iuncta rosis.
Ille genis inerat atro perfusa colore,
Candida quem pariunt lilia iuncta rosis.

Dicet se vidisse Musas lachrymantes.

Eius et ante fores stantem et vos inspicientem,
Inspiciebatis me lachrymasque meas.
Sed tamen et lachrymas fundebant lumina vestra,
A nimio fletu fluxit et iste cruor.
Lumina sive licet turpi celestia fletu
Turbari, atque ullus pectora meror habet,
Sive istud Musae faciebat tum dolor, ut me
Aspectis lachrymis ureret iste magis
Et vestris certe visis (nam vera fatebor)
Ceperunt lachrymae largius ire meae.
Quin eciam magnos gemebundo pectore verbis
Non timui nostris sollicitare deos.

Precatio ad deos deasque pro Musis.

Aethera dii quorum est, et quorum nostra tueri,
Dii quorum Stygios perdomuisse lacus,
Quae nimium iacuere diu succurrite Musis,
Musis quae divum facta referre solent.
Quando patrem divum nisi Pierides cecinissent
Tot tua per cunctos cognita facta forent?
Et superatorum latuissent bella Gygantum,
Et tua sub tenebris dulcia furta forent.
Adde, pater, quod sis sacris pater ipse Camenis,
Num poteris natis ulla negare pater?
Diique deaeque aliae quibus illae sponte dedere
Nomina, ne tenebris delituisse queant,
Illarum sitis nunquam immemores pietatis.
Non est (accepti non meminisse) deum.[12]
Vos quoque fatales trahitis quae pensa sorores
Et cunctis sortem quam libet usque datis,
Vos precor obscurum [13] cepistis carpere vellus,
Sumite (reiecto hoc) candidiora nive.

Hegius Musas letanter excipit hospicio.

Vultibus ingressas iucundis excipit ille,
Declaratque sibi gratius esse nihil.

[12] A later hand changed this to *deorum.*
[13] A later hand added *si.*

Et veluti densus si fugerit aethere nymbus
Celorum facies letior esse solet,
Sic ubi vos vidit (nebulis e pectore pulsis)
Perspicue facies letior orta viro est.
Corporibus sordes, atrumque in fonte cruorem
Abluit, uda suis lumina tergit aquis.
Et laceras reficit vestes, stringitque capillos,
Innectitque vagis serta renexa comis.
Vulneribus medicas ponit crudelibus herbas,
Et discissa brevi est integra facta cutis.
Quis dicat quantas illi grates habeatis?
(Ingratas quis enim non neget esse deas?)
16r Illi qui pressas relevat, qui vulnere fedis
Auxiliatrices admovet usque manus?
(Atque hoc exiguum) qui quondam non bene nota
Nomina iam toto scirier orbe dedit?
Ipsius (at quantum est?) it totum fama per orbem,
Hinc nihil est toto notius orbe viro.

Alloquitur famam.

Cuique loqui parvis de rebus maxima mos est,
Ne dic iam meritis fama minora cave.

Respondet, ac si famam audiat negantem se dicere minora viri meritis

Nescio,[14] verum ipsas video trepidare Camenas,
Ut sibi ne non sis sic bene fida viro.
Nil (ut sepe soles) fari mentita necessum est,
Nam sunt plurima quae vera referre queas.
Imo ego, tunc linguas ubi tu laxaveris omnes,
Vera et [15] quae nosti dicere posse negem.
Est etenim terrae lumen, terrae decus unum,
Et nemo est toto maior in orbe viro.
Magna tuo (et merito) iactas te Graecia Homero,
Et quo te iactes dignus enim ille fuit.
Alta tuo (et merito) iactas te Roma Marone,
Et quo te iactes dignus enim ille fuit.

[14] A later hand added *scilicet: an dicas necne.*
[15] A later hand changed this word to *eciam.*

Illo se iactet Germania carmina Homero
Et quem Virgilio cedere docta vetant.

Dicit tandem nomen viri.

16v Nomen Alexandro est illi, ludique magistrum
Urbs habet, urbs, notam quam sua fama facit.
Urbs haud magna quidem est, sed fama celsior astris.
Non est hac una notior orbe puto.
Nobilior longe est, quondam quam Roma fuisti,
Unum tocius qum caput orbis eras.
Nobilior longe est quam vos quoque eratis Athenae,
Istic doctrinae qum decus omne fuit.
Ipsa eciam vobis tunc fama favebat Athenae,
Huic urbi sed vix non inimica nocet.
Cogitur [16] atque dolet se cogi ferre per orbem,
Quasque potest linguas detrahit ipsa sibi.
Ne tamen ignores, urbs haec Daventria dicta est,
Urbs est quae cunctis est bene digna bonis.
Italiam [17] vidisse potes, versusque Latinos,
Est hac Meonios edidicisse modos.
Noris at o multum felix Daventria noris,
Non tantam famam te peperisse tibi.
Illi illi debes certe omnia, quem male comptis
Carminibus dixit nostra Camena virum.

Dicit adesse finem sui cantus.

En cecidere (suo religantur carcere) venti,
Ut pronae in portum vela tulere ratis.
At sint preceptor (cui nostra carina cucurrit)
Grata a discipulo carmina facta tuo.
Dignus es et meritus cui transmittatur et aequor,
17r Cymba sed extimuit non bene firma moram.

Docet cur grata esse debeant.

Qui dedit et vitam, qui quae sunt commoda, dicunt
Letari exigui thuris honore Iovem.

Telos.

[16] The word *famam* was written above this word in a later hand.
[17] On the left margin was added *in hac urbe.*

VI *Carmen Saphicum ad magistrum Alexandrum, ludi literarii in Daventria moderatorem. Guielmi.*

Mox (adhuc crescens tenera et Camena)
Ad tuas doctas ubi sensit aures
Esse iter, misso facies rubore
    Pallida facta est.

Dicerem cecis latitantem in herbis
Non secus quam qui pedibus retectis
Praessit[18] imprudens nimiumque fugit
    Territus anguem.

At minor longe est, refugitque pallor
Ille certamen, timidusque pallet
Quamlibet magnum, quoniam Camenae [19]
    Eminet extra.

Crederes undis eciam receptam [20]
In solum algentem fluere a capillo
(Crede) sudorem fuerat videre
    Atque trementem.

17 v   Forte quid causae rogites subegit
Ne rapi tanto fugeret timore.
(Nam quis argumen valeat timoris
    (Inficiari hec?)

Quod minus compti volitent capilli,
Quod sonum reddat renuens petitum
Nec satis doctum lyra nec suavem,
    Causa timoris.

Plus tamen ne aequo trepida Camena,
Vade, agit (dices) tibi mille grates,
Mille quondam discipulus salutes
    Candidus adfert.[21]

[18] i.e. pressit.
[19] A later hand added *pallorem* after *magnum;* pallor is written above *Camenae.*
[20] Above this word was written *Camenam.*
[21] Above this word was written *optat.*

22 v VII. *Carmen buccolicum Erasmi*[22]

Rosphamus insano Gunifoldae captus amore
Stridenti tacita solus sub nocte cicuta,
Rumpebat longo lucubrantia sidera questu.
Quem circum simeae quondam unica cura capellae
Errant, et gelidis neglecti in vallibus agni.
Nec stabulis egisse pecus, nec culmina tecti
Vel sera meminit deserta revisere nocte.
Rore procul tantum madida proiectus in herba,
Crudeles querula meditatur arundine flammas.
Huc ades o Gunifolda, mei medicina furoris,
Huc ades extremum vel visere funus amantis.
Rosphamus ecce vocat tuus, o Gunifolda, peritque,
Et tu flammivomae duris in collibus Ethnae
Mollibus indignum refoves Poliphemon in ulnis.

23 r Ah tibi setosi ne candida colla lacerti
Barba ah ne tenerum tibi conterat hispida mentum.
Huc ades, o Gunifolda, hic vitrea flumina iuxta,
Gramine florigero viridi recubabimus umbra.
Rosphame [23] quid sterili iuvat indulgere labori? [24]
Desine, non tanto certasse licebit amanti.
Et certasse tamen, quid tum si vertice Ciclops
Sidera sublimi feriat? licet, audiat ipse
Quantuscunque, nec illi cessero carmine, sola
Voce velit, velit arguta cecinisse cicuta.
Molle pecus, nivei sunt et mihi vallibus agni,
Corpore Dametas, vultu mihi cedit Amyntas.
Non mihi taurinis cervix riget horrida pilis,
Pectora sunt nobis candentia, lenia nobis
Ora, quid amplexus quid amas insana caninos?
Rosphame, litus aras, aversis aspera (cerne) [25]
Auribus effusas refugit Gunifolda querelas.
Quid speras? sed et esto velit, vetat ille volentem.
Quin morere, et longos componito morte dolores.
Extremum hoc, Gunifolda, tui cape munus amantis.

[22] This word was written in Greek.
[23] On the left-hand margin was added *secum loquitur.*
[24] On the right-hand margin was added *Amantium instabilitas.*
[25] On the right-hand margin was written *iterum relatur a cepto.*

Eternum, Gunifolda, vale, dirae necis auctrix.
Sic ait, et pulsae referebant carmina rupes.
Omne nemus, Gunifolda, sonat, sonat arduus aether.
Thetidos interea Titonis ab aequore coniunx
Paulatim croceis subvecta iugalibus, alto
Iam rarescentem pellebat ab aethere noctem.
Et iam Phebeae ferientia sidera rupis Parnassi
Culmina, vix dubio cepere rubescere sole.

23v Cinctus et ecce senex viridanti tempora mirto
Letus agit teneras ad pascua nota capellas
Drales, pastorum quo non annosior alter.
Cui iam depositis niteat frons nuda capillis,
Qui iam tergeminos cum Nestore computet annos.
Una viro serae requies et cura senectae,
Tortilis hirsuto pendebat fistula collo.
Hic ubi roranti resupinum Rosphamon herba
Conspicit, his miserum dictis compellat amantem.
Quenam [26] sub gelido tenuit Iove Rosphame causa
Teque pecusque tuum? fluitas quia totis et ecce
Nocturno madet omne pecus sua vellera rore.
Si vacat o Siculum pastorum gloria Drales
Una, tibi nostros referam moriturus amores.
Qum sol hesternus medium transmensus Olympum
Ureret ignivomis arentes aestibus herbas,
Atque ego (ne noceat quicquam calor ille) capellis
Condensi nemoris capto sicientibus umbram,
Illic forte sacrae video sub tegmine lauri
Naiades Aonidesque simul Driadesque puellas,
Ducere solemnes cantu modulante choreas.
Pan calamo, pulcher Cythera ludebat Apollo,
Omnis et in numeros agitabat brachia cetus,
Pulsabatque humiles pedibus salientibus herbas.
Viderunt oculi, rapuerunt pectora flammae.
Ibat formosis formosior addita nymphis
Et gracilis toti extabat Gunifolda coronae,
Digna dea facies, ipso dignus Iove vultus.

24r Non illi igniferi Citherea parens pueri (me
Iudice) non illi certavit pulchra Dyana.
Viderunt oculi, rapuerunt pectora flammae.

[26] On the left-hand margin was written *Drales*.

Germanam quantum Phebi lux aurea Pheben
Luciferum roseo quantum Phebe aurea vultu,
Caetera quam radians praecellit Lucifer astra,
Tam forma socias vincit Gunifolda puellas.
Viderunt oculi, rapuerunt pectora flammae.
Caesaries capitis fulvo crispantior auro
Undique cervicem circumvolitabat eburnam,
Ardentes oculi, liquido caro lenior amne.
Candidiorque nive, superis rutilantior astris.
Viderunt oculi, rapuerunt pectora flammae.
Adfuit et mediis puer improbus ille choreis
Nudus membra, genas lenisque, et captus ocellis,
Armatus facibus, levibusque volatilis alis.
Adfuit, et medius medio stetit improbus orbe.
Viderunt oculi, rapuerunt pectora flammae.
Is mihi fulgenti promens sua tela pharetra,
Flammifera stupidum traiecit arundine pectus.
Pectora traiecit, calidumque per ossa cucurrit
Virus, et in medias serpsit furor ille medullas.
Serpsit, et insuetis caluerunt intima flammis.
Hinc perii, atque gravis cepit mihi vita videri.
Et iam virgineas me conspectante choreas,[27]

24ᵛ Ibat supremi spacia ultima Phebus Olympi.
Quid facerem? iam tempus erat quo septa capellae
Quo repetant pasti praesepia nota iuvenci
Me dirus retinebat amor, sequor invia saltus.
Perditus, et questu Gunifoldam sector inani.
Et vano clamore voco, fugit illa vocantem.
Nil lacrimas miserata meas, nil flexa querelis.
Cautibus his mariis immotior, aspide seva
Surdior, aereae summis in rupibus Ethnae
Immani sese Polyphemi condidit antro.
Hinc perii, atque gravis cepit mihi vita videri.
Tum redeo tandem, sequitur grex tristis euntem,
Atque hic qum iam spes misero mihi nulla supersit
Mortem oro superos, certe aut (quod gratius esset)
Improba permutent Gunifoldae pectora nostrae.

Finis eglogae buccolicae.

[27] On the right-hand margin was added *vel coronas.*

APPENDIX B

THE "BOOK AGAINST THE BARBARIANS"

(See Chapter XV)

The earliest known version of the *Book against the Barbarians* was written in the back of a printed volume by one of the Brethren of the Common Life at Gouda, and the book was the property of the brotherhood. It now reposes in the City Library of Gouda. Part of the title-page reads thus: Tomus Nonus / Operum Divi Hieronymi Euse- / bii Stridonensis comple / ctens commentarios / in Matthaeum et Marcum, / et in divi Pauli / Epistolas, vi- / delicet ad / Galatas, / Ephesios, Ti- / tum, Philemonem; / necnon commenta- / rios in omnes Pauli / Epistolas sed . incerto authore. Postremo Didymi / de spiritusancto librum a Hieronymo versum.

At the bottom of the page we find this note: "Pertinet ad librariam domus fratrum Collationis Sancti Pauli apostoli in Gouda."

The *Opera* of Jerome were printed in the year 1516 by Froben at Basel. On the title-page of the first volume there is a note to the effect that they were edited by Erasmus.

In Volume IX, at the end of the book, on folio 203 verso, there appears this note: "Pertinet ad librariam domus fratrum Collationis in Gouda civitate Hollandie."

Then follow 37 pages, all of which originally were blank. On the first of these is found an extract from a letter by Erasmus addressed to Cornelius Aurelius of Gouda. The next 31 pages contain the *Book against the Barbarians*. The size of the pages is 23 × 35 cm. The manuscript has illuminated capitals in blue and red.

The binding of the volume is vellum.

We may assume that the version of the *Antibarbarorum Liber*, as it was first written down in Volume IX of Jerome's works in the library of the Brethren of the Common Life at Gouda, is very nearly an exact duplicate of an older copy of the same composition. The purpose of the present edition is, therefore, to indicate as far as is now possible just what Erasmus said in the original version of this work, and also to show what changes of importance he introduced in the version which he permitted to be printed afterward.

Unfortunately there appears to be extant only one copy of the *Anti-*

barbarorum Liber in its original form, namely, the manuscript that has just been described. And this manuscript presents not only the difficulties common to manuscripts of the late fifteenth century, but also some peculiarities of its own. It is not surprising to note that several words are spelled in at least two different ways, and usually in the most inconsistent manner. This is the case, for example, with *nihil, mihi, etiam, litera*, and generally with all words in which a *t* may become a *c*, or where one might write either *t* or *tt, l* or *ll, m* or *mm*. *Cur* sometimes becomes *qur*, and remains *qur* on a whole page, only to change back to *cur* for apparently no good reason. It must be admitted, however, that the letter *e* is consistently used for the classical *ae* or *oe*. Wherever the manuscript now has the latter spelling, except in two or three instances, one can easily detect that a change was introduced by a later hand.

The word *mihi* sometimes appears as *michi*, but in expanding abbreviations of this word I have used the classical form. In filling out the first syllables of abbreviations for such words as *umquam, tamquam*, and *quamquam* I have used *n*, which appears in editions of Erasmus' works, rather than the classical *m*. Sometimes *n* is written in abbreviations. The letter *m* does appear in an occasional abbreviation, but in general the presence of an *m* rather than an *n* signifies that it occurs in uncontracted words in the manuscript.

It is the later hand that has made the manuscript so difficult to edit. The Brethren of the Common Life at Gouda became acquainted with the printed version of the *Antibarbarorum Liber* after one of their members had written the earlier version in one of the volumes by Jerome. So it naturally happened that the two copies were compared. Some industrious scribe took it upon himself to show in the manuscript what changes had been made by Erasmus. If he had only indicated all the changes, or if he had done the work more carefully in general, or if the older hand had been more careful, it would still be possible to tell exactly what Erasmus had originally written.

A few examples may explain how difficult it is to follow any definite rule. On lines 14–15 of page 23 (p. 307, l. 29, in this volume) the manuscript read first: *Iubeo reliquos suos auctores ostendat, recusat ipse. De decretis....* The word *ipse* was struck out, and a period placed after *recusat.* A new sentence began with *Ipse.* The word *de* was struck out, and above it was written: *Ipse de a,* but that was not satisfactory either, so the word *de* was eliminated. It is evident that the first copyist made several errors. Some of these he corrected himself; others were corrected by the second hand. It is not always easy to tell at the present time which hand made the corrections, nor what were the reasons for the numerous changes in the manuscript. On page 29, line 41 (p. 323, l. 25, in this volume), the first hand originally had: *Utere, inquit Battus, utere.* It may be assumed that the first word was considered superfluous even by the first copyist, but since both this and the next word were crossed out and the word *et* was written above them and the word *inquit* above the line but behind the second *utere*, it is not clear what the version contained from which the present copy was made. Then on page 31, line 46, we find that the name Herasmo was changed to Erasmo, although in all other cases the name has the earlier spelling. It would, therefore, be unwise to follow the hand which caused this one change.

The punctuation is often inconsistent and sometimes even misleading. Furthermore, in many places words are written together which obviously should be separated, and others will have to be put together. In short, it has been necessary to take a number of liberties with the manuscript in order to go back as far as seems possible to the original version of the *Antibarbarorum Liber.* For the convenience of the reader it has been shown in a good many places what was added or eliminated in the printed editions, although it appeared unnecessary to indicate every deviation.

It would seem that some of the inconsistencies are due to the inadvertences of a scribe who was trying to reproduce faithfully a copy which had usages different from his own practice, but he could not keep his mind from lapsing into its accustomed grooves.

Most of the changes in the manuscript are made in a lighter and more careless handwriting than that of the original. From this fact one may conclude that in general the heavier stroke in words crossed out and in other corrections is due to the original scribe.

A comparison between the original draft and the printed versions of the *Book against the Barbarians* will show that the differences are numerous and important at first, but afterward they become fewer and fewer. Consequently the two versions have been printed side by side in the present work until a point has been reached where it is no longer necessary to give both readings.

Beyond this point those words which appear only in the manuscript are printed in italics, and those which are found only in the printed version have been inclosed in square brackets. The curved brackets appear in the original.

The printed edition with which the manuscript has been compared is the one published in 1540, edited by Beatus Rhenanus. In the footnotes it will be referred to as B.R.

2 Liber apologeticus Desiderii Herasmi Roterodami in quo refelluntur rationes inepte barbarorum contra poesim et literaturam secularem pugnantium.

Antibarbarorum liber primus, autore Des. Erasmo Roterodamo.

Cum adolescens admodum, pestilentie (que tum apud nostrates mirum in modum seviebat) defugiende studio Brabantico rure et salutari et ameno quandam quasi academiam mihi meisque edificarem, quod locus qum saluti tuende tum studiorum secessibus vel maxime ydoneus videretur.

Cum adolescens, pestilentiae quae tum apud nostrates inclementissime saeviebat, defugiendae studio, in rusculum quoddam Brabanticum me contulissem, tum salubre, tum amoenum, quod is locus non solum tuendae saluti, verumetiam studiorum secessibus vel maxime videretur idoneus, hoc nomine vel Platonis Academia potior, quod ocio par, salubritate vinceret, cum illam pestilenti coelo fuisse legamus, hic praeter salubris aurae commendationem habebat et silentii plurimum, amoenitatis etiam quantum philosopho satis esset, fortassis et musis, quae lympidis fontibus, ac ripis smaragdinis, et opacis nemorum umbris delectari feruntur: hic latitantem, ac suaviter rusticantem, praeter spem invisit Hermannus Guilhelmus, tum aequalium meorum unus longe mihi

Nam silentii habet plurimum amenitatis etiam quantum philosopho satis esset fortassis et Musis.

Hic igitur qum agerem invisit me Hermannus Guielmus, equalium meorum unus et optimus et doctissimus et de quo dubitare possis, moribus ne sit amabilior, an ingenio admirabilior, illis enim nichil candidius, hoc sublimius nichil. Sed a coniunctissimi hominis laude temperasse prestiterit, ne quid amici studio in amicum peccem. Peccarem autem, si virtutem eius eximiam mea predicatione elevarem. Que enim ab amante vel inferiora vero dicuntur, amori potius quam

PLATE VII

Facsimile of the second page of *Antibarbarorum Liber*, Gouda version

iudicio tribui solent, et aut falsa aut minora putari. Verum nec mih quidem ipse de Guielmo satis. Accedo integris, credo doctioribus qui qum multo minus ament plus videant, longe tamen audacius et predicant et mirantur. Cum hoc igitur a teneris (ut est in Greco proverbio) unguiculis, singularis quedam charitas, saneque iucunda studiorum societas accreverat mihi cum ipsa prope etate, iis vinculis ea fide conglutinata, ut nec Horresti Piladem, nec Pirithoo Theseum, nec Patroclo Achillem, nec Damoni Pythiam, nec Eurealo Nisum coniunctiorem fuisse crediderim.

Ex huius ergo expectatissimo[1] adventu,

qum incredibilem cepissem voluptatem, ne hoc tanto bono solus adeo fruerer, communi amico Jacobo Batto, qui tum erat opidi Bergensis publicus a secretis, per puerum renuncio, homini qum non indocto tum candidissimo, qui iampridem partim mea predicatione, qua de vetere amiculo libens apud recentem uti solebam, partim ipsius literis accensus, incredibili quodam Guielmi videndi desiderio ardebat.

charissimus, qui cum mihi a teneris (ut aiunt) unguiculis, singularis quaedam charitas, saneque iucunda studiorum societas, sic cum ipsa prope aetate accreverat, ac penitus iis vinculis, ea fide, ea benevolentia conglutinarat, ut nec Oresti Pyladem, nec Pirithoo Theseum, nec Patroclo Achillem, nec Damoni Pithiam, nec Euryalo Nisum coniunctiorem fuisse crediderim. Adeo copulat arctius animos hominum, puerilium studiorum communio, quam ulla cognationis, aut affinitatis propinquitas. Ex huius igitur adventu, vel hoc etiam gratiore, quod esset inexpectatus, cum incredibilem cepissem voluptatem, ne hoc tanto bono solus adeo fruerer invidus, communi amico Jacobo Batto, qui proximae civitatis Berganae tum erat publicus a secretis, confestim renunciandum curo, homini, deum immortalem, quo candore, qua morum suavitate, qua doctrina, quam felici facundia. Is iampridem partim mea praedicatione, qua de veteri sodali lubens apud recentem uti solebam, partim ipsius literis accensus, incredibili quodam videndi Guielhelmi desyderio flagrabat. Nemini enim adhuc mortalium vidi, qui sic admiraretur,

[1] The prefix *in* was added to this word by a later hand.

Is vero simul atque accepit,[1] ascito
e congerrionibus suis uno dumtaxat
non dicam accurrit, sed plane advo-
lat, idque adeo nocte fere concubia,
eo quod interdiu per negocia civilia,
egre ab urbe abesse licebat. Presertim quod nuper in reipublice
administratione vocato, omnia popularius accuratiusque essent obeunda. Minima eius noctis porcio
somno tributa est. Vix dum diluxerat consurgimus operisque ex more
distributis, ubi deinde edificium
demonstrassem, ut totius plane regionis faciem Guielmo ante oculos
ponerem, in agrum educo. Ibi nobis in diverticuli ponte consistentibus, de improviso Judocus medicus,
vir tum humanus tum eruditus, una
cum Guielmo Conrado viro primario de via sese ostendit.

Erat huic prope a nobis predium
rusticum, quo sese vir prudentis-
simus recipere solitus erat, quotiens
urbis urbanorumque negociorum
cepisset hominem sacietas, quotiens
fluctus illos civilium causarum voluisset paulisper effugere, quotiens
nugari liberius, ac discincto ludere
libuisset.

Porro perpetuum hoc tempus quod
ruri agebatur aut ille apud nos, aut
nos apud illum eramus, tum quod
hominis et comis consuetudine de-
lectabar, tum quod huius potis-

sic veneraretur, sic adamaret eruditos, praesertim in his literis, quas
non absque causa bonas appellant.
Is vero simulatque rescivit, ascito e
congerronibus suis uno duntaxat,
non dicam accurrit, sed prorsus ad-
volat, idque adeo nocte fere concubia, quod interdiu aegre liceret
abesse: praesertim quod nuper in
administrationem Reipublicae vocato, omnia popularius ac studio-
sius essent obeunda. Eius noctis
minima portio somno tributa est.
Vixdum diluxerat consurgitur, redi-
tur ad literatas fabulas, mox coeli
serenitas ad prodeambulandum invitat. Obambulatur, ac loci situm,
regionisque faciem hospiti demon-
stro. Ibi forte fortuna in diverticuli
ponte consistentibus, de improviso
Jodocus medicus, vir cum primis
humanus atque eruditus una cum
Guilhelmo Conrado, eius urbis cive
primario, de via nobis sese ostendit.
Erat huic haud procul a nobis prae-
diolum rusticanum, quo vir pru-
dentissimus recipere sese solitus erat,
quoties eum urbis, urbanorumque
negociorum cepisset satietas (nam
apud suos summo magistratu subinde fungebatur) quoties fluctus illos
civilium causarum voluisset paulisper effugere, quoties nugari liberius,
atque (ut ait Flaccus) discincto ludere collubitum esset. Porro perpetuum hoc tempus, quod ruri agebatur, aut ille apud nos, aut nos apud
illum eramus, tum quod hominis et
comis et eruditi consuetudine delec-

[1] Correction reads *recepit*.

simum ope atque opera ad id quod parabamus uteremur. Is ubi nobis conspectis blandius suo more arrisisset. Quo[1] tam mane (inquam) fugitive? Male (ita me deus amet) cum republica agitur, que tibi sit tradita, qui tanquam lucinia quedam nemoribus nichil anteponis, urbem non secus quam caveam odisti. Quid tibi cum rure homo omnium qui vivunt turbulentissime?

Tum ille prorsus (inquit) tuis deliciis invideo homo hominum qui vivunt felicissime, qui dum nos miseri turbulentissimis illis negociorum undis sine fine iactamur, beatus interim ruri cum tuis te Camenis oblectes.

Quo minus miror si nobis persepe vocantibus tu a tuis istis nemoribus in urbem extrahi nequeas. Hic ego familiarius arridens sane inquam tu tuis collegis paulominus desipis, qui istoc sis animo, quod si tue te Syrenes sinerent, cupiditas atque ambitio mirum in fluctus istos plane cum totis urbibus contemneres.

tabar, tum quod essent mihi quaedam communia cum illo negotia. Is ubi nobis conspectis, suo more blandius arrisisset, mox ego: Quo tam mane, inquam, fugitive? Male (ita me deus amet) cum repub(lica) agitur, quae tibi sit tradita, qui tanquam luscinia quaedam nemoribus nihil anteponis; urbem non secus quam caveam odisti. Quid cum rure consuli, quid tibi cum hoc ocio, homo hominum qui vivunt turbulentissime? Ad haec ille exhilaratus, prorsus, inquit, tuis deliciis invideo, homo hominum qui vivunt felicissime, qui dum nos miseri turbulentissimis illis negociorum undis sursum ac deorsum iactamur, ociosus interim, ac vacuus, cum tuis Camoenis obambulas, et animum oblectas, nunc cum amiculo quopiam, quicquid libuit garriens, nunc cum veterum scriptorum aliquo confabulans, interdum poeticam aliquam cantilenam modulans, nonnunquam chartis ceu fidis sodalibus committens, quod animo versaris. Quo minus miror, si nobis persaepe vocantibus, tu a tuis istis nemoribus in urbem extrahi nequeas. Hic ego: Nae tu, inquam, non paulo minus desipis, quam tui collegae, qui isto sis animo. Quod si tuae te Sirenes sinerent, cupiditas atque ambitio, mirum ni istos fluctus plane cum totis urbibus facile contemneres. Sed dum parum optimatem videri pudet, parum recte quid ad iucundam vitam sit optimum, eligis. Tum

---

[1] *Et* before *quo* is crossed out.

Excutiam me fortassis aliquando et Scipionem illum tuum quem mihi predicare non desinis, imitabor. Verum interim qum per dies aliquot ferias futuras scirem et heri forte vespertinus occasus serenitatem polliceri videretur, sub auroram rus cum tota familia me contuli.

Ac mox Battum quoque intuitus. Et unde (inquit) tu huc? aut qui nam cedo obsecro, qui nobiscum heri ad multam usque noctem cenaveris?

Mirari (inquit Battus) non debes, si nocturnum compotorem tuum mane ruri offendas. An ignoras quanta soleam esse noctua? Adest qui me Dedalum fecit. Et si quid est Dedalo ingeniosius, simulque Guielmum conveniens significabat.

An tu Battum a tam desiderati capitis conspectu tenebellas istas remorari potuisse censes? quas levioribus eciam in rebus magno contempsit animo.

Quod simul atque consul intellexit, continuo ipse quidem una cum medico de rheda descendit, uxorem vero cum sua pompa (ut aiebat) in
3 villam premisit. ¹Tu, inquam, de nostro rure permaligne sentis qui tantum puellarum gregem tecum portaveris? Quid ita? respondit ille. Satis apparet te credere, neque Pieridum neque Charitum neque

ille: Non ita procul, inquit, a scopo tua aberrat oratio. Atque utinam inficiari liceret quod dicis, sed excutiam me fortassis aliquando, et Scipionem illum tuum, quem mihi praedicare non desinis, imitabor. Verum interim cum per dies aliquot ferias a negociis futuras scirem, et heri forte vespertinus occasus serenitatem polliceri videretur, sub auroram rus me cum tota familia contuli. Simul autem et Battum intuitus, ex insidiis se proferentem. Et unde, inquit, tu huc? aut quinam cedo tam mane, qui nobiscum heri ad multam usque noctem potaris? Hic Battus homo ad iocos factus. Mirari, inquit, non debes, si nocturnum compotorem tuum mane ruri offendas. An ignoras quanta soleam esse noctua? Adest qui me Daedalum fecit. Apud Nasonem cuidam pedibus timor addidit alas, mihi amor, alas plusquam Daedaleas assuit. Atque interea Guilhelmum connivens subindicabat. An tu putas fieri potuisse, ut Battum a tam desyderati capitis conspectu, tenebellae illae remorari possent, quas levioribus etiam in rebus saepenumero fortiter contempsit? Arrisit consul, conscius Battum in prima adolescentia, ad furtivos puellarum amores fuisse propensum, a quibus tamen mox avocarunt literae. Porro ubi de Guilhelmo sensit consul, continuo ipse quidem cum medico de rheda descendit, uxorem vero cum sua pompa (ut aiebat) in villam praemisit. Hic

Driadum neque Naiadum ullam in nostris versari nemoribus. Imo chorum inquit facere volui.

Tum Batto paululum seducto, familiarius in aurem: Scelerate, inquit, cur non passus es me Icarum tuum una tecum volare? Battus. Quia, inquit, terrebar omine. Consul. Presertim, ait, qum me scires non minus teipso hominis videndi desiderio teneri, idque adeo tua opera. Ingenue fateor (Battus inquit) invidebam tibi expletus, tum denique te vocassem. Quare ne quid dolo dicam, nunc venisse quoque molestum est. Vereor enim ne homo negociosissimus ocium nostrum non nichil sis interturbatus.

Judoci quoque quem tecum ducis tetricam philosophiam odimus. Nos quoque[1] perpetuum hoc triduum meris nugis iocundissimisque susurris transigere decreveramus. Nichil nobis interim cum fascibus tantundem cum supercilio philosophorum. Consul. Imo (inquit) in tempore assumus, una nugabimur omnes.

ego: An non, inquam, de nostro rure perquam maligne sentis, qui tantum puellarum gregem tecum apportaris? Quid ita respondit ille? Quia satis apparet, inquam, tuo iudicio, neque Pieridum, neque Charitum, neque Dryadum, neque Naiadum ullam in nostris versari nemoribus. Imo chorum, inquit, facere volui, et vestras semideas cum his humani generis Nymphis coniungere. Sub haec Batto paululum seducto, familiarius in aurem: Scelerate, inquit, cur non passus es me Icarum tuum tecum huc advolare, praesertim cum scires me non minus teipso hominis videndi desyderio teneri, idque adeo tua opera. Primum omine terrebar, inquit, deinde, ne dolo dicam, invidebam tibi tam opiparam voluptatem, ipse adhuc famelicus: expletus, tum denique sodales advocassem, quare (ut ingenue fatear) nunc quoque venisse te submolestum est. Vereor enim ne homo negociosissimus, quo non solum ut Caecias quispiam attrahas negocia, verumetiam ultro sequentia fugientem, nusquam non tecum circunferas, ocium nostrum nonnihil sis interturbaturus. Jodoci quoque, quem tecum adducis tetricam philosophiam odimus. Nos perpetuum hoc triduum meris nugis, liberrimisque susurris transigere decreveramus. Quid inter haec nobis cum fascibus, aut quid cum supercilio philosophorum? Tum consul: Imo, inquit, in tempore adsu-

[1] This word is crossed out.

Nam et ego domi consulem reliqui et Judocus philosophiam omnem uxori commisit. Que cum risissemus.

Agite (inquit Battus) si fidem datis ita futurum recipimus vos in gregem nostrum. Deinde qum Guielmum meum uterque magnifice salutavisset, vulgatoque iam more salvum venisse gratulatus esset, obambulare visendi studio cepimus, non sine variis (ut fit) sermonibus, de regionis situ, de soli,[1] de coelo, de coepti operis ratione, tandem (ut solet inter fabulandum alius ex alio sermo incurrere) in veterem[2] quidem illam sed prorsus iustissimam nostrorum temporum querelam incidimus. Querebamus non sine vehementi admiratione, que tam vasta calamitas, tam optimarum artium frugem dissipasset. Quod tam dirum proluvium omnis prope veterum literas, olim purissimas, tam turpiter confudisset. Qui fieret ut nos veteres illos scriptores tam immenso intervallo sequeremur, ut qui nunc doctrine arcem tenerent, vix idonei viderentur, quibus olim latrine committi debuerint, et qui nunc imperatores exercituum, apud illos ne inter gregarios quidem milites asscribendos fuisse decebat.

mus, una nugabimur omnes. Nam et Jodocus quicquid severioris philosophiae uxori commisit (habebat autem submorosam) et ego consulem domi reliqui. Quae cum risissemus: Agite, inquit Battus, si fidem datis ita futurum, recipimus vos in gregem nostrum. Deinde consalutato Guilhelmo, perreximus obambulare, non sine variis (ut fit) sermonibus, de regionis situ, de soli natura, de coeli salubritate, de calamitate nostrae Hollandiae: tandem (ut solet in huiusmodi fabulis alius ex alio sermo incurrere) in veterem quidem illam, sed prorsus iustissimam nostrorum temporum querelam incidimus. Quaerebamus non sine vehementi admiratione, quae tam vasta calamitas, tam uberem, tam florentem ac laetam optimarum artium frugem dissipasset, quod tam dirum et immane proluvium, omnes prope veterum literas olim purissimas, tam turpiter confudisset. Qui fieret, ut nos priscos scriptores tam immenso intervallo sequeremur, ut qui nunc doctrinae tenerent arcem, pauculis quibusdam exceptis, vix idonei viderentur, qui cum priscorum mulierculis, aut pueris elementariis, in palaestra literaria possent decertare, et qui nunc imperatores exercitum ducerent, apud illos ne inter gregarios quidem milites asscribi mererentur, quique nunc disciplinarum clavum moderarentur, tunc ne in sentina

---

[1] The word *felicitate* appeared after *soli*, but was crossed out later.
[2] Corrected from *uterem*.

At medicus quidem ut erat astrologie qum studiosus, tum inter primos peritus, omne negocium in sydera reiicere moliebatur, permulta in eam rem disserens, tum acute tum probabiliter, ab hiis rerum humanarum vicissitudines proficisci, hinc orta atque extincta rursus imperia, hinc regna aliunde alio translata, hinc tociens immutatos mortalium animos, mores, habitus, studia fortunas fluxisse dicebat.

Syderum vices esse certas quasdam, nec vim omnibus eandem, alia studiis amica, alia contra infensa. Ita fieri ut illis vicissim imperia alternantibus, studia quoque invicem modo fugere, modo vigere, modo iacere, modo in preciis esse contingeret, et a mundi inicio usque repetens, singularum prope etatum mutationes doctissime collegit. At consul literarum interitum multis coniecturis in Christianam potissimum religionem conferre nitebatur quod Christianos olim ethnicas nescire literas, neutique turpe, contemnere pulchrum eciam dixisse crederet,

quidem locum invenissent. Ac medicus quidem, homo promptae quidem facundiae, sed astrologiae mire deditus, cui nihil non tribuebat, alioqui vir pius ac probus, totius mali causam in sydera reiicere moliebatur, permulta in eam rem disserens, cum acute, tum etiam probabiliter: ab his rerum humanarum vicissitudines proficisci, hinc orta atque extincta rursus imperia, hinc regna aliunde alio translata, hinc toties immutatos mortalium animos, mores, habitus, studia, fortunas fluxisse docebat. Syderum certas quasdam esse vices, nec vim omnibus eandem, alia studiis amica, alia rursus infensa. Ita fieri ut illis imperia vicissim alternantibus, studia quoque invicem modo frigere, modo vigere, modo iacere, modo in precio esse contingeret: et ab orbe condito prope repetens, singularum aetatum mutationes magna admiratione memoriae, collegit. At consul non improbatis usquequaque quae disseruerat medicus, literarum interitum multis coniecturis in Christianam religionem conferre nitebatur. Non quod de hac parum pie sentiret, cui et si quis alius erat addictus, sed quod ab hac crederet ansam esse porrectam. Videbant exordia nostrae religionis non a philosophis, non ab oratoribus, non a dialecticis, aut mathematicis, sed a simplicissimo Christo nata, ab idiotis apostolis propagata. Proinde mundanas disciplinas prisci religionis cultores, ut rem Christo inimicam horrebant partim quidem fidei zelo quodam vehementi magis quam sapienti, et adversariorum odio cum quibus usque adeo nichil commune esse voluerunt, ut vel optima relinquerent, partim quod natura abhorrerent,

partim vero laborem fugientes inerciam honesto religionis nomine pretexebant.

Nonnulli fortassis (et haud scio an multo maxima pars) non alia de causa oderant quam quia non didicerant. Alii in pietate omnia collocantes simplicitate sua contenti, cetera superis permittebant.

et pulchrum habebatur, nescire prophanas literas, neque minus laudis erat, negligenti philosophiam Aristotelicam aut Platonicam, quam contemnenti regna, calcanti divitias, sperneti voluptates. Quicquid enim mundus suspiciebat, hoc fastidiit religio, cuius studio vehementi magis quam sapienti, et immodico quodam adversariorum odio, cum quibus adeo sibi nihil voluerunt esse commune, ut vel optima relinquerent, neglectae sunt disciplinae liberales, nihilo prudentius agentibus quam si Gallus odio Britannorum mallet nudus incedere, quam panno apud Britannos texto vestiri, aut si Britannus mallet siti disrumpi, quam vinum bibere apud Gallos natum. Et fortassis erant, qui simpliciter errantes, negligerent studia literarum, erant et qui laborem fugientes, inertiam suam honesto religionis nomine praetexerent, quando sub nulla umbra melius tegitur iners ocium et segnis ignavia. Nonnulli fortassis, et haud scio an multo maxima pars, non alia de causa oderunt bonas literas, quam quia non didicerant, et pigebat simul ac pudebat discere. Huc adiuverunt primum tyranni quidam qui Christianis scholas praecludebant, existimantes fore, ut religio destituta doctrinae, facundiaeque praesidiis, sponte sua consenesceret, et tandem aboleretur. At cum sentirent se per adversarios eruditionis et eloquentiae praesidiis urgeri, coeperunt et ipsi iisdem armis ac telis communire

Postremo, inquit, non optime religioni cum eruditione per se convenit. Habet enim fere relligio sine literis nescio quid supine stoliditatis adiunctum, a quo qui literas sapiunt longe abhorrent.

Quibus rebus factum fuisse auguror, ut neque studiosis suis honos haberetur, et optimi libri utique literarum custodes, aut perderentur aut neglecti interirent.

sese, ut hostem suo quod aiunt gladio iugularent. Deinde secuti sunt homines impense pii, qui cum animadverterent ex ethnicorum libris, vehementer adamatis ob eruditionis splendorem, et illecebram eloquentiae, hauriri etiam nonnihil paganismi, iamque sic ubique propagatam esse religionem Christianam, ut eorum librorum usus non magnopere desyderaretur ad confutandos adversarios, huc incumbebant, ut extincta superstitione Judaeorum et ethnicorum, simul et literae et linguae tollerentur. Fortassis et illud perspexerunt, non optime convenire purae religioni, et perfectae doctrinae. Pietas fide nititur, eruditio vestigat argumentis, et rem in quaestionem vocat. Postremo fit, nescio quo pacto, ut minus tractabiles sint eruditi quam idiotae. Atque hinc est, quod abbatum vulgus hodie nihil magis cavet, quam ne monachi altius penetrent ad bonas disciplinas. Malunt enim ovibus quam hominibus imperare, nec ob aliud malunt, nisi quia facilius est. His rebus factum est, ut neque studiis suus honos haberetur, et optimi quique libri unici literarum custodes, aut data opera perderentur, aut neglecti interirent. Mox eo deducta res, ut turpe etiam sibi ducerent principes ac praesules, scire literas. Ne tamen omnino caeca esset hominum vita, si nulla extaret eruditio, omnis cura professioque literarum in monachos est relegata, a quibus aliquandiu non

Porro Guielmus tum plurimis coniecturis tum maximorum scriptorum auctoritate sese permoveri dicebat, ut omnium rerum quoddam senium esse crederet, mundum universum senescere, omnia sensim ab illa iuventa in deterius prolabi, Chibelem illam deorum parentem sterilescere et que[1] olim iuvenes deos gignebat, nunc longo pariendi usu effetam vix homines producere.

Non pauca in hanc sententiam e priscis illis theologis nostratibus tamen proferebat, sed que ad rem non admodum pertinent hic verbosa oratione recenseam. Eo evasit, ut nostri temporis homines ingenio minus valere dicerent, quam veteres illi valuissent naturamque quasi senescentem, quam dum non corpora modo prestantiora verum et ingenia magis (ut ita dicam) mascula felicioraque produxerit nunc homunciones ut pusillos corporibus,

omnino pessime tractatae sunt. Mox cum hi quoque supercilio turgidi ad luxum sese verterent, neglectis linguis, neglecta antiquitate, nata est nescio quae perturbata doctrina, et prorsus inerudita eruditio, qua non solum humanae disciplinae, verumetiam ipsa theologia miseris modis vitiata fuit. Haec aliaque in hanc sententiam cum disseruisset consul, Guilhelmus tum plurimis coniecturis, tum gravissimorum scriptorum autoritate sese moveri dicebat, ut omnium rerum senium quoddam esse crederet. Mundum universum, et quicquid hic gignit mundus, sua quadam iuventa subolescere, ac rursum postea quam ad summum vigorem suis auctibus pervenerit, tandem ad senium vergere, ac sensim in deterius prolabi; Chybelem illam deorum parentem iam sterilescere, et quae olim iuvenes deos gignebat, nunc longo pariendi usu effoetam, vix homines producere: huc enim referebat aenigma huius fabulae. Non pauca in hanc sententiam, et e priscis illis theologis, nostratibus tamen adferebat, sed quae ad rem non admodum pertinent, ut hic verbosa oratione recenseam. Breviter eo evasit, ut nostri temporis homines, ingenio minus valere diceret, quam veteres illi valuissent, naturamque quasi senescentem, quae olim non corpora modo praestantiora, verumetiam ingenia magis (ut ita dicam) mascula felicioraque producebat: nunc ho-

[1] *que* was added by a later hand. It is necessary to the sense.

ita ingenio non paulo deterioribus generare. Itaque demum fieri, ut que veteres invenire potuerunt nos nec percipere quidem possemus inventa.

Que qum admiram quadam quasi declamatoria ratione adeo scite a singulis disputata, ut nemo non concessa dixisse videretur, Battum iam 4 dudum dic- | turientem animadverti et nescio quid secum parturientem. Erat enim ut ingenua quadam dicendi libertate, non sine dicaci vehementia preditus, ita non secus ipse barbaris quam illi literis infensus.

Hunc ceteris expectantibus intuitus. Hierasmus. Dormis,[1] inquam, Batte et iam Battus non es.
Arrisit et caput movit. Deinde ut plane hominem excitarem rogabam: ecquid ista probarentur. Tum ille vultu quo solet faceto perquam magnifice quidem dixistis omnes (inquit) verum interim promissa non prestat fides. Convenerat ne quid preter nugas ageretur et in mediam philosophiam repente incidimus. Quanquam vestra ista vel iratum me non nichil delectarunt. Verum quid nostre cessaciuncule,

munciones, ut pusillis corporibus, ita ingeniis non paulo deterioribus generare. Itaque demum fieri, ut quae veteres invenire potuerunt, nos ne percipere quidem possemus inventa. Cumque illi mirabilem doctrinae vim cum eloquentia pari coniunxerint, nos alterum etiam horum parum feliciter tentare: Quae cum admirarer, quadam quasi declamatoria ratione adeo scite a singulis disputata, ut mihi nemo non confessa dixisse videretur, Battum meum iamdudum dicturientem animadverti, ac nescio quid secum parturientem. Erat enim ut ingenua quadam dicendi libertate, non sine dicaci vehementia praeditus, ita non secus ipse barbaris quam illi literis, infensus, adeo ut ad occursus horum frequenter aut nausearet, aut incandesceret, nonnunquam velut omen infaustum mutata via declinaret. Hunc igitur caeteris expectantibus intuitus: Dormis, inquam, Batte, et iam Battus non es. Videsne iamdudum equum in planitiem suam provocari? Arrisit ille et movit caput. Mox ut magis etiam hominem excitarem, rogabam, ecquid ista probarentur. Tum ille vultu quo solet faceto: Perquam magnifice quidem dixistis omnes, inquit, verum interim promissa non praestatur fides. Convenerat, ne quid praeter nugas ageretur, et in mediam philosophiam repente incidimus, quamquam vestra ista vel iratum me nonnihil de-

[1] *Dormis* is a correction above *Corvus*, which, however, is not crossed out.

cum istis tam impeditis ut vix
Chrisippus eciam ipse aut Carneades et ieiunus et helleboro purgatus
expediverit? Nam tu quidem Ju-
doce ita philosophum domi reliquisti ut astrologum nobis attuleris, et
tu ita consulem posuisti, ut philosophum (si superis placet) indueris,
Dyonisium credo imitatus.

Quanquam nec in sentiendo quidem
cuique vestrum accedo.
Alius enim sydera in crimen vocavit, alius optimam religionem incu-
savit, alius nature nescio quam
senectam causatus est. Iniquissime
quidem (quantum ego sentio) omnes.
Quale enim est hominum culpam in
res ipsas reiicere, quod nichilo est
equius,

lectarunt. Verum quid nostrae
cessatiunculae, cum istis tam impeditis, ut vix Chrysippus etiam
ipse, aut Carneades, et ieiunus et
elleboro purgatus expediverit. Nam
tu quidem Jodoce, ita philosophum
domi reliquisti, ut astrologum nobis
attuleris, et tu ita consulem posuisti, ut philosophum (si superis
placet) indueris. Dionysium opinor illum Syracusanum imitatus:
quanquam quod attinet ad sententias, nemini vestrum prorsus accedo.
Atque interim ingenium et eloquentiam miratus sum potius, quam
iudicium. Alius enim innoxia
sydera vocavit in crimen, alius optimam religionem poenae ream egit,
alius naturae nescio quam senectam
causatus est. Iniquissime quantum
ego quidem sentio omnes. Quale
enim est obsecro, culpam hominum
in res ipsas reiicere? Et quod nostro vitio commissum est, quovis
relegare potius, quam culpam nostram agnoscere? Quod si studio
nobis est, malorum causam, quae ne-
gari non possunt, a nobis depellere,
quin quicquid in vita mortalium accidit mali, in Aten Homeri-
cam reiicimus? Quemadmodum
apud eum poetam facit Agamem-
non et Jupiter, utque Christianorum vulgus, quicquid sua stulticia
designant, in cacodaemonem autorem et instigatorem reiiciunt.
Quam fenestram si patimur aperiri,
quid obstiterit, quo minus posthac,
libidinosus iuventam, avarus ac
sordidus senectam, ambitiosus
fortunam, iracundus corporis

quam si libidinosus iuventam, avarus ac sordidus senectam, ambiciosus fortunam, iracundus naturam
accuset.

Quin ego obmissis ambagibus, rei istius quem celo terraque queritis, auctorem vel indice (si libet) demonstrabo.

Herasmus. Quod ut faceret flagitantibus omnibus consulem digito significans. Tute, inquit, (si nescis) huius auctor es rei, in tuum caput omnis refunditur culpa, cui cum respublica suas fortunas omnes, suam salutem, dignitatem, amplitudinem

in manus dederit. Tu tam pestilentes homines in civitate impune sedere sinis.

Quos ais? Hos, inquam, assellos Archadicos quos publicis in ludis asinina

impudentia passim rudere vides, qui magna (ut est apud Fabium) confidentia atque auctoritate suam stulticiam perdocent. Qui se ob eam rem ludo litterario prefectos imo adeo natos arbitrantur, ut nos quicquid est bonarum literarum dedoceant, ut omnibus suam inscitiam inculcent.

Simulque permultos nominabat qui per id tempus insigni stoliditate nobiles habeantur,

quorum ego nomina prudens supprimo,

temperaturam accuset? Quin ego omissis ambagibus, istius rei autorem, quem coelo terraque quaeritis, vel indice, si lubet, commonstrabo. Quod ut faceret flagitantibus nobis consulem digito designans: Tute, inquit, si nescis, istius autor es mali, in tuum caput omnis haec culpa refunditur. Cui cum respublica suas fortunas omnes, suam salutem, dignitatem, amplitudinem, denique quo nihil habet charius, suos liberos in manus dederit, tu tam pestilentes homines in civitate sedere, quid autem dixi sedere, imo regnare sinis impune. Cumque consul admiratus interpellasset: Quos tandem istos ais tam pestilentes. Hos, inquit ille, asellos Arcadicos, sive mavis, Antronios, quos publicis in ludis, in quibus optimae literae tradi debuerant, impudentia plusquam asinina passim audis non loqui, sed rudere, qui magna (ut est apud Fabium) confidentia atque autoritate stulticiam suam perdocent, qui se ob eam rem ludo literario praefectos, imo adeo natos arbitrantur, ut nos quicquid est bonarum literarum, dedoceant, ut omnibus suam inculcent inscitiam, ac sui similes reddant. Simulque permultos nominabat, qui id temporis insigni stoliditate nobiles habebantur, cum quibus monstris Batto continuum et irreconciliabile bellum erat, donec publicum eius urbis ludum moderaretur (nam hinc ad secretarii munus erat ascitus) quorum ego nomina prudens supprimo, sive quod hoc ipsum

maxime quod huius generis maximus ubique sit numerus.

Hiscine inquit, belluis, miseri cives
sua viscera committunt? Hiis no-
bilissimi principes liberos suos gene-
rosissimis   ingeniis,   bonarumque
artium   avidissimos   adolescentes,
quos ex ingenuis rusticos, ex indoctis
indociles, ex stultis insanos reddant?
Hec, inquam, in tua republica fiunt,
te cive te primate te consule. Pri-
vataque adeo minimi momenti negocia, mirum est quanta vigilantia
curentur.

Hec pestis et publica et tanta
quanta in republica maior omnino
nequeat existere, negligitur, imo
fovetur.   In fontes alios, qui vel
paulum aliquid privati damni dederint, perquam severe animadverti-
tur. Hic mulctatur, ille vapulat,
alius in exilium eiicitur, alius laqueo guttur frangitur,

et eum qui liberos vestros, quibus
(ut par est) nichil habetis antiquius,
unam reipublice spem, tam indigne
corrumpit, non eiicitis.

famae illis invideam, dignis qui
sempiternae oblivionis tenebris se-
pulti iaceant, sive quod nolim meas
chartas spurcissimis nominibus in-
quinari, praesertim cum huius generis maximus ubique sit numerus, ut
semper fuit pessimarum rerum maxima foecunditas. Hiscine, inquit,
beluis miseri cives sua viscera committunt, his clarissimi principes
liberos suos credunt, his generosis-
simis ingeniis praediti adolescentes,
et iidem bonarum artium avidi
committuntur, quos ex ingenuis
rusticos, ex indoctis indociles, ex
stultis insanos reddant? Haec, inquam, in tua republica fiunt, te
cive, te primate, te consule? Pri-
vata, atque adeo minimi momenti
negocia, mirum est quanta vigilantia curantur: haec pestis et publica, et tanta quanta in republica
non queat ulla maior existere, negligitur, imo fovetur? In alios fontes,
vel qui paulum aliquid privati damni
dederint, perquam severe animad-
vertitur.   Hic aere mulctatur, ille
vapulat, alius ob aes alienum ultra
diem prolatum, in carcerem detru-
ditur, alius in exilium eiicitur, aliis
ob involatum poculum, aut numo-
rum pauxillulum, laqueo guttur frangitur. In his et huiusmodi valet
disciplinae severitas, valent leges,
vigilant magistratus, et eum qui
liberos vestros, quibus (ut par est)
nihil habetis antiquius, nihil dulcius, unicam reipublicae spem, tam
indigne corrumpit, non eiicitis, nullo
supplicio dignum ducitis? Capite

Qui tot chara civitatis pignora perdidit, eum non iugulatis?

Si villicus hic tuus, huius vicinus, felicem agrum zyzania ac iuncis sereret, quid faceres?

Profecto eiiceres, in ius vocares, damni dati reum ageres. Et nullo supplicio dignus videtur, qui generosam puerorum indolem, ita imperitie spinis ac vepribus occupavit, ut non sarculo nec incendio quidem repurgari queant? Qui in feriendo nummismate, paulum modo aliquid fraudis commisit horrendis exemplis penas legibus dare cogitur, at qui pueros in suam fidem acceptos pro ingenuis literis, nil nisi meram stulticiam docuit, premio dignus videbitur?

plectitur, qui equum abduxit, et qui tot tam chara civitatis pignora prodidit, imo perdidit, eum non iugulatis? In eum qui equum conductum secus quam debuit, habuit, ex legibus est actio, et filii male tractati, nulla est actio? Si villicus hic tuus, huius vicinus felicem agrum, tritici feracem, zizaniis ac iuncis consereret, dic mihi, te quaeso, quid faceres? Nimirum eiiceres, in ius vocares, damni dati reum ageres, et nullo supplicio dignus videtur, qui felicem ac generosam puerorum indolem, ita imperitiae spinis ac vepribus occupavit, ut non sarculo, ac ne incendio quidem repurgari queat? Qui in feriendo nomismate, paulum modo aliquid fraudis admisit, horrendis exemplis poenas legibus dare cogitur, at qui pueros in suam fidem acceptos, pro liberalibus et saluberrimis literis, nil nisi meram stulticiam docuit, praemio dignus videtur? Nec alia in re sunt vel oscitantiores, vel infeliciores, summi etiam principes. Adhibentur multi qui praegustent cibum, non adhibentur qui dispiciant, quid in animum ac pectus illorum infundatur. Periclitatur medicus aut chirurgus, si parum accurate tractavit principis corpus, et nihil est periculi istis, qui sic tractant animum tam multis imperaturum? Non temere committis equum curandum, ac fingendum, nec circumspicis, qui credas fingendum filium? Quasi patris officio functus sis, si modo genueris, ac non multo maxima pars sit officii pa-

terni, recte instituere quod genueris.
Quid enim refert bene natum esse,
nisi ad naturam accedat honesta
educatio? Non cuivis credis colen-
dum fundum, consulis probatos
agricolas, longoque rerum usu probatos, et filium praceptori tra-
diturus, ex ptochotyrannis istis
quempiam in consilium adhibes, et
viam quam ille caecus tibi mon-
straverit, ingrederis? Ex horum sententia quemlibet scholae publicae
praeficis, quorum iudicio non debe-
bas stabularium asciscere? Nihil
est similius regno, quam ludi literarii
moderator; et his tyrannidem per-
mittimus in liberos, quos si nosses,
nolles imperare canibus tuis? Magno
conducitur, qui iuventutem verberibus ac minis excarnificatam doceat
et scire nihil, et sibi videri nihil
nescire, quin saepenumero fit, ut
mores istorum nihilo sint meliores
literis. Quantum autem flagicium,
primam illam ac felicissimam aeta-
tem, bonis disciplinis a natura da-
tam, iis inficere, quae aut maiore
labore post dediscenda sint nobis,
aut magno nostro malo tenenda.
Tria sunt unde potissimum rerum
publicarum salus, aut etiam pestis
mihi pendere videtur, a principe
recte aut secus instituto, a concio-
natoribus publicis, et ludi magistris.
Sed huius postremi par erat potissimum curam agi, quod ludi magister
primum innoxiam ac rudem aeta-
tem curat, quae sibi nondum potest
prospicere, deinde optimae spei annos, qui et fugiunt ocyssime, et

Quin tanta pestis publicis manibus discerpitur. Qur non in solas terras publicitus deportatur? Cur tu consul Camillum illum tribunum militarem non imitaris ut quemadmodum ille infidelem ludi magistrum nudato a tergo corpore, vinctisque manibus pueris iisdem quos hostibus prodiderat, flagris in Faliscorum urbem tradidit redigendum, ita pari pompa istos ex tua urbe tradas exigendos? Miraris interire literas qum cerdones ludos teneant litterarios?

Miramur antiquam illam iam olim degenerare doctrinam, qum doctoribus ipsis nichil sit indoctius? Magis mirarer ni sic eveniret. Queso te quid a rudi preceptore possit expectari, nisi rudior discipulus? Et ut in vetere proverbio est: Quid a malo corvo nisi malum ovum? Quando asellus generosum equum progenuit?

Quando pavonem noctua? An potius ut vere scripsit Horatius:

5 Est | in iuventis, est in equis, patrum
Virtus, nec imbellem feroces,
Progenerant aquile columbam,
Fortes creantur fortibus.

redeunt nunquam. Apud Romanos olim atrocissimo supplicio necabatur, qui non ex usu publico gessisset imperium. Utinam extaret similis aliqua lex, quae in perniciosos pueritiae moderatores dignum aliquod exemplum statueret. Nunc honos etiam isti beluae, et sic merito, datur ex publico merces. Quin tanta pestis publicis manibus potius discerpitur? Cur non in solas terras aliquo deportatur? Cur tu consul Camillum tribunum illum militarem non imitaris, ut quemadmodum ille malae fidei magistrum, nudato a tergo corpore, vinctisque manibus, pueris iisdem, quos hostibus prodiderat, flagris in Faliscorum urbem redigendum tradidit, ita pari pompa pueritiae corruptores istos ex urbe tua cures exigendos? Miraris interire literas, cum cerdones, imo caudices, ludos teneant literarios? Miramur antiquam eruditionem iam olim degenerare, cum doctoribus ipsis nihil sit indoctius, magis equidem mirarer, ni sic eveniret. Quaeso te, quid a rudi praeceptore possit expectari, nisi rudior discipulus? Atque ut est in vetere proverbio: Quid a malo corvo, nisi malum ovum?

An hic verum non est quod scripsit Horatius:

Est in iuvencis, est in equis, patrum
Virtus, nec imbellem feroces,
Progenerant aquilae columbam,
Fortes creantur fortibus.
Atqui fieri videmus, ut filii non semper referant corporum vitia,

Quid hic sydera et celum innoxium in crimen vocamus? Quid immerentem naturam incusamus? Quid salutifera religio commeruit, ut in tantam invidiam adducatur? Tu modo preceptorem ydoneum para, videbis nimirum neque sydera, neque ingenia nostris seculis imo nec regionibus adeo defuisse.

Quod si ipsi nobis (ut facimus) defuerimus, frustra nobis vel universum arrideat celum.

Nichil itaque miror extingui literas, quas certatim omnes contendunt extinguere, vindicare perpauci.

Ubi nunc honos literis debitus? Ubi locus expolito ingenio dignus? Ubi fructus quem longos egregiosque labores consequi par fuit? Religiosi qui vocant summam inscitiam, consummatam pietatem arbitrantur.

quae erant in parentibus. Novi ipse fratres aliquot, caeco patre, matre clauda natos, quorum nemo tamen caecus esset aut claudus. Caeterum ubi animus in animum transfunditur, et ingenium ab ingenio formatur, fieri non potest, quin discipulus referat praeceptorem, velut animi parentem. Quid hic sydera et coelum innoxium criminamur? Quid immerentem naturam incusamus? Quid salutifera commeruit religio, ut in tantam invidiam adducatur? Tu modo advigila, ut parentur idonei praeceptores, dent operam principes, ut sit honos bonis literis, videbis nimirum neque sydera, neque ingenia nostris seculis, imo nec regionibus adeo defuisse: tametsi non inficior, vix aliam reperiri crassiorem, quod ad literas duntaxat attinet. Quod si ipsi nobis (ut facimus) defuerimus, frustra vel universum arrideat coelum, apud nos fatales illi cometae sunt, qui suo afflatu pestem invehunt optimis studiis. Nihil itaque miror extingui literas, quas certatim omnes contendunt extinguere, vindicare perpauci. Vere dictum est: Honos alit artes. Et illud: Sint Moecoenates, non deerunt Flacce Marones. Ubi nunc honos literis debitus? ubi locus expolito ingenio dignus? ubi fructus quem longos egregiosque labores consequi par fuit? Qui hodie professione religionis sese venditant, consummatam pietatem arbitrantur nihil scire, ac maxima ex parte aut quaestui serviunt, aut

PLATE VIII

Facsimile of the fifth page of *Antibarbarorum Liber*, Gouda version

Ecclesiastici Epicurum quam Crisippum malunt imitari. Principes quorum liberalitate studia et provocari solent[1] et foveri non Platones sed Gnatones sibi asciscunt.

ventri: ecclesiae proceres Epicurum fere quam Ciceronem malunt imitari. Principes quorum liberalitate studia literarum et provocari solent et foveri, non Platones iam sed Gnathones sibi asciscunt. Munera ferunt, moriones, palpones, voluptatum architecti. Pluris est qui canem bellum adducat, quam qui librum eruditum porrigat. Sacerdotiorum ampli census aut venalia sunt, aut malorum obsequiorum praemia. Ad abbatias, caeterasque dignitates, stupidissimi quique potissimum irrumpunt. Quaeritur Satyrographus, quod divites tantum admirentur, laudentque disertos, ut pueri Junonis avem. At hodie probro est, scire literas. Nusquam magis regnat, quam apud nos pestilens hoc hominum genus, quos merito ptochotyrannos dixeris: hi rerum omnium censuram sibi vindicant, praesertim apud stultas, atque etiam impudicas mulierculas, et apud imperitam multitudinem: his persuadent egregii sycophantae, haeresim esse, scire Graecas literas, haeresim esse, loqui quo more locutus est Cicero. Et quis tandem sani capitis cupiat sese tam diuturnis macerare laboribus, sine quibus nec mediocris literatura paratur, odium denique, summamque invidiam praemii vice reportaturus? Iam porro fac citra conatum, eruditionem dormienti contingere, quis non malit vel in ultimas Indiae solitudines profugere, quam hos litera-

Et quis tandem sani capitis velit sese tam diuturnis macerare laboribus sine quibus nec mediocris quidem literatura comparatur, odium denique et summam invidiam pro premio laturus? Iam porro fac citra conatum eruditionem contingere quis erit tandem qui non malit vel in ultimas Indie solitudines profugere quam hos literatorum simias

[1] The letter *a* in *soleant* is crossed out, probably by the original hand.

ferre? Equidem priscorum more inter pecora vitam transigere, non paulo prestabilius dixerim, quam inter hos brutorum omnium brutissimum hominum genus quibus apud nos omnia michi redundare videntur, qui alienam doctrinam contemnunt. En tibi alterum genus superioribus illis haud multo minus, tum odiosum, tum pestilens, qui religionis larva personati, si quando a parentibus super salute iuvenum consuluntur,

quibus artibus potissimum instituendos, quibus preceptoribus committendos censeant. Ut Demodocus ille Platonicus Socratem consulebat. Tum nichil Socratis preter vultum et taurinum intuitum imitantes, mira authoritate a poetarum oratorum lectione, ante omnia deterrent?

torum simios ferre? Equidem priscorum hominum more, quos e truncis arborum natos finxit antiquitas, non paulo malim inter pecora vitam transigere, quam inter hoc brutorum omnium brutissimum genus, quibus apud nos mihi differta videntur omnia, qui pari stoliditate et suam rusticitatem admirantur, et alienam doctrinam contemnunt. Sed inter has beluas verius quam homines, nullum odiosius aut pestilentius, aut Musis omnibus infensius, quam isti quidam religionis larva personati, de quibus modo dicere coeperam, qui venerando cultu, simultaeque sanctimoniae specie, non mediocrem autoritatem sibi pararunt apud idiotas, praesertim apud mulierculas, quarum et stultitia abutuntur, et libidini fortiter succurrunt, tauri egregie obesi, neque vulgariter mutoniati: hos adhibent in consilium, et si non adhibeant, ipsi qua sunt impudentia, ultro semet ingerunt, volentibus nolentibus. Consulitur igitur camelus de saltatione, de cantione asinus. Quid enim aliud fit cum Minorita, aut Jacobita, aut Carmelita, velut oraculum consulitur, cui puer ad optimas disciplinas destinatus, formandus tradi debeat, quibus rationibus et autoribus instituendus sit, non aliter quam Demodocus ille Platonicus consulebat Socratem. Ibi mihi consultor ille stupidus ac superciliosus, nihil Socratis referens praeter vultum et taurinum intuitum, mira severitate cum primis

Vestigia quibus ipsi sunt ingressi commonstrant, homines mera barbarie educati.

Deinde preceptorem si quem egregie indoctum noverint,

ad eum miserrimos adolescentulos mittent. Nec difficile persuadent, quippe qui sint callidissimi simulande probitatis artifices, et vulgus ignarum deterioribus facilius acquiescit.

Quem inter hec non pigeat vivere. Quem non ultra Sauromatas et glatialem oceanum fugere libeat? qui quidem veterum illorum et modes-

deterret a lectione poetarum. Porro bliteis istis poetae sunt et Quintilianus et Plinius, et Aulus Gellius, et Titus Livius, breviter, quicunque Latine scripserunt: adeo non intelligunt quid sit poetice, quam poetriam vocare solent, ut nec poetae qui sint, aut dicantur, intelligant. Vestigia quibus ipsi sint ingressi, commonstrant, homines ex mera barbarie nati, simul et educati. Alius iubet edisci psalterium, alius censet linguam Latinam petendam ex proverbiis Salomonis, alius vocat ad insulsissimum autorem Michaelem Modistam, alius ad Mammetreptum, alius ad Catholicon, ut quisque infectus est, ita dant aliis consilium. Deinde si quem noverint praeceptorem tam insigniter asinum, quam ipsi sunt insigniter hypocritae, ad eum mitti iubent miserrimos adolescentulos. Nec difficile persuadent, primum idiotis, deinde callidissimi simulandae probitatis artifices, postremo vulgus hominum fere deterioribus acquiescit libentius. Contra si quem olfecerint, politius eruditum abominantur: Cave, inquiunt, poeta est, parum Christianus est. Haec nusquam non instillant auribus hominum, in concionibus, in quibus regnant, populi stulticia freti, in privatis colloquiis, in arcanis illis confessionibus, in quibus sibi dii videntur. Quem inter haec portenta non pigeat vivere? Cui non lubeat et ultra Sauromatas et glacialem Oceanum fugere, si modo tiam et eruditionem, cum huius nostri seculi et arrogantia et inscitia componat?

Sed quid longam et inanem querelam ingredimur? In te (ut dixi) omnis hec culpa cecidit, qui si hos et indoctissimos doctores et consultores inconsultissimos vel eiiceres vel (quod dignius erat) culeis insutos in mare vicinum precipitares.

Ad quidvis supplicii deposci non recusaverim nisi mirabilem eruditorum proventum prope diem videas efflorescere. Quibus commemorandis qum vehementius Battus incandesceret,

subridens consul:

probe, inquit, intelligis me privatum hic adesse, qui tanta ista in me libertate audeas uti.

Verum ego vicissim te (si pateris) recriminabor, qui tuum officium preterieris. Tuum enim prorsus erat qui publico munere fungereris, ista tam nephanda ad consulem referre.

De referendo michi narras impudens respondit Battus, quasi ista in

veterum illorum et modestiam et eruditionem, cum huius nostri seculi tum arrogantia, tum inscitia componat? Sed quid longam et inanem querelam ingredimur? in te, ut dixi, omnis ista culpa recidit, qui si istos, et indoctissimos doctores, et inconsultissimos consultores vel eiiceres, vel quod illis esset dignius, culeis insutos, cimicibus et pulicibus differtis, in mare vicinum praecipitares, ad quidvis supplicii deposci non recusarim, nisi mirabilem eruditorum hominum proventum propediem cernas efflorescere. Quibus commemorandis cum Battus vehementius incandesceret, nam homo alias placidus ac lenis, hic sibi temperare nunquam potuit, sic adamabat bonas literas. Subridens consul: Quo supplicii genere perdendi sint isti Batte, inquit, post consultabimus: ego si Juppiter essem, omnes in asinos verterem et camelos. Sed interim probe videris intelligere, me hic privatum adesse, qui tanta ista libertate in me ausis uti, tanquam cum Conrado tibi res sit, non cum consule: verum ego te vicissim, si pateris, criminabor, qui tuum officium praeterieris. Si quidem tuum prorsus erat, qui publico munere fungereris, ista tam nephanda ad consulem ac senatum referre, nisi forte frustra sedes in consilio: certe tuae partes erant monere. Haec ideo consul, ut magis etiam inflammaret ardentem. Tum Battus: De referendo mihi narras impudens, quasi ista in re re non omnes Herculis labores suscceperim imo prope vicerim? Meminisse me scio (quanquam eciam falsus dissimulas) ut ante biennium fere a Parrhisiis reversus, ludi huius amministrationem vobis auctoribus inirem. Dii boni quas nugas? que somnia, que ludibria, quam barbariem, quos sentes infelicissimis adolescentibus inculcaverant, ii qui ante me docuerant.

Tum re quidem ipsa Fabianum illud approbavi: non paulo molestiorem dedocendi quam docendi esse laborem. Nam simul atque zizaniam illam, ita (ut erat necesse) evellere instituissem. Mirum dictu fuit, quam amaris odiis quam agmine, quam digladiatorio animo, sint coorti in nos illi imperitie magistri. Quid umquam in tua republica vidisti ea seditione turbulentius? Incitaverant in me de clero simili dementia imbutos, que maxima multitudo est, tum opidi primores quorum animi avitum adhuc rus sapiebant. Preterea iuvenum maiores plerosque, quorum pietatem religioso metu sollicitabant, ut filiorum pudori mature consulerent. Incenderant et fabros, fullones, sardones, pharmacopolas, mendicos, mimos, balatrones, aucupes, piscatores, essedarios, cetarios, coquos, fartores, bavilarios, tonsores, lenones, lenas, aniculas, et quos non?

non omnes Herculis labores susceperim, imo prope vicerim? Meminisse te scio, quanquam male falsus dissimulas, cum ante biennium fere reversus a Lutecia Parsiorum, administrationem ludi literarii suscepissem, quod ibi Augeae stabulum repererim. Deum immortalem, quas nugas, quae somnia, quae ludibria, quam barbariem, quos sentes, quam fecem infelicissimis adolescentibus inculcaverant ii, qui ante me nihil scire docuerant. Tum re quidem ipsa Fabianum illud nimium approbavi, non paulo molestiorem esse dedocendi, quam docendi laborem. Nam simulatque zizaniam illam, ita ut erat necesse, instituissem revellere, dictu mirum, quam amaris odiis, quam devoto agmine, quam gladiatorio animo sint coorti in nos illi imperitiae magistri. Age, quid unquam in tua republica vidisti ea seditione tribulentius? Incitaverant in me de clero simili dementia imbutos, quae maxima multitudo est: tum oppidi primores, quorum animi avitum adhuc rus sapiebant, praeterea iuvenum maiores plerosque, quorum pietatem religioso metu solicitabant, ut filiorum pudori mature consulerent: incenderant et fabros, fullones, cerdones, pharmacopolas, mendicos, mimos, balatrones, aucupes, piscatores, essedarios, cetarios, coquos, fartores, baiulos, a quibus non perinde ingenio differunt atque cultu. Ad haec tonsores, lenones, lenas, aniculas.

Vulgi infimi partem multo maximam. Id quod neutiquam ardui erat negocii, tum quod per se sit irritabile vulgus, tum quod pro insita stoliditate literas habet invisas. Tum quod pari temeritate absurdissima queque perlibenter et miratur et tuetur. Sed ducum virtutem prosequamur. Hii vero tantis copiis freti passim in me diras atque atroces voces iactabant, in foro, in compotationibus, in officinis, in lustris, publice, privatim, ebrii, sobrii, dictitantes. Extremum hominem nescio quem novam quondam heresim serere. Optimos illos auctores Alexandrum, Grecistam, Ebrardum, quibus et avi sui et proavi doctissimi evasissent, nunc indigne extrudi, inaudita quedam atque horrenda

Et quos non? Vulgi infimi partem multo maximam, id quod neutiquam ardui erat negocii, tum quod per se sit irritabile vulgus, tum quod pro insita stoliditate literas habet invisas, tum quod pari temeritate absurdissima quaeque perlibenter et miratur et tuetur. Sed ducum virtutem prosequamur. Hi vero tantis copiis freti, passim in me diras atque atroces voces iactabant, in foro, in compotationibus, in officinis, in tonstrinis, in lustris, publice, privatim, ebrii, sobrii, dictitantes externum hominem, nescio quem, novam quandam haeresim serere, optimos illos autores, Alexandrum, Graecistam, Ebrardum, Modistam, Breviloquum, Mammetreptum, Catholicontem, quibus et avi et proavi ipsorum doctissimi evasissent, nunc indigne extrudi, inaudita quaedam **atque** horrenda

6 | ethnicorum induci portenta, Flaccum, Maronem, Nasonem, iuvenibus iam nichil nisi de amando precipi, ea pueris inculcari, que ne *grandioribus* [gradibus] quidem scire fas esset. Nisi quamprimum profectum fuisset, actum esse de relligione Christiana, Antichristi seculum iam aut adesse, aut certe quam proxime instare. Venisse enim doctores, qui *prurirent auribus* [blandirenturiis, quibus aures essent novarum rerum aviditate prurientes: quique iuxta Pauli vaticinium] a veritate avocarent, ad fabulas traducerent adolescentes. Vidisti ipse, testis in eo tumultu, quantum[1] Herculem prestiterim, quot leones, quot sues, quot Stymphalidas aves, quos (*sic*) tauros, quot Antheos, quot Geriones, quot Dyomedes, quot Nessos confecerim, ut Cerberum e latebris illis, ubi exangues umbras territabat, extractum celo ostenderim,[2] quanta virtute Lernean hydram, fecundam suis mortibus, igne Greco vix tandem extinxerim, et haud scio an adhuc spiret pestis illa omnium perniciosissima. Urbis nostre Pompeius, [quanquam ille Midae quidem similior quam Pompeio,] quid moliatur, haud me preterit. Tot unus monstris

---

[1] *me* is crossed out after *quantum*.   [2] Original reading *ostenderem*.

obiectus, non cessi tamen, imo pervici, iis quibus sanior erat mens, persuasis, ceteris clarissima ratione confutatis, contemptis nonnullis.

Guiellmus. Que cum Battus dixisset, Moriar, inquit Guielmus, ni tu mi Batte non supplicatione modo, verum eciam triumpho dignissimus es. Iam si Ion ille rhapsodus apud Platonem, quod unum Homerum laudibus extulisset, meritum se iactitat, cui eius poete studiosi coronam auream imponerent: tu vero qui universam prope literaturam contra tot portenta strenue defendisti, quanto dignior es, cui Muse aut [ipse] eciam Appollo lauream triumphalem imponat. *Videor ego Hercules, respondit Battus, quanquam quod potui quidem sum conatus.* [Aut certe qui in omnibus Museis stes aureus. Ad quem iocum cum arrisissent caeteri, Battus quoque iam hilarior: Age, inquit, rideor Hercules, et vobis Pyrgopolinices quispiam videor, tamen qualis qualis sum, quod potui sum conatus.] Quod si Guielme huic animo tua lingua eruditioque fuisset adiuncta, melius fortasse cum literis ageretur.

Tum consul: Age, inquit, Hercules, quid si tibi pro rebus fortiter gestis triumphum decernamus, equidem speciosiorem quam umquam vel Paulo Emilio, vel Pompeio contigerit. Cras niveis equis vectus, urbem laureatus ingredieris, plaudentibus utrimque universis bonarum literarum studiosis: barbari duces tua virtute domiti, revinctis (ut digni sunt) [post tergum] manibus, triumphalem currum antecedent, victori populo supplices manus ostendent. Miles victor a tergo imperatoris laudes cantabit, preda circumferetur, trophea figentur Phebo, novemque sororibus optima spolia dicabuntur. Et quid? Deum te facimus, [ut ima non alter sis Hercules, iuxta proverbium, sed prorsus ipse sis Hercules: quid unquam simile promeruit ille?] verum ea lege, si hoc prius feceris, quod victores facere consueverunt, ut rerum abs te terra marique gestarum, et totius certaminis huius rationem nobis luculenta oratione exponas, quod eciam ut triumphum tantum contemnas, recusare tamen nequaquam debes vel nostra causa, qui tantopere id flagitamus, vel literarum amore, quibus scio tibi nichil esse antiquius, vel denique reipublice causa, in quam tu nuper receptus, sollicitudinem illi, et pietatis officium debere cepisti. Nam quod tu me modo insimulabas, quid me [posse] censes unum inter [tot] hominum capita longe aliter sentientium? An me vis (quod dici solet) adversum stimulum calces? presertim cum nec mihi [ipsi] *quidem ipsam* satis dum sit[1] hec confirmata sententia, ita nonnunquam istorum disputationibus labefactor ut partes vestras vix satis tutari queam. Et quod nunc quidem serio dicendum [sit] Batte, si vera sunt que michi de tuis eudoxis, adoxis, amphidoxis, soles disputare, non

1 A correction from *fit.*

minimam profecto turpitudinis partem causa vestra videtur obtinere, non apud vulgus modo, verum eciam apud literis equiores. Nam sunt vestri auctores (non mentiar) primum ethnici, quod tamen utcunque poterat defendi, deinde cognitu perquam difficiles, quod ipsum non paucis odium parit; postremo, quod est gravissimum, lascivi, imo etiam obsceni.

Nunc accipe rem, Christianos auctores eiicitis, inducitis ethnicos, notos expellitis, infertis ignotos, veteres extruditis, producitis novos, faciles tollitis, obscuros nobis obiicitis; denique quod caput est, castos interdicitis, lascivos iuvenibus proponitis. Quid oris tum esse mihi creditis, quotiens me consulem rogant mei cives, num ideo ludus sit in urbe publicus, ut iuvenes meretricios perdiscant amores, perinde quasi parum ipsi ad hac studia suopte sint ingenio proclives, ut assuescant technas fabre consuere, et veteratorie parentibus imponere, ut nichil pudere, mentiri, suum ponere vultum, alienum sumere, hec enim ex vestris comediis discunt, et domum memoriter referunt. Quin tu graviter hec ferre parentum *animos* [aures] arbitrare? Utrum in lupanar, inquiunt, liberos nostros mittimus, an in ludum literarium? Nam tres illas literas, quas senex Plautinus se didicisse gloriatur, domi facile discimus. Preterea si qui sunt paulo eruditiores, ii mihi pontificum decreta, et theologorum sententias memoriter decantant, tum quidem tergiversari soleo, sed plane ut victus, non [ut] insidiator.

Tu vero qum sis hac in palestra facile omnium exercitatissimus, fieri non potest quin plurima teneas tum lecta tum cogitata, quibus huiusmodi criminationes refelli queant: quare rem prorsus divinam feceris, si totam hanc controversiam a capite usque ad calcem explicueris, non quod causa vestra parum mihi probetur, verum patronum me paulo instructiorem reddideris.

Herasmus. Quod qum Battus, singulis quoque sua causa [vehementer] flagitantibus, defugere nulla ratione posset: Age, inquam, [de praemio plus etiam pollicemini quam postulo, mihi satis fuerit supplicii, si sola Ate studiorum pestis unco trahatur, ac mox in publicam cloacam praecipitetur: deinde procerum aliquot pro capitibus linguas duntaxat deposco. In quem usum, inquam? Ad nullum alium, inquit, quam ad abstergendum podicem, aut defricandas matulas, aut certe immundas patellas. Nihil, inquam, accommodatius: sed extra iocum hospites,] quandoquidem in rem tam preclaram fortuito incidimus, quin nos quoque hic Achademiam quandam Platonis exemplo instituimus? An quia deest nobis platanus illa vel Platonica, vel Ciceroniana, quarum altera facundissimi philosophi, 7 altera sapientissimi oratoris, literis ⌐ et sata est et crevit, potius quam humore aliquo. Quin ego nobis pro umbraticis veras, ac pro una arbuscula copiosum pomarium exhibebo, quod edibus nostris ab leva proximum videtis, proceris quercubus, et rivo limpidissimo cinctum. Quid si hinc quoque *aliquam* [locum] nostram disputaciuncula ita irrigemus, ut nulla umquam etate arescat. Nec desunt quidem sub ingenti illa piro mediis circiter hortis, commodissima sedilia, pulvinos quoque si videbitur, adferri iubebo. Iam vero [personarum] nichil me penitet vel ad Hierarchiam vel nedum[1] Achademiam, consul, medicus publicus, secretarius urbanus, theologus et idem orator, ego denique tam magnifici fundi *dominus* [colonus]. Nam ut de Platone taceam, (qui quoslibet eciam loquentes facit) quando umquam Tullius perfricte frontis homo, coetum magnificentiorem[2] ausus est convocare. Quod si Socratem philosophum gravissimum illa in Phedro loci amenitas potuit invitare, ut humi iuxta fonticulum in gramine disputandi gratia procumberet, quid ni nos hii horti, (quos vel Epicurus ipse laudare queat) certe ad considendum alliciunt, presertim qum nichil hic eorum, que Socrates illic miratur, desideretur, quippe ubi pyrus, ut videtis media, triplicem nobis voluptatem ministrabit. Nam ut est procera satis, et patulis diffusa ramis, amenissimam prorsus umbram prebebit, et frondibus opacis estum facile propulsabit, preterea ut est anni vernum tempus, non oculos modo flosculorum aspectu pascet, verum eciam nares gratissimo odore recreabit: tum nec fonticulo illo frigentis aquule a Socrate superari videamur, en pro fonticulo rivus leni murmure, circumlabens totos hortos irrigat. Hac aura quid possit esse spirantius, imo (quod medico teste dixerim) [quid] salubrius? Ibi Battus qui eius apud Platonem descriptionis pulchre meminisset, nostram orationem interpellans, Ut ceteris, inquit, Herasme rebus maxime superemus, una certe a Socrate illo Platonico vincimur. Nam et herbarum virentium, graminumque flosculis versicoloribus distinctorum, gryllorum[3] et cycadarum canorum murmur addas licebit, est tamen quo sumus inferiores. [Erasmus.] Quid nam [istuc], inquam? [Battus.] Puellarum Nympharumque imaginibus, inquit, [quas] Socratem illic video preterisse neutiquam. Quo ioco exhilaratus consul et medicus, per canem, inquiunt, et anserem Socraticum, dignum quod a Batto admoneretur, quanquam celaturis non magnopere solet delectari, [vivas opinor mallet, si detur optio]. Verum istud nostre disputaciuncule nichil obfuerit. Eamus. Ubi collaudata loci specie consedissemus Battum[que] certatim ut accingeretur, hortaremur, ille consulem fixius intuitus.

[Battus.] Merito, inquit, nunc meo iugulor gladio, nam [qui vos] modo magnifice nugari iubebam, eo per vos ipsos redigor, ut nichil me sit hodie

---

[1] B.R. has *Iarcae scholam non solum.*

[2] The word *eciam* follows in MS, but is crossed out.

[3] The MS reading *gratia* was corrected to *gryllorum* by a later hand.

futurum ineptius aut nugatius. Age, parendum video tum consuli, [tum medico,] tum amicissimis, [postremo tam multis]: sed pomarium prius concludatur,[1] ne quis nos videat. Neque enim vereor, ne vestrum quispiam me prodat, modo possit Herasmi stilus conquiescere, [qui quicquid noctu somniat etiam interdiu chartis suis illinire solet. Atqui, inquam, hic neque calamus est mihi neque charta. Fateor, inquit, at memoriam novi tuam, quam scio tibi esse commentarii vice. Quod etiam si quid suffugerit, tu facile de tuo fulcies hiatum, sed tamen aggrediar vobis fretus.] Deinde in pedes erectus, compositis ad dicendum et veste et vultu, et gestu, aliquamdiu defixis humi luminibus, cogitabundus hesit: dicturienti pallor quidam, ac trepidatio aborta, non stolidi nobis oratoris, et confidentis, sed cordati, et ut inquit Fabius periculum intelligentis dedit argumentum: mox inventis [ac] digestis orationis partibus (id enim egisse ex notatis articulis coniiciebam) subtussiens expuit (id quod habebat familiare). Deinde surrecto hilarius vultu, iamque vivacius singulos intuitus, summa cum omnium expectatione, ita exorsus est.

Orationis exordium. Battus

Nisi et apud iudices literatissimos dicturum me scirem, et ipsa cause bonitate non mediocriter adiuvarer, vererer ne in tanto stolidissimorum hominum odio non optimum hodie patronum litere fuerint habiture. Nunc vero tantum abest, ut omnia que ab istis antirhetoribus obiici vel soleant, vel queant, refellere me posse diffidam, ut in causa tam vincibili, ne principio quidem [mihi] utendum putarim. Idque non modo apud vos, quos qum amicissimos, eruditissimos, huius etiam dictionis efflagitatores habeam, benevolentes, dociles, attentos non habere non possum: verum etiam apud Sauromatas, et si quid hiis est [etiam] barbarius, modo homines dentur, certam mihi victoriam promisero, homines, inquam, qui rationis ductum, non *cum* [animi] impetu[m] sequuntur. Nam istos rabulas, qui obstinatis animis insaniam suam eciam confessam solent defendere, haud alio in numero quam Dyogenes suam contionem pono. [Ad quem cum hominum milia aliquot confluxissent, negabat se ullum adhuc videre hominem.] Pestifera est, inquiunt, mortalibus erudicio, optanda imperitia. Horatius: Nil intra est oleam, nil extra est in nuce duri.

De fide igitur facienda iamdudum securus, hoc unum mihi a vobis video postulandum, [ut] ne in re tam intractabili, tam spinosa, ullum orationis splendorem expectetis, quem alioqui ne in felicissima quidem materia a

---

[1] The word *volo* is here crossed out in MS, though it causes no difficulty in the construction.

Batto requirere debebatis. Nec delectari quidem postulabitis, nisi quid forte barbarorum ineptissime rationem risum movebunt. Herasmus. Tum ego veniam precatus, et licebit ne, inquit, aliquotiens [dicentem] interpellare? Battus. Licebit, inquit, per me quotiens videbitur [nec enim ad clepsydras dicimus, ut causae dispendium sit, si quid temporis intercipiatur].

Herasmus. Ita mihi principio supersedisse videris, inquam, ut hoc ipso quo non uteris, maxime sis usus principio: sed perge, obsecro, ne te primo statim cursu [diutius] remoremur. Battus. Istud vero tuum est, respondit Battus, haud meum qui vafriciem illam, et strophas rhetoricas perdidicisti, mihi sat habeo, rem ut est, [per] quam paucissimis ostendere. Non igitur hic altius repetam, quibus fatis, quorum opera, quo tempore, quibus 8 gradibus antique discipline ᐧ e tanto fastigio in hunc Tartarum deciderint, id quod vos paulo ante ceperatis: alias hec fortasse commodius: neque vero refert quo casu quispiam in puteum deciderit, sed quomodo qui cecidit, inde queat educi. Antiquis igitur literis contra novos hostes patrocinium feremus, quibus quidem a triplice potissimum hostium genere negocium exhiberi video. Alii enim literariam Rempublicam tanquam funditus deletam cupiunt, alii imperium non quidem prorsus extinguere, sed arctioribus finibus includere moliuntur. Postremi ita Rempublicam salvam esse volunt, ut afflictissimam velint, quippe in qua ipsi tyrannidem occupent, in quam (patriis legibus abrogatis) peregrinos et magistratus et mores inducunt.

Et primi quidem illi mihi videntur, qui plane rudes, haud scio invidia ne aut stoliditate maiore, religionis (nescio cuius) pretextu, literaturam universam poeseos nomine detestantur. Alteros ego intelligo, qui indocte docti, cetera quidem studia (hoc est sua) utrumque recipiunt, humanitatis autem literas, sine quibus ceca est omnis doctrina, angue peius oderunt. Postremos vero, quos alios esse dicam quam eos, qui quodvis literarum genus et mirantur, et probant, cum primis eciam poesim et rhetoricen, at ea lege, ut ipsi pro summis et poetis et rhetoribus habeantur, qum nichil sint minus: nec dictu interim proclive fuerit, quos ex hiis hostibus literaria Respublica gravissimos perniciosissimosque[1] patiatur, aut quibus maximam cladium suarum partem acceptam referre debeat.

Nam primi quidem illi (ne contemnendos putemus) tametsi neque ullo armorum genere, neque rei militaris scientia sunt instructi, quippe silvestris barbaraque multitudo, passim ex agris et montibus conflata, nescio tamen an ullum sit hostium genus infestius. Rabiose enim ferae in morem devotis animis in pugnam ruunt, non ingrediuntur, furore pro fortitudine utentes. Quatuor potissimum rebus valent, furore, quo Andabatas,

[1] An extra *s* appears after the first *o* in this word.

clamore, quo Stentorem Homericum, multitudine, qua Xerxis eciam copias vincunt. Postremo clipeo quodam simulate religionis sub quo perpetuo latent, quem unum ad omnia telorum genera obiiciunt.

Hii nimirum sunt qui qum ipsi sint omnis literature expertes, literatorum gloria peruruntur, aliorumque pulcherrimis studiis oblatrare, pulchrum in primis ac religiosum putant, ac mirum quam veteratorie suam vel inerciam, vel invidiam, vel superbiam speciosis titulis pretexunt simplicitatis ac religionis. Alteri [sunt] hiis quidem paulo instructiores, qui et eminus et cominus nos petunt. Eminus telis, sed plane deridiculis: nam stuppas, fumum et stercora in nos iaciunt. Cominus pugionibus appetunt, sed plumbeis. Pacem offerunt, sed superbissimis plane condicionibus, ut sine humanitatis literis perdocti simus,[1] sine quibus nulle constant litere, terminos nobis prescribunt. Omnem policiem interdicunt, et quicquid ipsi non didicerunt: hoc sunt molestissimi, quod prehendi nequeant. Consistunt nusquam, Parthis ipsis fugatiores, modo annuunt[2] modo negant, tergiversantur, aliquo cavillo elabuntur, et Prothei in morem, omnia transformant sese in miracula rerum. Porro postremos illos fortassis aliquis parum infestos hostes iudicarit, quod sedulitate peccent non odio, at mihi quidem videntur inter omnes longe nocentissimi. Ceteri quidem, quia infestis signis nos appetant[3] arcentur a menibus, hii dum intra menia, intra presidia nostra versantur, dum armis et insignibus amicos imitantur, eternum *exterminum* [exitium] Reipublice mendaci pietatis specie moliuntur, et quo magis vindicande patrie student, eo turpiori impediunt servituti. Quare primi quidem hoc prope modum sunt amandi, quod ita literas oderunt, ut nullas attigerint. Posteriores hoc minus nocentes, quod ab optimis abstinuerint, nam poeticis et oratoriis, sua tanquam [sorte] contenti *simplicitate*. Postremi dum omnia scire voluerunt, permiscuerunt, contaminaverunt, perdiderunt omnia. Vere hoc dicunt, importuno officio nichil esse inofficiosius interdum.

Ita hii dum literis laborantibus succurrere studuerunt, perniciosa sedulitate funditus extinxerunt. Vires ante conveniebat expendere, consulere ingenium, quam rem tam arduam susciperent. Nunc Phaetontem imitari maluerint, qui dum ignarus auriga currum [paternum] conatur moderari, magno suo malo subvertit. Et sunt hii quidem, ut stulticia

---

[1] MS reads *predocti simus*, which was changed by a later hand to *perdocti simus;* B.R. reads *predoctissimus.*

[2] MS reads *annuunt*, which makes an effective contrast with *negant*, but the copyist probably did not understand the word, for he crossed it out and wrote *aiunt.*

[3] Corrected by a later hand to *appetunt*, obviously a better reading.

Phaetonti pares, ita pari exicio digni, aut etiam graviore. Horum enim temeritate, vetus illa et vera philosophia ad meras nugas, ad somnia redacta est. Per hos innumerabilium priscorum auctorum monumenta desideramus: quod scriptorum ut quisque est doctissimus, ita fedissimis mendis scatet, hiis acceptum ferimus: quod prisca illa theologia tantopere degeneravit haud aliorum est opus: quod grammatiste non nisi meram barbariem et scribunt, et precipiunt, hiis debemus.

Et ut semel finiam, quod in unoquoque genere literarum muti et infantissimi, pro doctissimis in precio sunt, horum opera effectum est, quorum dum alius in grammaticis, alius in rhetoricis, alius in dyalecticis, alius in physica, alius in theologia scribit, dum hic commentationibus optimos auctores non illustrat sed obscurat, non adornat sed contaminat, dum ille quod non intelligit, emendare nititur, dum alius ex bene Grecis, male Latina facit, lingue utriusque iuxta ignarus, dum ita, inquam, certatim tumultuantur, inutili officio omnia confuderunt, depravarunt, everterunt, et quo diligentius suum quisque officium prestitit, eo plus damni dedit, ut si quis manibus merda oblitis, pulvisculum e purpura conetur extergere, quanto volet esse officiosior, eo erit molestior. Verum hiis (quod res infinitam prope disputationem postulare videtur) dilatis, reliquas acies, totidem conflictibus adoriemur, hic vero efficiam, ut vel Pirrho doctiorem me esse iuretis. Nam rusticanam illam cohortem tumultuario tantum milite dissipasse sat habebimus, et clipeo illo ficte
9 religionis nudatos, in fugam adegisse, id quod haud multi | fuerit negocii. Imbellis enim est multitudo e senibus contracta, qui ubi etatem per luxum effluxisse intelligunt, iuvenibus ad meliora proficientibus invident inepti. Hos igitur primum quidem validissimis rationibus tanquam telis, terga dare cogemus, deinde prelium (ut solent) redintegrantes, sacrarum literarum testimoniis, velut ensibus confodiemus. *Dein* [Sub haec] exemplorum copia [obrutos] castris quoque deturbabimus, quibus confectis, eodem quasi Marte et impetu posteriores aggrediemur, et omnibus exutos armis, omni dimicandi genere superabimus. Sed iam primi illi sunt lacessendi, si prius fecialis paterque patratus iusta peregerint [quibus, ut arbitror, huiusmodi quaedam oratio congrueret, si res serio gereretur].

Oratio fecialium.

Quo tandem iure o vos Gothi, e vestris egressi limitibus, non modo Latinorum provincias occupatis (disciplinas loquor liberales) verum eciam ipsam urbem rerum dominam, Latinitatem audetis incessere? Quanam[1]

---

[1] The original reading was *Quam nam.*

iniuria lacessiti, quid petitis? Quod si bellum placet, iusto Marte discernite, facite pugnandi copiam. Sin pugna diffiditis, desinite molesti esse, excedite *patriam* [solo, regionem hanc] purgate, vestris finibus continemini. Quod si hostes quam latrunculi dici malitis, prodite e latebris, conserite manus, et publico certamine finis queratur odiis, aut vos victi quiescite, aut nos vobis victoribus concedemus.

Quod litere compluribus tantopere sint invise, nichil [aliud] esse in causa, nisi quod ignorent.

Iam non auditi (proiecta hasta), bellum indixere feciales, iam ad pugnam est hostis evocandus. [Hic ego interpellans, Vide, inquam, ne nimium hoc sit calidum, nondum omnes tibi peractae ceremoniae, porcus tibi saxo feriendus, priusquam ad arma prosilias. Probe mones, inquit, Utinam ex istis haris, in quibus passim tot crassi validique sues ociosi saginantur cibo populi, mihi liceret insignem aliquem deligere. Eum ego bipedem libentius mactarem quam ullum porcum quadrupedem. Sed agite, factum putemus, quod ex animo factum volumus, et hostem bonis avibus aggrediamur.] *Equidem.* [Nam interim] perinde agam, ac si cum ipsis presentibus mihi res esset. Vos modo huius nostre dimicaciuncule spectatores sedete. [Atque adeo ne tubam deesse queratur Erasmus meus, superstitiosus ut video ceremoniarum observator, esto convitium hoc tubae loco.]

Dicite, queso, brutissimi homines, Mide progenies, statue marmoree, quid ita commeruere litere seculares (sic enim vos appellare soletis, quicquid non didicistis) ut vos eas tam obstinatis odiis insectemini, tanquam homines ad id unum sint nati, ut eruditionem oderint? An quia et non didicisse piget, nec discere licet, odisse libet? Quod si ipsi per ignaviam desperatis, aliis invidere pulchrum arbitramini? Quin [potius] accingimini, et gloriam hanc nobis quam invidetis, preripitis? Sed veremini ne in vos antiqua [illa] scommata iaciamus, asini ad lyram, boves ad ceroma. Quid graculo cum fidibus? quid cum amaricino sui? At non mirum facitis, quod odistis, mirum facturi si amaretis. Vere illud ut cetera, princeps [ille] Peripateticorum *scripsit:* Scientiis nisi inscium neminem esse inimicum. Non gallus miratur iaspidem, non sues delectant rose, non pictura simiam, non iuvat lippum lux, non placet Mide cantus, Apollinis.

Cur inepti auriculas vestras asininas ultro proditis, vel Mida patre stultiores [qui celare studuit]? Cur non magis terre infoditis inscitie vestre dedecus? Cur non potius quorundam calliditatem imitamini, qui *bonas artes* laudant ut scire videantur? Cur saltem non tacetis, ut philosophi putemini? Nunc ipsi vestromet iudicio, tanquam sorices comprehendimini. An vero eo dementie provecti estis, ut bellum eciam facinus putetis, res optimas, *usque* [quas] sapientissimi [quique] sibi tantis laboribus expetendas putarint, odisse, invidere, oblatrare. Ista vero gloria, [si nescitis,] cum baiulariis, cum cerdonibus, cum nautis et fossoribus vobis est communis: quippe oderunt et illi *secularia* [politiora] studia, contemnunt, execrantur, hoc *in nobis* [vobis] meliores, primum quod moderatius oderint, deinde quod suarum artium amore, nostra studia contemnunt. Vos ita *seculares* [elegantiores] artes odistis, ut nullas teneatis. Illi artem arti, studiis studia preferunt, vos scientie ignorantiam antefertis, sane menti insaniam anteponitis, pecudem homini. [O contemptores servum pecus, quos vel ipsi derideant asini.] At videte interim, quam iniquum sit odisse, nec scire neque quid oderitis, neque cur oderitis. Damnatis rhetoricen, quid autem sit ea, ne per nebulam quidem vidistis. Odistis poesim, quam neque quid sit, neque cuiusmodi sit, intelligitis. Odistis antiquitatem, omnis antiquitatis imperiti. Breviter, totum hoc quod docti magnis vigiliis sequuntur vos contemnitis, et totum hoc quantum est ignoratis. Nam si quando hec eadem ipsi didicistis, cur volentes discere reprehenditis? Si non didicistis (quod etiam gloriamini, nedum confitemini) quid de incompertis tam stolide pronunciatis? Sed opinor audistis, mala esse hec studia. Esto sane, dummodo a vestris simillimis, invidis, ignaris, inimicis: videlicet sus suem docuit, cecus ceco dux fuit. At proferte si potestis, vel unum qui has literas, ubi probe perceptas habuit, accusavit: qui insumpte [in] eis opere se penitere dixit? Cur autem stolido de incompertis blateranti creditur, erudito de perceptis disserenti fides negatur? An putatis [esse] obscuram rem cuicumque vestram invidentiam? an nos fucum vestrum fallere creditis? an fugere nos, quid morbi vos urat? Liceat tandem, queso, rebus sua dare nomina, desinite aliquando pro invidentissimis et ignavis, religiosos ac pios vos velle videri.

Invidum esse, haud religiosum odisse literas, quas nescias.

Tum medicus *inquit:* Utar [inquit] iure concesso, interpellabo. Preclarum te velitem declarasti, ne temere te Battum appellatum iam puto. Rogante illo, quid ita putaret: Non sunt, inquit, hec enigmata tibi qui fabulas perpulchre tenes. Ita probe barbarorum furta prodidisti, ut altera methamorphosi te ex iudice[1] illo lapide rursum in Battum revixisse

[1] The original reading *iudice* is an obvious mistake for *indice*.

propemodum credam: deinde scite istud hominum genus ad pugnam
evocasti. Nulla enim re perinde in rabiem agi solent, quam si stoliditatis,
si imperitie, si invidentie opinionem illis impingas, hoc est si maxime
vera ' audiant. Recte sentis, inquit Battus, nec mirum adeo, si tacto
[h]ulcere scabiosi commoveantur. Tum vero videres homines super-
bissimos, oculis ardescentibus, totiusque vultus immanitate, animi testari
furorem; *nec* [etiam si ne] inter hec quidem a simulande religionis artificio recedunt: hac tanquam personati, suas tragedias agunt. Nam ut
[est] res omnium optima religio, ita (nobili historico teste) ad quidvis
vitii pretextendum commodatissimum pallium, eo quod si quis in ipsa
vicia conetur animadvertere, religionem qua sese obumbraverunt violare
plerisque videatuŕ: sepe ita tuto latet vicium proximitate boni. [Cum-
que ipsi longe gravioribus vitiis madeant, quam ulli mortalium, quos isti
semidei pro prophanis habent, tamen in alienam vitam petulantissimis
linguis invehuntur, nulli parcentes, nec aetati, nec sexui, nec genti, nec
ordini, denique nec homini, nec nomini. Caeterum quoties illos depre-
henderit aliquis aut ebrios, aut scortantes, aut aliud his etiam sceleratius
designantes, excusant, tegunt, mussari volunt, ob honorem, inquiunt,
ordinis, quasi caeteri mortales omnes sint extraordinarii. Cum seditiosis-
sime vociferantur in vitia clericorum, et imperitam multitudinem ad la-
pides provocant, non putant esse periculum, ne succenseat Christus eius
ordinis autor, nam is sacerdos fuit, Iacobita non fuit. Si quis ausit efferre
quicquam de illorum mysteriis, et Augiae stabulum movere, periculum
denunciant, ne Franciscus, aut Dominicus, aut Helias, si diis placet,
iratus perdat hominem. Ex hoc grege quidam nuper miris laudibus vexit
sui ordinis sodalem, quod in concione publica nihil non vociferatus in
sacerdotes concubinarios populo ac magistratibus conatus sit persuadere,
ut sacerdotum concubinae in laevo humero rubram crucem gestare com-
pellerentur. Cumque hac narratione sibi mire placeret, rogabat quispiam,
colaudata illius oratione, quo colore vellet esse crucem Iacobitarum,
Carmelitarum, ac caeterorum. An placeret ut Minoritarum concubinae
gestarent crucem cinericii coloris, Carmelitarum candidi, Iacobitarum
nigri. Ibi abominatus homo religiosus omen, longa cruce se signavit.
Tum alter: Nunquam efficies, inquit, quamlibet magna cruce, quin
plurimi norint, quae dedecora a vestris sodalibus aliquando designentur.
Neque enim fieri secus potest, in tanta hominum ac nationum colluvie.
Verum haec, inquit, fortassis ob honorem ordinis efferri fas non est. Id
cum alter magnopere comprobasset, quaerebat, an putaret et sacerdotum
esse ordinem. Cum negare non posset, rogabat, cur existimaret horum
comissa seditiosis clamoribus apud populum elatranda? Sed ne longius ab

instituto divagemur, eodem pallio tegunt crassissimam inscitiam suam, quo caetera vitae dedecora.]

Hanc igitur [Ubique falsam] pietatem pro clipeo obtendunt, hanc mirificam quandam assimilant, adeo quidem vafre, ac veteratorie, ut non aliis modo, verum etiam sibi astutissimi homines imponant, non quod ullo religionis studio moveantur, quippe qui nusquam alibi quam hac una in re religiosi videri cupiunt, sed quod, Fabius inquit, *ut* sub magni nominis umbra delitescant. Nocentum est ista religio, furum, homicidarum, qui simul atque facinus aliquod designavere, tum demum ad aras ac templa solent confugere, ut servus ille apud Plautum sceleratissimus. [At quo tandem consilio? an quod loci religione delectentur? Imo vero ut crucem effugiant, ut impune sint flagitiosi.] Haud aliter nostri censores, quin ceteris in rebus et Dyonisii sint et Clodii, *qum* [quoties de bonis]*secularibus* studiis agitur, tum demum Nume videri volunt, tum denique se *tyrannos* [Christianos] esse meminerunt, tum demum Evangelicas sententias canere incipiunt, et res fedas speciosis vocabulis palliantes, zelose, haud invidentia dicunt moveri, nec odisse studia nostra, sed contemnere, id homine Christiano dignum ac pulchrum in primis. Apostolorum simplicem rusticitatem nobis proponunt. Singulare inter celites premium illos manere dicunt, qui disciplinas istas ethnicas ad ostentationem et superbiam inventas, religionis amore possint [pro] nichili ducere. Rudem pietatem superis esse gratissimam: quasi vero aut superos rusticitas nostra quicquam delectet, quod si est, cur non bruta in primis amplectimur? An ad ullam vite amministrationem utilis sit ignorantia, ac non potius insulsissimum sit, ac plane *puerile* [dementi], rem pulcherrimam quam nec habeas, nec habere speres, in aliis contemnere.

Errant vehementer, si cuiusvis rei contemptum laudi sibi duci volunt. Quid enim si Thersites Grecorum ultimus, Achillis partam armis gloriam una cum ipsis armis, pro quibus Aiaci cum Ulisse certamen erat, dicat se homo ignavissimus contemnere, nonne universis cachinnum moverit? Quis enim non rideat, si limax equi velocitatem contemnat? si noctua aquile, si talpa capree rideat oculos? si psitaci colorem corvus despiciat? Si asellus elephanti sensum nichili *ducat* [faciat]? si stolidus ac fatuus, viri cordati prudentiam contemnat? nunquam laudem merebitur. Equidem opere precium puto barbaris, ne mihi perpetuo de suo contemptu glorientur, contemnendi rationem ostendere.

Que res cum laude contemnantur, et que secus.

Sunt enim in rebus humanis quedam, que mortalium animos *insita* [insitiva] quadam sui cupiditate sollicitant, sive quod honesta ac speciosa videantur, sive quod dulcia, sive alioquin utilia, cuius generis sunt, opes, claritas, dignitas, voluptas[1]: ista quidem si habeas, aut certe in proclivi sit [ut] potiaris, eatenus dumtaxat, quatenus a virtute avocent,[2] contemnere, res est forti proboque viro digna. Pari item cum laude [tristia] ut dulcia contemni solent, ab hiis avelli posse, illa vero adire laudi est. Lacedemoniorum institutum Plato minus probat, quod cum durissimos labores facile contemnerent, contra voluptates non perinde exercitati viderentur? at hii nostri Cathones, ad utrumvis femina quavis molliores, ad solas literas contemnendas viros se prebent. Quodque magis rideas, contemnunt non modo res honestissimas, verum eciam *amenas* [alienas]. Ciceronianam contemnunt eloquentiam, homines mutis *animalibus* [piscibus] mutiores, Chrysippi contemnunt acumen, cum sint ipsi quovis pistillo retusiores. Poesim contemnunt prophani, et (ut inquit Plato) longe a Musis alieni. Contemnunt veterum theologorum policiem, quam assequi desperant,[3] et si sperent, tum magis insaniant.

O contemptorum *servum* [stolidum] pecus: dic queso michi, que nam ista nova magnanimitas? Quod inauditum contemnendi genus? nummulum non potes contemnere et de eruditionis contemptu gloriaris? Scorti molli suaviolo superaris Hercules, ducit te captivum puerilis voluptatula, rapit te quolibet assentatio, consternat conviciolum, et fortem te visum iri credis, si res maiores eciam quam ut assequi queas, possis contemnere? [Non libet superbire oratione compta, sed interim pallio compto te venditas mulierculis: vis orationem ieiunam ac squalidam, sed interim cuticula distenta nitet. Abhorres a mentione puellarum in legendis poetis, at interim non abhorres a comprimendis uxoribus alienis, aut Vestalibus etiam virginibus. Non placet nitor in stilo, at non displicet in marsupio.] Audi magnifice contemptor, prius literas disce, postea contemne: si quidem fortis videre studes, prius habe quod contemnas. Nisi forte et in isto te *credis* apostolos imitari [iactitas], quod in cupiditate relinquenda, non [in] modo [rei] virtutis laus consistat. Age nichil intersit inter opes et literas. Apostoli rem mediocrem, et spem maiorem contempsere, idque sine [nulla] invidentia, neque ipsi nudi aliis locupletibus invidebant. Vobis ne mediocris quidem est erudicio, quam possitis recte contemnere, summa despe-

---

[1] The word *honor* is crossed out after *voluptas*.
[2] MS reads *avocant*, but was corrected by a later hand.
[3] MS reads *desperent*, but is corrected.

ratio, tum quod res sit in primis ardua, et infiniti laboris, tum quod vobis sint ingenia quovis plumbo inertiora. Postremo si recte contempsistis, cur aliis invidetis? Si invidetis, profecto cupitis: si cupitis, cur non in eandem nobiscum [h]arenam descenditis, et nobiscum potius felices esse curatis, quam nostra causa miseri? Certate, vincite, triumphate. Sed vident homines ignavissimi duris undique laboribus [ac vigiliis] septas literas nostras, quas quidem si possent contemnere non tam stolide de eruditionis contemptu sese iac[ti]tarent.

11   Ubi summam mihi literaturam comparavero, tum demum incipiam cum laude contemnere, non quo minus | utar, sed ne quid insolenter[1] efficiam ut cum omneis antecedam eruditione, anteponam me nemini, ne stolidissimo quidem. [Mediocribus conatibus candide favebo, victori gratulabor, non] *Mediocrium* invidebo. Quanto maior ero, tanto me geram summissius, quo plus sapiam, eo alienam inscitiam modestius feram, ipse ferens omnes dabo operam, ut nemini sit ex me quod ferat. Cum studiosis eruditione, cum omnibus modestia, comitate, verecundia certabo. Ita me geram, ut hoc melior intelligar, quo sum doctior. Quanto magis alii me suspiciunt, tanto magis ipse me despiciam. Denique cum omnia scire curavero, ipse me scire tanquam nesciam. Ita demum qum laude contempserimus, si non alienam, sed nostram doctrinam contemnemus: sic non erudicio modo verum etiam virtus ipsa contemnenda est, et post omnia contemptus etiam *ipse* contemnendus.

Sic contempsit Augustinus ethnicas disciplinas, *at* [sed] tum posteaquam principatum esset in hiis assecutus. Sic literas Ciceronianas et Platonicas Hieronimus, ut nichilominus et egregie teneat, et passim utatur. [Sic Basilius sic Chrysostomus rhetorum ac philosophorum ingenia neglexerunt, ut ex monumentis agnoscas eos haec non ignorasse.] Isti vero quamobrem tandem se contemnere gloriantur? An more vulpis illius que in apologis est, quia frustra cupiunt? Illa enim asini testiculos tum demum cepit abominari, posteaquam sperare desiit. [O foedum inquit cibum, nunquam esse potuissem.] At istud (si fas est rebus sua dare nomina) mera invidia est, haud contemptus. An quia (ut sunt molliculi) laboris asperitate deterrentur, sine quo nec ad virtutem, nec ad eruditionem cuiquam est aditus? At istud ignavi simul atque maligni hominis esse, quis non videat? An tandem pro innata rusticitate, literarum mundiciem oderunt? Nec id quidem Christiano pioque (ut isti dicunt) sed agresti, ac plane bruto animo dignum puto. Eya sit pudor tandem, cedant meliora conantibus. Sit satis istis, [quod] suam ignorantiam ignosci[2] sibi, ne eciam ultro

---

[1] This word is changed to *insolescam*, the reading of B.R.

[2] This word is changed to *ignoscunt*, which is necessary when *quod* is added to the sentence.

nobis obstrepant, ultro quos venerari debebant ac suspicere, despiciant:
ac si ipsis nichil habetur prius ac dulcius somno et ocio, sint [aliis] equiores:
nobis saltem tristes vigilias et insanos labores relinquant, quandoquidem
[nos] istorum deliciis nichil invidemus: quo maioris invidentie est, alienis
uri *laudibus* [laboribus].

Absurde reprehendi quippiam [non ob aliud nisi] quod ab ethnicis inventum.

Hoc aceto perfusi, mirum est dictu, quanto clamore in nos irruant,
Christianos esse negant, sed ethnicos, sed ydolatras, et ipsis *hereticis*
[ethnicis] pestilentiores. An vero, inquiunt, is Christianus censendus qui
disciplinis prophanis, et ab impiis hominibus ad superbiam excogitatis,
tantum opere impartit, tantopere se oblectat? In hiis totus conquiescit, in
hiis ocium, in hiis negocium, in hiis solacium omne reponit? Et quis non
videat, quantum sit sacrilegium, hominem, qui iam Christiane milicie
nomen semel dederit, semel Christo imperatori sit et iniciatus et inauc-
toratus, ad hostes demones transfugere, et cum ydolorum cultoribus
habere commercium? an non habet (inquiunt) qui in dicendo Ciceronianum, in carmine Vergilianum aut Horatianum se nominari gaudet, in
philosophia Arestotelicum, Academicum, Stoicum, Epicureum? Audistis
Chrisippeum enthimema. Audistis sillogismum cornutum. Videtis quam
captiosis laqueis vos simplices irretire moliantur.

Enimvero helleboro illo Carnead[e]o opus esse intelligo. Quid dicitis
Antichrysippi? continuo ne malum et Christianis interdictum, quicquid ab
ethnicis profectum erit? Ita ne ulla gentilium inventa usurpare licebit,
nisi protinus Christiani esse desinamus? Scilicet igitur *fabros* per contionem [vestros fabros] admonendos censeo, ne post hac serris, securibus,
asciis, terebellis, ne cuneis, ne regulis, ne perpendiculis, *ne fornicibus*, ne
post hac amussibus suis audeant uti. Ne rogaveris, quid ita? et artem
hanc et artis arma Dedalus homo ethnicus excogitavit. Quiescant fabri
ferrarii, fabricam ferream invenere Cyclopes homines prodigiosi. Erariam
fabricam nemo exerceat, hanc Calybes monstrasse tradunt. Figulinam
Chorebus [ferientur figuli]. Sutrinam Boetius [quidam, nemo Christianus
consuat calceum]. Fulloniam Niceas [nemo sordes vestium eluat].
Textoriam Egyptii, [redeamus ad ferarum pelles]. Tinctoriam Lydii
[nemo lanam ab ove detonsam, fuco adulteret]. Metalli conflaturam
Cadmus Phoenix invenit. Metuant figuli, sutores, fullones, textores, tinc-
tores, conflatores.[1] Nautis, si fieri possit, religionem iniiciamus ne consue-

---

[1] This sentence is crossed out in the manuscript. The printed version reads
frigeant officinae conflatorum.

tis utantur armis. Aurigas admoneamus, ne Erichthonium imitentur. Pictores, celatores, vitriarios, breviterque ceterum[1] quantum est opificum, ne sese suosque post hac ethnicis artibus contaminent, si queant alios questus excogitent, sin minus, esuriant potiusquam Christiani esse desinant. Quid si et militibus hominibus impiis scrupulum iniiciamus, ne clypeis, loricis, galeis, gladiis, ocreis, cristis, arcubus, sagittis, lanceis, hastis utantur? hec omnia ab impiis reperta perhibent. Verum quis ferat puellis Minerve studium simul et arma eripi, pensa, colos, fusos, radios, telas, quorum nichil est a Christianis inventum.

Iam et agricolatoribus, vel cum vite periculo ferias indicendas video: aratrum Osiridis inventum est: nemo post hac ausit terram invertere, inversam serere, satammetere, horum Saturnum auctorem ferunt. Nemo vitem coluerit, id enim a Libero *inventum* [excogitatum]. Vinum merum nemo bibat, ne aqua quidem dilutum, monstravit hoc Staphilius. Egroti medicos non advocent, medicina Apollinis inventum est. Et hos quidem non impios modo homines, verum eciam cacodemones fuisse vulgus credit. Vobis igitur demonum inventis uti licet, nobis studiosorum hominum literis uti non licebit? [Atqui nihil] *Non* pudet, nec eos quidem qui et dyalectici et theologi videri volunt, studiosis hec obiicere, que si in pagis apud fossores messoresque audeant disputare, moriar ni rustici ipsi ligonibus et falcibus eos conficiant. Si gentilium inventis uti vetamur, quid tandem, obsecro, in agris, in urbibus, in templis, in edibus, | in officinis, domi, belli,[2] privatim aut publice relinquetur? adeo Christiani nichil habemus ab ethnicis non traditum. Quod scribimus, quod utrumque Latine loquimur ab ethnicis accepimus: ab illis reperti caracteres, ab iisdem orationis usus inventus. Egone, inquiunt, damnatorum hominum libros in manu, in sinu habebo, lectitabo, venerabor?

Ardet apud inferos Virgilius, et eius poemata cantat Christianus? quasi non et multi Christiani illic ardeant quorum si qua bene scripta supersunt, nemo tamen iccirco respuenda putet. Sed quis istam iudicandi petulantiam ferat, ut tanquam virga Mercuriali quos velint ad inferos demittant, quos velint ad superos evocent? Non hic ingrediar rixosam illam disputationem de ethnicis, que ne mulieribus quidem sit digna, non est nostrum de damnatione ethnicorum disputare, eorum, inquam, qui fidem nostram precesserunt. Tum si coniecturas sequi velimus, facile convicero aut illos viros ex ethnicis, aut omnino nullos salvos esse: quam bene preceperint, non quam recte vixerint laboramus.

---

[1] MS reading *ceteros* is changed to *ceterum*, a better reading.

[2] MS reading *bello* is changed to *belli*, a locative form, which is normal in classical Latin when this word is used with *domi*.

Hyppocritas magistratus, quorum vitam condemnat ipse qui novit, audiendos tamen iubet. Originis [libros in multis] iam hereseos damnatos,[1] *ut* [ad] eruditionis fructum[2] Christiana legit[3] ecclesia, et eorum divina scripta fugimus, de quorum moribus sine summa temeritate iudicare non possit. Imo ut melius dicam, de quibus in bonam partem cum laude, in malam non sine maximo vicio quisquam iudicet. Apage, inquiunt, ego me Ciceronianum aut Platonicum appellari feram, qui semel Christianus dici constitui? Quid ni monstrum hominis? Si te quod Sardanapali perditam molliciem imitaris, [recte] Sardanapaliacum dicimus, aut quod assentator es, Gnat[h]onicum, aut potius ut es stolide gloriosus, T[h]rasonicum appellamus, cur alium Ciceronis linguam imitantem, Ciceronianum pudeat denominari, aut Virgilianum, si quid illius queam emulari? Tu tibi barbaras istas appellationes asciscas, teque vel Albertistam, ut[vel] Thomistam, vel Scotistam, [vel Occanistam, vel Durandistam] vocari gaudeas, dummodo a Christianis denomineris. Ego me a quovis ethnico denominari paciar, dummodo doctissimo, dummodo facundissimo: nec me huius professionis penitebit, modo me prestantiora doceat ethnicus, quam Christianus.

Sed ut rem aliquando finiamus, nisi adversarios nostros talpis ceciores sua redderet invidentia, certe [viderent quod vel caeco apparet,] viderent in rebus ab ethnicis inventis, aliquod inesse discrimen, alias esse inutiles, dubias, pestiferas: alias perutiles, salutares, imo necessarias. Mala illis relinquamus, bona vero quid ni nobis usurpemus? hoc demum est homine Christiano, homine prudenti, homine studioso dignum. At nos, si superis placet, prepostere agimus, gentilium[4] vicia, libidinem, avariciam, ambitionem, *superbiam* [superstitionem] passim imitamur, imo vicimus: at eruditionem quam vel unam imitari par erat, unam aspernamur, stultius ne an superbius, non[dum] satis scio. Nam si res mediocri usui futuras, ab illis ad nos traduximus, idque citra culpam, quid impedit quo secius idem de *gentilium* [illorum] artibus faciamus? quibus (si quid Hieronimo credimus) nichil est in rebus mortalium aut utilius, aut prestantius.

Divino consilio disciplinas ab ethnicis expolitas, ut nos uteremur, non ut contemneremus.

Quin ymo admirabilem rerum ordinem et harmoniam (quam vocant) paulo penit[i]us introspicienti, videri mihi prorsus solet, nec mihi adeo

---

[1] The original reading is *damnati*.

[2] After *fructum* the words *intellexit vel precepit* are crossed out, presumably by the original hand.   [3] The original reading is *leget*.

[4] The printed version reads *ethnicorum*.

soli, visum est idem et plerisque gravissimis auctoribus, non sine divino consilio disciplinarum inveniendarum negocium ethnicis datum esse. Immortalis enim ille rerum moderator (ut est ipsa sapientia) ratione summa constituit universa, pulcherrima quadam vicissitudine distinguit, aptissimo ordine digerit, ut omnibus omnia miro quodam modo respondeant, nec quicquam in tam immensa rerum varietate fieri temere sinit. Hic aureo illi seculo, quo nasci decreverat, voluit ut omnes et anteacte et sequture servirent etates, ad huius unius felicitatem decusque cumulandum quecunque in rerum natura essent, referri placuit: quod ipsum se perfecturum pollicebatur. Qum, inquiens, exaltatus fuero a terra, omnia traham ad me ipsum. Ubi mihi aptissime trahendi vocabulo videtur usus, ut intelligas omnia, vel inimica, vel ethnica, vel alioquin aliena, eciam si non sequantur ad Christi cultum, invita trahi debere. Et ubi est illa rerum harmonia, qua fit (divo Augustino teste) ut ne mala quidem ociose creata videantur. Quorsum ab ipsis mundi rudimentis tot figure, tot prodigia, [tot] misteria spectabant? nempe ad seculum Christianum. Quid deinde tota lex Mosaica, tot ritus, tot cerimonie, tot sacrorum genera, tot promissa, tot oracula? nonne Paulo teste hec omnia *in* figura[1] contingebant illis? Iam ut imperiorum translationes preteream, quorsum pertinuit tanta mole Romanam condere gentem, tantis cladibus, [tot] tam cruentis victoriis urbi rerum domine universum subigere orbem? nonne divino prorsus consilio? nimirum ut iam nata Christiana relligio, facilius in singulas terrarum partes dimanaret,[2] si ab eodem capite tanquam in membra diffunderetur.

Age nunc, qua mente tandem orbem prope totum, tam vesanis, tam pudendis *sunt* religionibus [sivit] irretiri? *Nempe* [Nimirum] ut una exorta, universas summa cum gloria everteret. Adeo nichil sine dimicatione 13 fit egre-| gium. Artes studiosa Grecia repperit, cum qua deinde Latium certamine suscepto, bellicis quidem rebus superavit: at litterarum dicendique laudibus[3] [propemodum] equavit. Aliis rerum latentes causas rimari cure fuit, alii Promethei vinculis alligati, celestium ignium vagos recursus observarunt. Fuerunt qui divinitatis archana tentaverunt, hic disserendi, ille dicendi rationem invenit: nonnulli mortalium mores doctissime depinxerunt, quibusdam rerum gestarum memoriam ad posteros transmittere studio fuit. Iam vero in legibus, in philosophia, quantus sudor antiquis fuit? Quorsum tandem hec omnia? num ut nos exorti contemneremus? an potius ut optima religio, pulcherrimis studiis tum honestaretur, tum

---

1 B.R. reads *figurae*.
2 The original reading *omanaret* is corrected in the manuscript to *dimanaret*.
3 After *laudibus*, *certe* is crossed out, presumably by the original hand.

fulciretur? Omnia *gentilium* [ethnicorum] fortiter facta, scite dicta, in-
geniose cogitata, industrie tradita, sue Reipublice preparaverat Christus.

Ille ministraverat ingenium, ille querendi ardorem adiecerat, nec alio
auctore quesita inveniebant. Hanc artium frugem illorum etas tulit, non
tam sibi quam *nostre Reipublice profecturam* [nobis]: si quidem ut non que-
vis regio suppeditat omnia, nec omnis fert omnia tellus, [ut inquit Maro,]
ita seculis sue quibusque dotes michi distribute videntur. In summo
bono querendo plerique philosophorum et etatem et ingenium triverunt.
Sed id quod erat [vere] summum et prestantissimum, sue Christus etati
servavit, non ita tamen, ut ceteras inutiles, ac sine fruge actas voluerit: id
quod oculis quoque testibus videmus vel corporis in rebus diligenter cavisse
naturam, ne qua portio temporis inutilis effluat. En arbores (admoneor
enim aspectu ab hiis exemplum petere) primo iam vere frondibus alendis
succum suppeditant. Nunc videtis additi frondibus flores quantum voluptatis nobis spectantibus edant. Accedente etate, hii ipsi flosculi paulatim
in pomi carnem turgescunt: autumno mitibus malis stabunt [arbores]
gravide, que simul atque posuerint, rursus id intervalli, quod ex autumno
in hyemem superest, sub futuram estatem novis creandis surculis datur.
Hyems ne ipsa quidem ociosa, alterna quiete rerum vires reficit: idem
celestium orbium discursus ille tam varie temperatus efficit. Summa in
rebus *concordia* [discordia], sed qua nichil concordius. Eodem feruntur
et singula et universa eodem spectant, ad unum quiddam tendunt.

Optimus igitur ille moderator Christus cum suo seculo summi boni cognitionem peculiariter destinasset, proximis ante seculis id tribuendum
putavit, quod ad summum bonum proxime accederet, summam videlicet
erudicionem. Quid enim secundum virtutem potest homini prestabilius
contingere scienciam? qua quidem in re deus Christianorum [sive] ignavie
[sive mavis ocio] consultum voluit, [ut] qui essemus aliunde occupandi,
bonam laboris partem adimeret. Non paulo enim proclivius est, rem iam
ad unguem expolitam perdiscere, quam invenire. Quod nisi illi literarum
segetem sevissent, nobis fortassis nichil esset quod meteremus. Quid enim
ipsi reperissemus, qui illorum inventis non modo nichil unquam adiecimus,
verum detrivimus permulta, perturbavimus omnia? Quo turpius ingrati
sumus, imo invidi, qui res summo usui futuras ne gratis quidem oblatas
accipere velimus, qum istis magno constiterint: nec munus solum pul-
cherrimum recusemus,[1] verum eciam auctorem [muneris], pro gratia quam
debebamus, summa contumelia afficiamus.[2]

---

[1] Changed to *recusamus*.   [2] Changed to *afficimus*.

Homines ignorantia potius quam eruditione insolentiores fieri.

Herasmus. Hic ego, perdocte tu quidem [inquam] et vere Batte: at vix
crediderim ullos esse tam omnis humane rationis expertes, ut universam
literaturam a religione segregandam putent, modo sit Christiana. [Battus.]
Quasi vero, inquit Battus, ulla sit erudicio Christiana, que non eadem
[sit] ineruditissima [loquor autem non de mysteriis nostrae religionis, sed
de disciplinis repertis]. Quid enim (si vera fateri velimus) post ethnicos
illos novi a nobis repertum, quod non idem sit indoctum? Quid autem in-
veniamus bene, qui aliorum inventa tam male tuemur? Ego igitur nullam
[esse] eruditionem puto, nisi que sit secularis (sic enim appellant antiquam)
aut certe seculari literatura condita et instructa. Eam (si perversa et
impia absit opinio) Christianam eciam patiar appellari, quanquam non
paucos adeo stolide religiosos comperio, ut ne Christianam quidem istam,
id est ecclesiasticam multi faciant. Quid enim (inquiunt) si non simus
theologi, si Christum bene scis, satis est, si cetera nescis. Non doctis,
sed innocentibus promissa est immortalitas.

Num idcirco damnabor, si divi Pauli scripta parum sublimiter intelligam? Quid si Hieronimianam dictionem non capiam? quid si Augustini
et Ambrosii scripta ne legerim quidem? quid si ne Evangelium quidem
intelligam? stolide, imo quid si ne teipsum intelligas, quid si camelus sis,
non homo? Confide, eciam pecora celum obtinebunt. Hominum (me
Hercule) genus non modo stolidissimum, verum etiam impium. [Atque
utinam isti Christum bene scirent, qui se gloriantur nihil scire literarum.
At saepe fit, ut qui in literis simplices haberi volunt, in rebus mundanis
sint astutissimi nebulones.] Sed cum hiis mihi interim res non erit. Eo
hunc sermonem interieci, ne mirareris si huiusmodi nostram illam quam
descripsimus eruditionem execrentur, qui Evangelia quoque contemnunt.
Verum ut modo dicebam, cum hiis mihi res non est in presentia: de hiis
loquor, qui ecclesiastice docti videri cupiunt, et [tamen] ab omni seculari
disciplina tanquam Iudeus ab immundis abstinent, illud interim Paulinum obliti, et omnia munda esse mundis. Horum ego eruditionem ita
exiguam esse puto, ut nullam esse iudicem et quavis ruditate peiorem.
Hii vero omnem nostram doctrinam ut malam, ut ethnicam, ut impiam,
14 abominantur: quod ipsi *faciunt* [sciunt], id non humano studio, sed |
tamquam celitus accepisse [videri] volunt.

Iam eciam vulgo dici audio, ut quisque literatissimus sit, ita iniquissimum[1] esse. Que quidem contumelia non magis ad rhetoricos et poeticos,
quam ad theologos, ad iureconsultos, ad dyalecticos, ad ceteros [item]

---

[1] Above this word *nequissimum* is written.

studiosos attinet, dignum quod ab omnibus confutetur. Si mala est erudicio, utrum tandem per se mala est, an per aliud? Si per aliud, cur simpliciter erudicionem reprehendimus? Si per se, cur igitur [iudicio gravissimorum auctorum] in numero bonorum honestorum ponitur? cur opibus anteponitur, que per se male non sunt? *Sed ne* [Adde quod] veritas[1] [n]ulla per se mala esse potest, discipline *seculares* [liberales] cum sint veritates, bone sint necesse est. Quod si per se bona scientia, mala est ignorantia, si mala, igitur fugienda, quanquam si naturam audiamus, quis est qui non malit esse scientissimus, quam ignorantissimus? Hic nobis dyalectici incipiunt esse barbari: non reprehendimus, inquiunt, simpliciter eruditionem, sed quod astutos efficiat, intractabiles, elatos, insolentes, fastidiosos.[2] Quid enim aliud petitis, inquiunt, quam vulgus effugere, eminere inter ceteros, predicari, celebrari, nos nostrique similes pro pecudibus ducere?

Audistis quid istos religios[ul]os mordeat, contemni nolunt: imperare et ducere, non parere neque duci volunt, et ita demum publice paci consultum putant, si nemo extiterit, qui possit alienam insciciam emendare. Intelligitis (ut arbitror) *istam superbie* [eruditionis] calumniam non aliunde quam a superbia proficisci. Iniquissimum [autem] fuerit si lippus solem accuset, cuius luce offenditur. Scientia, inquiunt, inflat, charitas edificat. Utrum igitur insolencia, scientie, an nostrum est vicium? Non audebunt, [ut] opinor, eruditionis dicere, alioquin nemo unquam fuisset eruditus, nisi idem insolens: [et] quo quis[que] evaderet doctior, eo superbior redderetur. Ad istud preterquam quod absurdum est dictu, per quam contumeliosum eciam videri potest. In quos? In Augustinum, in Hieronimum, in plerosque alios, quos quia doctissimi fuerint, superbie nefas sit [ob id eos superbiae] insimulare. At inquies, de *seculari* [prophana] eruditione ago. Et quidem nos accipimus, nempe qualem in hiis, quos modo dixi, religionis Christiane principibus et miramur et veneramur, tue dissimillimam, qui ecclesiasticam doctrinam profiteris. Quid queris? quod si nostropte, non rerum vicio insolescimus, utrum animus erit castigandus, an res sine causa accusande? Nonne modestius faceres tu modestie preceptor, si ingenue tuam insciciam fatearis et non optimis rebus calumniam struas, quo tuo vicio patrocineris? nunc ad omnia rudis, ad hanc calumniam disertus [es].

Attamen, inquis, insolentie materiam ministrat erudicio secularis. Quis negat? At istam quidem materiam undecunque licebit sumere vel ab optimis sanctissimisque rebus. Iccirco [ne] res protinus incusande? An tu potius qui rebus optimis abutare pessimus. Animus per se insolens,

---

[1] The word *quidem* is here crossed out.   [2] MS reads *fastigiosos.*

exerendi sui *videlicet* [undelibet] occasionem arripit. Pecunia quot viciorum genera ministrat? nemo tamen hanc ut malam accusat, sed male utentium animus reprehenditur. Quid erit tandem tam bonum, quod non aliquando mali occasionem ministret[1]? Non ieiunium, non elemosina, non castitas, non virtus ipsa. Superbiunt philosophi, sibi placent poete. Eho tu, nulli superbiunt theologi? An in ullo genere supercilium arrogantius? Quis tamen audeat sanctissimam theologiam in crimen vocare? Superbiunt hac permulti sed suo non theologie vicio. Nulli [ne] superbiunt illitterati? Quid istos insolentiores facit? Nempe ipsa impericia? Quid igitur facerent, si literas[2] didicissent?

Ignorantiam esse superbie matrem. Eruditionem contra modestiam parere.

Nunquam [Quanquam] quid minus verum dici potest quam homines literatura astutos, elatos, et fastidiosos fieri. Si astutiam prudentiam appellant, nichil pugno, qum et in Evangelico consilio serpentum astutiam imitari iubeamur. De fastidio vero, cui non absurdum videatur? Quis igitur saxeos illos et agrestes homines ad humaniorem vitam, ad mansuetius ingenium, ad mores modestiores adduxit? nonne litere? He animum nostrum fingunt, affectus mitigant, frangunt indomitos impetus, mollitum[3] et ingenium non sinunt esse ferox. An vero hoc illi fastidium appellant quod ipsorum barbariem non miramur, quod imperitissimorum hominum nugis delectari non possumus, quod stercora pro gemmis non amplectimur? Utrum hoc fastidiosi est hominis an sani potius, et ab optimis pessima decernetis[4]? De modestia vero idem ego sentio, quod divum Hieronimum [ex Graeci cuiusdam sententia] et recte sensisse, et eleganter scripsisse video, impericiam adducere confidentiam, scientie vero timorem esse comitem? Quod idem Quintilianum probe vidisse intelligo. Quo quisque, inquit, ingenio minus valet, eo magis attollere *et* [se ac] dilatare *se* conatur. Videmus enim permultos, *quam* [priusquam] quid sciant aut nesciant, satis cognitum habeant, iam sibi consummate doctos videri. [Hi] Postquam et sibi persuaserunt, et dementia sua nonnullam apud vulgus eruditionis opinionem sunt aucupati, et sibi non parum tribuant, et alios fastidiant necesse est. Docent audacter que nesciunt, scribunt, orant, interpretantur, nichil non tentant, nichil non audent, suis applausoribus freti, erudi-

---

1 MS reads *ministrat*.
2 After *literas*, *non* is crossed out, presumably by the original hand.
3 B.R. has *molliunt*, a better reading.
4 B.R. has *discernentis*, a better reading.

torum, et iudicia, et paucitatem contemnunt, pestilens hominum genus et
sua [mente suaque] stoliditate dignum.

Guielmus. Dabis veniam [vel ex pacto, Batte,] si disputationis tue
cursum paucis remorabor. *Guielmus inquit:* Aut ego fallor Batte, aut
15 diversa et inter se pugnan- ¹ tia loqueris. Ais enim istos sibi placere, et
fastidire meliores, eo quod sibi docti videantur: at istud ipsum est argumentum, erudicionem adducere superbiam. Quanam enim alia re sibi
placent isti quam scientia etiam tenui, et prope nulla? Battus. *Certe*
[Recte] nulla. Inscitia sua superbiunt isti, haud eruditione: adfert enim
eruditionis [peritiae] illa persuasio plane confidentiam quandam, que ipsa
summa *inerudicio* est [imperitia]. Recte enim Socrates dixit nullam
inscitiam esse maiorem, quam qua quis se credit scire quod nescit. Quod
si vere docti essent (ut sibi videntur) iam alios mirari, sibi minus in-
ciperent placere. Nil mirum est si venti plurimum concipiant, qui sunt
inanes. Solida virtus seipsa*m* contenta est, suo se precio, non aliorum
opinione metitur. Isti igitur si doctiores essent, essent et modestiores.
Quod nolim mihi credatis, nisi ipsi in nobis [idem] experimur. Quid
enim hoc aliud est, quod in inicio studiorum nostrorum, ubi disciplinas
vix a limine (ut dici solet) salutavimus, statim efferimur, et [iam] tum in
ipsis rudimentis magis nobis placemus, quam ubi iam [multo usu, mul-
tarum rerum certam scientiam] comparaverimus, iuvenum more qui quo
minus habent prudencie, plus habent animi. Unde id? Profecto quia
nondum hoc ipsum scimus,[quam multa]quod nesci[a]mus: quanquam hec
inanitas non temere a natura nobis insita videri potest, ut hac falsa glo-
riola excitati, ad summos labores capessendos provocemur. Alioqui qui[s]
tantas tam[que] diuturnas vigilias adiret, si nichil magni sibi promit-
teret? Neque in hac re plane cum Stoicis sentio, qui universos affectus non
supervacaneos modo, sed et perniciosos arbitrantur. Michi ad virtutem
tendenti[bus]*nostris*[animis], tanquam pedagogi quidam videntur adhibiti.
Hec igitur fiducia gloriaque, si modo non sit immodica, in tyronibus quidem
non prorsus videtur inutilis, eo quod calcar et stimulum quendam ingeniis
nostris subiiciat, nam freno vix invenias qui indigeant. [At eandem
gloriam] *Quam* iidem ubi saniores sumus effecti, et ridemus ipsi, et dam-
namus.

De me fateor: equidem qum puer essem, prope¹ sciolus eram, et mihi
placebam, qum hec studia vixdum summis, ut aiunt, labiis degustassem.
Nunc post tantum annorum, accedo enim ad annum undetrigesimum,
in dies mihi magis magisque displiceo, et Socraticum illud amplector.
Hoc unum scio, quod nichil scio. Tum mihi videbar arcem tenere sum-

¹ MS reading *prope* seems better than the correction *probe.*

mam, nunc me ne vestibulum quidem adhuc preteri[i]sse puto [ac iuxta Graecorum proverbium, ne in apiis quidem consistere]. Tum me nichil nisi exactum, perpolitum, absolutum delectabat, nunc prope nichil non miror. Tum quosvis ultro provocabam, nunc Milium senescentem imitor, minus audeo, trepido magis: ex quo facile coniicio, ubi copiosior eciam, quam que nunc est, erudicio accesserit, minus eciam mea *mihi* placitura. Quod si mihi evenit homini ventosiore ingenio nato (est enim apud familiares simpliciter fatendum) quid aliis meliore mente preditis accidere putatis? Tum Guielmus: Astipulor, inquit, ista in re tibi Iacobe: istuc enim ipsum, quod tu doctissime disseruisti, in me ipso et agnosco, et fateor, nec in paucis animadverti. Maturescunt erudicione ingenia, reddunturque tum molliora, tum mitiora. Battus. Ita prorsus (ait Battus) cuius rei nusquam non copiosissima exempla offerunt sese, sive nostra, sive veterum secula respiciamus. Quid enim dici potest, aut cogitari superbius, quam summa confidentia docere alios, quod ipse nescias? Quod isti nostri anthiacademici passim faciunt, qui qum nichil sciant, nichil non precipiunt. Ita me deus amet, ad vomitum usque nauseo, quoties quorundam delicias, et stultam gloriam ex operum inscriptionibus colligo. Qui qum nichil nisi meram barbariem evomuerint, audite queso quam splendidis titulis suas nugas adornaverint, ut facile intelligas quam delicate simii[1] isti suos catulos adamaverint. Alius quod somniavit Gemmulam, alius Margaritam appellavit, hic Floretum, ille Rosetum inscripserit, at in medio ([o] bone deus) ut nichil nisi carduos et lolium invenias. Est qui speculum operi suo nomen dedit, est qui omnium errorum silvam, Catholicon ausus est appellare. Ineptius eciam quidam Mammetrectum [velut haustum lactis gallinacei pollicens. Sunt qui summas et summarum summas appellent, quasi lectori non sit alius scriptor requirendus, ubi tales sit nactus lacunas. An non eandem insolentiam deprehendas in autorem titulis, quos ideo magnificos illis tribuunt, ut ipsi praeclarum aliquid ac supra hominem profiteri videantur? Basilium, Originem, Chrysostomum, et his consimiles viros, aut non citant, aut contemptim citant, veluti censores: verum cum crepant illos suos doctores sanctos, doctores irrefragabiles, doctores subtilissimos, doctores seraphicos, tum sibi videntur adferre nescio quid, cui cedere debeat etiam maiestas Evangelica.]

Quod si in antiquis et eruditis has inscriptionum delicias docti non tulerint, quis in hiis barbaris ferat, qui ad contaminandas literas geniti videri possint? Quis non (ut est in proverbio) suspendio trabem eligat, ubi videt huiusmodi voluminibus refertas passim bibliothecas, perstrepere

---

[1] MS reads *delicatissime*, an obvious error, which was corrected later.

ludos? [Ex his contexi conciones ecclesiasticas, ex his colligi dogmata, quibus gubernator orbis, ex his nos censeri Christianos, aut secus?] Adde quod in tradendo nusquam herent, nichil addubitant, omnia constant, omnia precipiuntur? Credas eos non docere, sed legem prescribere. En modestiam quam secum adfert supina ignorantia, quanto satius [erat] Academicorum verecundiam imitari, ad quos cum isti ne componendi quidem fuerant, nichil tamen se scire professi, omnibus de rebus pudenter disputare, quam confidenter affirmare maluerunt. Nec me fugit, esse qui hoc philosophorum genus parum probent, michi vel omnibus anteferendum videtur, cur videatur alias fortasse. Iam si prisca repetimus, quid tam abfuit ab insolentia, quam Socratis doctum pariter ac facundum ingenium, quem nunquam puduit undecunque doceri, ne iam senem quidem?

16 Non sibi turpe duxit rhetoricen virilem |[utique] disciplinam, a femina Aspasia¹ doceri. Idem iam grandis natu, fidibus operam dedisse legitur, [praeceptore, nisi fallor, Cono]: preterea vox illa tam nobilis: Hoc unum scio, quod nescio, utrum, queso, sibi placentis, an modestissimi potius hominis videtur. Hac modestia promeruit, ut solus ab Apolline sapiens iudicaretur, quod qum alii sibi [ea] viderentur scire, quod nescirent, hoc tanto esset ceteris verecundior, quanto sapientior. Id quod illius apud Platonem disputationes facile iudicant, in quibus [omnibus] apparet studiosi quidem et acuti, sed inquirentis potius, quam precipientis oratio.

Et o utinam nostri temporis philosophastri, qui nobis fastum obiiciunt, huius omnis philosophie parentis verecundiam, quam Gorgie promptam garrulitatem mallent imitari, qui qum ne suam quidem ipsorum vocem intelligant, magna fiducia quavis de re pronunciant, probant, damnant, precipiunt, prescribunt: sed aliorum exempla prosequamur. An fuit quicquam uno Pythagora vel acutius, vel doctius? Hoc certe superiores philosophos quam eruditione vicit, tam modestia superavit. Qui qum ante id temporis sophi, id est sapientes, soliti essent appellari, ipse primus nominis arrogantiam recusavit, et se φιλοσοφον,² id est, sapientie studiosum, quam sapientem dici maluit. Platonem nonnulli ob ingenii divinam quandam sublimitatem fastus insimularunt: at in hoc ipso, quanta modestia? Ubi omnem preceptoris disciplinam ad plenum hausisset, perinde ac si nichil actum, quot maria, quot terras emensus legitur: dum ubique querit quod discat. Qui Athenis magister fuerat, et potens (Hieronimianis enim verbis libenter utimur) cuiusque doctrinas Achademie gymnasia personabant, fieret denuo peregrinus atque discipulus, malens aliena verecunde discere, quam sua impudenter ingerere.

Quid de Solone et Herodoto loquar, quos iam natu grandes, omnes orbis

¹ MS reads *Alpasia*.   ² The copyist wrote φιλοσοφουμ.

angulos pervagatos videmus, laboriosa utique peregrinatione, tanquam
impigros sapientie mercatores. Theophrastus philosophorum facile
precipuus, moriens, cervis et cornicibus invidisse legitur, quibus natura
vitam tam diuturnam tribuisset, homini tam exiguam. Et qui omnium
opinione consummatam sapientiam tenere putabatur, is se tum querebatur
extingui, qum iam quid esset sapere videre cepisset. Et [e]unde in
tantis ingeniis tanta modestia, ab imperitia ne (ut isti dicunt) an a doc-
trina¹ quadam singulari? Quis iam Virgilio palmam inter poetas invidet?
At [non] huius modestia*m tantam fuisse legimus,* [factum est,] ut dum in
vivis ageret multis indoctioribus inferior haberetur? Idem a Filisto mediocri oratore, conviciis salibusque agitatus, [ab insulso Perone famosis etiam
versibus impetitus,] a Cicerone summo oratore laudatus, pari modestia,
et illius scommata, et huius laudes tulit.

Quid autem de ecclesiasticis commemorem? quorum longe princeps
Hieronimus, incredibili discendi aviditate, quem tandem preceptorem
recusavit? Num Iudeum? num hereticum? [num Latinum? num Grae-
cum? num Hebraeum?] Adeo vir doctissimus discere, quam docere putavit pulchrius. Augustino quid eruditius? at quid eodem modestius?
qui [iam multorum annorum episcopus et doctor,] non solum se vel ab
anniculo *puero* [episcopo] doceri paratum fatetur, verum nec ipsum² errata
[sua fateri] puduit, et scriptorum suorum tanquam palinodiam canere.
Quis hanc modestiam e nostri temporis criticis unquam est imitatus? An
sunt Augustino vel cauciores vel doctiores? Ac non potius quanto indoc-
tiores, tanto arrogantiores? qui quicquid scripserint, hoc ipso³ verum videri
volunt [quod scripserint], pro celestibus oraculis sua somnia recipi volunt.
De parum doctis hec loquor, nam egregie doctum neminem adhuc repperi,
quin in eodem singularem modestiam agnoverim. Superbus igitur et
arrogans, indoctus vocabitur, [iuxta sapientis Hebraei sententiam,] haud
doctus: et sapientior sibi stultus videtur septem viris loquentibus sententias. Cave igitur tu quisquis es, qui mihi vultu religioso immodestiam
obiicis, ne ista ipsa tua modestia, summa sit immodestia. [Nam quaeso
te per Musas, uter superbior, isne qui dives invitat ad opum suarum
communionem, an tu qui mendicitate tua superbus ob hoc ipsum tibi
videre regulus, quod nihil habeas? Isne qui doctrina utitur ad Christi
gloriam, an tu, qui cum proximi contumelia contemnis alienam doctrinam,
ne apud idiotas, in quo theatro te venditas, parum semideus habearis?
Postremo fac utrumque placere sibi, uter arrogantior, qui sua effertur

---

¹ After *doctrina*, the word *potius* is crossed out, presumably by the original hand.
² After *ipsum*, the word *quidem* is crossed out, presumably by the original hand.
³ The original reading is *ipsi*.

eruditione, an tu, qui tua inscitia tibi insolentissime places? Ille nulil
obstrepit, si quis nolit meliora discere: tu coelum terrae misces, si quis
ausit docere, quod tu cum tuis sodalibus non didiceris. Huic animos facit
sua facundia: tibi cristas maiores addit infantia. Uter superbior? Ille
per omnes disciplinas obambulat, ut vere doctus esse possit, tu vix gustata
grammatica, eaque misera, vix gustatis tribus syllogismis, ad haec quaes-
tionibus aliquot Thomisticis aut Scotisticis, repente prosilis in theatrum,
paratus cum quovis, quavis de re dimicare. Et homo verecundus aliis
exprobras arrogantiam?] Verum ego dum de immodestia disputo, modestie sum oblitus: altius enim in re clarissima disputationem repetisse
me video. Sed ut finiam, ego sic mihi persuasi, si quem arrogantem et
sibi placentem videro, eum perdoctum esse non credam. Itaque quod isti
superbiam adducere putant, id mihi ne superbiamus solum remedio
videtur esse.

Illud Pauli, scientia inflat, quomodo accipiendum.

Verum instant interim suo more, et illud Paulinum constanter ingerunt:
Scientia inflat, charitas edificat. Non mentitur (inquiunt) apostolus,
inflat scientia, [Nemo negat, sed] inflat [et] inscitia. Quid dicitis, o
theologi, et iidem inscii, ita ne nichilo plus una sententia e Paulo decerp-
sistis, non venit in mentem, eundem alio in loco dicere: et si imperitus
sermone, non tamen scientia? Non audistis gloriantem, quod ad pedes
Gamalielis legem didicerit? Non libros [in] membrana scriptos sibi
postulantem? Quid ita Paulo in mentem incidit, ut qum fuerit vel unus
inter apostolos omnium rerum scientissimus, tum sepius nos ad sui imita-
tionem provocarit, hoc uno in loco volu[er]it a scientia deterrere? Quid autem
est charitas spoliata scientia? nempe navis sine clavo. Quis unquam
amavit quod nesciret? denique quorsum unquam fuit utilis ignorantia?
Neque mentitus est Paulus, sed parum intellectus, cuius quidem mentem
ita demum accipiemus, si et priora, et consequentia cum mediis conferamus.

Age, theologum interim Battus aget, mota erat divo Paulo de ydolo-
ticis questio, a quorum esu Christiani nonnulli infirmitate quadam conscientie sese continebant. Alii peritiores, qui intelligerent ydoloticum
nichil esse et mundis nichil esse immundum, sine discrimine vescebantur.
Et recte quidem illi sentiebant, sed interim supersticiosior, et infirmior
quispiam eorum offendebatur firmitate. Hinc inter fratres seditio.
17 Res- | pondit Paulus: quantum ad nostram ipsorum conscientiam attinet,
nichil referre, utrum de ydolis immolato, aut non immolato vescamur,

interesse tamen fraterne charitatis. Offendi enim fratrem infirmiorem (qui nondum ydoloticum queat contemnere) aliena conscientia, cum videat fratrem in ydolio recumbentem. Eoque satius censet apostolus hac in re fraterne infirmitati obsecundare, quam fratre neglecto, nostra uti scientia, gratiorem esse superis morigeram charitatem, quam superbam et contumacem scientiam. Huiusmodi enim inflare scientiam, si fratrem prudens offendas: at charitatem edificare, si sine tuo detrimento fratris infirmitati concedas. [Ut ne dicam interim quod ea res fuerit illorum temporum peculiaris. Altius a maioribus insederat superstitio, quam ut subito posset revelli, et ad confirmandam Evangelii doctrinam, omni obsequio erat opus. Postremo materia offendiculi reperta erat, non a nobis ministrata. Hic Christianae charitatis erat, ad tempus obsequi fratris infirmitati, sed hac spe ut post resipisceret.] Quid hec ad nos? quid ad philosophiam? quid ad oratoriam aut poeticam? sed tamen (si libet) ad liberaliorem eruditionem torqueamus, quando quidem didicere quidvis archane litere pati.

Quantumlibet inflexeris, Paulus non vult scientiam esse nullam, sed incomitatam esse non vult, nempe sine charitate. Quod si alterutra sit carendum, tollerabilius esse scientia quam charitate privari, cui interpretamento divus astipulatur Augustinus. Per se, inquiens, inutilis est scientia, cum charitate utilis. Quis enim tam demens, ut argentum reiiciat, quod aurum preciosius esse cognoverit? Num *igitur* [ideo] saxa nullum habent usum, quod gemme sint prestantiores? Num idcirco non optima quedam res est scientia, si melior sit charitas? Nam alio quodam in loco, ubi charitas peana Paulus decantat, scientiam inter precipua charismata ponit, puta prophetiam, fidem, miraculorum gestionem, *dona* linguarum [dotem], atque id genus alia. Num facturus, si scientiam tanquam pestiferam fugiendam iudicasset? Atqui, cur igitur inflare dixit scientiam [inquies]? Cur ipse fuit scientissimus, num continuo inflatissimus? Periculum ostendere voluit, quo cautiores redderet, non ut deterreret.

Tutior est charitas, necessaria quidem scientia sed periculi nonnichil habens, ut que posset esse perniciosa, ita si charitati repugnet. Equius erat indoctiorem scienti concedere et parere, at nunc ultro imperito concedit doctior. Quid tu cum tua charitate tibi places? quid scientiam calumniaris? Huius charitas laudatur, qui te scientia precedit, non tua. Nam quantum quidem in te fuit, tua ignorantia iam charitatem extinxerat, qui cred[eb]as esse aliquid, quod nichil erat, nisi huius scientia tue stulticie ultro concessisset: tolleraris, non preferris. Nunc uter vestrum est inflatior, tu qui imperitus doctiori recusas obtemperare, an hic qui tam indulgenter indoctiori concedit doctior? An vero semper imperitis concedendum? Minime, sed [in his] dumtaxat, in quibus neque nisi violata charitate obsisti non potest, et indulgentia ea nichil videtur incommodi allatura.

Non igitur deterritos a scientia Paulus voluit, ad quam nos suo provocavit exemplo, verum ne imprudentes in periculum incideremus, scopulos et cautes prudens navigator ostendit. Cur nos simplicem et castam scripturam ad nostra vicia trahimus? cur nobis ignorantia placemus? cur literis et ydoneos et deditos, ab optimis studiis deterremus? cur non potius, si quem remis et velis (ut inquit Plautus) ad literas properantem viderimus,[1] huiusmodi oratione premonemus: I bone quo virtus tua te vocat, i pede fausto. Ad *seculares* [humanas] disciplinas plenis velis raperis, sed caute naviges facito. Scopulos habet istud mare, aurum et smaragdos [habet istud nemus], sed per deum immortalem, cave tibi a veneni radicibus. Disces egregias artes, at ita demum utiles si parem probitatem adiunxeris, citra eam parum utiles, aut eciam pestilentes. Cave sic illis studeas, ut recti tibi cura recedat, stude non minus melior esse quam doctior, bona est scientia, charitas melior. Utramque alteri si comitem adiunxeris, rem absolutam conficies.

Medicus. Hec qum Battus dixisset, Medicus iamdudum subridens (est enim vir in primis *facetus* [festivus], multique ioci). Quis [inquit], Batte, credidisset umquam te hominem tam poeticum tantum tenere theologie. Ita me Muse tue [bene] ament, ut mihi Pauli mentem appositissime videris explicuisse, nec te prorsus fugere [video] verba theologica, preterea quantum audivi, equidem te pulchre concionari posse crediderim: quod si resciscant nostri cordigeri [Iacobite], vereor ne certatim te rapiant, et cucullum iniiciant. Battus. Et arridens Battus. Ista, inquit, Musarum hostibus eveniant,[2] verum ne tu impune Battum lacessiveris. Quid te uno impudentius, qui in me homine poetico, theologie scientiam admireris, qum te medico nichil sit theologicum magis? Ego si theologus essem nichil a poete partibus prevaricarer. Antiquitus enim theologi habebantur [iidem] qui poete, et ingenue fateor eloquentium theologorum scriptis, me non minus quam Ciceronianis delectari. Recentiorum vero tento quidem persepe ac mihi impero, sed vomitus oboritur[3] legenti, adeo me tum barbaries orationis, tum [rerum] perturbatio offendit. Tu vero partes egrederis tuas, et theologis adeo iniuriam facis. Nam cum illis animorum, vobis corporum cura sit tradita, tu totum hominem tibi vindicas.[4]

---

[1] The original reading is *videremus*.

[2] In this clause the original reading *Ista . . . eveniant* is changed by a later hand to *Istud . . . eveniat.*

[3] MS reads *aboritur*, an obvious mistake.   [4] MS reads *vendicas*.

Sed pergam (si sinis) theologari vel apud te medicorum omnium doctissi-
mum theologum, efficiam ut me neges ullos preter theologorum libros
evolvisse.

[Medicus.] Age, respondit Medicus, percupio: sed te iam unde depuli
in viam restituam. Hoc erat tue disputationis extremum, ut charitatem
cum eruditione copulandam esse diceres. Ipse quidem in ea prope sum
opinione, quam divum Augustinum in suis dialogis notasse video, ut cre-
18 dam vix a virtute divelli posse ¹ scientiam: verum ut scis mee professionis
[esse], inter *omnigena hominum* [omnium mortalium] genera versari, in
nonnullos [quosdam] religiosos nonnunquam incido, qui sibi hoc constanter
habent persuasum, non coherere cum pietate Christiana, literaturam
[quam illi vocant] secularem.

Battus. Nec aberrant isti, inquit Battus, in ipsis enim male coheret,
quibus utraque deest, at cohesit in Hieronimo, Cypriano, Augustino,
aliisque mille, quorum pietatem quis audeat cum istorum ignavia com-
parare?

Medicus. Age, inquit Medicus, scio tibi quidem cucullatos istos
omnes invisos haberi: verum [ut] ego religionem ut fatali quodam amore
(sum enim benigno Iove natus, et item Venere) et [ad]miror, et veneror,
ita non omnibus viciis libero. Video enim nonnullos ad Epicuream illam
rationem proxime accedere, qui incredibili laborum fuga, ignaviam quandam et umbratilem vitam amplectuntur. Tutos se credunt si tanquam
coc[h]lee intra testudines perpetuo delitescant, commodis corporum vel
minutis morosius etiam consulentes: Abunde se religiosos arbitrantur, si
literarum *secularium* [politiorum] nichil prorsus attigerint, suis bene
consultum putant, si ea que in sc[h]olis didicerunt, obliviscantur. Iam
vero civibus suadere non desinunt, si¹ liberos suos ad externas scholas
(quas universitates vocant) ire sinant. Perisse propemodum illos,² qui sese
illuc tanquam ad manes demiserint, aut non redire, aut redire deteriores.
Simplicitatem, nescio quam, illis predicant; literas a virtute revocare
animos, nec bonam *prestare* [parare] mentem, sed eripere magis. Stultum,
inquiunt, est disertam habere linguam, mores incompositos, dyalecticis cap-
ciunculis morti neminem imposuisse, rhetoricen et poesin nec nominare
quidem audent: insanire geometras aiunt, qui qum scite agros metiantur,
animi more [sui modum] ignorent; astrologos delirare dicunt, quod ea
que supra se sunt, curiosi scrutentur: physicos impietatis accusant, quod
divina rimantes opera, ipsum rerum opificem negligunt. Ne sacris
quidem theologie professoribus parcunt, hos insimulant, quod cum magna

¹ The word *ne* is written above this word.
² After *illos*, the word *utpote* is crossed out, perhaps by the original hand.

auctoritate virtutem doceant, ipsi non perinde vivant. Ita isti Cinici nostri universum genus hominum contemnunt, censent omnes. Moriendum est, inquiunt, omnibus. Quid tum si sis Salomone doctior? quid conferent nexus dyalectici? quid oratorie complexiones? moriendum est.

Battus. Per anserem homines pistrino digni, subiecit Battus. Quis istud ignorat, omnibus esse moriendum? nichil ne interea agendum? Malim ego doctior mori, quam natus sum. Isti perinde disputant, ac si quis doctus sit, eum continuo malum esse sit necesse. Num qui lingua erit incomposita, mores protinus incompositos habebit? Num qui dyalecticen contempsit, statim mortis laqueos effugit? [Num qui poetas non attigit, protinus erit Hippolytus? Num protinus sibi notus est, cui ignota est geometria? Quid prodest non fuisse philosophatum in astris, si interim philosopheris in patinis? An pulchrius esse ducis, scrutari sapores ganearum, quam arcanas rerum causas?] Et ne singula persequar, num qui erit indoctissimus, continuo religiosissimus habebitur? Erudicio nos in celum non levat: an eo levabit inscitia? an rusticitas?

Non prestat bonam mentem *literatura* [peritia], num igitur imperitia prestabit? Non prestant bonam mentem litere: *concedamus* [ut donemus] istud, [at] nec malam *quidem* prestant. Nonne recepta est calceolaria sutrina, textrina, fabrica, sartoria, fullonia? Nonne etiam in honore est coquinaria? Quid horum bonam mentem prestat mortalibus? Laudamus doctum pictorem, laudamus fabrum scientem, textorem callidum laudamus, laudamus etiam si sit [vir] improbus. Nec artem ideo malam dicimus, si forte sit malus qui in ea versatur. Et litteraturam [damnamus], que ut bonam mentem non prestet, ad eam tamen non mediocriter conducit. Quod si quem literis abutentem viderimus, non ut eruditionem relinquat admonendus est, sed [ne] in usus perversos torqueat. [Quanto rectius admonet ille philosophus, absque Christo sapiens. Sic vive, tanquam cras moriturus, sic stude quasi semper victurus. Occupabit mors, sed malo occupet studentem quam cessantem.] Hoc tamen adversariis concessero, ut pusillo, aut vehementer tardo ingenio natos, liceat a difficilibus [disciplinis] dehortari, ne si asinus ad lyram ducatur, et discens et docens simul operam luserit: eos autem, quorum ingenia magni aliquid polliceri videntur, a pulcherrimis conatibus retrahere, quid aliud est quam (quod Palus fieri vetat) spiritum extinguere? Quod idem si in summis illis (quos iam sepe nominavi) doctoribus factum esset, singulari profecto et presidio et solatio iam orbata esset ecclesia [quanquam interim patronus barbarorum, doctius ac modestius pro illis respondes, quam ipsi soleant loqui. Nam hoc ferme genus hominum, ne noverunt quidem cuiusmodi sint disciplinae in quas debacchantur. Poeticen existimant artem esse meretriciam, rhetoricen nihil aliud esse putant quam assentatoriam, geographiam, astrologiam curiosas et improbatas artes esse credunt, qualis necyomantia.]

Medicus. Tum medicus: Probabiliter tu quidem. Batte, id est, plane rhetorice: verum ut interim tibi pro istis imperitie admiratoribus respondeam, qui in summam invidiam *nos inducunt*, huiusmodi seditiosis condicionibus [imperitam multitudinem concitantes]. Quid igitur, inquiunt, tandem futurum est? Num soli literati celo potientur? Ita ne vos soli qui ventosa doctrina turgetis, Gygantum exemplo celum occupabitis, detrusis superis, exclusis inferis? Quid fiet imperite multitudini? [quid simplicibus fratribus] qui apostolorum vestigiis ingressi, non didicit[1] Aristotelicos laqueos, non spinas Chrisippinas, non salem Atticum, non Plautinam eloquentiam? Non[ne] hec est illa simplicitas, quam deus unice sibi delegisse videtur, qui asino vectus Iherosolimam ingredi voluit, cuius et illa exhortatio est: Discite a me, quia mitis sum et humilis corde. Non

19 dixit, discite compositam orationem, | metiri celum, nectere sillogismos, sed humilitatem discite. Multa nobis preterea de agno et columba, quorum appellatione rudis animi tractabilem simplicitatem significatam voluit,[2] verum ego iamdudum memorem moneo [qui haec quotidie audias ab istis deblaterari apud indoctam plebeculam].

Battus. Pape, tu me mediam in theologiam vocas, Battus inquit, Medicus poetam: sed quod asinum se *isti* imitari dicunt, iam hoc primum mihi satis quadrare videtur, nisi quod [iidem] ignavia ut tarditate asinum facile representant, ceterum et leonis, et tygridis et scorpii non exiguam partem isti asino admiscuisse videntur, tanquam Chymera, ex variis monstrorum figuris compositi. Quod si vacaret in presentia istius asini, istius columbe, istius agni misteria persequi, facile appareret isti hominum generi in hoc ordine nullum esse locum. Hoc ad refellendum satis [arbitror] istas misticas appellationes non ad scientiam sed ad mores esse referendas, hoc est (ut magis theologice dicam) non ad intellectum sed ad affectum. Quid enim potest esse *istius* [eius] modi mente magis (ut ita dicam) asininum, que istorum hominum importunas nugas possit et [dis]simulare, et perpeti? Quid eque columbinum, quid agninum magis? Istis vero quid cum asino preter stoliditatem commune est, qui neque duci a sanioribus *sese* patiuntur, et omne laborum genus tanquam pestem fugitant. Quid simile habent ad columbam, qui tanta amaritudine fraterne invident virtuti? Quid illis cum agno, qui nichil habent quod aliis possit esse usui? Hieronimus qui tantum laborum in adaugenda relligione *nostra* [Chris-

---

1 B.R. reads *didicerunt*.
2 MS reads *velint*, which is corrected to *voluit*.

tiana] exhausit, asinus fuit. Augustinus qui perpetuam operam Christianis prestitit, asinus fuit. Hos asinos imitemur. Quid homines ignavi et numero tantum nati sue inertie hiis commentationibus blandiuntur? [Appellant se simplices fratres cum possint cum quovis veteratore certare, si quid agatur quod ad ventris et gloriae negotium pertineat. Non recuso meum nomen quo minus inter mendacissimos scribatur, nisi quod dico fatebuntur omnes quibus cum istis simplicibus fuit proprio conflictatio.] Verum ut dolorem [quoque] illorum placemus qui sese ob imperitiam extrudi putant, recipimus, adiungimus, amplectimur, at ita si aures mihi paulisper commodarint, dum paucis rem absolvo. Haud temere multis auctoribus video placuisse nobilem illam Hesiodi sententiam, tria hominum genera constituentis.

Primum quidem eorum, quicquid rectum sit, ipsi per se intelligunt idemque sequuntur. Alterum eorum, qui per se quidem parum sapiunt, at sapientum monitis obsequuntur. Tercium ad nichil utile appellat [videlicet] horum, qui neque ipsi sapiunt neque credunt recta monenti. Primi boni sunt, iidemque docti. Alteri boni quidem illi, verum indocti. Postremi neutra re, neque doctrina, neque probitate prediti. Primum hoc genus, ut multo prestantissimum, ita precipue extendendum. Secundum ferendum quidem, at ita solum, si doctoribus acquiescat: quod si intractabiles (ut fere solent) esse pergunt, iam tercii generis esse incipient. Doctrinam itaque edico necessariam, sed quo mittis indoctos[1]? in malam crucem (ut comici dicunt) si doceri recusent.[2] Si dociles sint, admitto, verum penes aliquos erudicio perseveret necesse est. Quod si omnes erimus illiterati, quis castigabit errores imperitorum? Sunt in pictorum officinis, qui artis ignari, tantum quod iussi sunt faciunt, terunt, miscent, purgant. Est quidem nonnulla ex parte utilis horum opera, at ita demum, si monstrator assit, alioquin ociosa. Nec audiendos puto, qui dicunt non passim [esse] discendas esse literas, neque enim opus esse tanta turba eruditorum. A paucis plurimos duci posse. Cur enim quod in paucis pulchrum est, non multo erit in multis prestantius[3]? Cur quisquam vetet ad id (quod omnes prestantissimum fatentur) eniti?

Sapiens imperator tametsi gregariorum militum utitur opera, et ignavos strenuis misceri patitur, [ac] nec lixas quidem et calones eiicit, multo tamen malit omnes Scevolas, omnes *Sicinos* [Siccios], omnes Decios, [si dentur]. Intollerabile vero nephas, si gregarius miles egregii commili-

---

[1] After *indoctos*, the word *inquiens* is crossed out, perhaps by the original hand.

[2] Before *recusent*, the verb *contemnunt* is crossed out, obviously by the original hand.

[3] An original correction of *pulchrius*.

tonis fortibus factis invidens,[1] dicat: Quid si omnes insignes erimus, quo mittimus gregarios? Si omnes literati, quo illiteratos eiicimus? quasi non illiteratis usquam sit opus. Si quibus aut non licet aut non contigit erudicio, quiescant potius, ac desinant alios pulchrius aliquid conantes impedire: illum sinito precurrere, tu ducem sequere, eodem tamen perventurus. Vulgi quidem imperitia non laudatur, sed si tractabilis sit, non contemnitur. Quod autem fertur, id placet, collatum quidem deteriori: placiturum tamen amplius, si ipsum in melius quippiam [com]mutetur. Si rudes sumus,[2] et doctis auscultemus, bene [quidem] est, at meliores erimus si ipsi eciam indoctos docere potuerimus. Qua[re] rem paucis sic habeant: qui et indoctus et indocilis est, si quidem ignavia sit in causa, aut in eo vite genere versetur, quod eruditum hominem postulat, iam hoc ipso malus est, quod ignarus.

Tu in publico ludo *secularem eruditionem* [bonas literas profiteris, et harum inscitiam] predicas? Tu libros audes scribere, in quibus nos a literis dehorteris? Tu populo prefectus [es], et quod doceas non vis discere? Quod si privatus sit, et erudicio non neglecta quidem, verum non contigit, iis sibi unus satisfaciat, sibi uni natus, sibi uni vivit, non fastidiendus a doctioribus, modo suam agnoscat[3] impericiam. Qui vero probitati erudicionem adiunxit, is tanto erit prestantior, utilior, ornatior, quanto id fecerit cumulatius. [Nunc nulli magis exercent tyrannidem, quam isti apostolice simplicitatis histriones. Abbates indocti non patiuntur ut monachorum quisque attingat bonas literas, quo magis illis quicquid collubitum fuerit imperent. Malunt enim in beluas quam in homines habere imperium. Ptothotyranni cupiunt populum esse stultissimum, quo facilius imponant, et quidvis persuadeant, quoque magis superstitione territent. Nam eruditio fere liberat hominem superstitione.]

Medicus. Tum medicus. [Vera sunt fere quae narras, sed] Quandoquidem simplicium istorum causam semel suscepi, non patiar me prevaricatorem videri: nam tu Batte, que pro te faciunt, diligenter exponis: at que ledunt, dissimulas. [Ad partitionem tuam redeo:] Quid si literatus sis, et idem malus, quonam in genere te ponemus?

Battus. Immo si neque doctus sim, inquit Battus, et malus, quo in genere numerabor? Sed istic ibam. Age et quartum istud tribus Hesiodi generibus addamus, si placet: fieri enim potest, ut recta quis intelligat, nolit tamen intellecta sequi, ut optima sciat, pessima faciat. Sed mane,

---

1 The original reading is *invident*.

2 B.R. reads *simus*, which is obviously the correct reading, as is shown by the subjunctive form *auscultemus*, which has the same construction.

3 MS reading is *agnoscit*.

20 iam quid paraveris[1] [colligere], video: non igitur bona est eruditio, que malis contingat. Probe consequeretur,[2] si malos facit, mala est: aliud est eruditio, aliud virtus: ut qui bonus [est], non continuo doctus est: ita qui doctus, non continuo bonus. Sed latius explicande rei gratia quatuor hominum genera statuamus. Loquor [enim] iam tibi Medice, tanquam imperitorum patrono, tu causam tuorum clientum, ita ut cepisti, tuere. Statuamus, inquam, utrimque binos, hinc duos, alterum doctum et malum, alterum indoctum et item malum, uter alteri preferendus videtur?

[Medicus.] Ac medicus. Nempe is prior multo erit nequior (inquit). Atqui istuc ipsum sat est signi, non bonam esse literaturam, que reddat nequiorem. Tuo te iugulo gladio.

[Battus.] Equidem uter altero sit nequior, inquit Battus, vix ausim diffinire. Certe uterque accusandus mihi videtur: alter quod optimis rebus abutatur, alter multo fortassis amplius, quod ne scire quidem curaverit. Priorem tangit prophete criminatio: Sapientes sunt ut faciant malum, bene autem facere nesciunt. Alterum eque Davitica illa: Noluit intelligere, ut bene ageret. Nam ex illitterata *nequicia* [malitia] nihil potest expectari commodi, literata *nequicia* [malitia] etsi sibi perniciosa est, aliis tamen aliquid commodi afferre potest. Impericie si mala mens accesserit, peccatur confidentius, pudetur minus. Imperitus quicquid magnopere cupit, id recte fieri putat. At eruditio tametsi pravas cupiditates omnino non prohibet, temperet tamen necesse est. Fieri enim non potest, ut qui honesti et inhonesti discrimen scite intelligit, non aliquando et turpitudinem exhorrescat, et virtutis speciem admiretur.

Preterea qui doctus est, vel simulat honestatem, quod est virtuti proximum, indoctus e viciis suis eciam sibi laudem pollicetur. Ille morbum suum probe intelligit, quo sanabilior est: hic pene desperandus [est], quod sibi sanus videatur. Illi ad virtutem arma sunt instructa, hic nihil habet ad virtutem adiumenti, verum hoc ad nostram disputationem nichil interest. D[on]emus minus esse perniciosam rusticam *nequiciam* [maliciam] docta malicia, num igitur male litere? Immo vel hoc uno argumento sunt optime, ut telum quo me iugulare parabas, in te retorqueam. Primum [enim] non adferunt *nequiciam* [maliciam] litere, verum addite tanquam fax prelata, reddunt conspectiorem. Ut exempli causa, duos video adulteros, alterum celibem, coniugatum alterum: cum non dispar sit admissum, non par tamen culpa erit, nempe in coniugato turpior. Cur ita, an quia malum est coniugium?

---

1 MS reads *dicere* before *paraveris; colligere* was added by a later hand.
2 MS reads *consequerit.* It is corrected to *consequeretur.*

Minime quidem, verum quo res sanctior est coniugium, eo gravior est noxa illud adulterio temerare. Qui rem sacram inuncarit, gravioris piaculi tenetur quam furti, nempe sacrilegii: ergo ne prophanum *sacro* anteponendum. In sacerdote gravioris est culpe stuprum, quam in layco, ergo ne malum sacerdocium? Quid ni? fecit nequiorem, imo nisi melius esset sacerdocium, non faceret hoc pacto nequiorem. Quo namque res queque erit sanctior, eo abutens erit turpior. Sed iam alteros duos componamus. Pone duos utrosque probos, at alterum rudem alterum literatum, uter utri anteponendus? Tergiversantur, hesitant: modo, inquiunt, inveniatur doctus, et idem probus. Fateor quidem huius generis summam esse inopiam, nam indoctorum et improborum magna ubique est copia. Verum quid hesitant, ubi nichil hesitavit Hieronimus, qui libere, et plenis (ut aiunt buccis) sancte rusticitati, sanctam eruditionem anteposuit. Daniel, inquit, in fine sacratissime visionis ait iustos fulgere quasi stellas, et intelligentes, id est doctos, quasi firmamentum. Vides quantum inter se distant iusta rusticitas, et docta iusticia? alii stellis alii celo comparantur. Idem paulo ante: Sancta rusticitas solum sibi prodest, et quantum edificat ex vite merito ecclesiam tantum nocet, si destruentibus non resistat.

Vere profecto Hieronimus hec ut omnia: nam quo quodque bonum latius patet, eo prestantius sit necesse est. Qui vivit integrê, magnam[1] quidem [ille] rem agit, *aut* sibi uni confert, aut certe paucis quibuscum victitat. Quod si huius integritati doctrina accesserit, quanto iam pulchrius ac latius quasi face adhibita virtus pollebit? Si vero eiusmodi erit, qui possit pulcherrimas animi cogitationes mandare literis, hoc est si preter quam quod doctus, eciam disertus fuerit, huius demum hominis utilitas latissime manet necesse est, nempe non ad convictores modo, non tantum ad equales, [non tantum] ad finitimos, verum [etiam] ad peregrinos, ad posteros, ad ultimos orbis incolas. Indocta probitas nisi scriptis posteritati commendetur cum suo auctore demoritur. Docte eruditioni non terra, non maria, non seculorum longa series obstat, quo minus ad universos mortales pervolet. Nolo hic invidiosam suscitare comparationem, plus ne contulerit nostre religioni martyrum sanguis, an eruditorum hominum stilus? Non elevo martyrum gloriam, quam ne copiosissima quidem oratione quis[quam] assequi queat: at quantum ad nostrum attinet commodum, nonnullis etiam hereticis plus prope debemus, quam *nostribus ipsis* [quibusdam martyribus]. Et martyrum quidem summa fuit copia, doctores perpauci. Martyres moriendo Christianorum numerum imminuerunt, docti persuadendo, [ad]auxerunt. In summa,

---

[1] After *magnam*, the word *hic* is crossed out, presumably by the original hand.

frustra illi [pro Christi doctrina] sanguinem fortiter fudissent, ni hii
ab hereticis [eam] suis literis vindicassent. Quare non tam integra[1] erit
Christiana religio, ut *seculares* [bonas] literas, quas in rebus afflictis tam
salutares experta est, nunc in pace *et* rebus[que] florentibus in exilium
extrudat, per quas et pacem et felicitatem sit assequuta. Quo magis
nonnullos demirari compellor, qui prudentes eciam eruditionem se fugere
fateantur.

Nam quod ab ethnicorum inventis abstinere se dicunt, id quidem plusquam insanum esse iam demonstravimus. An vero est aliquid, quod
insolentiam aiunt, sese velle effugere? At vide ne *tam* ista sit [non tam]
infirmi animi trepidatio, quam inertie *vicium* [fucus], culpam fingere,
ubi culpa non est. Istos ego [ita] demum simpliciter errasse intelligam,
21 si moniti | ac correpti corrigantur: alioquin quenam erit ista religio, mi-
nimi mali metu, in maximam incidere perniciem? Ita inepti dum mulie-
briter trepidantes curiositatis vicium student defugere, in diversum sed
multo perniciosius decidunt. Frustra vicium vitaveris illud, si te alio
pravum detorseris, ait Horatius. Male Scyllam effugeris, si in Charibdim
incidas; male procellam declinaveris, si ad littoris scopulos navim fre-
geris. Hii sunt quorum puerilem, ne dicam perversam trepidationem,
sanctissimus ille et regum et prophetarum David notavit: Illic inquiens,
trepidaverunt timore, ubi non erat timor. Nam qui superstitiose ventum
observat, is nunquam se mari credat: et qui nubes anxie considerat, is
metet nunquam. Quid autem *perversus* [perniciosius], quam illic metum
fingere, ubi honestissimi sint capiendi labores, hic ubi summum et certum
est periculum supinum stertere? Illi inepta *stoliditate* [sedulitate]
nostris ex oculis curiositatis festucam volunt educere, ipsi in suis ignavie
trabem non sentientes. Nos criminantur, quod plusquam sat est scientes
[semper plura discere cupiamus, ipsi nec illa scire curant, sine quibus nec
homines sumus, nec vivimus].

Iam fac nos modum oblitos, utrum honestius est in rebus honestis
ultra limites esse an citra? Utrum prestabilius excedere, an deficere?
Verentur necubi in libris ethnicis aliquid forte minus severum tetricis
auribus insonet, nec verentur terrificam illam domini vocem, Serve
nequam, quare non dedisti ad mensam pecuniam meam, et ego utique
veniens cum usura exegissem illam? Adeo nihil eque aversatur deus, ut
ignaviam. Filium perditum, qui universam substantiam in scorta[2] leno-
nesque [et popinas] dissipaverat, in gratiam letus recipit: servum qui
talentum integrum eciam restituit, tam *minaciter* [immaniter] obiurgat.

---

[1] This word is corrected to *ingrata* by a later hand.
[2] After the word *scorta, et* is crossed out.

Semina quedam bonarum artium indidit nobis parens deus, intellectum, ingenium, memoriam, ceterasque animi dotes, que talenta sunt ad usuram credita, que si exercitatione ac studio quasi duplicaverimus, ut impigros servos dominus reversus laudavit, peculium esse sinet: sin acceptum talentum in terram defoderimus, quo tandem animo domini redeuntis oculos, ora, vocem feremus, ubi ceteris pro accepta sorte lucrum annumerantibus, nos inutile talentum referemus ignavi? Hic erit cur trepidare merito potuissent isti meticulosi homines, non illic ubi commodi plurimum periculi perparum.

Confutat auctoritates auctoritatibus.

Hic qum Battus collectis oculis, aliquandiu intersiluisset, Deum immortalem, inquit, quantum disputationis campum aperiri video, sed sit modus. Dextrum igitur cornu (ut arbitror) vel profligavimus, vel [certe] inclinavimus: urgent tamen hostes, et sinistram alam infensis *armis* [animis] admovent, sacrarum literarum armis nos eminus *et* cominus[que] territant. Primum igitur erit, hostibus sua tela eripere: deinde suomet ipsos, ut (inquit comicus) gladio iugulare. Rationibus cedere coacti, ad ecclesiasticas literas confugiunt et nobis occinunt, quod ipsi non intelligunt. Hic mihi Catho nescio quis, reducto mento, labiis prorectis, oculis stupidis, supercilio *sublato* [adducto], dextera prelata, leva cingulo iniecta: Facessant, inquit, humane cavillationes, audiamus quid divina scriptura iubeat. [Paulum audiamus.] Non altum, *sapere* (inquit) sapien[te]s, sed humilibus consentientes. *Item alibi. Non aliud sapere sed sapere ad sobrietatem. Et:* [Idem sapere iubet ad sobrietatem. Iterum alibi.] Noli altum sapere sed time. Rursum alibi. Qui se existimat aliquid scire, nondum scit quemadmodum oporteat eum scire, et qui sibi videtur sapiens, stultus fiat ut sit sapiens. Ad eundem modum Esayas, Perdam, inquit, sapientiam sapientium et prudentiam prudentium reprobabo.

Item divus Iacobus. Non est enim ista sapientia desursum descendens, sed terrena, animalis, dyabolica. Que autem desursum est sapientia, primum quidem pudica est, deinde pacifica, modesta, suadibilis, bonis consentiens, plena misericordia et fructibus bonis, non iudicans, sine simulatione. Huiusmodi aliquot sententiolas homines ineptissimi in nos iaciunt, quas omnes recensere, tum ociosum sit, tum [ad] nichil utile, presertim quod et eodem spectent, et eadem ratione dissolvi possint, universa quidem ista et *vere* [iure] et recte scripta. Verum nos alio torquemus depravamus[que] que recte dicta sunt: siquidem ad nostram *palliandam* [tegendam] ignaviam deflectimus, qum tam evidens sit, ut (quod inquiunt)

sentiri possit manibus, hiis sententiis non vituperari eruditionem, sed
[admoneri nos, ne mundi successibus sublatis animis, parum meminerimus
Christianae modestiae. Opes addunt cristas, hic metuendum quod monet
Paulus, imo ad eos haec pertinent, qui profecerunt in virtutibus. Neque
tamen inficiabor, haec ad eruditos quoque pertinere, verum non omnes,
sed] eos [duntaxat] qui aut efferunt sese, quod paulo sint eruditiores, aut
eis in studiis vel immodici, vel intempestivi inveniantur, aut sue sententie
tenaciores audeant ab ecclesiasticis opinionibus desciscere, aut certe
alioqui bonis literis abutantur. Invisa est superis impia, superba, impu-
dica literatura. Scimus istud, adde et mortalibus odiosa, merito in hanc
fulminat scriptura. Horreant et corrigantur, qui nox[i]am agnoscunt,
gaudeant immunes. Quid hec ad imperitos, qui prope nichil didicere?
scilicet hoc credo triumphant, quod egregie caverint, nec quicquam horum
in se dici possit. Neque enim reprehendi potest, quo male rem [ad]ministret,
cui nihil unquam rei fuit. Ridicule profecto, perinde quasi iste sententie
peritos literarum magis quam imperitos feriant.

Ita ne in solos eruditos cadit, altum sapere, at non multo maxime in
stolidissimum quemque? Quid tandem est altum sapere, alte doctum
esse, an potius sibi placere? Eis ista canantur, non qui bene docti sunt,
sed hiis potius qui qum nichil didicerint, doctioribus imperare contendunt.
Non studiosis, sed divitibus, inquit Paulus, non altum sapere. Eruditis
ista non apte canuntur, stolidis ista cantentur, qui alienam eruditionem
fastidiunt, suam rusticitatem mirantur. Et que tandem est illa sciencia
animalis dyabolica? Utique que zelum amarum habet, que contentiones
et simultates parit, que adversus veritatem dimicat: hoc apostoli sentie-
bat animus, hoc ipsa sermonis series ostendit. Quid simplicem scripturam
torquemus? quid invitam et reluctantem trahimus? Non hic de literis
secularibus [liberalibus], sed de theologicis questiunculis agitur, quas nichil ad rem pertinentes, nonnunquam inter se pertinacissimis contentioni-
bus agitant [quo stulto popello sublimiter eruditi videantur, cum eruditio
Christiana nesciat supercilium. Quid autem istis contentiosius, qui coelum terrae misceant citius quam usquam cedant? protinus haereticum
vociferantes, si quis ab illis dissentiat.]

22 Atque hoc quidem e scripturis, quas [1] appellant canonicas, depromere
solent: nunc pauca proferam, que de ceteris scriptoribus arma soleant
mutuari: at ne iuxta Grecorum proverbium, harenas metiamur, plurimos
repetendo, unius Gratiani meminisse sat fuerit, qui preter ceteros nos
terrere poterat, si non auctoritate certe voluminis immanitate. Nuper igitur qum e scola Parrhisiorum in patriam reversus essem, incidit mihi cum
quodam *sacerdote* concertatio, homine capitaliter nostris studiis infenso,

alioquin humano, comi, *non* [nec] ineleganti, bello, lepido, festivo, et quod hiis
virtutibus convenit, amatore strenuo, pot*at*ore invicto, comessatore assiduo,
scortatore, aleatore [fortissimo], et multis id genus virtutibus exornato. Accreverat mihi cum hoc Sardanapalo iam inde a puero coniunctior familiaritas,
cui quidem adhuc tribuo, ut nomini parcam congerronis vetusti. Consuevit
mihi, comicorum militum more, sua iactare facinora, quot eadem in urbe
haberet amicas, quoties et quibus artibus ad alienas uxores penetrasset,
quot rivales superasset, quotie*n*s una nocte marem prestare potuisset, que
barat[h]ra bibendo quanta cum gloria vicisset. Hec erant hominis studia,
in hiis operam, curam, voluptatem, ocium et negocium, in hiis felicitatem
reponebat. Huiusmodi nugis cum iam biduum mihi aures calfecisset,
incidit inter prandendum, ut nescio quid amenius e poetarum fabulis pro-
ferrem. Ibi homo sui repente oblitus, novam quandam religionem cepit
assumere, execrari vero me quod *et* ethnicos illos et impudicos auctores
legerem, iam et serio hortari ut resipiscerem, ut illis relictis ecclesiasticos
evolverem. Miratus sum subitam hominis metharmophosim, ex Epycuro
mihi factum Zenonem. Rogabam quid ita censeret, et nunquid ipse eosdem legisset, abominatus est perquam religiose.

Nunquam, inquit, in vita, nec attigi istos, nec attigero, sic mihi superi
sint propicii. Istud, inquam, vel citra iusiurandum facile tibi creditur.
Sed quid tu illos tantopere fugis? Nam si pudici sunt, non habent cur
vitentur: sin impudici, quid ita fugitas eos qui eadem scribunt que tu
facis? Qur non amplecteris potius tuarum virtutum precones? ibi tuorum
morum ymaginem expressam agnosces. Eho Sardanapale, non te pudet
tandem cum istis factis mihi frontem istam ostendere? An me vero
iubes tuam religionem imitari, qui gravius flagicium putas ethnicum librum
attingere, quam uxorem non tuam permolere, potare, amare, constuprare
virgines, tu ludum et pueriles nugas iudicas, legere poetam pro capitali
flagicio ducis. Tibi licebit ethnica flagicia designare, mihi non licebit
ethnicas literas perdiscere? Dissimulavit homo bilem, dicens, huiusmodi
cavillaciunculis lautum prandium non esse corrumpendum, post spacium
pomeridianum duxit me tanquam officiosus in bibliothecam publicam:
ubi qum me videret homo Ciceronianis quibusdam dyalogis (qui mihi
forte in manus inciderant) attentius incumbere, tandem irritatior, Gratianum, quem unum legebat, mihi obiicit. Iam, inquit, te confutabo
planissime. Commonstrant distinctionem tricesimam octavam, in qua de
liberalibus disciplinis nescio que questio tractatur: [at ita tractatur,] ut
pariter omnes in dubium vocentur. Quod quam sit absurdum quis non
videat? Iubeo pronunciet, vix legebat, tantum aberat ut recte
intelligeret. Episcopus gentilium libros non legat, hereticorum autem

perlegat pro necessitate ac tempore. Rogabam hominem quid sibi vellet pro necessitate ac tempore. Ait si forte contra hereticum aut disputandum esset aut scribendum. Et quid, inquam, si itidem contra ethnicum usu veniat? Quid si nec theologorum libros intelligere queas? Non iam vides oriri necessitatem? Non placebat ratio, iussi pergeret legere. Nonne videtur in vanitate sensus et obscuritate mentis ingredi, qui diebus ac noctibus in dialectica arte torquetur, qui phisicus perscrutator oculos trans celum levat, et cetera que sequuntur? Item *aliud* [illud], sicera[1] inebriantur, qui abutuntur *sapientia* [scientia] seculari et dyalecticorum tendiculis. Hic ego. Et non vides, inquam, abutuntur dictum, non autem habent, ut intelligas sapientie secularis plane usum quendam esse, neque vetitum neque ociosum.

Post multa congesta, ita suo more doctissime colligit Gracianus: ex quibus omnibus concluditur, quod non est ab ecclesiasticis secularium literarum querenda peritia. Iam perinde ac si debellatum esset, ita cepit ineptus *sibi* [se ad] triumphum preparare, vix exoravi ut paucis me auscultaret. Et non intelligis, inquam, hanc ipsam collectionem contra te vehementer facere. Primum non mirandum fuisset, si homo secularium literarum ignarus, eas condemnasset, presertim in hac parte ubi (vestigandi gratia) data opera, adversus illas pugnat. Nec tamen ausus est concludere, interdictam esse ecclesiasticis ethnicam literaturam, verum non esse querendam, frustra enim ibi queras ubi minime sit, sed extra iocum querendam, id est, exigendam. Non hic igitur in questionem vocatur, sit ne ecclesiasticis concessa erudicio secularis, sed an sit exigenda: non an habere, sed an carere liceat. Adiecit ecclesiasticis, ne quid dubites hanc a scolasticis prorsus exigendam. Vobis ignoscitur si careatis, nos si careamus, damnamur. Vides igitur quod tua ista conclusiuncula pro nobis faciat, sed mane paulisper etiam nunc accusationem audivimus, defensionem audiamus, nondum satis pernosti Gracianicam eloquentiam: de unaquaque re non in utramvis, sed in utranque partem disputat, et quidem[2] pari copia, pari[que] facundia: quod idem [olim] Gorgyam et Carneadem fecisse legimus. Nunc huius palinodiam audi. Iussi paginam evolvi, consequuntur enim illa: sed contra legitur, quod Moyses et Daniel omni sciencia Egypciorum et Chaldeorum eruditi fuerint, et post pauca: turbat acumen legentium et deficere cogit, qui eos a legendis secularibus libris omnibus modis estimat prohibendos, in quibus si qua inventa sunt utilia, quasi sua sumere licet, alioquin Moses et Daniel sapientia Egypciorum et

---

[1] MS reads *cicera.*

[2] MS reading of *et quidem* is *equidem,* but over the first *e* there appears the letter *t* in the heavy stroke characteristic of the first hand.

C[h]aldeorum non paterentur erudiri, et alia que sequuntur. [Rursum] Paulo inferius ex Ambrosio; Si quis artem noverit grammaticam, vel dialecticam, ut recte loquendi rationem habeat, et inter falsa et vera diiudicet, non improbamus. *Item ex* [Mox de] eodem: Qui de vino et mensa regis nolunt comedere, ne polluantur: utique si scientiam Babiloniorum scirent esse peccatum, nunquam acquiescerent discere quod non licebat. Et iterum aliquanto inferius ex synodo Eugenii pontificis. De 23 quibusdam locis ad¹ nos refertur, neque magistros neque curam inveniri pro studio literarum: iccirco ab universis *ipsis* [episcopis] subiectis plebibus et aliis locis, in quibus necessitas occurreret, omnino cura et diligentia habeatur, ut magistri et doctores constituantur, qui studia literarum liberalium artium dogmata doceant, quia in hiis divina maxime manifestantur [atque declarantur] mandata.

Hec ubi ostendissem, rogabam nunquid peniteret Gratianum obiecisse rhetor[culo]. Nunquam, inquit, ista antehac animadverti. Nec miror, inquam, si non capis venatu, que minime [venaris: quae] pro te faciunt ea demum excerpis: que pro tua causa facere videntur [legis], nec perlegis, nec intelligis ea que legis: quod non ita tibi eveniret, nisi tam in fugiendis literis ethnicorum esses religiosus. Audisti modo a sanctissimo consilio cautum esse, ut omnibus in locis [com]parentur, qui liberales disciplinas doceant, et quidem assidue. Nulla autem ex liberalibus disciplinis Christiana est, quia neque de Christo agunt, neque a Christianis invente: ad Christum autem omnes referuntur. Nec est *cur* [quod] tergiverseris, nullam artem excepit, non rhetoricen, non poesim, omnes in genere edicti forma complectitur, nisi cavillaberis poesim liberalem non esse, ut que in ludis trivialibus inter eas non numeretur. Ego vero contempta ista prescriptione, non liberalem modo, verum eciam liberalissimam iudico, quippe que libris olim non inter ceteras, [sed ante caeteras] tradi consuevit. Obmutuit meus iureperitus, iubeo reliquos suos auctores ostendat, recusat.¹ Ipse a decretis ad decretales [epistolas] duco, *locum* [titulum] de magistris ostendo [ubi diligenter cavetur de parandis linguarum doctoribus: cum isti Christianum non putent, nisi sit elinguis].

Hinc igitur ad Anthoninam summam, ad Pisanam, ad Astexanam, ad Angelicam, ceterosque non auctores [modo], sed congestores: omnes fere eandem cantilenam canunt, et *cuculus cuculo* [coccyx coccyci] succinit. Est enim huic scriptorum generi moris nichil suum ponere, sed diversorum dicta hinc *inde* [atque hinc] decerpta congerere, non modo diversa, verum etiam aliquotiens inter se pugnantia: sat habent coaceruasse, ceterum iudicii onus lectori relinquentes. Cui ubi iam longa lectione

¹ At this point MS reads ... *recusat ipse. De decretis* ...

cerebrum vertigine rotari, et caligare acies cep[er]it, non multo certior
surgit, quam Demipho ille Therentianus, *ut* [qui] ex tribus advocatis
consultis, qum unus suasisset, alter negasset, tercius deliberandum cen-
suisset. Fecistis, inquit, probe: incertior sum nunc [multo] quam dudum.
Horum igitur odiosas disputationes qum iam complures legissemus, huc
evadebant omnes, ethnicarum literarum usum nemini vicio verti, imo
laudi potius ducendum: verum abusum perniciosum esse, eoque vetitum,
id quod nemo puerorum nesciebat.

Iam mitis erat, sed libebat hominem paulisper illudere, rogabam nunc
ubi in suo Graciano legisset, licere viris ecclesiasticis amare, potare,
scortari, mechari? Negabat. At ista iam vulgo faciunt, et dormiunt
decreta, nobis qui oratores *aut* [et] historicos ethnicos legimus obiiciuntur.
Sed obsecro te, quandoquidem tibi morem gessi, michi iam mutuam
operam redde, et meos theologos paulisper consulamus. Hieronimum
aperio, locum forte obvium ostendo, ubi de muliere captiva disputat,
quam *sapientiam secularem* [eruditionem prophanam] vir doctissimus et
apte et festive interpretatur. Quid ergo, inquiens, mirum si [et] ego
sapientiam secularem propter eloquii venustatem et membrorum pul-
chritudinem, de ancilla atque captiva Israhelit[id]em facere cupio, et si
quid in ea mortuum *est* ydo*lo*latrie, voluptatis, erroris, libidinum, vel precido,
vel rado, et *nixos* [mixtus] purissimo corde vernaculos ex ea genero
domino sabaoth. Labor meus in familiam Christi proficit, stuprum in
alienam numerum auget conservorum. Neque orationis methaphoram, nec
vocabula quidem intelligebat: ancillam ministram domesticam putabat,
vernaculos, quo sane vocabulo Hieronimus elegantissime usus est, quid
sibi vellet, nichil potuit suspicari. Hic iam, inquam, ulciscuntur contu-
meliam *suam* [in se admissam] litere seculares: erat autem locus in ea
epistola in primis nobili, quam ad magnum oratorem inscripsit, [an
scripserit nescio,] in qua vir sanctissimus sicubi [alias] sententiam invidie
placande gratia vafre dissimulavit, hic certe non perplexe proloquitur.

Repetamus, inquam, a capite (non enim perlonga est epistola). Quod
autem queris in calce epistole tue qur in opusculis nostris secularium
literarum interdum ponamus exempla, et candorem ecclesie ethnicorum
sordibus polluamus: breviter responsum habeto, numquam hoc quere-
res, nisi te totum Tullius possiderit, si scripturas sanctas legeres, si
interpretes earum omisso Vulcacio evolveres. Quis enim nesciat et in
Mo*ss*e et in prophetarum voluminibus quedam assumpta de gentilium
libris, et Salomonem philosophis Tyri et nonnulla proposuisse, et aliqua
respondisse. Unde in exordio Proverbiorum commonet, ut intelligamus
sermones prudentie, versutiasque verborum, parabolas, et obscurum

sermonem, dicta sapientum, et enigmata, que proprie dialecticorum et philosophorum sunt. Pauloque inferius Paulum collaudans, Ac ne parum hoc esset, inquit, doctor Christiani exercitus, et orator invictus pro Christo causam agens, inscriptionem fortuitam arte torquet in argumentum fidei. Didicerat enim a vero David, de manibus hostium extorquere gladium, et Golie superbissimum caput proprio mucrone truncare. Legerat in Deuteronomio, domini voce preceptum, mulieris captive radendum caput, supercilia, omnes pilos et ungues corporis amputandos, et sic eam habendam coniugio.

Deinde post ea verba, que paulo superius recitavimus: Osee, inquit, accepit uxorem fornicariam Gomer filiam de *Belaim* [Balam], id est, dulcedinum: et nascitur[ei]de meretrice filius Israel qui vocatur semen dei. Esayas novacula acuta barbam et crura radit peccantium. Et Ezechiel in typo fornicantis, Iherusalem tondet cesariem suam, ut quicquid in ea[1] absque sensu et vita est, auferatur. Horum (me legente) qum nihil ille intelligeret, rogabat et quorsum istao mnia spectarent. Eo, inquam, ut nullas ethnicas literas fugiamus, sed repurgatas, ad Christianorum eruditionem transferamus: quod si tu fecisses, non hic marmoreus astares. Quod autem repurgatas dixi, non ad scientiam, sed ad opinionem referri volo. Non enim *gentilium* [ethnicorum] philosophorum errores legere perniciosum est, sed eos ecclesiasticis disputationibus immiscere (non confutandi, sed approbandi gratia) id vero nequaquam licuerit. Deinde illustrium scriptorum cathalogum texit, tum Grecorum, tum Latinorum, et Grecorum quidem hoc elogio claudit. Qui omnes in tantum philosophorum doctrinis atque sententiis suos refarciunt libros, ut nescias quid in illis primum admirari debeas, eruditionem seculi, an scientiam scripturarum. Latinorum ita concludit: De ceteris vel viventibus, vel mortuis taceo, quorum in scriptis et vires manifeste sunt, et voluntas. *Et* [Mox] callidam imperitorum calumniam excludens, addit. Nec statim prava opinione fallaris, contra gentiles hoc esse licitum, in aliis disputationibus dissimulandum, quia omnes pene omnium libri (exceptis [iis] qui cum Epicuro literas non didicerunt) eruditionis doctrineque plenissimi sunt.

Mordax quidem illud, quo epistolam claudit, sed plane barbarorum stulticia dignissimum. Cui queso, inquit, ut suadeas, ne vescentium dentibus edentulus invideat, et oculos caprearum talpa contemnat. Ostendi et eam prefationem quam Exodo preposuit, in qua adeo non dissimulat, ut eciam nominatim predicet artes liberales. Taceo, inquiens, de grammaticis, rhetoribus, philosophis, geometris, dialecticis, musicis, *astronomicis*, astrologis, medicis [quorum scientia mortalibus]. Quid hic

---

1 MS reads *ro.*

expectas dicturum Hieronimum? Pestifera est vel utilissima est, inquit. Rogabam ecquid hec placerent: qum tantum ac talem habeamus auctorem, exoriere tu nobis, et nescio quod glos[s]ema e tuis barbaris auctoribus, contra liberalem eruditionem obiicies? Astrologiam vestra decreta damnant, at Hieronimus *affert* [approbat] disciplinam et prope curiosam, et ad pauca utilem. Quid igitur de rhetorica, de poetica sensisse credis? Commonstravi homini eiusdem de viris illustribus opus, ubi in permultis scriptoribus miratur eloquentiam, predicat poetarum philosophorumque cognitionem, effert literaturam secularem. Que si pestifera esset, non tam diligenter eam [in autoribus ecclesiasticis] vir piissimus commemoraret. In eiusdem opusculi prefatione tantum abest ut improbet, ut etiam adversus et ethnicos et hereticos magnifice iactare sit ausus, Christianorum in ethnicis literis prestantiam. Discant ergo, inquit, Celsus, Porphirius, Iulianus, rabidi adversum Christum canes, discant sectatores eorum, qui putant ecclesiam nullos philosophos et eloquentes, nullos habuisse doctores, quanti[que] et quales viri eam fundaverint, instruxerint, adornaverint, et desinant fidem nostram rustice tantum simplicitatis arguere, suamque imperitiam potius *agnoscant* [recognoscant]. Non pudet, inquam, te Christianum obiicere Christiano, et quidem layco, quod Hieronimus non dubitavit apud *posteros* [hostes] gloriari vir ecclesiasticus, iam sanctitatis opinione celebris, postremo monachus, [et] *heremicola* [eremi cultor], presertim ea tempestate, qum Christiana adhuc religio cum ethnicis conflictaretur. Si mala est erudicio secularis, nichil Hieronimo stultius, qui hoc apud adversarios iactat, quod illi pro summo crimine poterant [ret]orquere: verum de compotore meo iam nimium.

Ad cetera properabimus, si prius alterum testem citaverimus: nam [nunc] decrevi contentus esse duobus, gravissimis tamen. Aurelius Augustinus vir sanctimonia iuxta ac eruditione singularis, tum arcte adeo, ne dicam meticulose conscientie, ut sepe numero michi (bona venia tanti viri dixerim) ab[s] re trepidare videatur, id quod tum ex eius vita tum ex confessionum retractationumque libris coniicere proclive est. Is, inquam, talis vir, utique literaturam secularem, [ut vocant,] dissuasisset, si aut noxiam, aut ociosam, aut suspectam habuisset. Hic in hiis libris, quos de doctrina Christiana inscribit, proponit duo genera doctrinarum, que in gentibus etiam, inquit, moribus exercentur, id est ethnicorum,[1] vel ut isti dicunt, secularium: unum earum quas instituerunt homines: alterum earum, quas animadverterunt, aut iam peractas aut divinitus institutas. Illud, inquit, quod est secundum institutiones,[2] partim supersticiosum est,

---

[1] Original reading was *ethnicarum*.

[2] The word *hominum* was crossed out after *institutiones*, which appears as *constitutiones* in B.R.

partim supersticiosum non est. Sed ne omnem disputationem, que verbosissima est, repetam verbis illius omissis, rei summam paucis complectar. Sub hoc ultimo genere, quod supersticiosum appellat, maleficia, incantationes, excantationes sortilegia, aruspicia, auspicia, auguria, nicromantiam,[1] [pyromantiam,] alphitomantiam, hydromantiam, geomantiam, chiromantiam, et id genus alia comprehendit: hec [quia] phitonum sunt et maleficorum, nec sine commercio scelestorum spirituum exercentur, iure Christiano fugienda censuit.

Illas quoque observationes *qum et* [quod] plurimum habeant et anxietatis et vanitatis, huic generi adnumerat: qualia sunt visorum et insomniorum interpretatio, extorum inspectio, volatus avium cantusque, monstrorum, tonitruum, fulgurum, syderum, sortium, sternutamentorum, mustelarum, murium occurrentium, aut stridentium, aut aliquid arrodentium, aurium tinnientium, oculorum salientium, foliorum crepitantium, nominum et ymaginum et *eiusmodi* [his similium] nugarum observatio. Sub altero genere, id est ab hominibus quidem instituto, minime tamen supersticioso, hec fere collocat, caracteres, vocabula rerum, consuetudinem loquendi, leges, plebiscita, et si qua id genus sunt alia: hec enim non modo non reprehendit, verum etiam Christiani hominis interesse putat, ut hec quam maxime scire curet. In primo genere, id est annotatis, omnes fere liberales disciplinas collocat, logicen, rhetoricen, phisicen, arithmeticen, geometriam, astronomiam, musicam, historias denique [et antiquitatis cognitionem].

At ne de singulis quidem pigebit divi Aurelii sententiam pronunciare, modo ne vos audire pigeat. De grammatica quidem dilucidius est, quam ut in eo debeat disputari, porro quod ad dialecticen [attinet] libro de doctrina Christiana secundo, capite (si bene [com]memini) vigesimo de dialecticis rationibus, de veritate, de falsitate connexionum, de consequenti et inconsequenti, de repugnanti, de diffiniendo, [de partiendo,] verbose et curiosiuscule suo more disputat, petitis etiam e divo Paulo connexionis formis (sic enim appellat) ut nos si dialecticen ignoremus, docere voluisse videatur. Hanc disciplinam in ipso disputationis capite hiis verbis commendat (nam puto me ea ut nuper relecta posse reddere). Sed disciplina, inquit, disputationis ad omnia genera questionum, que in literis sanctis sunt penetranda et dissolvenda plurimum valet, tantum cavenda est ibi libido rixandi. Pauloque inferius. Sunt etiam connexiones ratiocinationis, inquit, falsas habentes sententias, que consequuntur errorem illius cum quo agitur, que tamen ad hoc inferuntur a bono et docto homine, ut in hiis erubescens ille cuius errorem consequuntur,

---

[1] For *necromantiam*, which appears as *necyomantiam* in B.R.

25 eundem | relinquat errorem, quia si in eodem manere voluerit, necesse
est ut eciam illa que damnat, tenere cogatur. Hec de dialecticis. Pro
poetis et rhetoribus, que multa dixit, hic consulto pretereo, suis ea locis
redditurus. Ceteras autem artes minutiores quidem illas, attamen acutas,
ut Quintus Fabius oratori, ita Aurelius theologo putat non mediocriter
conducere, et quidem de musica hec fere sunt que tenemus. Et numerum,
inquit, et musicam plerisque in locis in scripturis honorabiliter positam[1]
invenimus. Non enim audiendi sunt errores gentilium superstitionum,
qui novem musas Iovis et Memorie filias esse finxerunt. Deinde auctore
Varrone, unde [ea] sit fabula [nata], aperit subiiciens: Sed sive se ita
habeat, quod Varro retulit, sive non ita, nos tamen propter superstitionem
prophanorum non debemus musicam fugere, si quid inde utile ad intelli-
gendas scripturas rapere pot[u]erimus.

De arithmetica hoc est disputationis inicium.

Ast numerorum eciam, inquit, imperitia, multa facit non intelligi,
translate ac mistice posita in scripturis. Omnes harum disputationum
ambages, qu[a]e[que][2] de geometria et astronomia in eundem fere
modum disputat, parvi refert meminisse.

Porro phisicen in primis ad sacrarum literarum cognitionem necessariam
arbitratur, quod passim scateat vocabulis tum animantium, tum herbarum, tum lapidum, quorum omnium [nisi] (monstratrice phisica) vim
naturamque teneas, temerarius videberis, si ea coneris interpretari. Et
huius quidem loci hoc est caput. Rerum autem ignorantia facit obscuras,
figuratas locutiones, qum ignoramus vel animantium, vel lapidum, vel
herbarum naturas, aliarumve rerum que plerumque in scripturis similitu-
dinis alicuius gratia ponuntur. Cetera idem et apte et erudite prosequitur.

Historiarum vero cognitionem adeo sacre scripture studioso putat esse
necessariam ut qui sine illis divinas literas tractare velit summo cum periculo
et errare et falli sit necesse. Porro de philosophis quid tandem, penes quos
beate vite professio [potissimum] est, mirum *an* [ni] istos legendos
negabit: qui qum se veri magistros [ut] omnium rerum [peritos] profiteri
sint ausi, omnium errorum auctores extiterunt, e quorum disciplinis nulla
fere non heresis nata est [nobis], quorum contortis enthimematibus quasi

---

[1] MS reads *positam*, but *m* is crossed out, although it is necessary for the sake of
the agreement with *musicam*. B.R. reads *posita*.

[2] The manuscript reads $\hat{q}$, the conventional abbreviation for *quae;* the printed
version has *quaeque*. The addition of *-que* provides a ready solution of the syntactic
difficulty.

quibusdam arietibus Christiane fidei menia totiens sunt pulsata: audite[et] quid et de hiis dicat vir equissimus. Philosophi autem, inquit, qui vocantur, si qua forte vera et fidei nostre accommodata dixerunt, et maxime Platonici non solum formidanda non sunt, sed ab eis tanquam iniustis possessoribus, *in* [ad] usum nostrum vindicanda. Et quod sequitur, non iniucundum de Egipcia suppellectile, utinam vobis verba ipsa possem annumerare, sed tamen bona cum fide appendam. Legimus, inquit, in Exodo, Hebreos, cum duce Moyse ab Egypcia servitute furtim fugam molirentur, plurimam omnis generis suppellectilem, immensam vim signorum, vestium, vasorum, a suo quemque vicino commodato cepisse,[1] itaque spoliatis Egiptiis, demigrasse clanculum: quam fugam, quod furtum, quia deo auctore patratum novimus, aliquid portendere creditur: scilicet iam tum divina providentia quorundam trepidationi consulebat, qui fortassis Egyptum spoliare, hoc est, ethnicorum sapientiam usurpare timuissent, nisi huius rei tantum imperatorem, tantum ducem, tantum exemplum habuissent. Migrant ex Egypto, qui relictis supersticionibus prophanis, ad Christianam sese religionem convertunt. Egypcias opes tollunt, qui *gentilium* literas [ethnicorum] ad nostre fidei decus et *numen* [usum] transferunt. Si ridebunt barbari interpretem, iure id facerent, nisi divi Augustini non meum interpretamentum protulissem. Ut enim, inquit, olim Hebrei ea que sibi usui fore iudicassent rapuerunt, relictis iis, que aut molesta, aut inutilia, aut prophana existimassent, ita *nobis* [nos oportet] sua quidem ethnicis vicia relinquenda, supersticiones, libidines, ambitionem, cupiditates, hec [inquam] apud dominos sunt relinquenda. At si quod sapientie aurum, si quod eloquentie argentum, si qua bonarum literarum suppellex penes illos erit, eam omnem *corradere* [convasare], et in nostros usus accommodare debemus, nichil furti calumniam veriti, quin potius pulcherrimi etiam facinoris et laudem et premium sperare ausi.

Hic rursum ne nodum in scirpo querentes cavillari inciperemus, que sint ethnicis pro perniciosis relinquenda, [quae pro utilibus transferenda,] Augustinus de sua partitione nichil excipit, preter ea que supersticiosa nominat. Ceterum a sua [illa] divisione non recedens ille, et hoc suo more, auro *et* [atque] argento eas disciplinas sibi videri significatass cripsit, que essent ab ingeniis humanis animadverse, sicut dyalecticen, rhetoricen, phisicen, historiam, et id genus plura, quod hec homines non ipsi quidem produxissent, sed tanquam aurum et argentum de quibusdam [quasi] metallis divine providencie, que ubique infusa est, eruissent. Vestes autem Egyptiorum interpretatur disciplinas a mortalibus quidem institutas, sed vestium in morem accommodatas humane societati, puta leges

---

[1] MS originally read *accepisse.*

loquendi, *leges vivendi*, plebiscita, decreta pontificum, que quidem omnia
quoniam plurimum habent usus, ab ethnicis quoquo pacto rapienda censet. Postremo festivo exemplo rem et confirmat et locupletat. Quod
inquiens, fecerunt multi boni nostri fideles. Nonne aspicimus quanto
argento et veste suffarcinatus exierit de Egypto Cyprianus, doctor
suavissimus, et martyr beatissimus? quanto Lactantius? quanto Victori-
nus, Optatus, Hylarius? (ut de vivis taceam) quanto innumerabiles
Greci? Quod prior ipse fidelissimus dei famulus Moyses fecerat, de quo
scriptum est, quod eruditus fuerat in omni sapientia Egypciorum. Quibus
omnibus viris supersticiosa gentium consuetudo, et maxime illis tempori-
bus, qum Christi excutiens iugum persequebatur Christianos, disciplinas
quas utiles habeba[n]t nunquam commodaret, si eas in usum colendi unius
dei, quo vanas ydolorum cultus excinderetur, conversum iri suspicaretur.
Hec quidem e pluribus pauca (ut potui) brevissime, perstrinxisse satis
putavi.

Ceterum sexcentos citare testes possem, ni et vestris parcerem auribus,
et horum duorum *auctorum* ea esset auctoritas, ut tam sacris, tam eruditis
viris nolle accedere summa sit impietas. Sed ita ab ethnicis abstinent
barbari, ut nec *hos* [sacros] quidem attingant, aut si tangunt contaminent.
Immo quod indignius [est], iam Hieronimum non in theologorum numero,
26 sed oratorum ponunt[1] *non ob aliud nisi quia non intelligunt Scoticis
commentis et Acursianis glosematis insenescunt, in quibus preter barbariem
nichil mirantur* [atque e suo sacro sancto senatu depulsum grammaticis
annumerant, ipsi nescio quorum confusissimis collectaneis ac summulis
insenescunt, nihil eruditum existimantes, nisi quod idem sit barbarum].
Nos [Et] qum tantos duces utrunque sequamur, veniant et apostolicum
nobis illud cantitent, non altum sapientes, scientia inflat. Si theologi
videri cupiunt, quin illud potius proferunt: Estote prudentes sicut ser-
pentes, et simplices sicut columbe, non [sicut] asini, tardi, inertes, ignavi.
Cur non illud: Malicia parvuli estote, sensibus autem perfecti. [Cur
non illud: Sapientia vincit malitiam, et sapientiam stulti despiciunt.]
Cur non illud Daviticum *dissilant* [adferunt]: Bonitatem et disciplinam
et scientiam doce me domine. Cur non illud *quidem* ecclesiastici sapientis:
Sapientiam omnium antiquorum exquiret sapiens, et in prophetis vacabit.
Narrationem virorum nominatorum conservabit,[et] in versutias parabola-
rum introibit. Occulta proverbiorum exquiret, et in absconditis parabo-
larum conversabitur. In medio magnatorum ministrabit, et in conspectu
presidis apparebit. In terram alienigenarum pertransibit, bona et mala in
omnibus tentabit.

In eo libro qui dubio auctore Sapientia inscribitur, quanta laus eruditionis, ut quod gravissime a Platone scriptum est, sapientiam incredibili esse specie, que si oculis videri queat, admirabiles sit exci[ta]tura sui amores, hic quisquis fuit scriptor non infacundus, sapientie [quasi] quandam effigiem expressisse videatur, quo nos ad illius amorem accenderet. At *de*negaverit quispiam hic [secularem] laudari sapientiam secularem, verum aliam quandam celestem ac divinam: imo certe eam, que sit nostri temporis philosophia[e] [pars] difficillima, que omnium rerum tum divinarum, tum humanarum cognitionem copularit. Mentior nisi id ipsa sonant verba, Deus,[1] inquit, dedit mihi horum que sunt scientiam,[2] ut sciam dispositionem orbis terrarum, et virtutem elementorum, inicium et consummationem et medietatem temporum, [et eorum mutationes, divisiones temporum,] anni cursus, et stellarum dispositiones, naturas animalium, et iras bestiarum, vim ventorum, et cogitationes hominum, differentias virgultorum, et virtutes radicum, et quecunque sunt absconsa et improvisa, didici. Hiis sane verbis describi mihi videtur, non perturbata et ieiuna erudicio quedam, sed polita et copiosa, et que preter omnium disciplinarum scientiam plurima sit antiquitate condita. Capite insequenti multo significantius exprimit, virtutem cum eruditione liberali coniunctam, vocari sapientiam. Et iusticiam, inquit, qui plus diligit, labores huius magnas habent virtutes: sobrietatem enim [et] sapientiam docet, et iusticiam, et virtutem, quibus utilius nichil est in vita hominibus. Et si multitudinem scientie desiderat, quis scit preterita, et de futuris estimat, scit versutias sermonum, et dissolutiones argumentorum, signa et monstra scit antequam fiant, et eventus temporum, et seculorum.

Sed *nos ne* in [hac] re tam clara, pro ipsa quidem nimio plus satis, pro istorum pertinacia parum, quanquam quid frustra rem infinitam prosequar, qum ex unoquoque auctore permulta loca depromi possint[3]? Nec inficias ivero tamen eosdem ipsos [non]nullis in locis perinde disserere, ac si a seculari doctrina nos conentur dehortari, et ita rhetorica contentione incandescant contra curiosam, superbam, ventosam, obstinatam, eruditionem, ut non in abutentium vicium, sed in rem ipsam invehi *in*videantur. At non venit in mentem istis, ea ipsa que contra doctrinam disputata videntur, non a doctissimis modo viris, verum etiam doctissime disputata [esse]. Quonam igitur ore a literis secularibus dehortentur, qum ipsi in ea dehortatione secularem literaturam exhibeant [ut interim nobis ius fiat hoc verbo utendi]: sed viciis nostris libenter blandimur. Dic mihi tu marmorea statua, et fruges consumere nate, ita ne credis summis illis

---

[1] The word *enim* is crossed out after *Deus*.
[2] The word *veram* is crossed out after *scientiam*.
[3] MS reading *possent* is corrected to *possint*.

viris, et in omni literarum genere consummatissimis cordi fuisse, ut tuam illam supinam oscitationem atque ignaviam predicarent. Dictum est recte, nempe ad deterrendos curiosos ab nimio, ab inani studio [ab intempestivo]: dictum est ad compescendam arrogantiam: dictum est fortassis ad consolandam simplicitatem columbinam, non ad fovendam stoliditatem asininam. Quid tu gestis? quid triumphas inepte? quid alio torques ac dicitur? Audisti notari peritiam impiam? quid tu tibi plaudis, quasi pietas sit imperitia? Si deus reprobat ac perdit prudentiam huius seculi, stulticiam seculi amabit scilicet? Nichil profecto minus, imo *potius* [peius] oderit. Damnatur is qui doctus ignarum fastidit: *ita* [tu] tibi places, quod doctos ignarus contemnas ac iudices. Ille reprobus habetur quod virtutis negligentior abutatur scientia, te iisdem viciis ornatum et fortasse pluribus, una absolvet inscitia? Hic accusatur, quod omissis Evangeliis plurimus sit in evolvendo Aristotile, tu culpa vacas, qui ne Evangelia quidem intelligis, [imo adeo] nec legis. Ille sciens voluntatem domini, plagis vapulabit multis, tu neque faciens, neque scire curans, num paucis vapulabis? Ille sedulitate quadam modum officii egressus castigatur, tu tua non contentus inertia, [et] aliorum industriam impediens laudaberis? Sed ut aliquando mee loquacitatis modum faciam, et stomachum effervescentem cohibeam, nusquam nobis ista obiicerent imperiti, si relicta oscitatione sua sacris literis legendis invigilarent.

Hic qum Battus brevi interiecto silentio, nos familiarius esset intuitus, Bone Deus, inquit, iam prope exciderat apud quos dicerem, ita nescio quo furore correptus, in presentes hostes mihi visus sum debachari. Equidem tam disertarum aurium patientiam admiror, que me puerili more tot verba fundentem, tum diu ferre quea[n]t.

Guielmus. Et nos, inquit Guielmus, nescio quo tua disputatio impetu abripuerat suo: itaque propera queso, ac periculum facito, *an tu* [utrum] nos prius dicendo, an nos te audiendo superemus.

Herasmus. At ego iamdudum, inquam, mecum admiror, quanquam orationem currentem interpellare nolui, qui tot versus e tot ecclesiasticis auctoribus, tam apte, tam ad verbum reddere valueris, quod quidem a summo theologo tam scite fieri posse vix crediderim. Desino enim iam mirari, quod Medicus dudum,[1] te hominem Musis penitus devotum, theologorum libros evolvisse: tantum[2] memoria complecti potuisse mirandum videtur.

Battus. Tum Battus [mihi] arridens, Non frustra, inquit, tuum

[1] MS reads *se mirari dudum aiebat,* but all these words except *dudum* were crossed out by the heavy stroke of the original hand.
[2] Before *tantum*, the word *et* is crossed out.

calamum metui, iam enim mihi subolet, quid animo destines. Nugas
nostras vis prodere, et de verisimili laboras: vereris enim, ne ubi hunc
nostrum sermonem literis mandaris (sentio enim te id velle) existat
aliquis, qui te dialogum Platonico ¹ aut Ciceroniano more finxisse putans,
neque decorum, neque probabile satis observasse calumnietur, qui me et
adolescentiorem et poetam tantum ecclesiasticarum literarum memoriter
reddentem feceris. Sed nichil est quod mireris, si homo non prodigiosa
quidem, sed tamen haud maligna preditus memoria, que legi tanto inten-
tius quanto irritatior, que decerpsi, que totiens contra barbaros deprompsi,
pauca potuerim memoria complecti. Age iam ad certamen ad quod me
provocavit Guielmus, accingamur.

Battus. Quoniam adversarios [inquit] primum rationibus, deinde
testibus revicimus, unicum illis profugium superest, exempla quorundam probatioris vite, quos aut citra eruditionem doctos habitos, aut
virtutis studio literas contempsisse obiiciunt, a quo illos presidio si
eiecerimus, reliquum est, ut aut in deditionem veniant, aut certe fuga
turpissima victos se profiteantur. Age accingamur certaminis huius
reliquias profligare.

Videtis, inquiunt, fidem Christianam non a physicis, non a dyalecticis,
non a poetis, non [a] rhetoricis auctoribus ortam, sed a rusticis hominibus,
[indoctis,] rudibus, denique piscatoribus, non e Platonica Academia, non
[e] porti[ci]bus Stoycorum, non e scolis Peripateticorum apostolos voca-
tos novimus, sed a navi et rethe, neque Christus ludos rhetoricos aut
dyalecticos aperuit, sed [tantum] vivendi precepta tradidit. O sacrilegam
impudentiam, audent rusticos dicere apostolos quo suam rusticitatem
tueantur, digni vero, quos ut pie sibi deditos ament apostoli. Adeo nichil
istorum refert, unde inertie sue patrocinium sint nacti, [vel] cum sacri
ordinis iniuria. Dic mihi os pestilens, et ferro inurendum, rusticos ais
fuisse apostolos? Aio, inquit, alioquin in quo tandem ludo didicerunt qui
repente sunt a piscatione ad apostolatum missi? Num a gubernaculo
scalmi [protinus] ad gubernacula mundi evecti sunt? Quorsum igitur
pertinuit, non Platonem aut Chrisippum, aut [alium] philosophum
aliquem, sed ipsum philosophie parentem tantum temporis sectari preceptorem, audire disputantem? videre monstra gerentem, convivere
assidue, assidue colloqui? Eam philosophie vim esse scripsit Seneca, ut
non sibi studentes modo, verum etiam conversantes, iuvet. Ut qui,¹
inquit, in solem venit, licet non [in] hoc venerit, colorabitur. Qui in
unguentaria taberna resederint, et paulo diutius sunt commorati, odorem
loci secum ferunt. At apostoli cum ipso scientie fonte tam diu commorati,

¹ MS originally read *vult* after *qui.*

[tam familiariter tam avide versati,] inscii eque ac rustici permansere, neque tam sedula tanti preceptoris opera quicquam confectum est? Lusit operam, qui bovem duxit ad ceroma. Ut resurrexerat, quadraginta dies in terris moratus, subinde discipulis suis apparuit, monuit, docuit, parum erat hoc quoque. Ipse in celum relatus paracletum dimittit, qui nichil illos iam nescire pateretur. Et audent post hec omnia homuntiones rusticitatem obiicere apostolis, obiicere quod piscando questum fecerint? Cur non eadem opera hamiotas illos et conchitas et fures maritimos appellant? Quandoquidem apostolos conviciari libet, rusticus [est] Paulus? unus est, inquiunt, qui liberalem literaturam apostolatui intulerit, at hic unus inter ceteros preminet, qua re, nisi doctrina? nam pietate pares arbitror fuisse. Unus hic vas electionis est appellatus, cur ita preter ceteros? Nempe quod hic in primis, ut homo tum doctus, tum disertus, visus est ydoneus qui contra literatas Athenarum scolas ferret arma, qui philosophorum supercilium ferret, qui Rhomanam eloquentiam sub Christi dictionem redigeret. Rusticus est Ioannes? Et unde illa vox sublimis, In principio erat verbum, et verbum erat apud deum, et deus erat verbum. An rusticus est Petrus? Illius certe epistole, etsi imperite sermone non tamen scientia. Iacobus rusticus fuit? Falso igitur huic illa tribuitur epistola, que videtur non modo sapientis, verum eciam diserti.

Sed fingamus rusticos fuisse apostolos. Ita ne nichil in apostolorum moribus imitatione dignum isti videre potuerunt, preter unam rusticitatem? Non enim me tam[1] contineo, quin id quod sentio proferam, ita risus mihi ingens oboritur, quociens horum qui nobis apostolicam impoliciem obiiciunt, perditissima vita in mentem venit. Quis enim ferat Esopum sibi de frugalitate precipientem, Sardanapalum de severitate disputantem? Quod si stomachus paulo mordacius erumpet, existimate me non in homines, sed in rem maledicere quanquam auctore Plauto, quod dignis maledicitur, benedicitur. Qui nobis apostolorum rusticitatem obgannire non desinunt, si virtutes tenerent apostolicas, ferri utcunque poterant, at nunc pudet me quorundam corruptissimam vitam cogitatione intueri. Qui qum ecclesiasticis sacris sint iniciati, ecclesiasticis stipibus alantur, adde senes, cani, rugosi, [quidam etiam cucullati,] cum Sardanapalo ipso certamen sumpsisse videntur. Me hominem adolescentem, prophanum, civilibus addictum negociis, et literas ipsas *seculares* [prophanas] profitentem, in ius vocant, nephandi criminis reum agunt,[2] quod antiquos philosophos, quod priscas historias, quod poetarum et oratorum scripta libenter lectitem. Ipsi qum iussi sint in lege domini, in sanctis literis die[3] noctuque

---

[1] B.R. reads *iam*.
[2] The word *rerum* is crossed out after *agunt*.
[3] B.R. reads *diu*.

versari, ab omni prorsus studio se cohibent, religioso quodam opinor metu adducti, ne si libros tractare ceperint, in ethnicum aliquem auctorem imprudentes incidant. At ita demum apostolos imitari se credunt, si usque adeo sint literarum ignari, ut nec ipsas quidem preces quas quotidie remurmurant, intelligere possint. Dic mihi *stolidissime* [stultissime] imitator, *servum pecus*, sic nobis apostolos refers? Ais rusticos et imperitos fuisse apostolos? Esto sane, donemus istud tibi,[1] habes quod glorieris, vicisti rusticitate piscatores, non invidemus tibi gloriam istam cum *farcinatoribus* [agricolis] communem, verum ubi simplicitas apostolica? ubi mores? Num quando venatos legisti apostolos? num isto ornatu usos accepisti? num pellicarum gregem domi aluerunt apostoli? num tantum opum in unum barat[h]rum demergebant apostoli? Tu si superis placet, apostolos imitandi studio sumptibus ecclesiasticis edes regales in celum erigis. Nitet amplissima in domo, suppellex Attalica, ministris militaribus omnia perstrepunt, cene Persico instruuntur apparatu, videas illic agi Sibaritica convivia, et quidem assidue, vincitur audacia perdende rei Cleopatra, vincitur Esopus cum filio haudquaquam degenere. Fastidiuntur illic acipenseres, non sapiunt murene, nauseam movent attagines. Noctes diesque estur, bibitur, luditur, saltatur, subatur, et qum vino immodico balbutire ceperint, videntur (opinor) sibi incultum sermonem apostolorum imitari. Cum hiis factis (quorum vel Neronem pudeat) audent nobis apostolos imitandos proponere.

28   [1] Nuper qum in Flandria legationem vestro nomine obirem, incidi in huiusmodi portenti convivia: ibi inter pocula, ut fit, qum hospitalitatem nobis suam iac[ti]taret, ut festiviore fabulatione convivium exhilararem, Tantali et Lycaonis et [his similes] nonnullas fabellas commemoravi: rogabat me, ubi nam illa legerentur? aio in poetis: oravit protinus, ne illos ethnicos ad suam mensam nominarem, ne fedis nominibus sanctum convivium prophanaretur. Gessi morem convivatori meo. Aderat theologus quidam, homo adolescens, sed plane doctus, nec ita ut hodie theologorum est vulgus, [quorum plerique] *ut* preter sophismata nichil didicerint, verum ita ut non minus rhetor esset quam theologus. Cum hoc mihi (assidebat enim proximus[2]) de scriptorum ecclesiasticorum eloquentia sermo incidit, dicebamus Aurelium Augustinum acute quidem, sed [sub]oscure [ac perplexe], et suo quodam more dicere [et huic tamen esse suam gratiam, ob schemata quae frequenter affectaret]. Hieronimi vehementem esse dictionem, variam, vafram, acrem, locupletem. Lactantium, Firmianum Ciceroniana facilitate fluere, nec a declamatoria illa palestra,

---

[1] MS reads ... *donemus istud. Tibi* ....
[2] This word was changed to *proxime* by a later hand.

in qua [fu]erat multos annos versatus, abhorrere. Ambrosii stilum plus obscuritatis, minus habere acuminis [delectare tamen allusionum aculeis]. Bernardi orationem facetam, nec incultam, ecclesiasticam tamen, *Guerrin*[1] *non perinde* [Hilarii vero parum] copiosam, verum cultiorem, preterea floridam. Bede equalem ac somniculosam [doctam tamen, ut eo sane seculo. Gregorii modulatam ac numerosam magis quam succulentam, quod identidem eadem repetere cogitur, ut expleat sermonis periodum].

Recentiores theologos, ne loqui quidem [adeoque non illustrare veritatem orationis adminiculis, ut quae per se praeclara sunt, infantia sua dehonestent]. Hec et alia quaedam qum nugaremur, risit nos homo severus ille, et curiosos appellavit, qui res ociosas et ad nichil utiles curaremus. Intellecta hominis improbitate, putavi malo nodo malum querendum esse cuneum, ac de industria quidem eum sermonem inieci, in quo illum sciebam ut plurimum valere, de vinorum generibus, de arte coquinaria, de venaticis epulis. Ibi ille (tanquam in re magna) erectus, magno silentio, magna autoritate diu disputavit acute, copiose, polite. Platonem ipsum dixisses, sexcenta vinorum genera memoriter reddebat. Preterea precia, qualitates, differentias, patrias, naturas, se[d]que ista non e physicorum literis, sed sapiente illo suo palato didicisse gloriabatur. Plinium (illum enim citabat) delirare dicebat, qui tanta in re alienis potius literis, quam suo palato fidem habuisset. Iam vero de epulis coquendis, condiendis, si disputantem audisses, quem tu non ibi coquum, quem non Catium, [quem non Philoxenum, quem non Apitium,] quem non Platynam, contemneres: hec nimirum sunt artes tetrice, et gravi sacerdote digne, has didicerunt ipsi, nobisque tradiderunt apostoli, non sylogismorum laqueos nectere, non Ciceronem, non Virgilium evolvere, non aliorum ingenia dictionemve taxare. Hec non in poetarum fabulis, sed in sacris literis discuntur scilicet. Ferendum hoc quoque, si non inter epulas, senes, sola libidine fortes, antiqua sua *flagicia* [facinora] iactarent invicem, et quod facere per etatem nequeunt, fecisse se turpiter glori[ar]entur. Hii sunt quorum poetarum fabulas religiose refugiunt aures, qui nos ad apostolicos mores provocant, horum peritam rusticitatem et simplicitatem fraudulentam divus Hieronimus quodam in loco scite notat. Venerationi, inquit, semper mihi fuit, non verbosa rusticitas, sed sancta simplicitas. Qui in sermone se imitari dicit apostolos, prius imitetur virtutes in vita illorum. In loquendo simplicitatem excusabit sanctimonie magnitudo, et sillogismos Aristotilis, contortaque Chrisippi acumina resurgens mortuus confutabit. Ceterum ridiculum, si qui se nobis manens in[ter] Cresi opes, et Sarda-

---

[1] This probably refers to Guerricus, a disciple of St. Bernard, and abbot of Igny. See J. P. Migne, *Patrologia Latina*, CLXXXV, cols. 9–10; CLXXXVIII, cols. 983–984.

napali delicias, de sola rusticitate se iactet, quasi omnes latrones et diversorum criminum rei diserti sint, et cruentos gladios philosophorum voluminibus, et non arborum truncis occulant.

Hec per digressum tangere volui, quo intelligatur, qui apostolorum imperitiam nobis ingerunt, eos non id apostolos emulandi studio facere, sed ut sunt superbi, sue rusticitatis patrocinium ab apostolis petere. Alioquin si id recte fit quod multorum fit exemplo, quot et quantos habemus quos imitemur? A Moyse repetamus, quid eo imperatore sanctius? *at* [et] hic omnem Egypciorum disciplinam a puero doctus legitur: non huic fraudi fuit secularis, [ut vocant,] erudicio, quo minus e mortalium genere unus in domini familiaritatem ascisci meruerit. Daniele quid castius? et [hic] C[h]aldeis disciplinis non recusavit institui. Docto patre, doctiorem Solomonem accepimus. Et Iob et omnes prope prophetas, non illiteratos fuisse, qum Hieronimi Augustinique testimonio constat, tum ipsa scriptorum monumenta declarant. At ne cavillentur, id cum lege Mosayca desiisse fas esse, Paulum apostolum eis proponam, Pauli[1] discipulum Dyonisium, quorum uterque quanta doctrina, quanta[que] fuerit eloquentia, ipsi [sibi] sunt testes. Quadratus apostolorum auditor, eruditionem in primis admirandam illis preceptoribus non dedidicit. Qui cum esset Atheniensis antistes ecclesie, Adriano imperatori librum porrexisse *creditur* [traditur] tante eruditionis ut acerrimam in Christianos persecutionem suo ingenio sedaverit. Fecit idem huius equalis, Aristides philosophus gravissimus et idem summus orator. Iustinus, etiam habitu philosophus, in disciplinis liberalibus artifex precipuus, ad Christi tutandam religionem non modo eruditissimum vertit ingenium, verum eciam animam impendit.

Clemens preceptor Origenis, Alexandrine ecclesie presbyter, vir omnium longe doctissimus, idque iudice viro omnium [longe] doctissimo Hieronimo, ad sacre religionis defensionem, que tum negocium exhibentibus ethnicis, in summo discrimine versabatur, non parum adiumenti contulit tum eloquentia, tum libris eruditionis plenis. Sed plane harenas metiar, si hic tendam omnem eruditorum cathalogum revolvere. Bis mille recensere possem, quorum insignis eruditio nisi fidei laboranti succurrisset neque tam amplam, neque ita confirmatam, fortasse et nullam haberemus: et postea trepidant isti discere *seculares* disciplinas [humanas], quasi desint quorum exemplo id faciant. Deflectant paulisper obtutum ab exemplis domesticis, evolvant veterum Chronicas, evolvant eos qui de scriptoribus scripserunt illustribus, invenient Originem, Gregorium Nazianzenum, Didymum, *Hylarium*, *Basilium*, Iohannem Chrisostomum, et ut ad
29 Latinos veniam, Lactantium, | [Hilarium,] Severum, Paulinum, ad sum-

1 The original hand wrote *Paulum*, an obviously incorrect reading.

mam, omnes prope ad unum qui in defensanda fide ac tractandis misteriis scripturarum operam navarunt, scolasticis fuisse disciplinis instructissimos: quorum omnium ethnicam eruditionem, ymmo et Christianam effert [ac] miratur Hieronimus, ne nos contemnamus: at nos qua sumus religione nichil quantumvis politum eruditione movere potest nisi sit idem pium. At Origines hereseos notam non effugit. [Habent quod causificentur.]

Age ne huius quidem generis deerunt exempla. Hylarius in divorum numerum relatus est, hunc nobis proponamus. Cyprianus etiam martyrio, nec minus literatura seculari clarus, hunc sequamur. Ambrosio quid sanctius? hunc emulemur. Hieronimo vel Augustino quid vel magis pium, vel literatius? horum similes esse curemus. Quantum in hiis omnibus compositionis, linguarum, philosophie, historiarum, antiquitatis, Latinitatis, Grecanitatis, auctorum quanta peritia, et hec quidem ethnica adhuc. Conferamus, queso, cum hiis viris vel scolasticos, vel theologos nostri temporis. Videbimus utroque genere adeo inferiores, ut umbras dicas non homines, et in tanta gravissimorum hominum multitudine soli apostoli nobis in mentem veniunt, quos ita demum imitari nos credimus, si indocti simus. A moribus vero apostolicis tam absumus quam a nobis India. Quod si nos apostolorum rusticitatem imitandi tantopere studium habet, miror cur non etiam piscari incipiamus. Sed extra iocum, Ambrosium imitari metus est? Hieronimum imitari religio est? Isti, inquiunt, nondum Christiani, et pueri adhuc, literis illis sunt imbuti.

At Hieronimus parentibus Christianis natus, a puero Christianus, se tamen inter grammaticos et rhetores educatum fatetur, immo gloriatur. Verum quid istud refert, [cum iis] *qum* qui ante baptismum didicerunt, non modo Christiani, verum et episcopi et senes sunt usi. [Cur] Omnes libros suos ethnicis literis resperserunt? cur [ut] recte factum defendunt? Si taciti fecissent, ignoscendum potius quam imitandum videri potuisset, nunc et recte, et optimi cuiusque exemplo fecisse [se] testantur. Augustinus ipse iam non ethnicus de singulis artibus liberalibus singula volumina scripsit. At scripsit, inquiunt, cathec[h]uminus, non Christianus. Commode vero admones. Tum igitur ne cogitandum quidem de studiis ethnicis erat, *quando* [cum] novus tyro ad Christianam religionem exercebatur. Sed esto sane peccaverit, erraverit, ignoraverit, cur iam sanior et senior hunc errorem non reprehendit? Cur autem consulto eciam a se factum fatetur, ut hiis tanquam vestigiis ad summe veritatis cognitionem gradatim *ascenderet* [accederet]? Has enim disciplinas scintillas quasdam ait esse ab immortali illa luce promicantes, quarum indicio ad fontem illum perveniatur. Et quanto religiosius ille quam nos, qui animis rudibus, repente ad divinitatis archana non ingredimur, sed irrumpimus, non ascendimus sed involamus, et tanquam gigantes, extructis in celum molibus, invito Iove arcem illius occupare conamur: eoque ille (quia gradatim ascendit) receptus est, nos repellimur, deiicimur, precipitamur.

Beda monachus, vir Anglus quidem, [aut certe Scotus,] sed et vite probitate, et doctrine non contemnende, adeo scolasticas disciplinas non contempsit, ut de schematis grammaticis et carminibus condendis scribere non piguerit. Post hos quidem nitor politiesque theologie sensim in deterius degeneravit, *ut* [et] non parum rubiginis cepit contrahere. Non defuere *tamen* aliquot seculis docti, verum ut rariores, ita inferiores. Laboriosorum nunquam non fuit copia. Thomas Aquinus scriptor nobilissimus in Aristotilem ethnicum philosophum commentarios edidit, atque adeo in ipsis theologicis questionibus, ubi de summo principio, de Trinitate disputat, Ciceronis ac poetarum testimonia profert. Scotus tametsi a Musis prorsus alienus fuisse videtur, scolasticus tamen est, ac [ne in] mediis quidem misteriis, et archanis theologie, philosophorum suorum oblivisci non potest. Et quid attinet vel recentiores, vel vivos commemorare? quorum licet sit inferior multo eruditio, is tamen inter ipsos videtur prestantissimus, qui secularibus doctrinis instructissimus fuerit. Hec summa est, multis quidem summis viris non contigit eruditio secularis, at cui contigit, nemo non est usus, *nec omnino* [nemo] veritus est Christianorum templum *gentilibus* [ethnicis] opibus exornare.

[Hic] Cunctante paulisper Batto,[1] consul [interloquens]: Per deum, inquit, immortalem, quid si et ego e consule philosophus fiam? [Et] Battus: Utere [inquit] promisso. Subiicit consul: Longis tu quidem ambagibus circumactus mihi videris, callido opinor consilio, ut apostolice interim simplicitatis oblivio nobis obreperet. Verum quod in hac re precipuum erat preteritum non oportuit. Demus sane complures pios viros literatura gentili [prophana] cum laude usos, attamen haud temere (ut reor) apostolos rudes, et nullis instructos literis nostre religionis et auctores, et *iudices* [duces], et principes nacti sumus, quos tu me vetas imitari. Ego vero summe laudis et prime iudicio, primos ac summos emulari. Subridens Battus: Quantus, inquit, apostolorum imitator hec michi obiicit. Egon[2] apostolos imitari te veto? Immo iubeo, at ita ut moribus apostolos exprimas, eruditione Hieronimum, nunc apostolicam ruditatem imitantur omnes, vitam nemo. Prime laudis ais esse, summos emulari, nichil pugno: sed tu perperam facis, qui e primis et summis viris, id quod est extremum et infimum, tibi proponas. Diligens imitator qui

---

[1] The word *tam* is crossed out after *Batto*.
[2] After *Egon*, *aut* is crossed out.

sit, non solum quam accuratissimum sibi deliget exemplar, verum in eo
ipso quod optimum putav[er]it, excerpit, quedam preteribit, quedam repre-
hendet. Summa [modo] conabitur imitari. Primus est Petrus, primus
Hieronimus, hic doctorum, ille apostolorum. [In] Petro summus erat
ardor fidei, in Hieronimo summa doctrina, alterius animum, alterius
studia imitare. At tu mavis apostolorum quam doctorum ordinem tibi
proponi, propono [et quidem] et primo ordine precipuos, Petrum et
Paulum. Paulus omnium literarum genere refertissimus erat. Petrus
auctoritate superior a Paulo reprehensus, scientiori et credidit et paruit.
Imitamur hos, sed plane prepostere. Indocti literatos ultro reprehendimus, quando parum est quod parere recusamus. At non temere cura tum
est, ut Christiana religio a rudibus auctoribus inicium caperet. Istud
quidem [recte], ne scilicet tanti facti gloria penes humanam esset *sapientiam*
[industriam], sed omnis divine virtuti tribueretur. Ea res illi quidem
tempori erat apta, verum quid ad nos? hic dies aliam vitam, alios mores
postulat. Non percalluerunt seculares disciplinas apostoli, at nunquid
reprehenderunt? Num quando literatos a suo contubernio exclussise
leguntur? Rudes erant literarum apostoli, quid istud ad te, qui ipsas
profiteris litteras. Neque enim de apostolis, sed de ludi magistris agimus,
quanquam quis Christiane pietatis amator ferat ab istis nebulonibus,
totiens insimulari viros celestes et nostre salutis auctores? Age nunc si
placet, eorum rusticitatem cum nostra eruditione componamus. Nempe
illos linguarum species [omnes] calluisse legimus, nos unica vix balbutimus.
Illi tantum valuerunt dicendo, ut tyrannos, ut populos immanes et bar-
30 baros permoverent, [1] nos pecudibus ipsis fere mutiores. Illi testamenti
utriusque misteria memoriter tenuere. Nos vix prima literarum elementa
percepimus, et audemus postea homines ipsa ruditate rudiores, imperitos
fuisse apostolos dicere.

Consul. Tum consul. At tu, inquit, Batte, in ista disputatione,
vehementi magis quam apta, bis mihi peccare videris: nam et de *gentili*
[prophana] literatura instituta erat disputatio, non divina, quam apostolos
accepisse constat: et eam [ipsam] non humano studio, sed celesti munere
sunt consequuti.

Battus. Profecto tu istorum mentem pulchre tenes, istud enim ipsum
ineptus aliquis theologus fuerat responsurus. Huc enim confugiunt,
quotiens eis Hieronimiana facundia, Augustini eruditio, et veterum litere
obiiciuntur. Istis enim, inquiunt, celestis spiritus ministravit. Equidem
admirari soleo in hominibus, qui sibi perquam acuti videntur, quippe
dialectici, tam [h]ebes ingenium, nisi forte perperam ista faciunt. Quid
enim ista tandem oratione sibi volunt? An nullam nobis expetendam

scientiam, nisi que celitus infundatur? frustra igitur nocturnis diurnisque
maceramur studiis. Quorsum autem attinent ludi litterarii, e[t] quidem
publici, quorsum tot sumptuose bibliothece? Quid meliores annos,
atque adeo totos, insanis lucubrationibus consumimus? quid frustra
pallemus, frustra libris insenescimus? Resipiscamus vel sero, *vel* [et]
moniti meliora sequamur. Missos faciamus inutiles labores, compen-
diarum viam astutum hoc genus hominum indicat. Nos cutem curemus,
ac vini somnique benigni (ut ait Flaccus) celitus expectemus, donec oscitantibus nobis spiritus illabatur ethereus, ac deinde perinde ac fonte
Aonio poti repente theologi prosiliamus, nisi malimus[1] expectare, dum
Pauli more vel in paradisum, vel in tercium usque celum rapiamur,
audituri que nephas sit hominem homini prodere. Sed statuamus oportet,
utrum semel nobis omnia infundi iubeamus, an quotiens usus erit, totiens
presto fieri spiritum malimus.

Equidem posterius hoc longe commodius esse censeo: nam si semel
infundat, noster erit labor meminisse. Quare ut memoriam ea sarcina
levemus, satius erit celesti spiritui omnia permittere, ille modo presto fiat,
vocatus et invocatus *ubi* [ut] res postula[bi]t, quantum satis non amplius
suggerat. Scribendus erit liber, advolet, ut nobis securis calamum regat.
Habenda erit oratio, tum vero in columbe figura ad aurem assideat, linguam ipse temperet, nos modo hiscere meminerimus, ut cum psalmographo
rege canere liceat: Os meum aperui, et attraxi spiritum. Erunt fortasse
quibus hec acerbius dicta videbuntur. Quid autem acerbum in homines
tam arrogantes dici potest, qui contemptis aliorum egregiis laboribus
ipsi cum nichil sciant, celitus tamen docti videri volunt? nec ego quidem
homo poeticus auderem istos deos lacessere, ni divus [ipse] Augustinus in
prefatione in libros de doctrina Christiana istorum amentiam multis
salibus prior elusisset. Quo, *siquidem* [inquit] error iste demum evasis-
set, si semel animos hominum occupasset? Nemo a scientiore se doceri
passus fuisset. Nullus ad ecclesiasticam contionem properasset, nec quisquam evanglium pronuncianti prebuisset aurem. Hec [enim] ociosa
fuerant futura, si celitus eruditionem expectandam putassent. Addit
ibidem vulgo iactatam fuisse fabulam, de nescio quo, cui citra humanam operam litterarum pericia contigerit, quam ille quidem non magnopere confutat: parvi tamen ducit, propterea quod eciam si maxime
vera fuisset, non cuivis idem sperandum esset. Nec [putat] illius unius
felicitatem nos ab industria debere avocare: nam quod commode possis

---

[1] The original reading *malimus* is corrected to *malumus*. In classical Latin the
subjunctive mood would be required by attraction if for no other reason. In this
sentence all the other verbs, numbering six, are in the subjunctive mood.

ab homine doceri, id e celesti afflatu postulare, hominis est aut stulti, aut quod fedius *est*, arrogantis.

Consul. Tum consul. Libet scolastico more tecum obiect[at]iunculis *agitari* [argutari]. Quid igitur sibi vult, quod *Christus* ipse sollicitos suos discipulos esse vetat, quid coram regibus atque presidibus essent dicturi? Dabitur enim, inquit, vobis in illa hora quid loquamini, neque enim vos estis qui loquimini, sed spiritus patris vestri, qui loquitur in vobis: quid quod Petrus spiritu sancto instructos loquutos dei homines, scripsit? Quid illud Iacobi: Qui indiget sapientia postulet a deo, qui dat omnibus abundanter, et non improperat? Hec (nisi fallor) longe aliud quam tua oratio, sonare videntur.

Battus. Recte tu quidem admones, et in tempore, verum ista perfacile dissolvi poterunt. Cedo num tibi C[h]ristus istis verbis, que modo recitasti, discipulos deterruisse videtur, ne apud principes [dicturi] quid essent dicturi cogitarent, quod nemo nisi freneticus non fecit, cum Christus ipse quatenus homo erat, non sine premeditatione sit loquutus. Non igitur apostolos, *ab eo* quod prudentis hominis proprium videtur, *deterrere* sed metum adimere studuit, ne quid homines contempti et imperiti apud principes et doctos et facundos dicere trepidarent, [apud] quos summi et exercitatissimi oratores solent exalbescere: se enim non deserturum patronos suos, ipsi modo magno animo essent. Ergo non industriam et vigilantiam interdicere, sed animum addere voluit. Imo ausim dicere, tum reliquos apostolos, tum vero Paulum meditata et fortassis scripta oratione nonnunquam dixisse, id quod ex eius defensionibus, que sunt in Actibus apostolorum, haud obscure licet coniicere: tum neque Petri, neque Iacobi, neque Iohannis huiusmodi sunt epistole, ut *non* sine cura scripte videri possint. Sed hic mihi illud obiicies, quod spiritu sancto instructi, loquuti sunt dei homines. Quo nam igitur modo tu eos loquutos fuisse arbitraris? Num vaticinantium *Phebedarum* [Phoebadumve] more, ut furore quodam correpti, ipsi quid dixerint non intelligerent? Sed hec paulo post commodius excutientur. Illud autem Iacobi de postulanda a deo sapientia, perquam insulse accipiunt. Postulanda est a deo sapientia, accedo, at quomodo postulanda? Nempe ut victus, ut[1] vestitus, ut cetera humano usui necessaria. Iubemur a deo panem quotidianum quotidie petere, et datur quidem quotidie, at nunquid oscitantibus? Vestitum petimus, prestatur, sed laborantibus. Hac ratione quoque sapientiam postulamus, at ita [ut] de humana [industria nihil diminuamus. An vero quae corporis sunt, non nisi] industria tua tibi obveniunt, que animi sunt bona, gratis accipies? Panis nisi sudanti non prestatur, sapientia dormienti

[1] Original MS reading was *et*.

infunditur? Perditus et homicida sui iudicatur, qui celestem alimoniam expectans, fame mori maluit, quam pane humano labore quesito mortem effugere, et religiosus habe[bi]tur, qui turpiter nescire preoptet [magis], quam ab homine salutarem doctrinam accipere? At apostolis sine mortali opera sapientia infusa est. Demus istud, et Hebreis in heremo [ab] ethere cibum depluisse legimus.

Sed quam impium est velle manna illud de celo prest[ol]ari, tantundem aut etiam magis impium fuerit, apostolorum more sapientiam e nubibus ociosos expectare: nam vetamur evangelica voce, de crastino victu vestituve esse solliciti, nusquam sapientiam querere prohibemur. Nec vicio tamen vertitur, quod non modo in crastinum, verum eciam in multos annos parcimus, querimus, serimus, edificamus, non nostre modo vite, verum eciam posterorum consulentes, et vicio dabitur, si quis idem in querenda sapientia fruge longe meliore facit? Illic sanam interpretationem admittimus, non panis industriam [1] querendi nobis interdictam esse, sed inanem et anxiam sollicitudinem, hic cur idem non facimus? Promissa erat sapientia celesti oraculo Solomoni, promissum erat patri regnum Israheliticum, neuter tamen ita oraculo confi*dit* [est], ut vel hic quicquam humani conatus preterierit,[1] quo se dignum prestaret, vel ille sapientiam languidiore studio quesiverit: intelligebant nimirum quod gravissime a quodam scriptum est, deus omnia nobis laboribus vendere. Dabunt igitur, sed laboranti, addent sapientiam, sed annitenti, prestabunt continentiam, sed conanti, docebunt, sed studiosos, adiutabunt, sed dimicantes. Neminem deserent, ita quidem, nisi ipse sibi defuerit, alioquin cur ipsi scripsere apostoli? cur evangeliste? cur Hieronimus? cur Augustinus? cur ceteri [nobis] *divini* ingenii sui monumenta reliquerunt? preclara si studio comparanda est sapientia, ociosa si per somnum ociosis expectanda. Iam dedimus apostolis infusam sapientiam, mitto enim quod ante resurrectionem, et post resurrectionem assiduis preceptionibus ab optimo doctore Christo sunt formati, mitto quod apud se assidue legerint, et inter sese de scripturis contulerint, cur non equam omnibus partem immisit? cur plus sapuit Paulus quam Petrus? cur facundior est Iacobus Petro? cur divinius scripsit Iohannes ceteris evangelistis? cur in ceteris sanctis doctoribus alius est alio eruditior? alius alio facundior? Eodem certe numine *instincti* [instructi] scripserunt.

Nimirum in causa est, quod spiritus ille adorandus, non parem apud omnes eruditionem offendit. Auget enim ille, que nostra peperimus industria, promovet studia nostra, aspirat [nostris] conatibus. Quod si fas

---

[1] Original MS reading was *preteriret*, but the verb should have the same mood and tense as *quesiverit* in the next line.

est hoc loco poetarum fabulas admiscere, Prometheus est nobis imitandus: qui simulachro illi suo luteo, vitam ex astris ausus est petere, sed tum demum ubi quicquid humano artificio prestari potuit, adhibuisset. Nos rudem massam offerimus, et spiritum omnia nobis dormientibus confecturum speramus: nec meminimus Paulum ipsum, cui in tercium usque celum rapi contigit, libros, qui in membranis essent,[1] per literas petiisse, ac postea cum Petro ceterisque apostolis de fidei doctrina contulisse. Apostolos ipsos non semel inter se de religione nova communicasse. Petrum Pauli voce castigatum. Ubi *tum* [tunc] cessabat spiritus sanctus? Cur legere Paulum, cur errare Petrum, cur herere omnes sinebat? Videtis ut operam humanam spiritus huius munus non excluserit, sed adiuverit. Adfuit tamen nonnunquam prodigioso quodam more, sed tum demum, qum aut miraculum res postularet, aut studium humanum vinceretur, et ex studiosis multos eruditos evasisse, adiutore hoc spiritu legimus. At ex asino theologum repente factum, quis umquam aut audivit, aut legit? Nec quicquam hiis exemplis moveor, que vulgo narrant, alii columbam ad aurem dicentis scribentisve conspectam, alii per somnium librum traditum. Sint ista sane vel conciliande auctoritatis gratia a benevolis conficta, sint vel vera, si quis pugnet, equidem haud pugno. Nichilominus tantum unumquemque eruditione valuisse videmus, quantum ingenio polluisset, quantum studio contendisset. Ingenium et indoles multis contigere gratis, sunt enim nature dotes, virtus et eruditio nullis.

Consul. Hic consul. E duobus, inquit, scrupulis, altero me propemodum liberasti si hoc unum expedias, quod nemo barbarorum mihi non obiicit, divum Bernardum preter sanctitatis laudem, virum ex recentioribus nec indoctum, nec infacundum, nescio quo nam in loco ipsum fateri, se quercubus et fagis usum pro magistris.

Battus. Sapientes profecto arbores, inquit Battus, que talem discipulum nobis reddidere, et [in]digne prorsus [2] que in montibus senescerent, [ac sues alerent, dignae quae] in [3] cathedris theologorum [potius] presiderent, aut certe, ut de navibus illis Enee fabulatur Maro, in Nymphas transformarentur. Deum immortalem, ut nichil pudet homines ipsis quercubus hebetiores, quique iuxta poetarum fabulas ex arborum truncis nati videri possint. Quid arbores homines docent?

Herasmus. Inter hec qum Battus inardesceret, Guielmus meus aderat, Socratica quadam vafricie, festiva tamen magis quam mordaci, preditus.

---

[1] After this word *scripti* is crossed out with a heavy stroke.
[2] After *prorsus*, *non* is crossed out, presumably by the original hand.
[3] The word *sed* is crossed out before *in*.

Guielmus. Age, inquit, ignosce Batte, fieri potest, qui scis enim an ex illa paradisiaci nemoris arbore fuerint propagate, que boni malique scientiam non habuisse modo, verum et ministrasse legitur. Aut si id non placet, quoniam [1] species non convenit (quanquam nec apud nos species nominatur) et crebra plantatione degenerare potuerunt, [ex] illarum certe genere, que canentem Orpheum admirate consequuteque fuisse narrantur, inter quas quercus in primis fuisse compertum est. Postremo scis homines olim vulgo in arbores transmutari solere. Quid si quercus ille et fagi, summi olim fuerint philosophi, quorum longa incommoda miserati dii arbores eos esse iusserunt: sed utcunque res habet, unum hoc vehementer optarim, ut essent Herasmo aliquot ex sapientissimis illis arboribus surculi, quos in novis pomariis, que molitur, inserat, haberet domi (ut comicus ait) unde disceret.

Battus. Ad que vix arridens Battus (erat enim commotior). Iure, inquit, ridetis in re risu potius quam argumentatione confutanda. Sed extra iocum miror Bernardum, si doceri cupiebat, ad arbores potius quam ad homines se contulisse, ac non Socratem potius illum [quam] Platonicum imitatum. Huic enim qum Phedrus locum in agris per quam amenum ostendisset, iamque Socratem eius specie vehementer captum sentiret, mirari se dicebat, quod non antea urbe relicta, rus concessisset. Cui quidem ille scite respondens, Ignosce, inquit, mihi optime Phedre, nam discendi cupidus [sum], agri vero et arbores nihil me docere possunt, sed homines qui in urbe versantur. Quid igitur Bernardus inter quercus versari maluit, nisi forte (quando ridere libet) Gallia doctiores habet arbores, quam olim habuit Grecia. Figurate dictum est, inquiunt, orabat sub arborum umbraculis, immo et legebat, et lecta animo volvebat, et scribebat, et scribenda suo cum animo tractabat: ergo non tam discendi quam docendi cupidus ad quercus confugiebat, secessum videlicet et silencium scribentibus necessarium captans. Qua quidem in re non ille supersticiosum agebat hominem, sed poetarum institutum imitabatur, qui carmen scripturi silvas et fontes captare consueverunt. Hic si maxime pugnant, sacros scriptores orando eam eruditionem esse consequutos, iam ipsi nobis laqueum quo capiantur ministrant. Qum enim divus Bernardus literis non modo philosophicis, verum etiam poeticis fuerit institutus,[2] utique *gentilibus* [prophanis], quis iam ausit nos reprehendere, quod id nostra industria conemur assequi, quod celestis ille spiritus aliquot felicibus impertivit. *Sed gentilis* [Si ethnicorum] eruditio spiritus sancti munus est igitur bona atque expetenda: malorum enim non est auctor deus,

[1] This reading was changed to *quando* by a later hand.
[2] B.R. reads *instructus*.

quod si in hiis ethnicas[1] fuisse negabis, ego oculos esse tibi negavero: sin divinam scientiam illis orantibus infusam esse, humanam vero sibi peperisse dixeris, ridebo commentum, et te vicissim criminabor qui contra tantorum exempla | virorum preteritis humanis literis, ad divinam scientiam tam stolide irrumpas.

Consul. Hic qum Battus dicendi finem facturus videretur: Perge, queso, consul inquit, me etiam altero levare scrupulo: nam nodum ipsum modo tua sponte tetigisti: nulli apostolorum spiritus celestis prophanas literas infudit, de quibus hic erat instituta disputatio, non dialecticen, non rhetoricen, non poesim, infusurus haud dubie si[cubi][2] hec usui futura fuissent.

Battus. Ad que conversus Battus, Nemini infudit, inquit, donemus istud, at cui umquam ademit? Petro non inspiravit, Paulo cur non ademit? cur uti non vetuit? vetiturus utique, si perniciosas videri voluisset, *non* [quanquam quid] refert, an infuderit ethnicas literas? id certe infudit, cuius gratia *seculares* [ethnicae] litere sunt discende. Si datum esset quavis lingua et integre loqui, et loquentes intelligere, nichil esset cause cur grammatici miseros adolescentes excarnificarent: si is esset mortalium animus, qui nulla nube prepeditus, facile statimque verum et videret, et ostenderet, frustra et ratio[cinatio]ne, et dialecticis argutiis exerceremur. Si nobis esset in manu, quos vellemus animorum motus et sumere nobis, et aliis excitare, sine causa rhetorum precepta disceremus. Verum *qum* [quando haec] multo secus se res habent, nec ille nobis spiritus *sit* [est] expectandus, disciplinis liberalibus opus est, ut vel longis ambagibus eo tandem perveniamus, quo spiritus apostolos compendio perduxit. Non desideravit Petrus nostras literas, Paulum tamen adiuverunt. Sed in re puerili plus satis est disputatum: nam qui istam divinam scientiam nobis solent obiicere, adeo tum ab humana, tum a divina absunt, ut Hyppocraticis potius vinculis sint alligandi quam rationibus coarcuendi. Ita simplicitatem predicant, ut docti tamen haberi velint: ita se nichil didicisse fatentur, ut nichil non sciant tamen. Sed hos cum sua dementia relinquamus, quod reliquum est, de poetica et eloquentia disputetur.

Battus. Hic qum Battus paulisper intersiluisset: Unam, inquit, aciem (ut arbitror) profligavimus, quam tamen non ita magni negocii fuit vincere, quippe neque satis armatam, neque ita capitaliter *infensam* [infestam]: reliquum est, ut confutemus eos, qui negant eloquencie dare operam Christianum oportere, verum huic bello non paulo difficiliori imperatorem preficiendum censeo tum integrum tum meliorem. Ut enim in causis non

---

[1] After *ethnicas*, the word *literas* was crossed out, apparently by the original hand.
[2] After this word *quorsum* is crossed out.

optimis optimus patronus: ita in bello durissimo, peritissimus dux queren-
dus. Qui eloquentie studium damnent, et plurimi sunt, et habent fortasse
que dicant, si non vera at certe verisimilia. Et iam tantum verborum a me
factum video, ut mirer aurium vestrarum duriciem, que me tot horas
blaterantem ferre potuerint. Quare successorem mihi peto, qui que
restant, dissertius possit disputare.

Guielmus. Tum Guielmus pudenti risu. Tene, inquit, Batte, iniussu
senatus ante negocium confectum de tradita provincia decedere, ac qum
iam prope debellatum sit, successorem tibi nullo exempto petere penes
quem omnis belli profligati sit gloria? Quod vero de meliore imperatore
querendo dicis, ambiciosus tu quidem videri non vis, ceterum eum adhuc
te ducem prestitisti, cui prorogandum [etiam] sit imperium, [tantum
abest ut] *nedum* successor ante tempus [sit] mittendus: quare volente
senatu perge ac strenue ut cepisti tuo munere defungere. Tantum autem
abest ut tua oratio cuiquam e nobis visa sit longior, ut mira quadam cum
voluptate omnes habuerit attentissimos. Dum hec inter se cavillantur
illi, consulis puerum ab illius villa recurrentem conspicimus: is qum domi
instructa esse omnia, corrumpi prandium, uxorem iamdudum nos operiri
renunciasset. Age, inquit consul, eamus omnes: ad prandium philoso-
phicum non consulare vos voco: quod reliquum est disputationis, id
pomeridiano consessu in hortis meis conficiemus.

Herasmus. [Hic ego,] Ita ne mecum agitur, inquam, ni tam esses
iurisconsultus, in ius te vocarem, iniurie tecum agerem, qui tam charos
hospites sic abducas, quia luxuriosior sit tibi culina, quasi domi nostre, si
frugaliter, tamen non lautissime sint accipiendi.

Consul. Tum consul. Equus, inquit, esse debes, ego hac pomeridiana
disputatione villulam meam nobilitari cupio, hanc glorie partem si mihi
non invides, libenter nobis concede. Tum uxor id iubet, cuius huiuscemodi
in rebus imperium nosti.

Τελοσ

Finitum Anno Domini XV^c et[1] *XIX in translatione beati Benedicti, ad
usum et librariam Domus Fratrum Collationis in Gouda.*

[1] This word is crossed out.

BIBLIOGRAPHY

ACQUOY, J. G. R., Het Klooster te Windesheim en zijn Invloed, 3 vols· Utrecht, 1875–1880.

AGRICOLA, RUDOLPH, Lucubrationes, ed. by Alardus. Cologne, 1539.

ALLEN, P. S., The Age of Erasmus. Oxford, 1914.

—— Opus Epistolarum Des. Erasmi Roterodami, vols. I and II. Oxford, 1906, 1910.

BROCKWELL, M., Erasmus, Humanist and Painter. Privately printed [New York?], 1918.

BURIGNI, J. L. DE, Vie d'Érasme, 2 vols. Paris, 1757.

COEVERINCX, G., Analecta, ed. by G. van den Elsen and W. Hoevenaars. 's-Hertogenbosch, 1905.

DOES DE WILLEBOIS, A. VAN DER, Studiebeurzen, vols. II and III. 's-Hertogenbosch, 1905.

DUMBAR, G., Analecta Daventria, vol. I. Deventer, 1719.

EMERTON, E., Desiderius Erasmus of Rotterdam, New York, 1899.

ERASMUS, D., Opera, ed. by J. Clericus, 10 vols. Leiden, 1703–6.

—— Silva Carminum, ed. by Ch. Ruelens. Brussels, 1864.

—— Compendium Vitae, ed. by P. S. Allen, Opus Epistolarum Des. Erasmi Roterodami, I, 47–52.

FRUIN, R., "Erasmiana," Bijdragen voor Vaderlandsche Geschiedenis en Oudheidkunde, Nieuwe Reeks, X, 1880, 85–118.

GANSFORT, W., Opera. Groningen, 1614.

HEGIUS, A., Dialogi. Deventer, 1503.

HENSEN, A. H. L., "Henric Gysbertszoons Kronyk van het Fraterhuis te Gouda," Bijdragen en Mededeelingen van het Historisch Genootschap te Utrecht, vol. XX, 1898.

HETTEMA, B. F., EN TELTING, A., Een Bezoek aan een Nederlandsche Stad in de XIVde Eeuw. The Hague, 1906.

HEUSSEN, H. F. VAN, Historia Episcopatuum Foederati Belgii, utpote Metropolitani Ultrajectini, vol. I. Antwerp, 1733.

HYMA, A., The Christian Renaissance: A History of the "Devotio Moderna." New York, 1925.

JONG, J. DE, "Een Nederlandsche Godsdienstige Beweging: De 'Devotio Moderna,'" Nederlandsche Katholieke Stemmen, XXVIII, Zwolle, 1928, 99–109, 138–147.

KESPER, L. A., Geschiedenis van het Gymnasium te Gouda, Part I. Gouda, 1897.

—— "De Oorsprong der Librye," Dagblad van Gouda, August 12–14, 1912.

KNIERIM, P. H. J., Dirc van Herxen. Amsterdam, 1926.

KRAFT, C., UND CRECELIUS, W., "Mittheilungen über Alexander Hegius und seine Schüler," Zeitschrift des Bergischen Geschichtvereins, VII, 1871, pp. 213–286.

KRONENBERG, H., "Wanneer is Alexander Hegius te Deventer aange-komen?" Verslagen en Mededeelingen der Vereeniging tot Beoefe-ning van Overijsselsch Regt en Geschiedenis, Second series, Deventer, 1913, XXIX, 1–7.

—— "De Bibliotheek van het Heer-Florenshuis te Deventer," Neder-landsch Archief voor Kerkgeschiedenis, Nieuwe Serie, IX, 1912, pp. 150–164, 252–300, 313–322.

LIEBERT, A., Giovanni Pico della Mirandola. Jena and Leipzig, 1905.

LINDEBOOM, J., Het Bijbelsch Humanisme in Nederland. Leiden, 1913.

—— Erasmus: Een Onderzoek naar zijne Theologie en zijn Godsdienstig Gemoedsbestaan. Leiden, 1909.

LOOS, C., Illustrium Germaniae Scriptorum Catalogus. Mainz, 1582.

MANCINI, G., Vita di Lorenzo Valla. Florence, 1891.

MANGAN, J. J., The Life, Character, and Influence of Desiderius Erasmus of Rotterdam, 2 vols. New York, 1926.

MEINSMA, K. O., Middeleeuwsche Bibliotheken. Amsterdam, 1902.

MELANCHTHON, "Declamatio de Erasmo," Corpus Reformatorum (Halle), XII, 1844, cols. 265–271.

MESTWERDT, P., Die Anfänge des Erasmus: Humanismus und "Devotio Moderna." Leipzig, 1917.

MOLHUYSEN, J. C., "Cornelius Aurelius," Nederlandsch Archief voor Kerkgeschiedenis, II, 1903, 1–35; IV, 1907, 54–73.

MOLL, W., Johannes Brugman en het Godsdienstig Leven onzer Vaderen in de vijftiende eeuw, 2 vols. Amsterdam, 1854.

MONNIER, PH., Le Quattrocento, 2 vols. Paris, 1901.

NICHOLS, F. M., The Epistles of Erasmus, 3 vols. London, 1901–18.

PINEAU, J. B., Érasme, Sa pensée religieuse. Paris, 1924.

POT, G. J. J., Geillustreerde Gids voor Gouda. Gouda, 1923.

PUSINO, I., "Ficinos und Picos Religiös-philosophische Anschauungen," Zeitschrift für Kirchengeschichte, XLIV, 1925, pp. 504–543.

—— "Der Einfluss Picos auf Erasmus," Zeitschrift für Kirchengeschichte, XLVI, 1927, 75–96.

REICHLING, D., Johannes Murmellius: Sein Leben und seine Werke. Freiburg in Breisgau, 1880.

RHIJN, M. VAN, Wessel Gansfort. The Hague, 1917.

RÖMER, R. C. H., Kloosters en Abdijen van Holland en Zeeland, vol. I. Leiden, 1854.

RUELENS, CH., Erasmi Roterodami Silva Carminum, avec notice sur la jeunesse et les premiers travaux d'Érasme. Brussels, 1864.

SASSE VAN YSSELT, A. F. O. VAN, De Voorname Huizen en Gebouwen van 's-Hertogenbosch, vol. III. 's-Hertogenbosch, 1914.

Schepenprotokollen van 's-Hertogenbosch. Rijksarchief, 's-Hertogenbosch.

SCHOENGEN, M., Jacobus Trajecti alias de Voecht, Narratio de Inchoatione Domus Clericorum in Zwollis. Amsterdam, 1908.

—— Die Schule von Zwolle von ihren Anfängen bis zu dem Auftreten des Humanismus. Freiburg in Breisgau, 1898.

—— Geschiedenis van het Onderwijs in Nederland. Amsterdam, 1911 —.

SCHUTJES, L. H. C., Geschiedenis van het Bisdom 's-Hertogenbosch, vol. IV. St. Michiels-Gestel, 1873.

SMITH, PRESERVED, Erasmus: A Study of His Life, Ideals, and Place in History. New York, 1923.

SYMONDS, J. A., The Renaissance in Italy, vol. II: The Revival of Learning. London, 1877.

VAHLEN, J., "Lorenzo Valla," Almanach der Kaiserlichen Akademie der Wissenschaften, XIV, 1864.

VALLA, L., Opera. Basel, 1540.

VELDEN, H. E. J. M. VAN DER, Rodolphus Agricola. Leiden, 1909.

VILLARI, P., Niccolò Machiavelli e i suoi Tempi, 3 vols. Milan, 1914.

VORSTMAN, M. A. G., "De Geboorteplaats van Erasmus," Archief voor Kerkelijke Geschiedenis, XVI, 1845, 233–239.

—— "Stukken betreffende de Broeders des Gemeenen Levens te Gouda," Archief voor Kerkelijke Geschiedenis, XVIII, 1847, 65–167.

—— "Het Klooster Steyn of Emmaus bij Gouda," Kerkhistorisch Archief, I, 1857, 327–342.

WALVIS, I., Beschryving der Stad Gouda. Gouda and Leiden, 1714.

WIESE, J., Der Pädagog Alexander Hegius und seine Schüler. Berlin, 1892.

WOLFF, M. VON, Lorenzo Valla: Sein Leben und seine Werke. Leipzig, 1893.

WYBRANDS, A. W., "Een onuitgegeven Brief van Johannes Brugman," Archief voor Nederlandsche Kerkgeschiedenis, I, 1885, 226–228.

INDEX

INDEX

A

Academy, Platonic, in Greece, 186, 188, 199, 201; in Florence, 45–47, 120
Adam, 33
Adelbold, bishop of Utrecht, 75
Aeneas, 170
Aeneas Sylvio, 109, 158
Aesop, 106, 165
Africa, 4
Agricola, Rudolph, 36, 37, 41, 57, 87, 96, 111; and Erasmus, 48, 56, 105, 127, 154, 218; and Hegius, 112–113; and Gansfort, 125; and the Devotio Moderna, 120
Alanus, 106
Alardus of Amsterdam, 157
Albertus Magnus, 178
Alexander the Great, 4, 175
Alexander de Villedieu, 108, 192
Alfonso, of Naples, 43
Allen, P. S., 36, 53, 55, 56, 60, 72, 74, 82, 160, 173
Alps, 3, 10, 18, 37, 48, 210, 218
Ambrose, 121, 198
America, 3, 4, 11, 32
Amersfoort, 26
Amsterdam, 4, 17, 63, 65
Andrelinus, Faustus, 206
Angelo, 165
Angers, 125
Anna of Borselen, 170, 212
Anthony, 165
Antonius, fictitious name for Peter, brother of Erasmus, 146
Antwerp, 4, 13, 20, 75
Aquinas, Thomas, 88, 178, 203
Aristotle, 5, 46, 110, 115, 190, 200, 203
Arme Fraterhuis, house for poor students at 's-Hertogenbosch, 134
Arti Legi, at Gouda, 62
Artois, 13, 18, 82

Asia, 4
Athenaeum Library, Deventer, 207
Athens, 120, 202
Atlantic, 4
Auctarium, by John Butzbach, 98
Augustinian Canons Regular, 21, 30, 145, 150, 173, 202, 217; protect the Brethren of the Common Life, 100–101; and Hegius, 106; befriended by Erasmus, 152, 194; not ascetic, 168
Augustinian rule, 31
Augustus, Emperor, 4
Aurelius, Cornelius, 157, 158, 183, 184, 205, 206
Aurispa, Giovanni, 41
Austria, 17
Ave Maria, 94
Avernus, Lake of, 211
Averroës, 47, 110
Avicenna, 47
Avignon, 6

B

Babylon, 214
"Babylonian Captivity" of the popes at Avignon, 6
Balkan Peninsula, 4, 6
Baltic Sea, 65
Bartholomew of Cologne, 107, 113
Barzizzi, 109
Basel, 185
Basel, Council of, 6
Basil, 141, 165, 197
Batavia, by Cornelius Aurelius, 157
Batt, James, 170, 171, 186, 191, 194; character and education of, 188, 189; and Erasmus, 195, 199; attacks the "barbarians," 196–198, 200, 201, 203; defends classical learning, 195, 198, 201.
Bavarian house (Wittelsbach), 13
Beatitudes, 122

339

UNIVERSITY OF MICHIGAN STUDIES

HUMANISTIC SERIES

General Editors: JOHN G. WINTER AND EUGENE S. McCARTNEY

Size, 22.7 × 15.2 cm. 8°. Bound in Cloth.

VOL. I. ROMAN HISTORICAL SOURCES AND INSTITUTIONS. Edited by Henry A. Sanders. Pp. vii + 402. (*Out of print.*)

VOL. II. WORD FORMATION IN PROVENÇAL. By Edward L. Adams, University of Michigan. Pp. xvii + 607. $4.00. Postage extra.

VOL. III. LATIN PHILOLOGY. Edited by Clarence Linton Meader, University of Michigan. Pp. vii + 290. (*Out of print.*)

Parts Sold Separately in Paper Covers:

Part I. THE USE OF IDEM, IPSE, AND WORDS OF RELATED MEANING. By Clarence L. Meader. Pp. 1–112. $0.75.

Part II. A STUDY IN LATIN ABSTRACT SUBSTANTIVES. By Manson A. Stewart. Pp. 113–178. $0.40.

Part III. THE USE OF THE ADJECTIVE AS A SUBSTANTIVE IN THE DE RERUM NATURA OF LUCRETIUS. By Frederick T. Swan. Pp. 179–214. $0.40.

Part IV. AUTOBIOGRAPHIC ELEMENTS IN LATIN INSCRIPTIONS. By Henry H. Armstrong. Pp. 215–286. $0.40.

VOL. IV. ROMAN HISTORY AND MYTHOLOGY. Edited by Henry A. Sanders. Pp. viii + 427. (*Out of print.*)

Parts Sold Separately in Paper Covers:

Part I. STUDIES IN THE LIFE OF HELIOGABALUS. By Orma Fitch Butler, University of Michigan. Pp. 1–169. $1.25 net.

Part II. THE MYTH OF HERCULES AT ROME. By John G. Winter, University of Michigan. Pp. 171–273. $0.50 net.

Part III. ROMAN LAW STUDIES IN LIVY. By Alvin E. Evans. Pp. 275–354. $0.40 net.

Part IV. REMINISCENCES OF ENNIUS IN SILIUS ITALICUS. By Loura B. Woodruff. Pp. 355–424. $0.40 net.

VOL. V. SOURCES OF THE SYNOPTIC GOSPELS. By Rev. Dr. Carl S. Patton. Pp. xiii + 263. $1.30. Postage extra.

Size, 28 × 18.5 cm. 4to.

VOL. VI. ATHENIAN LEKYTHOI WITH OUTLINE DRAWING IN GLAZE VARNISH ON A WHITE GROUND. By Arthur Fairbanks. With 15 plates, and 57 illustrations in the text. Pp. viii + 371. $4.00. Postage extra.

Orders should be addressed to The Librarian, University of Michigan, Ann Arbor, Michigan. Postage extra.

VOL. VII. ATHENIAN LEKYTHOI WITH OUTLINE DRAWING IN MATT COLOR ON A WHITE GROUND, AND AN APPENDIX: ADDITIONAL LEKYTHOI WITH OUTLINE DRAWING IN GLAZE VARNISH ON A WHITE GROUND. By Arthur Fairbanks. With 41 plates. Pp. x + 275. $3.50. Postage extra.

VOL. VIII. THE OLD TESTAMENT MANUSCRIPTS IN THE FREER COLLECTION. By Henry A. Sanders. With 9 plates showing pages of the Manuscripts in facsimile. Pp. viii + 357. $3.50. Postage extra.

Parts Sold Separately in Paper Covers:

Part I. THE WASHINGTON MANUSCRIPT OF DEUTERONOMY AND JOSHUA. With 3 folding plates. Pp. vi + 104. $1.25. Postage extra.

Part II. THE WASHINGTON MANUSCRIPT OF THE PSALMS. With 1 single plate and 5 folding plates. Pp. viii + 105–349. $2.00. Postage extra.

VOL. IX. THE NEW TESTAMENT MANUSCRIPTS IN THE FREER COLLECTION. By Henry A. Sanders. With 8 plates showing pages of the Manuscripts in facsimile. Pp. x + 323. $3.50. Postage extra.

Parts Sold Separately in Paper Covers:

Part I. THE WASHINGTON MANUSCRIPT OF THE FOUR GOSPELS. With 5 plates. Pp. vii + 247. $2.00. Postage extra.

Part II. THE WASHINGTON MANUSCRIPT OF THE EPISTLES OF PAUL. With 3 plates. Pp. ix + 251–315. $1.25. Postage extra.

VOL. X. THE COPTIC MANUSCRIPTS IN THE FREER COLLECTION. By William H. Worrell. With 12 plates. Pp. xxvi + 396. $4.75. Postage extra.

Parts Sold Separately in Paper Covers:

Part I. THE COPTIC PSALTER. The Coptic Text in the Sahidic Dialect, with an Introduction, and with 6 plates showing pages of the Manuscript and Fragments in Facsimile. Pp. xxvi + 112. $2.00. Postage extra.

Part II. A HOMILY ON THE ARCHANGEL GABRIEL BY CELESTINUS, BISHOP OF ROME, AND A HOMILY ON THE VIRGIN BY THEOPHILUS, ARCHBISHOP OF ALEXANDRIA, FROM MANUSCRIPT FRAGMENTS IN THE FREER COLLECTION AND THE BRITISH MUSEUM. The Coptic Text with an Introduction and Translation, and with 6 plates showing pages of the Manuscripts in facsimile. Pp. 113–396. $2.50. Postage extra.

VOL. XI. CONTRIBUTIONS TO THE HISTORY OF SCIENCE. By Louis C. Karpinski and John G. Winter. With 11 plates. Pp. xi + 283. $3.50. Postage extra.

Parts Sold Separately:

Part I. ROBERT OF CHESTER'S LATIN TRANSLATION OF THE ALGEBRA OF AL-KHOWARIZMI. With an Introduction, Critical Notes, and an English Version. By Louis C. Karpinski, University of Michigan. With 4 plates showing pages of manuscripts in facsimile, and 25 diagrams in the text. Pp. vii + 164. $2.00. Postage extra.

Part II. THE PRODROMUS OF NICOLAUS STENO'S LATIN DISSERTATION CONCERNING A SOLID BODY ENCLOSED BY PROCESS OF NATURE

Orders should be addressed to The Librarian, University of Michigan, Ann Arbor, Michigan. Postage extra.

WITHIN A SOLID. Translated into English by John G. Winter, University of Michigan, with a Foreword by Professor William H. Hobbs. With 7 plates. Pp. vii + 169–283. $1.30. Postage extra.

VOL. XII. STUDIES IN EAST CHRISTIAN AND ROMAN ART. By Charles R. Morey and Walter Dennison. With 67 plates (10 colored) and 91 illustrations in the text. Pp. xiii + 175. $4.75. Postage extra.

Parts Sold Separately:

Part I. EAST CHRISTIAN PAINTINGS IN THE FREER COLLECTION. By Charles R. Morey. With 13 plates (10 colored) and 34 illustrations in the text. Pp. xiii + 86. Bound in cloth. $2.50. Postage extra.

Part II. A GOLD TREASURE OF THE LATE ROMAN PERIOD. By Walter Dennison. With 54 plates and 57 illustrations in the text. Pp. 89–175. Bound in cloth. $2.50. Postage extra.

VOL. XIII. FRAGMENTS FROM THE CAIRO GENIZAH IN THE FREER COLLECTION. By Richard Gottheil, Columbia University, and William H. Worrell, University of Michigan. Text, with Translation and an Introduction. With 52 plates showing the different styles of writing in facsimile. Pp. xxxi + 273. Bound in cloth. $4.00. Postage extra.

VOL. XIV. TWO STUDIES IN LATER ROMAN AND BYZANTINE ADMINISTRATION. By Arthur E. R. Boak and James E. Dunlap, University of Michigan. Pp. x + 324. Bound in cloth. $2.25. Postage extra.

Parts Sold Separately in Paper Covers:

Part I. THE MASTER OF THE OFFICES IN THE LATER ROMAN AND BYZANTINE EMPIRES. By Arthur E. R. Boak. Pp. x + 160. $1.00. Postage extra.

Part II. THE OFFICE OF THE GRAND CHAMBERLAIN IN THE LATER ROMAN AND BYZANTINE EMPIRES. By James E. Dunlap. Pp. 164–324. $1.00. Postage extra.

VOL. XV. GREEK THEMES IN MODERN MUSICAL SETTINGS. By Albert A. Stanley, University of Michigan. With 10 plates. Pp. xxii + 385. $4.00. Postage extra.

Parts Sold Separately in Paper Covers:

Part I. INCIDENTAL MUSIC TO PERCY MACKAYE'S DRAMA OF SAPPHO AND PHAON. Pp. 1–68. $0.90 net.

Part II. MUSIC TO THE ALCESTIS OF EURIPIDES WITH ENGLISH TEXT. Pp. 71–120. $0.80 net.

Part III. MUSIC FOR THE IPHIGENIA AMONG THE TAURIANS BY EURIPIDES WITH GREEK TEXT. Pp. 123–214. $0.75 net.

Part IV. TWO FRAGMENTS OF ANCIENT GREEK MUSIC. Pp. 217–225. $0.30 net.

Part V. MUSIC TO CANTICA OF THE MENAECHMI OF PLAUTUS. Pp. 229–263. $0.60 net.

Part VI. ATTIS: A SYMPHONIC POEM. Pp. 265–384. $1.00 net.

Orders should be addressed to The Librarian, University of Michigan, Ann Arbor, Michigan. Postage extra.

Vol. XVI. Nicomachus of Gerasa: Introduction to Arithmetic. Translated into English by Martin Luther D'Ooge, with Studies in Greek Arithmetic by Frank Egleston Robbins and Louis C. Karpinski. Pp. vii + 318. $3.50. Postage extra.

Vols. XVII–XX. Royal Correspondence of the Assyrian Empire. Translated into English, with a transliteration of the text and a Commentary. By Leroy Waterman, University of Michigan.
Vol. XVII. Translation and Transliteration. Pp. x + 490. $4.50. Postage extra.
Vol. XVIII. Translation and Transliteration. Pp. iv + 524. $4.50. Postage extra.
Vol. XIX. Commentary. (*In press.*)
Vol. XX. Supplement and Indexes. (*In preparation.*)

Vol. XXI. The Minor Prophets in the Freer Collection and the Berlin Fragment of Genesis. By Henry A. Sanders and Carl Schmidt. With 7 plates. Pp. xiii + 436. $3.50. Postage extra.

Vol. XXII. A Papyrus Codex of the Shepherd of Hermas. By Campbell Bonner, University of Michigan. (*In press.*)

Vol. XXIII. The Complete Commentary of Oecumenius on the Apocalypse: Now printed for the first time from Manuscripts at Messina, Rome, Salonika and Athos. By H. C. Hoskier. Pp. viii + 260. $4.00. Postage extra.

Vol. XXIV. Zenon Papyri in the University of Michigan Collection. By C. C. Edgar. Pp. xiv + 211. With 6 plates. $3.50. Postage extra.

FACSIMILES OF MANUSCRIPTS
Size, 40.5 × 35 cm.

Facsimile of the Washington Manuscript of Deuteronomy and Joshua in the Freer Collection. With an Introduction by Henry A. Sanders. Pp. x; 201 heliotype plates. The University of Michigan. Ann Arbor, Michigan, 1910.

Limited edition, distributed only to Libraries, under certain conditions. A list of Libraries containing this Facsimile is printed in *University of Michigan Studies, Humanistic Series*, Volume VIII, pp. 351–353.

Size, 34 × 26 cm.

Facsimile of the Washington Manuscript of the Four Gospels in the Freer Collection. With an Introduction by Henry A. Sanders. Pp. x; 372 heliotype plates and 2 colored plates. The University of Michigan. Ann Arbor, Michigan, 1912.

Limited edition, distributed only to Libraries, under certain conditions. A list of Libraries containing this Facsimile is printed in *University of Michigan Studies, Humanistic Series*, Volume IX, pp 317–320.

Size, 30.5 × 40.6 cm.

Facsimile of the Washington Manuscript of the Minor Prophets in the Freer Collection and the Berlin Fragment of Genesis.

Orders should be addressed to The Librarian, University of Michigan,
Ann Arbor, Michigan. Postage extra.

With an Introduction by Henry A. Sanders. With 130 plates. The University of Michigan. Ann Arbor, Michigan, 1927.

Limited edition, distributed only to Libraries, under certain conditions. A list of Libraries containing this Facsimile is printed in *University of Michigan Studies, Humanistic Series*, Volume XXI, pp. 431–434.

SCIENTIFIC SERIES

Size, 28 × 18.5 cm. 4°. Bound in Cloth.

Vol. I. The Circulation and Sleep. By John F. Shepard, University of Michigan. Pp. ix + 83, with an Atlas of 63 plates, bound separately. Text and Atlas, $2.50. Postage extra.

Vol. II. Studies on Divergent Series and Summability. By Walter B. Ford, University of Michigan. Pp. xi + 194. $2.50. Postage extra.

Size, 16 × 23.6 cm.

Vol. III. The Geology of the Netherlands East Indies. By H. A. Brouwer. With 18 plates and 17 text figures. Pp. xii + 160. $3.00. Postage extra.

Vol. IV. The Glacial Anticyclones: The Poles of the Atmospheric Circulation. By William Herbert Hobbs. With 3 plates and 53 figures. Pp. xxiv + 198. $2.75. Postage extra.

MEMOIRS OF THE UNIVERSITY OF MICHIGAN MUSEUMS

Size, 26 × 17 cm. 4°. Bound in Cloth.

Vol. I. The Whip Snakes and Racers: Genera Masticophis and Coluber. By A. I. Ortenburger, University of Oklahoma. With 36 plates and 64 text figures. Pp. xviii + 247. $6.00. Postage extra.

Vol. II. Description of the Skull of a New Form of Phytosaur, with Notes on the Characters of Described North American Phytosaurs. By E. C. Case, University of Michigan. With 7 plates and 24 text figures. Pp. vi + 56. $2.00. Postage extra.

UNIVERSITY OF MICHIGAN PUBLICATIONS

HUMANISTIC PAPERS

General Editor: EUGENE S. McCARTNEY

Size, 22.7 × 15.2 cm. 8°. Bound in Cloth.

The Life and Work of George Sylvester Morris. A Chapter in the History of American Thought in the Nineteenth Century. By Robert M. Wenley. Pp. xv + 332. $1.50. Postage extra.

Latin and Greek in American Education, with Symposia on the Value of Humanistic Studies, Revised Edition. Edited by Francis W. Kelsey. Pp. xiii + 360. $2.00. Postage extra.

The Menaechmi of Plautus. The Latin Text, with a Translation by Joseph H. Drake, University of Michigan. Pp. xi + 130. Paper covers. $0.60. Postage extra.

Orders should be addressed to The Librarian, University of Michigan,
Ann Arbor, Michigan. Postage extra.

LANGUAGE AND LITERATURE

VOL. I. STUDIES IN SHAKESPEARE, MILTON AND DONNE. By Members of the English Department of the University of Michigan. Pp. viii + 232. $2.50. Postage extra.

VOL. II. ELIZABETHAN PROVERB LORE IN LYLY'S 'EUPHUES' AND IN PETTIE'S 'PETITE PALLACE,' WITH PARALLELS FROM SHAKESPEARE. By Morris P. Tilley. Pp. x + 461. $3.50. Postage extra.

VOL. III. THE SOCIAL MODE OF RESTORATION COMEDY. By Kathleen M. Lynch. Pp. x + 242. $2.50. Postage extra.

VOL. IV. STUART POLITICS IN CHAPMAN'S 'TRAGEDY OF CHABOT.' By Norma D. Solve. Pp. x + 176. Cloth. $2.50. Postage extra.

VOL. V. EL LIBRO DEL CAUALLERO ZIFAR: Part I, Text. By C. P. Wagner, University of Michigan. Pp. xviii + 532, with 9 plates. Cloth. $5.00. Postage extra.

VOL. VI. EL LIBRO DEL CAUALLERO ZIFAR: Part II, Commentary. By C. P. Wagner. (*In preparation.*)

VOL. VII. STRINDBERG'S DRAMATIC EXPRESSIONISM. By C. E. W. L. Dahlström. Pp. xii + 242. Cloth. $2.50. Postage extra.

HISTORY AND POLITICAL SCIENCE

(*The first three volumes of this series were published as "Historical Studies," under the direction of the Department of History. Volumes IV and V were published without numbers.*)

VOL. I. A HISTORY OF THE PRESIDENT'S CABINET. By Mary Louise Hinsdale. Pp. ix + 355. (*Out of print.*)

VOL. II. ENGLISH RULE IN GASCONY, 1199–1259, WITH SPECIAL REFERENCE TO THE TOWNS. By Frank Burr Marsh. Pp. xi + 178. Cloth. $1.25. Postage extra.

VOL. III. THE COLOR LINE IN OHIO: A HISTORY OF RACE PREJUDICE IN A TYPICAL NORTHERN STATE. By Frank Uriah Quillan. Pp. xvi + 178. Cloth. $1.50. Postage extra.

VOL. IV. THE SENATE AND TREATIES, 1789–1817. THE DEVELOPMENT OF THE TREATY-MAKING FUNCTIONS OF THE UNITED STATES SENATE DURING THEIR FORMATIVE PERIOD. By Ralston Hayden, University of Michigan. Pp. xvi + 237. Cloth. $1.50. Postage extra.

VOL. V. WILLIAM PLUMER'S MEMORANDUM OF PROCEEDINGS IN THE UNITED STATES SENATE, 1803–1807. Edited by Everett Somerville Brown, University of Michigan. Pp. xi + 673. Cloth. $3.50. Postage extra.

VOL. VI. THE GRAIN SUPPLY OF ENGLAND DURING THE NAPOLEONIC PERIOD. By W. F. Galpin, Syracuse University. Pp. xi + 305. Cloth. $3.00. Postage extra.

VOL. VII. EIGHTEENTH CENTURY DOCUMENTS RELATING TO THE ROYAL FORESTS, THE SHERIFFS AND SMUGGLING: SELECTED FROM THE SHEL-

Orders should be addressed to The Librarian, University of Michigan, Ann Arbor, Michigan. Postage extra.

BURNE MANUSCRIPTS IN THE WILLIAM L. CLEMENTS LIBRARY. By Arthur Lyon Cross, University of Michigan. With 4 plates. Pp. xviii + 328. $3.00. Postage extra.

VOL. VIII. THE LOW COUNTRIES AND THE HUNDRED YEARS' WAR, 1326–1347. By Henry S. Lucas, University of Chicago. Pp. xviii + 696. Cloth. $4.00. Postage extra.

VOL. IX. THE ANGLO–FRENCH TREATY OF COMMERCE OF 1860 AND THE PROGRESS OF THE INDUSTRIAL REVOLUTION IN FRANCE. By A. L. Dunham, University of Michigan. Pp. xiv + 409. Cloth. $3.00. Postage extra.

VOL. X. THE YOUTH OF ERASMUS. By A. Hyma. Pp. xii + 342. With 8 plates and 2 maps. $3.00. Postage extra.

CONTRIBUTIONS FROM THE MUSEUM OF PALEONTOLOGY

VOL. I. THE STRATIGRAPHY AND FAUNA OF THE HACKBERRY STAGE OF THE UPPER DEVONIAN. By Carroll Lane Fenton and Mildred Adams Fenton. With 45 plates, 9 text figures and 1 map. Pp. xi + 260. Cloth. $2.75 Postage extra.

VOL. II. Consisting of 14 miscellaneous papers, published between July 10, 1924, and August 3, 1927. With 41 plates, 39 text figures and 1 map. Pp. ix + 240. Cloth. $3.00. Postage extra.

Parts Sold Separately in Paper Covers:

No. 1. A Possible Explanation of Fenestration in the Primitive Reptilian Skull, with Notes on the Temporal Region of the Genus Dimetrodon, by E. C. Case. Pp. 1–12, with five illustrations. $0.30.

No. 2. Occurrence of the Collingwood Formation in Michigan, by R. Ruedemann and G. M. Ehlers. Pp. 13–18. $0.15.

No. 3. Silurian Cephalopods of Northern Michigan, by Aug. F. Foerste. Pp. 19–86, with 17 plates. $1.00.

No. 4. A Specimen of *Stylemys nebrascensis* Leidy, with the Skull Preserved, by E. C. Case. Pages 87–91, with 7 text figures. Price, $0.20.

No. 5. Note on a New Species of the Eocene Crocodilian *Allognathosuchus*, *A. wartheni*, by E. C. Case. Pages 93–97, with 1 plate and 1 text figure. Price, $0.20.

No. 6. Two New Crinoids from the Devonian of Michigan, by G. M. Ehlers. Pages 99–104, with 1 plate. Price, $0.20.

No. 7. New Brachiopods from the Warsaw Formation of Wayne County, Kentucky, by G. M. Ehlers and M. S. Chang. Pages 105–111, with 1 plate. Price, $0.20.

No. 8. The Richmond Formation of Michigan, by R. C. Hussey. Pages 113–187, with 11 plates, 12 text figures and 1 map. Price, $0.75.

No. 9. Devonian Cephalopods from Alpena in Michigan, by Aug. F. Foerste. Pages 189–208, with 5 plates. Price, $0.35.

No. 10. The Vertebral Column of *Coelophysis* Cope, by E. C. Case. Pages 209–222, with 1 plate and 9 text figures. Price, $0.25.

Orders should be addressed to The Librarian, University of Michigan,
Ann Arbor, Michigan. Postage extra.

No. 11. A New Species of Trionychid Turtle, *Amyda nelsoni*, from the Eocene Beds of Southwestern Wyoming, by E. C. Case. Pages 223–226, with 1 plate and 3 text figures. Price, $0.20.

No. 12. A Complete Phytosaur Pelvis from the Triassic Beds of Western Texas, by E. C. Case. Pages 227–229, with 1 plate. Price, $0.20.

No. 13. Discovery of a Hamilton Fauna in Southeastern Michigan, by G. M. Ehlers and Mary E. Cooley. Pages 231–236. Price, $0.15.

No. 14. *Anisotrypa waynensis*, a New Bryozoan from the Warsaw Formation of Kentucky, by Charles F. Deiss, Jr. Pages 237–239, with 2 plates. Price, $0.20.

VOL. III, No. 1. Indications of a Cotylosaur and of a New Form of Fish from the Triassic Beds of Texas, with Remarks on the Shinarump Conglomerate, by E. C. Case. Pages 1–14, with 1 plate. Price, $0.25.

No. 2. Fossil Fishes from the Triassic of Texas, by Aldred S. Warthin, Jr. Pages 15–18, with 1 plate. Price, $0.20.

No. 3. Contributions to the Geology of Foxe Land, Baffin Island, by L. M. Gould, Aug. F. Foerste and R. C. Hussey. Pages 19–77, with 17 plates. 1 text figure, and 1 map. Price, $0.75.

No. 4. Cystoids from the Trenton Group of Michigan, by R. C. Hussey. Pages 77–79, with 1 plate. Price, $0.20.

No. 5. Description of a Nearly Complete Skeleton of *Ostodolepis brevispinatus* Williston, by E. C. Case. Pages 81–107, with 3 plates and 12 text figures. Price, $0.35.

No. 6. The Color Patterns of Fossil Cephalopods and Brachiopods, with Notes on Gasteropods and Pelecypods, by Aug. F. Foerste. Pages 109– 150, with 5 plates. Price, $0.50.

No. 7. Additional Notes on Nephriticerina, by Aug. F. Foerste. Pages 151–154, with 1 plate and 1 text figure. Price, $0.15.

No. 8. On the Lower Jaw of *Brachysuchus megalodon*, by E. C. Case. Pages 155–161, with five plates and two text figures. Price $.30.

UNIVERSITY OF MICHIGAN COLLECTIONS

CATALOGUE OF THE STEARNS COLLECTION OF MUSICAL INSTRUMENTS (Second edition). By Albert A. Stanley. With 40 plates. Pp. 276. $4.00.

PAPERS OF THE MICHIGAN ACADEMY OF SCIENCE, ARTS AND LETTERS

(Containing Papers submitted at Annual Meetings)
Editors: EUGENE S. McCARTNEY AND PETER OKKELBERG
Size, 24.2 × 16.5 cm. 8°. Bound in Cloth.

VOL. I (1921). With 38 plates, 1 text figure and 5 maps. Pp. xi + 424. $2.00. Postage extra.

VOL. II (1922). With 11 plates and 7 text figures. Pp. xi + 226. $2.00. Postage extra. Bound in paper, $1.50. Postage extra.

VOL. III (1923). With 26 plates, 15 text figures and 3 maps. Pp. xii + 473. $3.00. Bound in paper, $2.25. Postage extra.

Orders should be addressed to The Librarian, University of Michigan, Ann Arbor, Michigan. Postage extra.

Vol. IV (1924), Part I. With 27 plates, 22 text figures and 3 maps. Pp. xii + 631. $3.00. Bound in paper, $2.25. Postage extra.

Vol. IV (1924), Part II. A Key to the Snakes of the United States, Canada and Lower California. By Frank N. Blanchard. With 78 text figures. Pp. xiii + 65. Cloth. $1.75. Postage extra.

Vol. V (1925). With 27 plates, 26 text figures and 1 map. Pp. xii + 479. $3.00. Bound in paper, $2.25. Postage extra.

Vol. VI (1926). (This volume contains papers in botany only.) With 28 plates, 4 text figures and 3 maps. Pp. xii + 406. $3.00. Bound in paper, $2.25. Postage extra.

Vol. VII (1926). (This volume does not contain papers in botany.) With 28 plates, 17 text figures and 7 maps. Pp. xii + 435. $3.00. Bound in paper, $2.25. Postage extra.

Vol. VIII (1927). With 32 plates, 35 text figures and 2 maps. Pp. xiv + 456. $3.00. Bound in paper, $2.25. Postage extra.

Vol. IX (1928). (This volume contains papers in botany and forestry only.) With 99 plates and 29 text figures. Pp. xiv + 597. $4.00. Bound in paper, $2.25. Postage extra.

Contributions to a Monograph on the Genus Helianthus. By E. E. Watson, Michigan State College. Reprinted from Vol. IX, pp. 305–476, with forty plates. Bound in paper, $2.00.

Vol. X (1928). (This volume does not contain papers in botany and forestry.) With 24 plates, 61 text figures and 13 maps. Pp. xvii + 620. $4.00. Bound in paper, $2.25. Postage extra.

Vol. XI (1929). (This volume contains papers in botany and zoölogy only.) With 55 plates, 30 text figures and 3 maps. Pp. xii + 494. $3.50. Bound in paper, $2.25. Postage extra.

Vol. XII (1929). (This volume does not contain papers in botany and zoölogy.) With 39 plates, 10 text figures and 8 maps. Pp. xii + 348. $3.00. Bound in paper, $2.25. Postage extra.

Vols. XIII–XIV (1930). (*In press.*)

Orders should be addressed to The Librarian, University of Michigan,
Ann Arbor, Michigan. Postage extra.